POSSESSING
POLYNESIANS

# POSSESSING POLYNESIANS

*The Science of Settler Colonial Whiteness in Hawai'i and Oceania*

MAILE ARVIN

DUKE UNIVERSITY PRESS   *Durham and London*   2019

© 2019 DUKE UNIVERSITY PRESS
ALL RIGHTS RESERVED

DESIGNED BY AIMEE C. HARRISON

TYPESET IN ADOBE CASLON PRO
BY WESTCHESTER PUBLISHING SERVICES

LIBRARY OF CONGRESS CATALOGING-IN-PUBLICATION DATA

COVER ART: YUKI KIHARA, *Nose Width with Vernier Caliper*, 2015. FROM *A Study of a Samoan Savage* (2015) SERIES. COURTESY OF YUKI KIHARA AND MILFORD GALLERIES DUNEDIN, AOTEAROA NEW ZEALAND.

FOR NATIVE HAWAIIANS AND
OUR KIN ACROSS POLYNESIA,
MELANESIA, AND MICRONESIA.
MAY WE CONTINUE TO FIND
WAYS TO BE IN GOOD RELATION
TO EACH OTHER, OUR MOANA,
AND ALL THE LANDS WE LIVE ON.

CONTENTS

*Acknowledgments* ix

Introduction: Polynesia Is a Project, Not a Place  1

PART I. THE POLYNESIAN PROBLEM: SCIENTIFIC PRODUCTION OF THE "ALMOST WHITE" POLYNESIAN RACE  35

Chapter 1. Heirlooms of the Aryan Race: Nineteenth-Century Studies of Polynesian Origins  43

Chapter 2. Conditionally Caucasian: Polynesian Racial Classification in Early Twentieth-Century Eugenics and Physical Anthropology  67

Chapter 3. Hating Hawaiians, Celebrating Hybrid Hawaiian Girls: Sociology and the Fictions of Racial Mixture  96

PART II. REGENERATIVE REFUSALS: CONFRONTING CONTEMPORARY LEGACIES OF THE POLYNESIAN PROBLEM IN HAWAI'I AND OCEANIA  125

Chapter 4. Still in the Blood: Blood Quantum and Self-Determination in *Day v. Apoliona* and Federal Recognition  135

Chapter 5. The Value of Polynesian DNA: Genomic Solutions to the Polynesian Problem  168

Chapter 6. Regenerating Indigeneity: Challenging Possessive Whiteness in Contemporary Pacific Art  195

Conclusion. Regenerating an Oceanic Future in Indigenous Space-Time  224

*Notes*  241
*Bibliography*  279
*Index*  301

ACKNOWLEDGMENTS

I wrote this book over many years while living on the lands of the Kumeyaay in San Diego, the Abenaki in New Hampshire, the Cahuilla in Riverside, California, and the Newe (Shoshone) and Nuche (Ute) peoples in Salt Lake City. I am grateful for how these Indigenous lands sustained me and this work. While this book focuses on an Indigenous Oceanic context, I hope the words I have written here remain in good relationship with the Kumeyaay, Abenaki, Cahuilla, Newe, and Nuche, as well as with the other Indigenous peoples of Turtle Island.

This book began as a dissertation, completed at the University of California, San Diego, in the Department of Ethnic Studies. My warmest thanks to my advisors, Denise Ferreira da Silva and Ross Frank, for critically pushing and caring for this project in its earliest stages. Mahalo as well to the rest of my dissertation committee—Adria Imada, K. Wayne Yang, Andrea Smith, and Cathy Gere—for their support. Lisa Yoneyama and Eve Tuck also provided important support. I wrote part of the dissertation at Meiji University in Tokyo, Japan, and am grateful to Mari Armstrong-Hough and Yoshi Hananoi for the library privileges there. I am also grateful to the Native American Studies Department and Native American students at Dartmouth College for their support during my year as a Charles Eastman dissertation fellow.

The University of California's President's Postdoctoral Fellowship allowed me crucial time to write and revise the dissertation into a book manuscript. Warm thanks to Stacy Kamehiro, who served as my mentor for the first year of the postdoc, as well as to many others who offered friendship and support during my time at UC Santa Cruz, including Neda Atanasoski, Julietta Hua, Christine Hong, Marcia Ochoa, and Felicity Schaeffer-Grabiel. At UC Riverside, the Ethnic Studies Department supported me during my second year of the postdoc as well as my first two years as faculty. My sincere thanks to the department faculty and graduate students, as well as Mariam Lam and Dana Simmons. I also received crucial support from my cohort of early career faculty at UCR and nearby schools, including Crystal Baik, Ashon Crawley, Donatella Galella, Liz Przybylski, Hyejin Nah, Megan Asaka, Antoine Lentacker, Jody Benjamin, Ademide Adelusi-Adeluyi, Eric Stanley, Emma Stapley, Yumi Pak, Emily Hue, Xóchitl Chávez, and Robb Hernández. Mahalo nui loa as well to the larger Indigenous Studies faculty at UCR, especially the warmth of Michelle Raheja, Jacqueline Shea Murphy, and Allison Hedge Coke.

I am finishing this book while serving on the faculty at the University of Utah, where I am privileged to be part of the Pacific Islands Studies Initiative. Mahalo nui to my PI Studies collaborators, with whom it is a such a pleasure to work with, including Hōkūlani Aikau, Kalani Raphael, Adrian Bell, Matt Basso, Nia Aitaolo, Kēhaulani Vaughn, ʻIlaheva Tuaʻone, Piʻikea Godfrey, Karen Mulitalo, among many others. I am also grateful to the ongoing support of my colleagues in history and gender studies at the university. Special thanks to Annie Fukushima and Sarita Gaytán for their friendship and Annie's cultivation of space for women of color academics.

I could not have completed this book without the help of many archivists. Thank you to the Newberry Library of Chicago, which supported my dissertation research there through the Frances C. Allen fellowship for Indigenous women scholars, and especially to Scott Stevens. Mahalo to the staff of the Bishop Museum's library and archives, and to Betty Kam and the cultural collections of the Bishop Museum as well. And an especially big thanks to Sherman Seki of the university archives at the University of Hawaiʻi at Mānoa for his help in accessing the Romanzo Adams Social Research Laboratory files.

David Chang, Julie Hua, Ty Kāwika Tengan, and Vernadette Gonzalez all provided important feedback on this manuscript that made it stronger. A special mahalo to Vernadette for her multiple reviews and encouragement. Thanks also to Cathy Hannabach for her feedback. Many audiences heard pieces from the book at invited talks and conferences and also offered meaningful feedback. Warm thanks to Denise Ferreira da Silva, Laurel Mei Singh, Ellen Wu, Samantha Frost, Neel Ahuja, Duncan Williams, Judy Wu, Karen Leong, Laura Briggs, Jessica Bissett Perea, Aimee Bahng, Brian Chung, Suzanna Reiss, and John Rosa, among others, for hosting me at their institutions and/or including me in symposia they organized. I am most grateful to my editor Courtney Berger at Duke University Press for supporting and shepherding this project from its earliest stages through publication. Thank you also to assistant editor Sandra Korn for so ably keeping track of all the details. At the University of Utah, thanks to Justin Sorensen of GIS Services for his assistance in creating a map of Oceania. My warmest thanks to Adrienne Keahi Pao and Yuki Kihara for allowing me to reproduce their artwork in this book, and especially to Yuki for allowing me to use her striking image on the cover.

So many other friendships sustained me through the writing of this book. These relationships continue to make this career meaningful to me, as I learn so much from thinking and organizing with these friends' brilliance and care. From graduate school through today, my love and gratitude go especially to Angie Morrill, for all the tears and laughter and karaoke, as well as to Ma Vang, Kit Myers, Laura Terrance, Ayako Sahara, and Kate McDonald. The wāhine of Hinemoana of Turtle Island are often in my mind: mahalo nui loa to Lani Teves, Liza Keanuenueokalani Williams, Fuifuilupe Niumeitolu, Kēhaulani Vaughn, and Natalee Kēhaulani Bauer for sharing this work we do. Lee Ann Wang, Brian Chung, Chris Finley, Kiri Sailiata, Ren-yo Hwang, Judy Rohrer, Tiffany Lethabo King, and Kim May have all been wonderful coconspirators as well. Aloha pumehana to you all, and to the many other Indigenous feminist and scholars of color, too many to list here, who have shared the work and laid the paths.

My families have made my work possible in more ways than I can count, and their support has mattered even—or especially—when the timing and frequent moves of this academic life have been difficult to explain. Thank you to my mom, Wanda Leilani Arvin, for always being my biggest fan. Mahalo nui loa to all my aunties, uncles, and cousins of my Awo 'ohana as well. I have such deep aloha for our Waimānalo roots. I am also grateful to my Arvin family and to my in-laws, the Morans. My deepest thanks are reserved for Ryan Moran, for his steadfast love through every up and down. It is a joy to share every day with you. Me ke aloha pau'ole.

INTRODUCTION

*Polynesia Is a Project, Not a Place*

What is a Polynesian? I've encountered this question many times in my life, from strangers and friends alike. For most, it's an honest question. Schools in the United States rarely teach much, if anything, about the Pacific Islands. From elementary school through college, even the history of how Hawaiʻi became the fiftieth state of the union usually remains unexplored. Unsurprisingly, then, the transnational histories of Polynesia, itself only one region of the broader world of Oceania, are even more rarely addressed. Yet Polynesia and Polynesians are everywhere in popular culture. To many Americans, Japanese, Chinese, and others, Polynesia (especially Hawaiʻi) is a magical vacation spot, destination wedding venue, and tropical honeymoon getaway. So-called tiki culture is popular again in the United States, that postwar invention expressing nostalgia for U.S. military service and R&R in the Pacific, now revived in everything from hipster tiki bars to a bewildering proliferation of tiki-themed lawn ornaments to supplement the familiar tiki torch. Perhaps most pervasively, *Lilo and Stitch* (2002) and *Moana* (2016) are two well-loved Disney franchises set in Polynesia and featuring Polynesian characters. Disney further capitalizes on these films at their resorts, including the Polynesian Village Resort at Disney World in

Orlando, Florida, opened in 1971, and their newer Aulani Resort and Spa in Kapolei, Hawai'i, opened in 2011.

So, when people ask me "What is a Polynesian," the question is tinged with an uneasy mix of familiarity and confusion. Polynesia is sometimes misunderstood as referring solely to French Polynesia, the French territory that includes Tahiti, rather than the broader region that encompasses over a thousand islands and more than a dozen independent countries or territories. Some questioners want me to authenticate exotic images or recommend the best hotels to stay at in Hawai'i. To them, Polynesians are natural travel agents. Others are unsure, after learning that I am Native Hawaiian, what that means exactly. Some insist: That means part Asian, right? What percent Hawaiian are you? But aren't all the Natives extinct? That I, like many Native Hawaiians, am multiracial with Chinese and haole (white) ancestry in addition to my Native Hawaiian ancestry, often seems proof to them that their suspicions about Hawaiian extinction are correct—however long I might spend explaining why such notions are both false and harmful.

There is a long history to such questions, and the attendant proprietary sense that many white Americans, in particular, display when they decide my answers are not sufficient and that they actually already know what a Polynesian or Native Hawaiian is. This book is a critical history of such Western knowledge production about Polynesians as a race, demonstrating how important such pursuits have been to the ideological work of settler colonialism in Hawai'i and other parts of Oceania. My goal in exploring this history, and its enduring legacies, is to challenge how Polynesians are made invisible as a people, despite their literal and imagined presence in many of the centers of American culture, from Disney cartoons to the many Polynesian men on the field during *Sunday Night Football*. While my analysis is relevant to the popular images of Polynesia noted above, this book takes a closer look at the history of Western scientific studies that similarly and repeatedly questioned: "What is a Polynesian?"

Indeed, since the earliest encounters between Europeans and Indigenous Pacific Islanders, white Europeans (and later, white Americans) expressed a fascination and partial identification with the racial origins of Polynesians. To British Captain James Cook and others, Polynesians seemed to represent "natural man" in his purest state. European painters such as William Hodges, for example, depicted Tahitian women in the style of classical Grecian bathers in his 1776 painting *Tahiti Revisited*. In later social scientific studies from the mid-nineteenth century through the mid-twentieth century, such ideas about the racial origins and classification of Polynesians became the subject of intense scrutiny and debate. While these theories shifted over time, the enduring logic that Polynesians could be understood as more "natural," "classical," or otherwise primitive versions of white civilizations remained throughout changes in social scientific trends.

This logic persists to this day, from the daily exotification of light-skinned Hawaiian "hula girls" as naturally available sexual conquests for visiting white tourists, to complicated matters of legal recognition for Native Hawaiian people.[1] The central argument of this book is that settler colonialism in Hawai'i and Polynesia more broadly is fueled by a logic of possession through whiteness. In the logic of possession through whiteness, both Polynesia (the place) and Polynesians (the people) become exotic, feminized possessions of whiteness—possessions that never have the power to claim the property of whiteness for themselves. Instead, the Polynesian race is repeatedly positioned as almost white (even literally as descendants of the Aryan race), in a way that allows white settlers to claim indigeneity in Polynesia, since, according to this logic, whiteness itself is indigenous to Polynesia. This logic naturalizes white settler presence in Polynesia and allows white settlers to claim, in various ways, rightful and natural ownership of various parts of Polynesia. Notably, this idea of whiteness making itself Indigenous in order to control and own a place violently attempts to replace the quite different definition of indigeneity held by many Polynesians and other Indigenous peoples, which emphasizes relationships and responsibilities to land as ancestor.

Today, white social scientists no longer claim that Polynesians are Aryan. Whiteness, like all forms of racial ideologies, has never been a completely stable or unchanging concept. Yet the historical production of Polynesians as very close to whiteness in science continues to authorize white claims to ownership over Indigenous Polynesian lands and identities. This is true despite the fact that whiteness is often unmarked as such in scientific discourse, more often operating through the language of the "universal" or "good of mankind." Nonetheless, as Toni Morrison has written about tropes of blackness in the writing of white American writers, "the subject of the dream is the dreamer."[2] So too, the Western racial construction of Polynesians from the nineteenth and twentieth centuries reflects the self-referential concerns of the West and white anxieties over their own shifting definitions of whiteness and humanity.

While whiteness is commonly the named referent, antiblackness is also always a significant part of the Western construction of the Polynesian race as almost white. Like indigeneity, blackness is so often simultaneously invisible and hyper-visible. Ideas about Polynesians being almost white were formed in distinction to ideas about Melanesians being black.³ Melanesia, a distinct Oceanic region west of Polynesia and south of Micronesia, includes the present-day countries of Papua New Guinea, West Papua, the Solomon Islands, Vanuatu, New Caledonia (Kanaky), and Fiji. Imperial and settler images of Melanesians projected fears about savage, dark-skinned cannibals, and were used to justify practices of kidnapping and forced labor. Blackness as understood in the continental United States in reference to African Americans also, at times, played a significant role in racial discourses in Oceania, especially in Hawai'i. For example, in the period surrounding the overthrow of the Hawaiian Kingdom in 1893, U.S. media repeatedly portrayed King Kalākaua and Queen Lili'uokalani as pickaninnies and spread rumors about their having African American ancestry in order to discredit them as legitimate rulers.⁴

Such racist images were enabled by discourses about Polynesians' proximity to whiteness, rather than being a break from them. For whiteness in relation to Polynesians always remained a question and a problem, despite accumulating social scientific knowledge over decades declaring various definitive answers. The question "What is a Polynesian?" was always implicitly or explicitly a question about whether Polynesians were white or black. White settlers wanted Polynesians to be whiter because it suited their own claims of belonging to Polynesia while it also soothed colonizers' racial anxieties about those they dispossessed. This book therefore analyzes how Western fears about Polynesian blackness, through ancestral or more recent relationships with Melanesians and African Americans, haunts the logic of possession through whiteness in deep and complex ways. These fears about Polynesians' potential proximity to blackness are also always wrapped up in fears about Polynesian indigeneity threatening and undercutting the claims to indigeneity, power, and resources made by white settlers in Polynesia.

Overall, *Possessing Polynesians* investigates narratives about Polynesian whiteness not to reveal truths about Polynesians per se, but to expose the foundations of settler colonial power in a possessive form of whiteness that must be divorced from its claims to indigeneity on the path to decolonization. My goal is not to provide a more appropriate racial classification for Polynesians, but to show how racial knowledge—never stable, but often shifting—has been and continues to be central to settler colonialism in Polynesia. In this sense, this book is a critical genealogy of whiteness in Polynesia, more than it is a history of Polynesianness, as self-determined by Polynesian peoples. Yet what I show here is the history of how, and with what consequences, constructions of Polynesianness, whiteness, and blackness have intertwined through enduring settler colonial ideologies, and how Polynesians have alternately accepted and refused them.

POLYNESIA AS A SETTLER, SCIENTIFIC PROJECT

To Thor Heyerdahl in 1947, the answer to "What is a Polynesian?" was: an ancient white race from Peru. A Norwegian self-styled "explorer," Heyerdahl sought to prove a theory, already discredited by other social scientists of the time, that Polynesia was settled by a mythical white race that left Peru centuries ago. His method of proving this theory was dramatic: he would himself attempt to drift on a simple balsa wood raft from Peru to Polynesia.[5] The raft, which he named *Kon-Tiki*, was ill-equipped for such a long sea voyage, and Heyerdahl could not swim. Ultimately, the raft reached the Tuamotu Islands of French Polynesia, where he and his crew were saved from starvation and dehydration by the local Indigenous people. This ill-fated voyage did not dissuade Heyerdahl from his theory or this style of "exploration."[6] In 1962, the *Honolulu Star-Bulletin* critically commented on a new Heyerdahl book in which he claimed that Peruvians first settled Hawai'i and then "mixed" with American Indians who arrived later. The article cited Bishop Museum ethnologist Kenneth Emory, who strongly dismissed Heyerdahl's claims, emphasizing instead the strong relationships between Polynesian languages and cultures.[7]

Yet the newspaper also disparaged Polynesians. In a political cartoon accompanying the article (figure 1.1), a Polynesian figure, depicted as a hulking, obese man, charges at a Peruvian, yielding a sign saying "Polynesians A-OK." The Peruvian man is drawn as much smaller in size, but unwavering, holding his own sign: "Peruvians SI, Polynesians NO." In this cartoon, the white social scientist or self-styled explorer disappears from view, while the two figures come across as holding tribal, "primitive" attachments to exclusive origin stories and racial divisions. In this way, the cartoon neatly illustrates how the social scientific knowledge that produces theories about Polynesians as a race so often disavows its own role in that production, instead blaming Polynesians (and Peruvians, in this case) for believing in race and racism. Meanwhile, white social scientists maintain their authority as experts on Pacific and South American cultures because of their seemingly distanced position, when in fact their work shores up white, colonial claims to lands and resources.

FIGURE 1.1. "Polynesians A-OK!" *Honolulu Star-Bulletin* cartoon, 1962.

Despite the apparent absurdity of Heyerdahl's research, his "exploration" was an outgrowth of what social scientists from the early nineteenth century had dubbed the "Polynesian Problem," that is, the problem of determining the geographic and racial origins of Polynesians. Until the revitalization of long-distance Indigenous oceanic voyaging, notably beginning with the Native Hawaiian double-hulled canoe *Hōkūle'a*'s successful navigation from Hawai'i to Tahiti in 1976, Western science maintained that Indigenous Pacific Islanders could not have purposefully traversed the Pacific Ocean, but instead likely settled the Pacific Islands randomly through "accidental drift." By navigating the *Hōkūle'a* with traditions based on reading the stars, taught to them by Mau Piailug, a Satawal (Micronesian) navigator, the *Hōkūle'a* crew proved that Indigenous Pacific Islanders had the skills to intentionally travel the Pacific.[8] The *Hōkūle'a* and many other revitalized canoes across the Pacific continue to demonstrate that Polynesia was not inhabited haphazardly by accidental rafts set adrift from Peru. Yet Heyerdahl's antics are still praised and promoted today. In 2011, his archives became officially part of UNESCO's "Memory of the World Register," which describes Heyerdahl as "one of the greatest communicators and renowned explorers of the 20th century."[9] Similarly, a 2012 film about the *Kon-Tiki* expedition emphasized that Heyerdahl's journey inspired the world and reanimated interest in exploration after the devastation of World War II. Neither UNESCO nor the film mention Heyerdahl's racial theories, nor the well-established and revitalized traditions of skilled Indigenous oceanic voyaging.[10] In this way, stories about white settlement of the Pacific and white racial origins continue to circulate today, erasing Polynesian, Micronesian, and Melanesian histories and present-day lives and imposing racial divisions both internally and externally, while acclaiming white "exploration" of the Pacific as valuable to all mankind.[11]

Martinican postcolonial theorist Édouard Glissant has reminded us that the "West is not in the West. It is a project, not a place."[12] In this vein, I see discourses, such as Heyerdahl's, about Polynesians as almost white as an attempt to make Polynesia into a Western, settler colonial project, not merely a place. In this project, Polynesia's origins can be traced to the imaginations of European imperialists, dividing the "almost white," friendly Polynesians from the decidedly more savage and hostile Melanesians. This Western project of Polynesia does not negate the fact that Indigenous peoples from across the areas of Polynesia maintained meaningful connections and identity, long predating Western contact and settlement and continuing through today, through shared or overlapping genealogies and cosmologies. Many

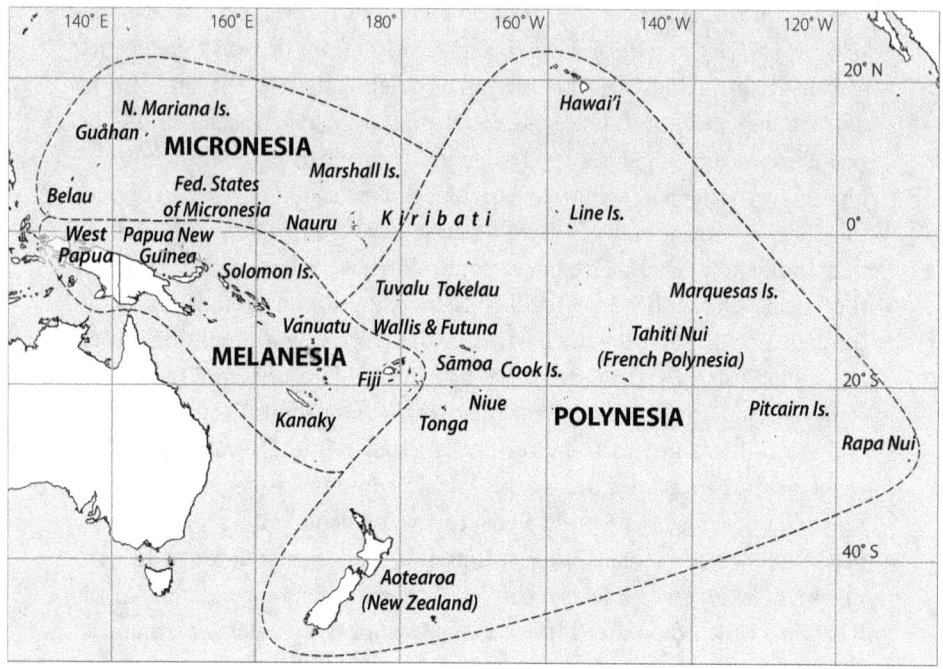

MAP I.I. Map of Oceania showing the regions of Polynesia, Melanesia, and Micronesia. Created by author and Justin Sorensen, GIS Services, Marriott Library, University of Utah.

Pacific Islands studies scholars have shown that Western ideals of Polynesia, Micronesia, Melanesia, and Oceania (map 1.1) are not totalizing and are irreconcilable with Indigenous epistemologies of the Moana, or Pacific Ocean, that emphasize the ocean as connection rather than barrier.[13]

It is important to know the origins and terms of Polynesia as a Western project not because it reflects the "truth" about Polynesia or Polynesians, but because it is a form of knowledge production that structures settler colonialism in many parts of Polynesia. Additionally, attention to the history of race in regard to the Polynesian/Melanesian divide analytically shifts understandings of race in relation to Pacific Islanders beyond the common U.S.-based racial categories, in which Pacific Islanders (including Native Hawaiians, Māori, Tongans, Sāmoans, Marshall Islanders, Chamoru, and many others) are usually understood only in reference to the incredibly broad U.S. designation "Asian/Pacific Islander."[14] Many scholars and activists have argued that Pacific Islanders are ill-served by the Asian/Pacific

Islander, or its abbreviation API, label, given stark, documented inequalities between Asian American and Pacific Islander groups as well as the distinction that Pacific Islanders are Indigenous peoples (whereas some, but not all, of Asian Americans identify as Indigenous).[15] Polynesian, Micronesian, and Melanesian can at times be labels preferred by Pacific Islander communities, since (despite their Western origins) these labels have been adopted in Oceania as identities of regional solidarity. These regional identities are often more relevant and grounded in local contexts than the Asian/Pacific Islander classification. Polynesian, for example, is a broadly used, coalitional identity used in many diasporic contexts to signal political and cultural affiliation, as in the Salt Lake City, Utah, area, where a large population of Tongans, Sāmoans, Native Hawaiians, Māori, and others live.

While I approach Polynesia and Polynesian identity as a transnational, regional formation, this book focuses most specifically on how the ideal of Polynesians as almost white has shaped settler colonialism in Hawai'i. This focus stems from my position as a Native Hawaiian feminist scholar. Yet, with my focus on Hawai'i, I also seek to connect the issues most relevant to the Kanaka Maoli context to other Polynesian and Indigenous contexts, because neither the structures of settler colonialism nor the Indigenous alliances formed against it are limited to Hawai'i. In the United States, there is often a problematic assumption that Native Hawaiians can stand in for all Indigenous Pacific Islanders, especially Polynesians, or that they easily fit into the category of Native American. This assumption reduces the complexity of Native Hawaiians, other Pacific Islanders, and Native Americans. Though there are long-standing, crucial alliances among all of these groups, sometimes under the broadly applicable identity of "Indigenous," Native Hawaiians, like all Indigenous peoples, are a distinct people with specific histories and cultures developed in relationship to the lands and waters of Hawai'i. This book uses Native Hawaiian and Kanaka Maoli (a Hawaiian language term literally meaning original people, and a preferred identity to some) interchangeably to refer to the Indigenous peoples of Hawai'i.

When I do analyze other Polynesian or Indigenous contexts, I do so not because these contexts are all exactly the same, but to attempt to regenerate meaningful connections, especially among Polynesians and other Pacific Islander peoples, and because of the political resonances that exist in our histories and contemporary moments. Tonga, for example, was never formally colonized or settled by white people; thus, settler colonialism as an analytic frame is arguably less relevant to the Tongan context.[16] Nonetheless, Tongans, as Polynesians, have undeniably been subject, at times, to the same ideologies about Polynesian almost-whiteness, especially through the influence of the Church of Jesus Christ of Latter-Day Saints.[17] In another example, in Tahiti and the other island groups of what is now French Polynesia, a territory of France, the Mā'ohi have maintained a demographic majority throughout white French settlement. This differs from the New Zealand and Hawai'i contexts, where Māori and Kānaka Maoli have long been minority populations in their own lands.[18] Still, French imperialism and settlement impacted Mā'ohi in many similar ways, including the use of French Polynesia as a site for nuculear testing. So too, the idyll of Polynesian women as the exotic, "dusky," almost white objects of European heterosexual male fantasies remains rooted in particular ways to Tahiti, especially through the works of the painter Paul Gauguin. This book is a starting point for further scholarship on these Oceanic connections.

A critical analysis of the Polynesian context also offers a valuable approach to scrutinizing broader, seemingly "inclusive" contemporary discourses on racial mixture, multiculturalism, and universalist notions of humanity. Too often, uncritical liberal discourses identify greater inclusion of women, queer folks, and people of color into white spaces, or the very existence of multiracial people, as the solution to the structural violences of white supremacy, heteropatriarchy, settler colonialism, and racial capitalism. Diversifying the faces of those in power is not nothing, but it is never adequate in and of itself in achieving structural change. Indeed, as Sara Ahmed has pointed out, too often "diversity" is deployed as a powerful rhetoric to preserve the status quo.[19] While many in the United States may tend to think of such superficially multicultural forms of maintaining white institutionalized power as a post–Obama era phenomenon associated with the nonsensical term *postracial*, the history of discourses that conditionally include Polynesians within whiteness provides a deeper genealogy to both the strategy of dispossession-through-inclusion and the resistance that always accompanied it.

One telling example of both the enduring logics and the global import of Western studies of the Polynesian race comes from shortly after World War II. Here again, that question of what a Polynesian is arose, namely in a booklet produced by United Nations Educational, Scientific and Cultural Organization (UNESCO) in 1952, titled *What Is Race?* The booklet was created in the context of UNESCO's directive to clarify for the world the scientific basis of race after World War II and the United Nations' passage of the Universal Declaration of Human Rights in 1948. Using diagrams and tables outlining Mendelian genetics, the booklet illustrated that "a race, in short, is a group of related intermarrying individuals, a population" that differs merely in the relative frequency of certain hereditary traits. Though UNESCO's first Statement on Race in 1950 had boldly stated, "For all practical purposes, 'race' is not so much a biological phenomenon as a social myth," physical anthropologists maintained the continued existence of biological, racial categories.[20] For such physical anthropologists, whose careers depended on the continuation of race as a matter of measureable, physical features, "it was not 'race' but racism that was the problem."[21] Thus, the 1952 *What Is Race?* booklet emphasized that there was no "single objective list of races," but nonetheless sought to further teach and test readers' understandings of scientific racial classifications.[22] The Polynesian race was utilized as an instructive example.

"What is the Polynesian race?" the UNESCO booklet asked readers, presenting them with a diagram of three circles (figure 1.2), labeled with racial classifications as determined by anthropologist A. L. Kroeber. There is one red circle each for the "Caucasoid," "Mongoloid," and "Negroid" races, filled with specific groups, such as "Nordics" in the Caucasoid circle.[23] In the dead center of the three circles is a dot labeled "Polynesians." While a cursory glance at the diagram might suggest that it is indicating Polynesians are an equal mix of the three racial groups, the Polynesian dot actually represents an assignment. The book instructs readers to investigate and classify the Polynesian race into one of the three circles.[24]

Readers were encouraged to seek answers to the proper classification for Polynesians in the book *Up from the Ape*, by E. A. Hooton.[25] Hooton described Polynesians as a "COMPOSITE RACE (Predominately White)." As "one of the tallest and finest-looking races of the world," Hooton explains Polynesians' "composite" racial nature as blending "Mongoloid, Negroid and European" characteristics "into a harmonious and pleasing whole." Yet this mixture is not equal, as he notes: "However, a careful consideration of Polynesian features in the light of what is known of the behavior of Negroid and Mongoloid characters in racial crosses suggests that the White strain in this composite race must be much stronger than either of the other two elements."[26]

Hooten's account here, emphasizing that Polynesians were fundamentally a broad racial mixture but also more white than Negroid or Mongoloid, concurred with other anthropological accounts at the time. Kroeber's 1948 textbook *Anthropology* (from which the *What Is Race?* booklet copied their three-circle diagram) similarly highlighted Polynesians' whiteness: "There is almost certainly a definite Caucasoid strain in them."[27] In this way, physical

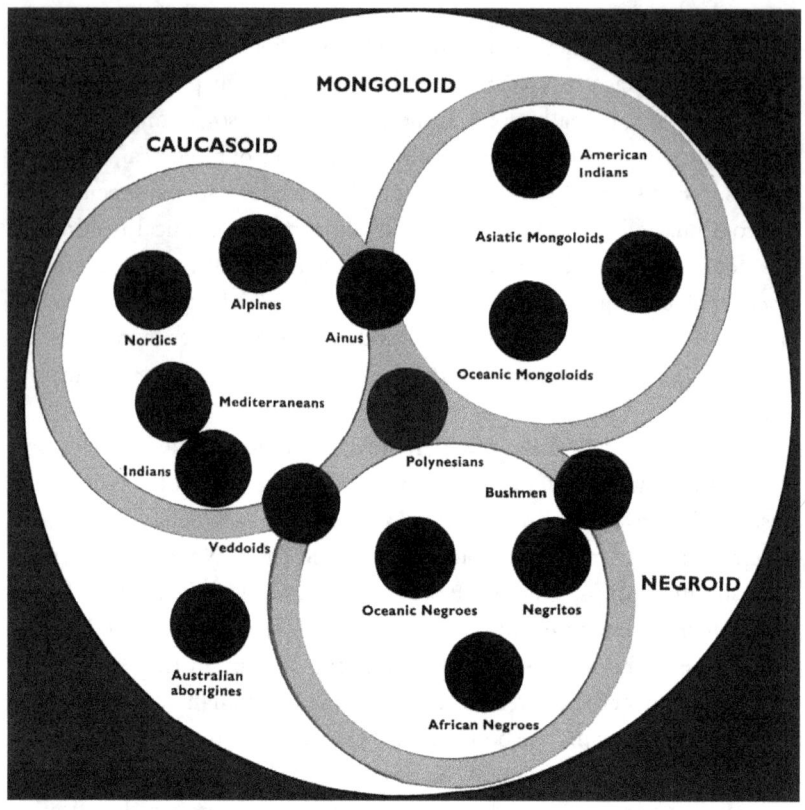

FIGURE I.2. "Classification of Races according to A. L. Kroeber," from *What Is Race? Evidence from Scientists*" (Paris: UNESCO, 1952). Illustration by Jane Eakin Kleiman, based on A. L. Kroeber's *Anthropology* (London: Harrap, 1949).

anthropologists combined "racial mixture" and whiteness as the Polynesian race's defining features.

Rather than being squarely in the center of the Caucasoid, Mongoloid, and Negroid racial classifications, the booklet therefore taught readers that the Polynesians should be included within the Caucasoid circle.[28] This lesson and its use of the Polynesian race raise a number of important questions. Why was the Polynesian race the ideal test case for a scientific and lay audience to contemplate the biological aspects of race? Why, despite the effort of UNESCO to show that race was significantly socially constructed, did Caucasoid, Mongoloid, and Negroid remain valid scientific categories in 1952? Why and how could Polynesians classify as both "composite" (a mixture) and as "predominately" Caucasoid?

Today, it may be easy for many to dismiss such arguments as those displayed in the UNESCO booklet as racist pseudoscience. Yet such a dismissal is premature and at times even naïve, as it risks overestimating how much contemporary ideas about race continue to be formed by that science. Today, most college classrooms across the humanities and sciences teach students that race is not a scientific truth, but a social construction. Social scientists and geneticists in fact largely agree on this point, often citing biologist Richard Lewontin's conclusion in 1972 "that of all human genetic variation (which we now know to be just 0.1 percent of all genetic material), 85 percent occurs *within* geographically distinct groups, while 15 percent or less occurs *between* them."[29] In other words, there is much greater genetic diversity within distinct racial groups than between them. Yet, in looking to genetics to confirm the social construction of race, have we forgotten to remain critical of how science itself is socially constructed and retains an enormous power for legitimizing truth?

This is why the UNESCO efforts to educate about race and science after the racial horrors of World War II are so instructive. Indeed, many of the physical anthropologists, such as Harry Shapiro, who contributed to knowledge production about Polynesians' almost-whiteness, were directly involved with the UNESCO initiatives on race and education in the 1950s. Their involvement partially explains the use of Polynesians in a UNESCO lesson about race. More generally, the Polynesian race was appropriate for UNESCO's purposes because Polynesians and their supposedly racially mixed but also white nature could easily represent a fundamental human unity and universality that UNESCO was eager to impress on their readers. From some of the most isolated islands in the world, Polynesians symbolized the post-racial decades before that term would come into vogue. To social scientists, Polynesians showed that the geographic isolation that caused biological racial difference could be overcome—that racial mixture could thrive and not only be socially accepted but herald the end of race and racism.

SETTLER COLONIALISM AS POSSESSION THROUGH WHITENESS

The use of Polynesians by UNESCO as an object lesson about race in 1952 illustrates how the questions raised in the Polynesian Problem literature from the early 1800s continued to circulate long after. This book analyzes that deep history of attributing (always approximate or partial) whiteness to the Polynesian race in Western scientific literature, popular culture, and law. Through bestowing partial, ancestral whiteness upon Polynesians in scientific knowledge, white settlers (and white settler nation-states) were able to claim that whiteness itself was indigenous to Polynesia. With these scientific declarations, white settlers established their own kind of ancestral claims to Polynesian lands, resources, and identities, while also projecting that the future of Polynesia was destined to be white again through "racial intermarriage" between white settlers and Polynesian women. Yet this Polynesian whiteness was constructed as a one-way conduit, transferring what was valuable about Polynesia in colonial, capitalist economics to white settlers. In turn, the value of whiteness was not accrued by or extended to Polynesians; rather, Polynesians became the feminized, exotic, possessions *of* whiteness, gaining no secure power to possess whiteness or identify as white themselves. This process of uneven racial alchemy was fueled by a logic of possession through whiteness. The agent(s) of possession in this process are not merely individual white settlers, but the discourse of Polynesians as almost white produced in Western scientific knowledge.[30]

To be clear, the discourse about Polynesian whiteness examined in this book is a serviceable construct for the interlaid structures of white supremacy and settler colonialism, not for Polynesians themselves. It has little to do with what Polynesians look like or are recognized as on the street. Polynesians do not uniformly "pass" as white individuals socially, legally, or economically. In most contexts, in fact, Polynesians decidedly do not pass. They face higher rates of incarceration, shorter life spans, less wealth, and more discrimination in workplaces and education.[31] The construction of Polynesian whiteness has even less to do with how Polynesians identify themselves and their own genealogies outside of such imposed Western frames. Perhaps this disjuncture between the Western construction of Polynesian whiteness and the lived experiences of Polynesian people explains, in part, why histories of the Pacific often fail to seriously engage the well-documented history of the construction of Polynesians as almost white. Or, perhaps, the lack of engagement is more simply due to a reluctance to examine the thoroughly discredited field of Aryanism. Contemporary studies of ethnologists and scientists working in Polynesia in the nineteenth and twentieth centuries often fail to mention, or note only in passing, that figures such as folklorist Abraham Fornander or physical anthropologist Louis Sullivan were fully committed to, and saw the bulk of their work as, proving that Polynesians were members of the Aryan family.[32]

Unfortunately, discourses about Aryanism and white supremacy are no longer quite as distant and disproven as many hoped. White supremacist rallies such as the "Unite the Right" event that took place in Charlottesville,

Virginia, in August 2017, highlight the fact that white supremacy has never been eradicated as either an openly racist ideology or a structuring foundation of the United States. While Charlottesville foregrounded violence against black people and nonwhite immigrants, that the white supremacists carried tiki torches as they marched demonstrated yet another way that the legacies of the Polynesian Problem continue to uphold latent associations between whiteness and Polynesianness. Polynesians were not foremost in these white supremacists' minds as they rallied. No doubt, the tiki torches were simply the most convenient consumer product for the angry mob to buy. Yet the fact that the ubiquitous tiki torch was so readily available to them is undeniably tied to the history of colonial images of Hawai'i as an idyllic vacation destination for white Americans—that is, of Hawai'i as a white possession. This example also calls attention to how the settler colonial logic of possession through whiteness is at once anti-Indigenous, anti-immigrant, and antiblack. The relation between the logics of possession through whiteness and antiblackness, and between anti-indigeneity and anti-immigration, is not merely one of analogy or comparison, even as they are distinct logics; rather, they are inextricable. This means they also must be challenged and undone together.

Given the increased but varied usage of *settler colonialism* as an academic term in recent years, it is worth explaining in detail here how this book defines and theorizes the concept. Settler colonialism, as a structure of dominance, is particularly set on the domination and exploitation of land.[33] Settler colonialism is not a structure limited to any discrete historical period, nation, or colonizer. Though never monolithic or unchanging, settler colonialism is a historical and a contemporary phenomenon. Its power usually operates simultaneously through economy (the turning of land and natural resources into profit), law (the imposition of the legal-political apparatus of a settler nation-state, rather than an indigenous form of governance), and ideology (culturally and morally defined ways of being and knowing resulting from European post-Enlightenment thought).

Possession through whiteness is one strategy deployed within the ideological power of settler colonialism, which is often in articulation with, but irreducible to, the economic and juridical forms of governance that also constitute settler colonialism. For example, in the Hawaiian context, economic and ideological components of settler colonialism preceded its legal-political expression, as Christian missionaries and plantation owners (often descendants of missionaries) worked within the existing legal-political structures of the Hawaiian Kingdom until it no longer adequately suited their needs. White plantation owners overthrew the Hawaiian Kingdom in 1893 because Queen Lili'uokalani began seeking stronger protections for Native Hawaiians against the power of the plantations.[34] Further, Hawai'i only officially became one of the United States' "new possessions" (along with the Philippines, Cuba, and Puerto Rico) in 1898, when annexed by a U.S. Congress that sought to secure a coaling station for the U.S. Navy on their way to fight the Spanish-American War in the Philippines.[35] This history of how Hawai'i became part of the United States shows that the economic, juridical, and political forms of settler colonialism may not always be automatically aligned. Nonetheless, the ideological components of settler colonialism often work to coordinate these different spheres of power, though creating an enduring racial and gendered "settler common sense" about Indigenous peoples.[36]

I emphasize the logic of possession in friendly contrast to other articulations of influential ideologies under settler colonialism. For instance, Patrick Wolfe's "logic of elimination" encompasses Indigenous genocide and amalgamation, through which the settler is the one who replaces the eliminated. Yet possession, rather than elimination, articulates more fully the ways in which settler colonial practices of elimination and replacement are continuously deferred. Though these processes are often taken on their own terms to be over and "settled"—the Natives long dead and vanished—they are not, and cannot ever be, complete.[37] Though Wolfe also acknowledges this incompleteness, famously noting that settler invasion is "a structure not an event," I see possession as expressing more precisely the permanent partial state of the Indigenous subject being inhabited (being known and produced) by a settler society. There is, as Scott Morgensen notes, a promised consanguinity (literally, "of the same blood") between settler and native that is often eclipsed in formulations that focus only on settler colonial "vanishing" and "extinction."[38] This imagined familial and racial affinity enables constant (sexual, economic, juridical) exploitation, by producing the image of a future universal "raceless" race just over the settler colonial horizon.

I also highlight processes of possession, rather than elimination, in order to foreground the gendered aspects of settler colonialism. The supposed consanguinity between the settler and the Native is necessarily produced through heteropatriarchy. Heteropatriarchy can be defined as "the social systems in which heterosexuality and patriarchy are perceived as normal and natural, and in which other configurations are perceived as abnormal, aberrant, and abhorrent."[39] As in the English legal principle of coverture, whereby a woman's property and rights are passed on to her husband upon marriage, through the logic of possession, an intimate relationship is forged that binds settler and Native, aiming to nullify Indigenous peoples' distinct "sense of being a people."[40] Settlers thus also come to possess indigeneity (making their presence and exploitation of land natural and nonviolent) through "racial mixture," enabled by sexual relationships with Indigenous women.

Too few scholars have recognized that policies encouraging "racial mixture" in and of themselves have never seriously threatened existing racial and colonial hierarchies, but can in fact be strategies of racial/colonial subjection.[41] As Jared Sexton argues, miscegenation provided structure to "the fiction of race purity."[42] Further, as Tavia Nyong'o has shown, racial hybridity, as a promised but continually deferred panacea for the historical ills of slavery and racism in the United States, is a venerable "American national fantasy" visible in antebellum history, not just contemporary millennial trends.[43] Nyong'o traces the ways that blackness is constructed through hypodescent, "in which each successive generation of mixed peoples are determined to be legally and socially black and held to the same discriminatory standard as everyone else of African descent."[44] Nyong'o persuasively argues that hypodescent thus "manages the racial future by promising a fusion that never comes."[45]

Complementary to the hypodescent of blackness is the hyperdescent of indigeneity, wherein successive generations of mixed-race Indigenous peoples are determined to be legally "white," through systems like blood quantum, though they are generally not socially or economically treated as white. This hyperdescent manages the racial future by promising a "fusion" that never was intended to be one. The end product of racial mixture determined by hyperdescent is whiteness, but a whiteness that remains accessible only to non-Indigenous, nonblack people. Hyperdescent accordingly maintains the line between black and white, managing white racial fears of the potential savage blackness of Indigenous peoples by constructing them as almost white, rather than black. This black/white split is replicated and gendered within Indigenous populations too, as evident in tropes about the light-skinned, sexualized Polynesian girl available to white settler men that ensure Polynesian women are subject to sexual violence while Polynesian men are viewed as dark, dangerous threats to white masculinity, as discussed further, particularly in chapter 3.

Racial mixture therefore provides a method for settlers to become native, thus possessing the "native" category in terms of both land and identity, while Indigenous peoples and Black peoples are continually dispossessed from claims of belonging to the settler colonial state. The logic of possession through whiteness is not only a logic of hyperdescent that specifically dispossesses racially mixed people; more broadly, it projects an imagined past and future of racial mixture in order to bolster white settler claims to belonging in settler colonies. Blood quantum laws in Hawaiʻi, for example, dictate that Native Hawaiians must prove that they are "more than one-half part" Hawaiian to be eligible for access to certain lands. This requirement places a burden of "race-saving" on Native Hawaiian women, who face pressure to have children with Native Hawaiian men of high blood quantum. Such projections are inherently heteropatriarchal, taking for granted that Indigenous women will "marry" white settler men and reproduce mixed-race children who will usher in this whiter future. Yet this discourse does not actually depend on large numbers of racial intermarriages but simply projects as inevitable a future horizon in which the Indigenous populace has been "whitened," and thus made "extinct."

The repeated use of discourses of racial mixture in settler colonial ideologies demonstrates that the places where settler colonialism appears to be "tender" and feminized are just as deserving of critical analysis as the forms of violence perceived to be more "masculine," such as war. Misogyny and homophobia are structural forms that continue to subtly shape many Western societies. Though academia often pretends that because it is "critical," it is more evolved and more immune from such oppression, institutionalized patriarchy, misogyny, and homophobia undoubtedly shape the lack of theoretical attention to gender and sexuality in academic accounts of settler colonialism. Heteropatriarchy's relationship to settler colonialism is far too under-theorized in conventional formulations of ethnic studies, gender studies, and even in the recent growth of interdisciplinary literature focused on critical theories of global settler colonialism.[46] For example, scholar Lorenzo Veracini, a founding editor of the *Settler Colonial Studies* journal in 2011, offers productive analyses about the differences between colonialism and settler colonialism.[47] However, Veracini has little to say about the place of gender or heteropatriarchy in either of these structures, and his theoretical framings of settler colonialism are less robust because of it.

Veracini characterizes colonialism as "a demand for labour," whereas settler colonialism is "a demand to go away."[48] But settler colonialism is more complicated than a demand for Indigenous peoples to "go away," and not only because Indigenous peoples were forced to labor for settler colonies in many contexts (e.g., California Indians forced to build Spanish missions, or blackbirded Melanesians forced to work on settler plantations in Australia and Fiji).[49] The so-called tender side of settler colonialism does not demand that Indigenous peoples "go away," but rather assumes the natural demise of the Indigenous "race," and the ultimate unification of settlers and Indigenous peoples in one nation. Through the logic of possession through whiteness, the "demand" is more a liberal statement of commensurability: "We are you. We are (almost) the same."[50] This requires additional labor of a different kind—primarily the sexual and reproductive labor of Indigenous women, who are expected to birth the new, successively less "raced" generations, through coupling with white settler men.

How whiteness and racial mixture relate to structures of settler colonialism is therefore under-theorized but holds the potential to clarify our theories of settler colonialism globally. The United States, Canada, New Zealand, and Australia are commonly taken for granted as the exemplars of settler colonialism. In each context, the settlers' national investment in whiteness is clear, suggesting that possessive forms of whiteness (the selective incorporation of Indigenous peoples into white settler societies) may be one of the most important features distinguishing settler colonialism from other forms of colonialism. Though I focus on possession through whiteness as applicable in Polynesia, possession through whiteness has wider potential applicability, though the specific contours of the racial category of possession may differ in Asian, African, Latin American, or Middle Eastern contexts such as Taiwan, Tibet, South Africa, Mexico, or Israel. While whiteness in Latin America, for example, is often understood through discourses of *mestizaje*, there are rich similarities in how racial mixture is understood, in both Latin America and Polynesia, as a mode of not simply "whitening" a native population but engulfing the human and natural resources of a place for the purposes of white settlers. This is not to say that whiteness across various settler colonial contexts is exactly the same, or even impacts the various Indigenous peoples under these countries' rule in the same way. Rather, I am calling on scholars to better interrogate whiteness in concert with how Indigenous peoples have been racially constructed (something whiteness studies usually fail to do) in each of these places, precisely because they are different. This book makes a modest contribution toward this goal by focusing on whiteness and indigeneity in Polynesia, and Hawai'i in particular. Yet in doing so, this study also hopes to contribute to the larger theorization of settler colonialism in fields including Native American and Indigenous studies, Pacific Islands studies, critical ethnic studies, gender and sexuality studies, and settler colonial studies, through attending to the structural importance of Western scientific discourses of whiteness and racial mixture.

## REGENERATION AS INDIGENOUS FEMINIST ANALYTIC

Though this book is attentive to the construction of Polynesia as a Western, settler project, it is also concerned with how Polynesians have made it their own project as well, far predating Western settlement. Not surprisingly, then, the meaning invested in Polynesia by Polynesians often has little or nothing to do with Western ideas about race and whiteness. Instead, Polynesianness is often grounded in shared political and cultural histories, living and organizing together in diasporic locations such as Auckland, Honolulu, Salt Lake City, Southern California, or the San Francisco Bay Area, and/or common genealogies especially in relation to our akua and kūpuna, gods and ancestors, who traveled across Polynesia, such as Maui and Pele.[51] This book cannot do justice to the variety of meanings Polynesia as a Polynesian project holds. Yet it does analyze what happens when Polynesian pasts and futures are interrupted by settler horizons. To better contextualize such interruptions, we must reorient ourselves to what Damon Salesa has called "Indigenous time," which is oriented by ancestors and descendants, not to a "disembodied calibration of time."[52] In Polynesian epistemologies, Salesa further notes that we might recognize a long-standing concept of wa, va, or vahaʻa, meaning something like "space-time," in which "places and time were not secular, but filled with the resonance of the spiritual and divine."[53]

Salesa's work reminds us that despite historical and contemporary colonial projects in Oceania, we can still meaningfully locate Polynesia within Indigenous frameworks as well. This book analyzes how Polynesians respond to, critique, and co-opt the settler colonial logic of possession through whiteness, through a framework of regeneration. Regeneration is an Indigenous feminist analytic, shaped by my engagements with other Indigenous studies' formulations of regeneration.[54] As Anishinaabe writer Leanne Simpson puts it, regeneration is a "process of bringing forth more life—getting the seed and planting and nurturing it. It can be a physical seed, it can be a child, or it can be an idea. But if you're not continually engaged in that process then it doesn't happen."[55] As Simpson's theory points out, regeneration is therefore a different conceptualization of time, reminiscent of Salesa's reorientation to Indigenous time, focused on embodied daily practices, incremental steps, and the nurturing of life. Regeneration within an Indigenous feminist frame is not a vanguard or prescribed political program. Regeneration signals new growth and life cultivated after destruction, as in the plants that gradually return to a charred landscape after a volcanic flow. Regenerative actions seek the return of function, balance, or power, as in the regrowth of a starfish's limb or moʻoʻs (lizard, gecko) tail.

In other words, regeneration is acting on the recognition of a responsibility to a people and a place to refuse the settler colonial order of things. This is relevant to this book's working definition of indigeneity itself. As particularly informed by the Kanaka Maoli context, indigeneity refers to the condition of being genealogically related to specific lands/oceans, which determines particular kinds of relationships between a people and a place, where the place is often understood as an ancestor that the people must care for.[56] Settler colonialism often disrupts the abilities of an Indigenous people to fulfill such responsibilities or kuleana. This happens in part through the production of Indigenous peoples as a race, rather than as a sovereign people, and the production of settlers as the native, natural owners/residents of a place (though without the same genealogical relationships and responsibilities to that place that Indigenous peoples do).[57] This process is deeply connected too, in the U.S. context, to the dispossession of kidnapped Africans who are transformed from Indigenous peoples of their own African nations into black slaves through the transatlantic slave trade. For Indigenous peoples of both the Americas and Africa, settler colonial law, society, and science turn a people's political claims (sovereignty) into a supposedly biological one (race).

Framing indigeneity through a lens of regeneration consciously centers the raced and gendered body in analyses of both settler colonialism and decolonization. Regeneration in this Indigenous feminist sense invokes the body, but does not center genetic, biological reproduction as the mode of building the future (though it also does not dismiss the gendered labor of birthing and raising children). Rather, regeneration takes a broader view of kinship and community that is rooted in good relationships with one's self, one's community, other communities, and the lands we live on. As Indigenous feminist Geraldine King writes, "dispossession is about breaking the relationship between bodies and land."[58] Accordingly, Indigenous decolonization efforts inside and outside the academy must center the body, not only land or issues such as Native governance that are often perceived as more central (and implicitly, more masculine).

Attempts at regeneration are also sometimes ugly, uncomfortable, conflicted, and co-opted. Because regeneration is not a political program or vanguard, regeneration in my framing also allows for analysis of actions that are not always straightforwardly "good," though they are always complex. *Regeneration* was in fact a keyword of the American eugenics movement, as in "race regeneration," signaling efforts to purify the genetics of the white race. While Polynesians in general do not adhere to imposed Western designations of race, gender, and sexuality, at times they do seek to use imposed categories to their own advantage, as in the *Day v. Apoliona* case examined in chapter 4. The *Day* plaintiffs went to court to further entrench and even extend the reach of blood quantum laws defining Native Hawaiians as those with 50 percent or more Native Hawaiian blood. While I find the politics of the plaintiffs deeply troubling, reinforcing the very racial and heteropatriarchal hierarchies that comprise their own colonization, their actions nonetheless betray a strong anticolonial critique and an interest in repossessing a Native Hawaiian future of their own making. In this way, it is oriented by a politics of regeneration that cannot be wholly separated from the other Native Hawaiian activist projects this book examines. I therefore find it useful to contrast the *Day* plaintiffs' actions with other, more expansive visions of regeneration in part II.

The attention to regenerative actions alongside the historical and contemporary presence of possession through whiteness allows this text not simply to document the colonial "damage" of attributing almost whiteness to Polynesians in Western scientific knowledge, but to further better understand what strategies have been and might be effective in unsettling settler logics.[59] Focusing on desire and not just damage is an Indigenous feminist approach, most eloquently described by Eve Tuck.[60] As this book attempts to highlight throughout, the racial designations imposed on Native Hawaiians and other Polynesian peoples have never been wholly or blindly accepted. In many Native Hawaiian contexts, historically and in the present, being "Part" or "*x* percent" Native Hawaiian is entirely nonsensical. Native Hawaiians have long been inclusive about their genealogical definitions of community and nation in a desire to grow their relations.[61] This inclusion rarely made sense to social scientists like Louis Sullivan, as I discuss in chapter 2, who often doubted and disregarded the self-identifications his Native Hawaiian subjects made, marking many of those who claimed to be "Pure Hawaiian" as likely "Part Hawaiian" instead.

That Native Hawaiians would want to hold onto their Hawaiianness, that they seemed to refuse the offer of nominal entry into whiteness, was often baffling to scientists and the larger American public. Salesa similarly writes of the continual self-identification of "half-castes" as Māori, as a development that was "fascinating to scholars, who wondered why, if given access not just to the colonial polity but the white race, literally thousands of people apparently refused, and not just day after day but (by the 1930s and

1940s) generation after generation."[62] This kind of refusal is what I term a *regenerative refusal*. Part II of this book examines how such regenerative refusals operate against the logic of possession through whiteness in law, art, and science today. I seek not to make such refusals legible to Western science, but to spend more time with refusal as a mode of promoting more life and joy to Indigenous communities, even or especially in the face of seemingly insurmountable settler colonial power.

Regenerative refusals attempt to capture how Polynesians negotiate entanglements with the logic of possession through whiteness, with an eye toward effecting meaningful change. Overall, this book's theory of change is in line with the sentiment expressed by Avery Gordon: "We need to know where we live in order to imagine living elsewhere. We need to imagine living elsewhere before we can live there."[63] My purpose in excavating the racial and colonial knowledge of "where we live" is oriented by the need "to imagine living elsewhere," in an Indigenous space-time where we have divested from such knowledge. My framework of regeneration attempts to reveal glimpses of a possible "elsewhere" through a thorough investigation of how Native Hawaiians respond to "where we live" now. As a Native Hawaiian feminist, I find these tasks urgent. Yet, while I am of the Native Hawaiian people, and Polynesian people more broadly, I do not seek to speak for all of them, or even part of them. Rather, under the rubric of regenerative refusals, I analyze several different actions that I see as connected through similar goals of decolonization, even when their strategies may be at odds. In other words, this book is about both understanding the colonial histories that shape the lives of Native Hawaiians and Polynesians today and, through listening to and learning from abundant regenerative refusals, planning for a different future for Oceania and its diasporas.

THE POSSESSIVE SPIRIT OF WHITENESS AND ANTIBLACKNESS

How do Indigenous Oceanic pasts and futures figure in contemporary scientific research about Polynesians? I take up that question further in chapter 5, but it is worth noting from the outset that researchers continue to ask "What is a Polynesian?" especially through tracing Polynesian origins in genomics and linguistics to Austronesia. *Austronesian* (literally meaning "southern islands") is a designation given to an extensive language family spanning from Southeast Asia to Madagascar in the west and Polynesia in the east. A significant amount of research about Austronesian origins is centered in Taiwan as a possible "homeland" or "birthplace" of Austronesian languages, which supporters of Taiwanese independence have at times used to further their political cause by pointing to Taiwan's ancestral racial distinction from mainland China. While contemporary Austronesian discourse does not center whiteness, its roots are in early twentieth-century discourses of Aryanism.[64] So too, the Austronesian discourse, as emanating from scientific and popular culture sources, has occasionally flattened rather than expanded notions of Indigenous identity. Narratives about Taiwan as a Polynesian homeland can be problematic for both Polynesians, who can be represented as immigrants to their native lands and therefore equivalent to other citizens of settler states like New Zealand and the United States, and for Indigenous Taiwanese, who are sometimes represented, as Mark Munsterhjelm has noted, as "ancestral living dead because their main significance is primarily as living conduits to dead Māori ancestors."[65] Ironically, as I show in chapter 1, this problematic construction of Indigenous Taiwanese people echoes nineteenth-century Polynesian Problem literature that constructed Māori and other Polynesians as the "ancestral living dead" to white settlers.

No one deserves to be framed by science as "living conduits" to another people's past. This gloss of Indigenous Taiwanese as repositories of Polynesian pasts is a more recent example of the kind of colonial possession that this book traces and critiques. Possession, in this respect, is the claiming of other peoples' bodies, identities, and other resources as one's own, without regard to those peoples' own histories and desires for the future. As I describe further throughout this book, the logic of possession through whiteness clearly continues to impact not only how white people see Polynesians and other Indigenous peoples, but also, and more devastatingly, how we see each other, as in the above examples between Polynesians and Peruvians or Indigenous Taiwanese peoples. What is at stake in my project, then, is ensuring that our relationships between Indigenous peoples in and beyond Oceania are not haunted at their foundations by settler colonial frameworks. By understanding the history of Western constructions of race in the Pacific, we build the groundwork for finding new ways to reject the imposed white/black racial and settler colonial binary that endures within and between Polynesia, Micronesia, and Melanesia.

In colonial conditions, knowledge is the important agent of possession—a word with which I purposefully invoke its bodily, haunting, supernatural connotation. Demons and spirits, rather than (and anathema to) the logic of science, are commonly identified as the agents of bodily possession. But many have noted that modernity and science are in fact haunted, obsessed with the eradication of the premodern and the exorcism of ghosts.[66]

Similarly, this book is a history of social science, what haunts it, and how this form of knowledge continues to haunt us, with a particular interest in how and why social science produced the idea of the almost white Polynesian.

In its approach to race and the history of social science, this book follows the critical interventions of Denise Ferreira da Silva, who has intervened into conventional conceptions of race by returning to accounts of the human in foundational post-Enlightenment European philosophy, which structured early social scientific texts. Silva particularly focuses on the importance of the transcendent human Spirit theorized by G. W. F. Hegel, which provided the conditions of possibility for the development of racial power.[67] By following how Hegel's Spirit haunts past and present concepts of race, Silva intervenes into conventional understandings of race as used in the United States as descriptive of particular forms of oppression by recuperating "scientific signification to introduce a conception of political subjects as an effect of symbolic, productive violence."[68] What Silva finds in the field of science is not simply the production of race as part of the "symbolics of blood," or physical characteristics, but "raciality" that operates via the production of minds."[69] For Silva, raciality is enabled by the scientific production of self-consciousness as Man's distinguishing attribute (which, after Hegel, is able to be understood as an interior quality that allowed Man productive power over exterior things).[70] Europe's Others would not be able to achieve transcendence in the same way, remaining "doubly affectable," because they would be subject to both exteriority (bodies and nature) and the European Man who had more successfully realized his own self-perfection (Hegel's Spirit).

Silva's approach illuminates the history of the social scientific construction of the almost white Polynesian well precisely because it attends to race as not merely a matter of skin color. While physical markers are certainly of consequence to the racialization of Polynesians, the creation of the almost white Polynesian had very little to do with the objective physical traits of Polynesian peoples, and much more to do with white settler claims to self-realization, over and against what white settlers saw as Polynesians' "exteriority" and "affectability," in Silva's terms. In other words, Silva's take on raciality helps explain the complex workings of possession through whiteness as a form of settler colonial power that did not simply discriminate based on color but created elaborate fictions about past and future relationships between white settlers and Polynesians. While on the surface such claims promoted a sense of equality between white settlers and Polynesian people, in actuality, they allowed a subtler form of raciality, as a "production of minds," where white settlers would be understood as self-determining and productive, and Polynesians would be understood as never having the ability to be self-determining. This kind of reasoning instituted a hierarchy wherein white settlers were understood to be necessary to making Polynesian lands and people productive, because Polynesians were supposedly incapable of this productivity themselves. Of course, this idea was demonstrably false, contravening the deep history of Polynesians creating self-sustaining ways of life for centuries before European contact.

By following Silva's formulations of raciality and spirit, this study differs in significant ways from other studies of race and whiteness, especially those structured by positivism or empiricism. For example, possession through whiteness, like Foucault's theory of biopolitics, is an extralegal, liberal, social form of governance. For Foucault, the biopolitical was a type of power/knowledge that focused on society and the management of society through technologies that produced and capitalized human life.[71] Foucault's account of biopolitics is largely an account of the management of life as positive knowledge, made most plain in statistics. Unlike biopolitics, however, possession through whiteness forces a spiritual and racial investment of human capital within the colonized, which cannot be fully produced through statistics alone. My theory of the logic of possession through whiteness relies on a different account of life from biopolitics—namely, Hegel's, which produced the human as Spirit.[72] Through the production of the colonized as almost (but not quite) white, the possibility of attaining transcendence is held out but deferred as impossible—indeed, attaining transcendence and whiteness would "obliterate" the colonized as such. This account of raciality helps explain why racial violence can continue haunting the present despite laws against racial discrimination or the lack of overt racism in some places. The extension of rights or social niceties to nonwhite people can be the very mechanism through which racial violence is perpetuated, as the achievement of full personhood for Europe's Others in Hegel's understanding of the human will always be indefinitely deferred.

Formative studies of whiteness in the United States and beyond have emphasized whiteness as a powerful legal, economic, psychological, and/or literary category. Emphasizing whiteness as a matter of scientific knowledge/power, this book alternately draws from, extends, or departs from these studies, with attention to their varying engagements with theorizing indigeneity and settler colonialism.[73] The structural forms of whiteness and white supremacy in my analysis are not reducible to a set of phenotypes or group identity labels such as haole.[74] *Haole* is a word commonly used to describe white people in Hawaiʻi, which can be merely descriptive or hold a pejorative implication, though its original meaning is simply "foreigner." This book is not about the history of the development of haole identity, but about the racial discourses haole settlers used to dispossess Native Hawaiians and other Polynesian peoples. I approach whiteness, after Rey Chow's description, as a historically and geographically changing, "ascendant" ideology, folding peoples into it, encouraging peoples to identify with the power/knowledge of whiteness even when they are individually excluded from identifying as white.[75]

Settler possession of indigeneity through whiteness is an oft-overlooked foundation of the legal protection of "whiteness as property," in the well-known formulation by Cheryl Harris.[76] Harris argues that the privileges of whiteness have historically been constructed as a kind of privilege-laden property that white people own and that the law acts to defend. Harris points out that white people are able to control whiteness as property, but Indigenous peoples or Black people who can at times "pass" as white have no equivalent control over their own identity.[77] As Harris puts it, this is "*tres*passing," because performing whiteness is not the same as owning it permanently. Performing whiteness requires sacrifice and, indeed, accepting the daily "risk of self-annihilation."[78] There is no guaranteed future in performing whiteness this way because those who pass do not have "continued control" over whiteness as ownable, permanent property. Indigenous peoples also at times "*tres*pass" on the property of whiteness in similarly damaging ways. But because indigeneity, as a natural claim to a place, is desirable within a settler colonial context (in contrast to blackness, which is defined as a negative opposite to whiteness), white people also routinely attempt to "pass" as Indigenous. I mean this not only in the sense of "playing Indian," but in a deeper identificatory process in which white settlers feel a natural ownership of a place. Within the structure of settler colonialism, this type of passing is far from risky—rather than "self-annihilation," possessing indigeneity is in fact a form of self-actualization for white settlers. In short, white settlers in Polynesia use this form of passing to steal Indigenous land and power.

My approach to whiteness and settler colonialism builds on other accounts in Indigenous studies, notably including Indigenous Australian scholar Aileen Moreton-Robinson's work. Moreton-Robinson argues that patriarchal whiteness operates through "possessive logics" that are "underpinned by an excessive desire to invest in reproducing and reaffirming the nation-state's ownership, control and domination."[79] Her attention to these possessive logics in law, such as Native title law in Australia, provides invaluable analysis for understanding deeply rooted ideologies about settler colonial nation-states as naturally white. Where Moreton-Robinson's scholarship locates the foundations of whiteness largely in early settler accounts such as Captain Cook's declaration of Australia as *terra nullius* (empty land) and in settler state law, this book turns to the construction of race and whiteness in the history of Western social and genetic sciences, as well as law and art. Whereas in the context of Australia, Indigenous people have been constructed as black in stark distinction to white settlers, in Polynesia, the racial construction of Indigenous peoples is in closer proximity to whiteness. While these racial constructions are superficially distinct and opposing (Aboriginal Australians as black and Polynesians as almost white), both are simultaneously structured by antiblack and anti-Indigenous settler colonial ideologies.

Antiblackness is generally under-theorized in critiques of settler colonialism, but it is central to my theory of settler colonialism as buoyed by a logic of possession through whiteness.[80] By antiblackness, I mean antiblack racism as it is globally, structurally embedded in societies, economies, laws, and ideologies, exposing people who are Black or read as black to what Ruthie Gilmore has succinctly described as "vulnerability to premature death."[81] In the context of the history of Oceania, "black" as an identity either imposed or self-attributed most often refers to Melanesians and/or Aboriginal Australians, both of whom, in the Western imagination, formed the contrasting image to the ideal of Polynesians as white. Tracey Banivanua-Mar describes Melanesianism as "the historical notion that Melanesians, or Kanakas, were essentially driven and motivated by the base instincts of tribalism, primitivism, and savage violence ... an idea that dehistoricized people's physical actions and essentialized Islanders' violence in a way that displaced it from its social context."[82]

Deeming Melanesians black and irrationally violent served Western purposes in many ways, perhaps most obviously in the forced labor practice of so-called blackbirding. About sixty thousand Melanesians were kidnapped, coerced, or otherwise forced into laboring on plantations in Queensland, Australia, from 1863 to 1906, and at least twenty-two thousand Melanesians were similarly forced into labor on plantations in Fiji in this period. While seemingly distant and largely taking place after the legal end of slavery in the United States, the United States played a role in these forced labors. Gerald Horne, for example, analyzes post–Civil War U.S. complicity with British and other European blackbirders in Fiji, showing how white U.S.

settlers in Fiji and Australia brought antiblack and white supremacist ideologies with them to the Pacific.[83]

While this book does not focus on the history of Melanesia directly, these racial discourses that Banivanua-Mar and Horne trace in relation to Melanesians as black, primitive, and violent are a constant counterpart to the logic of possession through whiteness that I analyze in the history of racial constructions of Polynesians. Against the lofty ideal of Polynesians having an ancestral Aryan genealogy and therefore holding kinship with white settlers, in practice Polynesians were always subject to binary classification as either a "true" Polynesian who was conditionally Caucasian, or a false Polynesian whose primitive habits and dark skin placed them more solidly with the Melanesian "type." In fact, Polynesians were, on occasion, also blackbirded. Matt Matsuda describes, for example, how the Rapa Nui people were forced to work in guano mines in Peru from 1862 to 1864, doing work that was so deadly that 90 percent of them perished.[84]

Given such histories, this book demonstrates that the relations between indigeneity and blackness are deeply bound, not just comparable as similar but distinct categories. They are, as scholars like to say, "mutually constitutive," but I attempt to show in this book how that does not simply mean that Melanesians and Polynesians are represented as eternal, static opposites. Rather, periodically or even regularly, Polynesians can fail to live up to their supposed conditional whiteness and then be treated as degenerate, black, primitive—all characteristics that in the Oceanic context of imperialism and colonialism are coded as Melanesian, and in Hawai'i and other U.S.-dominated islands can additionally be coded as African American. Within both Polynesian and Melanesian groupings, white settlers could create hierarchies that elevated some Polynesians or Melanesians over the rest, labeling certain Polynesians "black," or those deemed relatively advanced among Melanesians as "relatively civilized."

These contingent valuations could be internalized by Polynesian peoples, giving rise to a kind of Polynesian exceptionalism, wherein Polynesian peoples invest in the idea that Polynesians (or their specific ethnic group such as Kānaka Maoli, Sāmoan, Tongan, or Māori) are better than Melanesians and Micronesians. I discuss the complications of such internalized Polynesian exceptionalism throughout the book. On the other hand, there are also many notable cases in which Polynesians have identified explicitly as Black in order to signal both an anticolonial stance distinguishing Polynesians from white settlers and a meaningful solidarity with Black people from other colonial contexts, including Melanesians but also Africans and the African diaspora in the Americas. Robbie Shilliam, for example, examines how Māori in Aotearoa "grounded" with Rastafari and the Black Panthers in the 1960s and 1970s, forming a powerful activist movement under the banner of the Polynesian Panthers.[85] Nitasha Sharma further analyzes the solidarities between African Americans and Native Hawaiians in Hawai'i.[86] In some contexts, then, Polynesians have explicitly responded to the logic of possession through whiteness by investing in identities that emphasize both blackness and indigeneity as global forms of solidarity among colonized peoples. Such examples are hopeful demonstrations that these community divisions are not inevitable, and that actions challenging imposed colonial ideologies about race can work.

Further, we can see elements of a racial triangulation when we consider other immigrant populations in Oceania—primarily Asian immigrants. Yet this triangulation is also more complicated than simply assigning Asian immigrants an intermediate place in the preexisting black/white, Indigenous/settler binary. I argue in this book that white settlers used the presence of Asian immigrants in Hawai'i, particularly Chinese immigrants, many of whom found success as small business owners in the Hawaiian Kingdom and Territory of Hawai'i, as evidence that Hawai'i was whitening. While Chinese were not viewed as white, they were also, in the minds of haole setters, not Native Hawaiian and not black. As I discuss in chapter 3, white social scientists would take the presence of Chinese and other Asian immigrants, and especially their intermarrying with Native Hawaiians, as proof of a uniquely American melting pot transforming Hawai'i into a multicultural society that nonetheless adhered to white norms.

In the Hawaiian context, important coalitions have formed between Native Hawaiians and Asian Americans. A recent formation of self-identified "Asian settler scholars" including Candace Fujikane, Jonathan Okamura, and Dean Saranillio, have theorized Asian settler colonialism as a framework to grapple with the ways that Asian Americans have participated in settling Hawai'i and naturalizing American occupation.[87] I say "Asian American" here to make clear that these scholars are largely ones who in other contexts may identify as Asian American (that is, people who have Asian ancestry but were largely born and raised in the United States) and/or consider themselves part of Asian American studies as a field, but it is notable and instructive that these scholars emphasize "Asian settler" as their connecting force, not Asian American. There is much to unpack in that choice of term, but I read it as a critique of the way the identity Asian American can erase both differences within the label and complicity with settler colonialism more broadly. It is also consistent with the ways that Asian American holds less salience in the Hawaiian context, where people have often identified with specific ethnic identities rather than with Asian American as an umbrella term. Perhaps most notably, the choice to not identify with the "American" in Asian American appears to be a purposeful reorientation of those with Asian heritage to see themselves in relationship to Native Hawaiians and the Hawaiian Kingdom, rather than only in relation to the U.S. nation-state. For indeed, in contrast to histories that laud the first generations of Japanese and Chinese plantation workers as the foundation for the contemporary Asian American middle class in Hawaiʻi, these scholars seek to reposition themselves and their communities outside of U.S. national frames and within a squarely settler colonial one.[88] While criticism of the term *Asian settler* has denounced the potential for lumping Asians and Asian Americans along with white settlers into a category starkly opposed to Native Hawaiians, the Asian settler scholars repeatedly position their critiques as ones that do not seek to reproach Asian Americans in Hawaiʻi for their presence there but rather to challenge Asian American affiliations with the U.S. nation-state.

The usage of "Asian settler" is therefore not a determination that Asian immigrants are exactly the same as white settlers in Hawaiʻi, but rather that ideologically Asian Americans have also been placed in proximity to whiteness in the United States, and are working to undo the ways that this positioning invites violence against Asians and Asian Americans. The model minority myth, Victor Bascara writes, trots Asian Americans out as "miracle synthetic white people."[89] Of course, there are nuances within the incredibly broad label of Asian American. Historically, Filipinos in Hawaiʻi, for example, have always had much less capital and been much more distanced from whiteness than Japanese and Chinese Americans. Not being able to assume that synthetic whiteness in any secure, consistent way, however, puts Asian Americans in a similar if incommensurable position to Native Hawaiians in respect to whiteness. Each group is engaged in the project of America by being possessed through whiteness, while they themselves are not fully extended the possession of whiteness. Nonetheless, many Chinese and Japanese Americans in Hawaiʻi have secured middle-class or higher status. So too, international Chinese and Japanese investors continue to buy a large proportion of Hawaiian real estate, while Native Hawaiians continue to fall to the bottom of most socioeconomic scales and increasingly make up a majority of Hawaiʻi's growing homeless population. This incommensurability is what Asian settler colonialism attempts to acknowledge and work to change. I further engage with the theoretical and political possibilities of Asian settler colonialism in chapters 3 and 6, in relation to the history of the ideal of Hawai'i as a melting pot and the problematic Asian American use of *Hapa*, a Hawaiian word meaning "part," and commonly used as a self-identification of mixed-race Native Hawaiians to foreground their Native Hawaiian ancestry.

### TRACING POSSESSION THROUGH WHITENESS: METHODS AND STRUCTURE OF THE BOOK

Words and discourses do not exist separate from us, but infiltrate and shape the intimate and public spaces we live in. This wisdom is encompassed in the 'ōlelo no'eau (proverb), "i ka 'ōlelo ke ola, i ka 'ōlelo ka make" (in words is the power of life and death).[90] This book applies discourse analysis to Western social scientific literature about Polynesians from the mid-nineteenth century through the mid-twentieth century, as well as to more contemporary constructions of race in law, genetics, and visual representation. Discourse analysis of social scientific studies may sound rather dry and irrelevant to the daily lives of Polynesian peoples, and indeed, such texts are, by design, often abstract and removed from community concerns. My attention to the power of social scientific studies, in concert with law and popular culture, throughout this book follows the principle in Hawaiian epistemology that words and language (and by extension, discourses, which encompass words, representations, practices—specific modes of knowing) are powerful, with the ability to give and take life.

Indeed, this book is attentive to the power of discourse to bring about material, corporeal changes. I often employ the analytic of possession through whiteness through the metaphor of haunting, particularly the haunting of Polynesian bodies by the deep legacies of Western knowledge production about Polynesian whiteness. This colonial, racial knowledge as a discourse was always forcibly enacted on Polynesians. Rather than a distanced, historical, literary, or visual studies approach, conceiving of possession through whiteness with attention to the body and the corporeal reminds me of the many ways this knowledge is violently embodied, attached to people with devastating consequences, as in blood quantum designations and legislation, as I examine in chapter 4, or inevitably overlaying the erotic image of the hula girl onto an actual Native Hawaiian woman, as I examine in chapters 3 and 6.

These issues are constantly present, and deeply felt, in my own life as a Native Hawaiian woman. Yet the force of Western scientific constructions of Polynesian race and gender are not and never have been totalizing. Possession, in whatever its supernatural, scientific, legal, and/or other imperial forms, is unstable and never quite complete. Possession is nine-tenths of the law, as the popular maxim goes, but the one-tenth matters in sometimes surprisingly substantial ways. Science fiction portrayals of demonic or other kinds of possession, for example, enjoy showing the always-shifting battles between an occupying spirit and its unwilling host. Following these ideas about possession, this book is attentive to the instability and specificities of the discourse of Polynesians as almost white across time and place, especially through the many ways that Native Hawaiians and other Polynesians have refused to be wholly possessed by settler colonialism. In the acknowledgment that words can hold life and death, there is also an acknowledgment in Hawaiian epistemology that you always have a regenerative power to write, sing, or chant back.[91] The discourse of the almost white Polynesian race must be exposed, overturned, and thoroughly exorcised. Accordingly, I understand the words I offer here and the words and actions of other Polynesian peoples I highlight to be part of what kuʻualoha hoʻomanawanui has identified as a "hulihia discourse of ʻŌiwi agency" that counters and overturns settler rhetoric, while developing its own.[92]

In a similar vein, Nyong'o argues: "Race is a theory of history, so exposing its historicity will trouble its foundations and foreground its assumptions regarding time and temporality."[93] Exposing the historicity of the Western construction of the Polynesian race is the task I take up in part I of *Possessing Polynesians*, "The Polynesian Problem: Scientific Production of the 'Almost White' Polynesian Race." These chapters examine Western scientific studies of the Polynesian race from the nineteenth through the mid-twentieth centuries, where the logics of seeing Polynesians as simultaneously "Caucasoid" and as racially mixed developed, especially in studies based in Hawaiʻi. The use of Hawaiʻi as a social scientific model for supposed racial harmony before and after World War II is a central concern, especially in chapter 3, where I consider the ways that the sociological theory of Hawaiʻi as a racial melting pot was premised on the assimilation of Asians and Native Hawaiians into whiteness. Though the chapters of part I are roughly chronological, their goal is less to provide a comprehensive narrative history of all ideas about race in the Pacific than to show how settler colonial ideologies about Polynesian almost whiteness developed thematically, from the representation of Polynesians as Aryan "heirlooms of the past," to the physical anthropological theories of Polynesians as "conditionally Caucasian," and, finally, to the sociological construction of Polynesians blending into a whitening melting pot. All of these ideologies are underpinned by enduring logics that allowed white settlers to write themselves into Polynesian pasts and futures.

Part II of of *Possessing Polynesians*, "Regenerative Refusals: Confronting Contemporary Legacies of the Polynesian Problem in Hawai'i and Oceania," considers how the histories of part I continue to haunt the present by examining ongoing challenges Native Hawaiians and other Polynesians face in law, popular representation, and science. Mirroring many of the concerns of part I, part II demonstrates that the logic of possession through whiteness, though generated in sciences that are now often spoken of as debunked pseudosciences, is still very much alive in the structure of settler colonialism in Polynesia. Chapter 4, for instance, examines echoes of the eugenic construction of the "Pure" and "Part" Hawaiian in internal and external battles over legal recognition for Native Hawaiians. In the interplay between parts I and II, *Possessing Polynesians* impresses upon its readers that the role of science in constructions of race cannot be too easily dismissed or limited to the "bad" science of the past, but that both past and ongoing scientific projects naturalize white settlement of the Pacific, constructing Indigenous Pacific Islanders as almost-white relics rather than complex and contemporary Indigenous peoples.

The inclusion of historical and contemporary analysis is essential to this book because to many Polynesians, these histories are not over. This interdisciplinary approach enriches existing scholarship on the history of science in the Pacific. While largely overlooked in the U.S. academy, the history of the Polynesian Problem and the imposed white/black divide between Polynesia and Melanesia is well documented and described by European and Australian historians.[94] However, these studies focus on the history of European colonialism largely without engaging the scholarship of Indigenous Pacific Islanders or Indigenous studies, which has grown enormously in the past few decades.[95] This book covers some of the same ground as historians such as Bronwen Douglas, K. R. Howe, and Nicholas Thomas, but with a different purpose. I focus on unraveling the logic of possession through whiteness for the benefit of contemporary Indigenous peoples. This research is oriented by Polynesian epistemologies that value learning from both distant and more immediate ancestors, often metaphorically described as envisioning the future by walking forward into the past. Accordingly, part I's focus on the past is not intended to be an immersion in historical trauma and damage, but rather a caring, critical assessment of what needs to be done today to regenerate vibrant Polynesian futures.

PART I

# The Polynesian Problem

## Scientific Production of the "Almost White" Polynesian Race

Throughout the eighteenth century, Europeans sailed in search of Terra Australis, which they imagined as the last undiscovered southern continent accessible through some unknown part of the Pacific Ocean. Visions of this mythical continent had circulated as early as the Middle Ages, along with titillating projections of the monstrous, antipodean race of men who inhabited this land. Some fantasies portrayed these men with legs and feet that bent in directly opposite ways from European ones, while others conjured sciapods, creatures originating in Greek and Roman lore with single legs and giant feet they used to shade themselves from the sun.[1] In the wake of European encounters with the Americas, many would seek to be the first to actually discover Terra Australis and capitalize on its imagined wealth. This quest animated many European voyages by sea to the Pacific, at least through 1775, when James Cook's second voyage to the Pacific sighted Antarctica but, thwarted by ice floes, deemed the continent uninhabitable. Nonetheless, European curiosity and fear about the peoples of Terra Australis, who they suspected were diametrically opposite from them, colored the actual encounters they began to have with Indigenous peoples of Australia and the Pacific Islands.[2]

Indeed, as Europeans and Americans sought knowledge of the Pacific Islands for potential economic, religious, and scientific gain, their cartographic pursuits also simultaneously catalogued and categorized people, mapping imposed divisions upon the perceived "races" of the Pacific, which would endure in the labels of Polynesian, Melanesian, and Micronesian. Part I analyzes the development of these racial ideologies along with the development of social sciences in the nineteenth and twentieth centuries. Even as ethnology, physical anthropology, and sociology would approach race in the Pacific from distinct methodologies and concerns, each field's inquiry remained haunted by this older literature that laid the foundation for seeing Indigenous Pacific peoples in opposites—often, literally, in black and white.

RACIALLY MAPPING THE PACIFIC ISLANDS

As Europeans produced knowledge of the Pacific, they mapped not only geographic boundaries, but also racial ones. As early as 1595, Spanish navigator Pedro Fernandez de Quiros reported on the apparent beauty and fairness of the people he encountered upon contact with what he called the Marquesas, an island group in the southeastern Pacific.[3] In contrast, British navigator William Dampier in 1688 described Indigenous Australians as "coal blacks" who had the "worst features of all the savages."[4] As European contact with Pacific Islands grew in the eighteenth century, many would classify the people they met with tropes that either mirrored de Quiros's idyllic representation that emphasized a modicum of similarity with Europeans, or, like Dampier, maintained that Indigenous Pacific peoples were hostile cannibals.

Polynesia, Melanesia, and Micronesia were consciously invented as terms that connoted not only physical distances, but also cultural and racial separation. This is most obvious in the term *Melanesia*, literally meaning "black islands," which, as Serge Tcherkézoff notes, signified black by "using the Greek root melas rather than the Romance root ne(g)ro."[5] Yet *Polynesian*, a term that was formally in use earlier than Melanesian, was also, if more subtly, a racial designation. The French scholar and politician Charles de Brosses has been credited with the first use of the term *Polynesia* in 1756 (in French, Polynésie), having derived it from the Greek *polloi*, meaning "many."[6] To de Brosses, Polynesia signified not only "many islands," the literal translation, but "everything in the vast Pacific Ocean," incorporating not only the boundaries attributed to Polynesia today (commonly understood as a triangle spanning from Hawai'i in the north, to Aotearoa in the southwest and Rapa Nui in the southeast) but also Micronesia and much of Melanesia.[7] De Brosses further distinguished "Australasia" (the lands to the south of Asia) and "Magellanic" (the region around the Strait of Magellan at the southern tip of South America) as the other regions of the Pacific. The relatively "whiter" Polynesians in de Brosses's account were racially distinct from the relatively "blacker" Australasians.

This coinage of Polynesia was published in de Brosses's 1756 two-volume text *Histoire des navigations aux terres australes* ("A History of Voyages to the Southern Lands"), which was one of the first European texts to systematically condense and analyze all existing narratives of European voyages to the Antipodes.[8] Tcherkézoff has argued that *Polynesia* was a speculative term, as de Brosses "wanted to give the impression with the word 'Polynesia' that, apart from the famous Southern continent that would surely be found one day, the Pacific was likely to conceal 'many' lucrative spice islands."[9] At the invention of the term *Polynesia*, Western contact had not yet been made with all of the islands of the Pacific. For example, British Captain James Cook did not arrive in Hawai'i until 1778. Indeed, the *Histoire* argued for the further exploration and settlement of "the Southern lands," and arguably significantly influenced the subsequent Pacific voyages, including those of Cook (three voyages from 1768–71, 1772–75, and 1776–79), and French explorers Louis-Antoine de Bougainville (1776–79) and Jules-Sébastien-César Dumont d'Urville (1826–29 and 1837–40).[10] Polynesia entered the English lexicon first in 1766 with a plagiarized version of de Brosses's *Histoire* published by John Callender in Britain.[11] Scottish geographer John Pinkerton further popularized the label Polynesia in English with his *Modern Geography* of 1802.[12]

De Brosses helped popularize Western racial distinctions between Indigenous peoples of the Pacific in a period in which scientific study of "race" was beginning in earnest.[13] In the 1750s, at the time of de Brosses's writing, Western descriptions of race in the Pacific were understood as information that would illuminate not only knowledge about the Pacific but also the constitution of humanity itself. As Tom Ryan argues, to de Brosses, like his intellectual interlocutors Pierre Louis Moreau de Maupertuis and Georges-Louis Leclerc, the Pacific as "the largely unknown oceans and lands of the southern part of the globe, and their equally unknown human inhabitants, constituted the last major piece of this most important philosophical and scientific jigsaw"—namely, human variety and theories of race.

This view of the Pacific as a kind of missing piece to the puzzle of humanity was informed by a sense of the Polynesian as the ideal "natural man," or what Patricia O'Brien has dubbed "the Pacific muse," though this latter representation was more frequently applied to Polynesian women.[14] Certainly, as many other scholars have noted, the questions and theories about race, gender, sexuality, and humanity that Europeans brought to the Pacific were deeply shaped by the ideas that had already solidified from other colonial ventures. The split between the Indians of the New World and Africans, epitomized by the Valladolid debates between Bartolomé de las Casas and Juan Ginés de Sepúlveda in 1550–51, had determined that Indians were fully human and capable of being civilized, whereas Africans were inferior and appropriately enslaved.[15] This split, which structured violence against Indigenous peoples of the Americas and Africa in distinct but interlocking ways, would further map onto European understandings of Indigenous Pacific Islanders, thus reinvigorating the noble Indian and the enslavable African stereotypes two centuries later.

This mapping of racial ideologies onto the Pacific was due in part to European disillusionment about Indigenous peoples of the Americas, who rarely lived up to the impossible ideal of the noble savage. As O'Brien notes, by the late eighteenth century, Native Americans were less often understood in idyllic terms, due to "centuries of trade, warfare, competition for finite resources, and everyday interaction that both demystified and complicated the indigenes beyond the simplistic ideal."[16] Tcherkézoff similarly argues that especially after Louis-Antoine de Bougainville's voyage to the Pacific in 1776–79, Polynesians, usually represented by Tahitians, replaced Hurons, Mohicans, and Iroquois in Enlightenment philosophy as idealized figures of natural man and warrior chiefs.[17] Polynesian women were represented as sexualized, classical figures such as sirens or nymphs signaling both a "cultural difference and a resemblance to Europe's classical past."[18] At the same time, the peoples to the west of Polynesia (de Brosses's Australasia) were interpreted with many of the same tropes attributed to Africans—savage, black, and cannibalistic. Johann Reinhold Forster, the naturalist who accompanied the second Cook voyage to the Pacific, firmly established this distinction between the "exoticized primitivism" of nearly white Polynesians and the "hard primitivism" of the dark, savage Melanesians, with his influential travel account published in 1778.[19]

In the 1830s, the French navigator Dumont d'Urville modified the geographical boundaries used in regard to the Pacific into the boundaries more commonly accepted today, while also keeping to the notion that at least two distinctly different races existed in the Pacific. Presenting his work to the Société de Géographie in 1831–32, d'Urville was the first to suggest that Oceania be divided into four regions: Polynesia, Micronesia, Malaysia, and Melanesia. These labels would be widely influential, becoming common knowledge in French school textbooks, for example, by 1840.[20] With the label "Micronesia," d'Urville was following the invention of an Italian navigator Louis Domeny de Rienzi, who subdivided Polynesia into Polynesia and Micronesia (the area of "very small islands") in 1831. De Rienzi and d'Urville made this distinction (though they subscribed to different boundaries) based on the ideas that across Polynesia peoples spoke similar languages and that Micronesian societies were somewhat less advanced than Polynesian ones and did not follow the Polynesian custom of tabu.[21]

D'Urville's mappings also more systematically codified the racial distinctions between the Oceanic regions.[22] For d'Urville, Polynesia, Micronesia, and Malaysia were inhabited by a "yellowish, copper-skinned, straight-haired" race, whereas Melanesia was inhabited by a dark, frizzy-haired race. Melanesia was, in fact, d'Urville's coinage, though only a slight modification on Bory de Saint-Vincent's term for the dark peoples of Oceania (to distinguish them from Africans), noted in 1825, "Mélaniens."[23] Until at least the 1880s, the categories Melanesian, Papuan, or "Oceanic Negro" often included, or gestured toward, ancestral foundations in Aboriginal peoples of New Holland (Australia) and Van Diemen's Land (Tasmania).[24] Tracey Banivanua-Mar's analysis of what she calls "Melanesianism," incisively critiques the antiblack racial ideologies generated with d'Urville's mappings in the 1830s but that continue to haunt Melanesian lives today. As she put it, "representations of Islanders as black, savage, tribal, violent, and physical were intimately related to the colonial project of constructing and containing a colonizable, oppressable, and exploitable object and were more than just a set of haphazardly similar constructions."[25]

Banivanua-Mar's analysis of Melanesianism is a parallel to what might be termed *Polynesian exceptionalism*, as I discuss further in conjunction with the logic of possession through whiteness in part I. The so-called noble savage only makes sense in distinction from the so-called ignoble savage. It is important to see how central both antiblack (most obvious in relation to explicitly disparaging racist discourses about Melanesians) and anti-Indigenous logic (most obvious in relation to the exoticization and conditional white identification with Polynesians to undermine the power of Polynesians in their own lands) are to the settler colonial ideologies about the Polynesian race. In this respect, I examine antiblackness in historical writing about the Polynesian race not just as an analogy (as in, racist constructions of Polynesians are simply similar to racist constructions of Melanesians) but as essentially constitutive. The white settler construction of Polynesians as almost white is also always a claim about white racial superiority that is centrally an antiblack stance.

### THE POLYNESIAN RACE AS SCIENTIFIC PROBLEM

Later anthropologists did not adhere to the racial divisions sketched above in exactly the same ways, but undoubtedly the idea of two races with distinctly opposite coloring and character persisted through the twentieth century. Some scholars have cautioned against tracing an unbroken line of similarities between older labels and contemporary divisions because, as Bronwen Douglas argues, "the binary construction of Pacific humanity was never homogeneous or uncontested ... it has recurred, retreated, and mutated."[26] Indeed, ethnologist S. J. Whitmee would express dissatisfaction with the "confusion in the use of Geographic and Ethnographic names in the Pacific" as early as 1879.[27] Whitmee argued that Polynesia should be applied as a strictly geographic term to all the islands east of Australia, the Philippines, and New Guinea. Nonetheless, he maintained that there were ethnological divisions to be made between the "dark races" and the "brown stock," insisting only on further specifying this divide with designations such as "Negrito-Polynesian" and "Malayo-Polynesian."[28] So too, many scholars reject attributing the history of race to earlier periods than the late nineteenth and early twentieth centuries, when race moved more squarely into focus in the sciences and racial categories became systematized. Yet, in his analysis of de Brosses's *Histoire*, Tom Ryan has argued that even this systematization occurred earlier for Western ideas of race in the Pacific than has generally been acknowledged.[29]

Certainly, by the nineteenth century, Western writing about the Pacific had shifted from "first contact" travel narratives and recalibrations of geographical regions and names to a scientific fascination and investigation of Polynesian origins. This body of scientific inquiry, beginning in earnest around the 1830s, was nicknamed by scientists, in their publications and correspondence with each other, the "Polynesian Problem." This "problem" encompassed many seeming mysteries to Europeans at the time, including: What could explain why Polynesians' racial appearance was proximate to Europeans (from European perspectives)? Were Polynesians related to Europeans? Were Polynesians related to Melanesians—if so, why did they look and form societies so differently? How could Polynesians have navigated the immense expanses of ocean to populate some of the most isolated pieces of land on Earth? Did the first Polynesians set sail from mainland Asia, island Southeast Asia, or the western shores of North America or South America? Overall, Europeans were eager not only to figure out where Polynesians fit within established racial and gendered hierarchies of Man but also if Polynesians, as possibly a more authentic "natural man" than the American Indians had turned out to be, might offer a different or deeper insight into Man itself.

The Polynesian Problem literature and its legacies, from roughly the 1830s through the 1930s, are the focus of part I. Chapter 1, "Heirlooms of the Aryan Race: Nineteenth-Century Studies of Polynesian Origins," examines in detail several of the early studies of the Polynesian Problem. The chapter argues that theories about the migratory routes of the earliest people into Polynesia helped represent Polynesians as "settlers," analogous to European settlers. Indeed, such studies argued that Polynesians, in stark contrast to the more tribal, savage Melanesians, were ancestrally related to classical "European" civilizations, including, in different accounts, Egyptians, Greeks, and Aryans. Theories of Polynesian almost whiteness were also strategically employed by Polynesian leaders at the time, including King Kalākaua, in attempts to enhance international recognition of Hawaiian and other Polynesian sovereignties as modern and on par with European nation-states through a discourse of Polynesian exceptionalism.

The second and third chapters focus more tightly on the development of such logics for various political ends in the Hawaiian context. Chapter 2, "Conditionally Caucasian: Polynesian Racial Classification in Early Twentieth-Century Eugenics and Physical Anthropology," examines how the narratives established in the early Polynesian Problem literature continued into the early twentieth-century fields of physical anthropology and eugenics in the work of social scientists based in Hawai'i. These fields claimed to bring more precision to answering the question of where Polynesians came from through the new technology of anthropometry (the measurement of human physical features) and new knowledge of Mendelian laws of inheritance. In relation to Native Hawaiians, this research helped form the ideologies about blood percentages that would solidify blood quantum laws. Chapter 3, "Hating Hawaiians, Celebrating Hybrid Hawaiian Girls: Sociology and the Fictions of Racial Mixture," examines sociological literature that lauded Hawai'i as a "racial laboratory" alongside popular images of the "hybrid Hawaiian girl." The chapter argues that in the context of a long campaign toward achieving statehood for Hawai'i, both these sociological studies and the popular representations of Hawai'i's exotic, feminine "racial mixes" played an important role in downplaying the foreignness of Hawai'i's various ethnic populations and making white settler men feel welcome and in control. To actual multiracial people in Hawai'i, however, there is ample evidence that racism was alive and well.

Altogether, part I of *Possessing Polynesians* tracks the logic of possession through whiteness in Polynesia through the late nineteenth and early twentieth centuries, with attention to both continuities and adaptations to changes in social scientific methods and the ideological demands of settler colonialism in Hawai'i in particular. While the logic of possession through whiteness is never static over time, I emphasize the rhetorical consistencies that make this logic so foundational to settler colonialism.[30] The ideas I highlight in part I regarding the Polynesian race as ancestrally Aryan (chapter 1) or conditionally Caucasian (chapter 2), and the conduit for creating a new, whitened race in Hawai'i (chapter 3) are all enduring pieces of the logic of possession through whiteness that I further analyze in relation to twenty-first-century legal cases, genomic studies, and visual representations in part II.

CHAPTER 1

*Heirlooms of the Aryan Race*
Nineteenth-Century Studies of Polynesian Origins

In what consists the ever constant interest in the handful of people that comprises the Polynesian race? ... The answer is, no doubt, the mystery that surrounds their origin, their intelligence, their charming personality, and—one likes to think—their common source with ourselves from the Caucasian branch of humanity, which induces in us a feeling of sympathy and affection above that felt toward any other colored race.
—S. PERCY SMITH, "Polynesian Wanderings," 1911

What does Polynesia have in common with ancient Greece, Rome, or Egypt? Everything, according to white scholars of the nineteenth century, who argued repeatedly that ancient Polynesians were just like classical Grecians, Romans, or Egyptians. Though distant on maps, scholars emphasized the similarities in social and political organization, encouraging a view of Polynesia as a once-great civilization and empire. For example, Australian John Dunmore Lang wrote in 1834: "The South Sea Islands have, in all past time, been, like the ancient Greek democracies, the scene of frequent, if not perpetual civil war."[1] Such noble warfare portrayed ancient Polynesians as brave, masculine heroes who were thereby made relatable to European and American audiences. In this respect, Glissant's words about the West being a project, not a place, resonate strongly. Polynesia did not have to be located near Europe for Europeans to view Polynesia through a Western lens.

To many, Greeks and Polynesians were more than analogous societies, however—they were biological relatives. Scholars of this period argued that the connection between Polynesians and the fabled ancient civilizations of the Mediterranean was deeply ancestral. New Zealand–based writer Edward Tregear argued that Polynesians and Europeans were made of one Aryan stock, which he understood as the "outcome of that tribal intelligence, that vitality of mind and body, which evolved the art of Greece, the strength of Rome, the commerce of Britain."[2] By writing Polynesians into the classical mythology frame, Polynesians were mapped onto an invented past—a past that, like the ancient histories of Greece, Rome, and Egypt, was claimed as the natural heritage of Europeans.

As noted in S. Percy Smith's words in the epigraph above, research about Polynesians seemed so captivating to white settlers in large part due to a perceived link between Polynesians and white people—what Smith describes as "a common source" in "the Caucasian branch of humanity." Smith describes this common source as the explanation for Polynesian "intelligence" and "their charming personality." Yet he also clearly maintains a distanced view of Polynesians. They are, in his words, only a "handful of people," and despite their common descent from the "Caucasian branch of humanity," they remain a "colored race."[3] Indeed, though Polynesians had been viewed as almost white by some of the earliest European visitors to Oceania, this did not mean that Polynesians were seen as identical or equal to Europeans—far from it. As much as the so-called Polynesian Problem literature about Polynesian origins investigated the similarities between Polynesians and Caucasians, European scholars were at least as interested in delineating racial distinctions in order to rank Polynesians as inferior to white settlers who saw themselves as more deserving to rule and profit from Polynesian lands.

This chapter analyzes discourses that link Polynesia to Europe, particularly focusing on ideas about degeneration (how Polynesians supposedly fell from the heights of their grand civilization in ancient times) and Aryanism in the work of Lang, Tregear, and Abraham Fornander, a Swedish-born, naturalized citizen and judge in the Hawaiian Kingdom. As these scholars established Polynesians as related to ancient Mediterranean and Aryan civilizations, they also helped construct Polynesians as part of the heritage of white settlers in the Pacific. Heritage is commonly used today as a synonym for ancestry, but its meaning more fundamentally refers to possessions that are legally passed down: "that which has been or may be inherited; any property, and esp. land, which devolves by right of inheritance."[4] By attributing Aryan heritage to Polynesians, white settlers thereby wove a complex web of claims with legal, material, and familial overtones. If the relative greatness of Polynesian people could be said to have Aryan heritage, then white settlers could, by extension, claim Polynesian peoples, culture, and, crucially, lands, as their own heritage—because they were also descendants of Aryans. The tight connections between race, family, and material ownership indexed in the word *heritage* are key to the examples of Polynesian Problem literature examined in this chapter.

While many of the white settlers writing about the Polynesian Problem were earnestly seeking answers to ancient migratory history, their work was not merely an effort to precisely pinpoint Polynesian origins. I argue that a significant part of Western interest in Polynesian origins, lands, and cultures is structured by a strong desire to better know and define Man. I follow Denise Ferreira da Silva in using "Man" to denote not simply an apolitical notion of humans as a global collective, but the Western, scientific concept of humanity which is often presented as universal, yet actually remains tied to biological, racial, and cultural hierarchies that privilege European/white men.[5] Scientifically articulated desires to better know Man have both justified and helped realize the possession of Polynesia through whiteness. Historical and contemporary scholarship, popular culture, and law emphasize definitions of race and humanity that naturalize Western whiteness as the natural past and future of Polynesia. Within such discourses, the distinct bodies, lands, cultures, and politics of Polynesians are possessed through an insistence on an imagined ancient whiteness that justifies the present and future occupation of Polynesia by white settlers. This chapter analyzes the context and content of nineteenth-century white settler scholarship about Polynesian origins, including the work of John Dunmore Lang (1834), Abraham Fornander (1878), and Edward Tregear (1885). The chapter concludes with a focus on David Kalākaua, ruling monarch of the Hawaiian Kingdom from 1874 to 1891, and his engagement with scholarship about Polynesian origins, often with radically different aims from those of white settler scholars. However, Kalākaua's engagement with the Polynesian Problem literature also fostered a belief in a Polynesian exceptionalism that extended from Western values about whiteness and civilization.

IMPERIAL DREAMS AND DEGENERATION

In the nineteenth century, many Europeans envisioned Polynesia as an ancient empire, reminiscent of Rome or Greece, while at the same time angling to chart a new Polynesian empire under their own flags. The British, French, Spanish, and Americans, among other world powers, jostled for control over islands they saw as vital to their military or economic interests.

This fight was especially crucial to Great Britain, given its new settler colonies in the region, which included New South Wales (1788), Van Diemen's Land (Tasmania, 1825), South Australia (1836), New Zealand (1840), Victoria (1851), and Queensland (1859). The writings of the Scottish Protestant minister John Dunmore Lang must be understood within this context of the British settlement of Australia and dreams of further imperial expansion across the Pacific. Lang, who settled in Sydney in 1823, was a passionate advocate for white settlement in Australia and the Pacific, making trips back to England, where he lectured widely on his belief that "the grinding poverty of Britain could be readily relieved by the boundless opportunities in Australia."[6] He further envisioned a grand Australian empire that would spread across the Pacific, starting with New Guinea, Tahiti, New Caledonia (Kanaky), Fiji, and the New Hebrides (Vanuatu).[7] While various forms of the Polynesian Problem had circulated since Cook's first voyage into the Pacific to track the transit of Venus in 1768, Lang's writing encapsulates several commonly accepted scientific theories of the time that would shape how the world understood the "Polynesian race," including the idea of degeneration.[8]

In 1834, Lang was writing with the assumption that all humans were derived from a single, original pair: the biblical Adam and Eve. He quickly dismissed the idea "that the South Sea Islanders are indigenous, or coeval with the islands they severally inhabit," due to this Christian theology. "God made of one blood all the nations of men for to dwell on all the face of the earth," he wrote—therefore, no men could have originated in the Pacific independently.[9] From medieval times, Christian ideas of monogenesis promoted the view that Europe's Others were effectively failed or subhumans, but human nonetheless. These subhumans had sunk so low due to sin and rejecting the Word of God—but through missionary efforts, they were at least partially redeemable. Yet even if Indigenous Pacific Islanders were human to Lang, as Western explorers from the earliest encounters in the late eighteenth century also viewed them, he was nonetheless eager to slot Indigenous Pacific Islanders' into Man's Great Chain of Being. The Chain of Being was linear, and progression along it was possible for all, since eighteenth-century philosophers understood "mankind as capable of indefinite improvement."[10] As K. R. Howe explains, this meant that "societies that maintained the 'principles of education,' that increased and passed on knowledge, improved, while others degenerated."[11] But that improvement was not guaranteed, nor would stasis or progression be the only options. Societies could also fall down the chain. Yet the heights that those degenerated societies had once reached were the heritage of all humanity—in this respect, the arts, philosophy, and architecture of the Greeks, Romans, and Egyptians became the prehistory of all Western civilization.[12] As J. R. Forster, the natural scientist who accompanied Cook on his second voyage to the Pacific, put it, "all the improvements of mankind ... ought to be considered as *the sum total of the efforts of mankind ever since its existence.*"[13] Here we see the expansive claims of "heritage" that Europeans could make by lauding "mankind" as an obstensibly universal category. Through this logic, Europeans could claim all useful "improvements" as their own, while not necessarily claiming all humans as equal.

The very label *Polynesia* (with a Greek etymology) reflected a Greco-Roman comparison in terms of expressing a kind of wonder at the apparent "unity" of Indigenous cultures across "many islands" of the Pacific, which suggested to Western thinkers an ancient empire.[14] Indeed, Lang's fascination with the Pacific seems to have started with his wonder at how the "same primitive language is spoken, the same singular customs prevail, the same semibarbarous nation inhabits the multitude of the isles" from Hawai'i to New Zealand, and the Indian Archipelago to Easter Island—an expanse he noted was "exactly twice the extent of the ancient Roman empire in its greatest glory."[15] This unity across Polynesia was, notably, vastly overstated. Though Polynesian languages are highly cognate, they are not the same, and while some cultural traditions are similarly related, there are also important differences. The important point to Lang was that Polynesia could be mapped as an empire, in a way that not only made Polynesia an analogue of ancient Rome or Greece, but also painted the idea of empire as natural to Polynesia. Seeing Polynesians as imperialists, of course, also helped Lang ignore their status as the subjects of contemporary colonialism and imperialism.

Ultimately, these comparisons provided acceptable answers to where Polynesians came from, who first settled the Pacific Islands, and implicitly whose islands they really were. Lang argued that Polynesians came from the West—likely even ancient Rome or Greece itself—and they had traveled across Asia to get where they were today. Polynesians, then, were really descendants of ancient Romans and Grecians, through a line that was distinct from, but ultimately traceable to, modern Europeans. By this logic, the Pacific belonged to—and was destined to be repossessed by—modern Europeans. This justified Lang's push to gain British settlers for Australia and the other parts of the Pacific he viewed as intimately connected. By bringing civilization to the Pacific "wilderness," European settlers could reverse the degeneration that Polynesians had apparently suffered. In his words: "It is an easy and natural process for man to degenerate in the scale of civilization, as the Asiatics have evidently done in traveling to the northward and eastward. He has only to move forward a few hundred miles into the wilderness, and settle himself at a distance from all civilized men, and the process will advance with almost incredible celerity. For, whether he comes in contact with actual savages or not, in the dark recesses of the forest, his offspring will speedily arrive at a state of complete barbarism."[16]

As is clear in Lang's description, degeneration was closely associated with the notion of a white, civilized person "going native"—of losing the material, mental, and physical inherited trappings of civilized Man as they moved off the established map. In this narrative, Polynesians had not always been savage. Rather than something that was in their very nature, degeneration was caused by their migratory history and their residence in isolated environments, which had sparked their fall from the heights they had known as "an ancient and primitive civilization, of which both the memory and the evidences have almost passed away."[17]

From this lower state, Lang believed that Polynesians could potentially be saved, but only through outside influence. "No nation," he argued, "has ever yet risen from a state of savage barbarism to a state of comparative civilization, unless some lever, powerful enough to raise the nation from its lower level has been worked *from without*."[18] In his view, this lever specifically meant European missionaries and settlers. Though Lang acknowledged that the West had not yet uncovered a truly effective mode of redeeming the "savage," either in the "Indo-American" or the "South Sea Islander," he maintained that such work was both possible and desirable.[19] Lang's theory of change here operated within the ideology of what would come to be known as diffusionism.[20] Within diffusionism, change was understood as occurring only through the influence of people or technologies newly introduced from elsewhere. In the context of the Polynesian Problem, diffusionism emphasizes the dissemination of an "original" culture from a few, limited points of origin—usually, older civilizations that had been long established in India, Malaysia, or Papua New Guinea. By mapping Polynesians as offshoots of Asian (and later in the nineteenth century, as Aryan) civilizations, this logic allowed European settlers to understand their own presence in the Pacific as fitting naturally into the next stage of the Pacific's development. The ideology of diffusionism was part and parcel of imperial and missionary ideology since it advocated the importance of the transference of superior cultures to inferior ones.[21]

Other Kanaka Maoli scholars have shown that similar discourses about the degeneration of Polynesians around this time were crucial parts of missionizing work by many different denominations. Hōkūlani Aikau, for example, has demonstrated that in the 1850s the Church of Jesus Christ of Latter-Day Saints used similar logics about Polynesians being degenerated descendants of ancient civilizations. In particular, the Church understood Polynesians as one of the Lost Tribes of Israel.[22] Aikau demonstrates that the Church drew on preexisting Western knowledge about the distinction of Polynesians as relatively white in contrast to Melanesians and Micronesians. This knowledge was consolidated with Mormon doctrine through a vision by Mormon missionary George Cannon while he was visiting Maui in 1851. In the vision, Cannon learned from God that Polynesians were descendants of Abraham, which "made Polynesians become one of the chosen people who were among the noble and elite during the premortal existence. As such, the covenant of the priesthood could and should be (re)established with them."[23] This origin story would be developed further by the Church, through comparisons of Polynesian languages, mythologies, and other cultural forms to the Israelites, methodologies also used by social scientists.[24] This lineage continues to be important to how the LDS Church and its Polynesian members understand the preordained place of Polynesians within Mormonism. Notably, such discourses were employed during a time when Mormons themselves were often viewed with suspicion by other white Americans, who did not always see Mormons as "white like us."[25] Thus, the inclusion of Polynesians as "chosen" but still inferior to more civilized Mormon missionaries can be read as a move toward giving the Latter-Day Saints a greater claim to white superiority, in contrast to the racial Others they evangelized.

In another vein, Kealani Cook has illustrated how American Protestant missionaries, from soon after their arrival in Hawai'i in the 1830s, instructed Native Hawaiian converts to understand themselves as elevating their race out of na'aupō, or ignorance, and into ke ao, the light, and becoming na'auao, enlightened. He analyzes how Kanaka Maoli missionaries quickly internalized these discourses and deployed them during their own missions to other parts of the Pacific, including the Marquesas and Tahiti. Kanaka Maoli missionaries would use such rhetoric around themselves being na'auao to challenge racism they faced from haole missionaries whom they needed to remind were their equals. Yet they also understood most other Indigenous Pacific Islanders, and nonconverted Kānaka Maoli, as na'aupō, ignorant, backward, and at a much lower place on the scale of enlightenment. Cook notes that "Even among the hoahānau [Native members of the Congregational Church], the fear that they might *ho'i hope*, or backslide, into ka pō [the darkness] remained a constant fear."²⁶ Spreading this fear of backsliding into darkness and ignorance was thus a powerful use of the discourse of degeneration for Protestants in Hawai'i.

Aikau's and Cook's scholarship demonstrates how Western, Christian ideologies about degeneration and the place of Polynesians within the prevailing hierarchies of Man in the nineteenth century had real impacts on how Polynesians were treated by Europeans and Americans, as well as how Polynesians themselves treated each other. Whether missionaries promoted an acknowledgment of Polynesians as relatively civilized for Indigenous people, as Lang did, or advanced a more specific discourse around Polynesians being ancestral kin, as with the Mormon Church, these inclusive moves did not simply extend equality to Polynesians. Rather, such discourses merely allowed for the possibility that Polynesians could progress on the scale of Man's enlightenment, given the proper intervention and instruction from European or American missionaries. The lineage linking Polynesians to great civilizations justified the project of beginning to pull Polynesians out of their degeneration, but notably did not guarantee that project's success. In this logic, only white leadership would ensure the reversal of Polynesian degeneration.

THE ARYAN POLYNESIANS

The Pacific's supposed Mediterranean heritage would take on added significance in the late nineteenth century, as the influence of new developments in biology, archaeology, and linguistics, among other fields, would give new significance to the study of ancient proto-European civilizations, particularly through the discourse of Aryanism. Today, popular understandings of Aryanism are deeply entwined with the history of the Holocaust, as well as white supremacists and the "alt-right." The roots of Aryanism as an intellectual project, however, are actually in eighteenth-century linguistics. Sir William Jones is credited with the earliest Western study of the Sanskritic tradition in India, and with first establishing a common linguistic and cultural heritage between northern India and Europe, in the 1780s (at the very same time that the West would begin to "explore" and colonize the Pacific).²⁷

From Jones's work, the "Aryan concept" would become influential across many fields of European thought. Lang, for example, acknowledged Jones's scholarship but disagreed with Jones's contention that the Polynesian language and "Polynesian nation" had Sanskritic origins.²⁸ Where Jones understood Sanskrit as the "common parent" of both "Malay" and "Polynesian" languages, Lang argued that these two languages had originated in "Chinese Tartary," the area around present-day Mongolia.[29] By the time of Abraham Fornander's writing, as further analyzed below, the publication of the work of Max Müller had further developed the discourse of Aryanism into a popular subject in Europe. Another key difference in the works published by Lang in 1834 and Fornander in 1878 was the impact of the scholarship of biologist Charles Darwin, who published his *On the Origin of Species* in 1859.

While the reception of Darwin's *Origin* spurred the notion of positive human evolution, degeneration (as intertwined with Christian discourses, as discussed in the previous section) maintained an important place within ideas of progress in the late nineteenth and early twentieth centuries. Except now, degeneration was thought of as being a potential biological fate, as opposed to being a primarily historical, religious, social, or individual moral one. Fears about "biological collapse" and "social pathologies" were enabled by Darwin's theories of evolution and natural selection (and his cousin Francis Galton's extrapolations of social Darwinism) as well as a renewed passion for studying antiquity, brought about by other timely revolutions in geology and archaeology.[30] Geology had revealed that the Earth was much older than previous biblical understandings had held, and archaeology flourished as scientists attempted to piece together a better understanding of the various epochs of antiquity.[31]

The popularity of new ideas about human antiquity would come to shape more than just archaeology, however. For example, practitioners of anthropology also understood their task as "a sort of living archaeology."[32] Science studies scholar Cathy Gere evocatively describes this epistemology of science at the turn of the century as one of, in Thomas Huxley's terms, *retrospective prophecy*, in which one conjures the events of ancient history.[33] Gere notes that while the "effect was magical ... the method was eminently rational."[34] This retrospective prophecy could also be described as deductive reasoning, in the mode made classic by that still popular Victorian fictional hero Sherlock Holmes. Yet this technique would also characterize innovations in fields such as criminology—in Francis Galton's invention of fingerprinting, for example—and psychoanalysis—such as Freud's insistence on recovering and coming to terms with one's past, pre-Oedipal layers.[35]

The scholarship of Max Müller should also be understood within the context of this turn toward "retrospective prophecy." Müller's views on the significance of studying ancient India within a liberal education are particularly clear in a series of lectures he delivered in 1883 to Cambridge University students about to enter the British Indian Civil Service. He argued that such study had "not only widened our views of man, and taught us to embrace millions of strangers and barbarians as members of one family, but it has imparted to the whole ancient history of man a reality which it never possessed before."[36] Though he maintained a strict differentiation between the ancient Aryan race who produced the Vedas and contemporary Indians, he asked the young men about to travel to India to consider their work as part of determining "a history of the human mind."[37] Müller was interested in what Silva would term *transcendence*—in how Europeans as the epitome of Man had progressed inwardly, how they had realized their "true selves" from a long development over time.[38] In this formula, Indians represented humans in a stage of earlier intellectual development. While this kind of thinking may seem blatantly racist by today's standards, Müller clearly understood his work as both worldly and liberal. Gere notes that Müller later attempted to distance himself and his scholarship on Sanskrit and Aryanism from more explicitly political attempts to shore up the purity of the white race.[39] Yet understanding the Vedas as primarily the heritage of Europeans, rather than the heritage of contemporary Indians, was a colonial logic that often persists in the Western study of other peoples and their cultures and resources.

Müller similarly wrote of Polynesian mythology as a potential key to understanding the development of "the human intellect" in the 1876 preface to W. W. Gill's *Myths and Songs from the South Pacific*.[40] Gill's volume was a collection of myths and songs recorded during his twenty-two-year stay as a missionary on the island of Mangaia, part of what is now the Cook Islands. To Müller, Gill's compilation was invaluable, because Mangaia was seen as largely free from modern influence.[41] Müller argued that Gill's volume allowed scholars of religion and mythology to "find ourselves among a people who really believe in gods and heroes and ancestral spirits ... as if the zoologist could spend a few days among the megatheria, or the botanist among the waving ferns of the forests, buried beneath our feet."[42] This description demonstrates how Müller could approach Mangaian stories as "living archaeology." Gill's informants are "the last depositaries of the old faith," in Müller's account.[43] Though Müller thought Polynesians were largely savages, he also was willing to see in them the beginnings of the development of enlightened human thought. He concluded that Gill's book would "startle those who think that metaphysical conceptions are incompatible with downright savagery."[44]

The following sections further analyze the work of two white settler writers focused on Aryan–Polynesian connections in the late nineteenth century: Abraham Fornander, based in Hawai'i, and Edward Tregear, based in New Zealand. Fornander's 1878 three-volume work, *An Account of the Polynesian Race: Its Origin and Migrations and the Ancient History of the Hawaiian People to the Times of Kamehameha I*, contained detailed observations about the provenance and character of Polynesians, under the rubric of analyzing Hawaiian "folklore." Fornander's goal was to use the "folklore" of the Native Hawaiian people themselves to prove that Polynesians were "fundamentally Arian [sic] of a pre-Vedic type."[45] Edward Tregear's 1885 *The Aryan Maori* similarly asserted, through analysis of Māori language and "mythology," that Māori were Aryan. Why each wanted to make these claims was inextricably related to wanting to prove that whiteness naturally belonged in Hawai'i and New Zealand, respectively.

At the time of Fornander's writing, Hawai'i was an independent nation-state, ruled by King Kalākaua, but with a number of white settlers living in the kingdom, largely with connections to missionary work and/or the growing sugar plantation industry.[46] As a respected judge and "Knight of the Royal Order of Kalākaua," Fornander believed his well-known reputation in Hawai'i allowed him, as he stated in the text's introduction, "to speak on behalf of the Polynesian people, to unravel the past of their national life."[47] As ku'ualoha ho'omanawanui has shown, Fornander was one of many haole settlers who, by "[p]ublishing Hawaiian legends, myths, and folklore under their own names ... claimed an authority (kuleana) over the mo'olelo [narrative, story, history] they did not have, and reframed mo'olelo to forward settler agendas."[48] ho'omanawanui, like many other Hawaiian studies scholars, has shown that analyzing writing from this period by Native Hawaiians in Hawaiian-language sources offers rich reclamations of Native Hawaiian mo'olelo, and importantly destabilizes the authority of those like Fornander over Native Hawaiian histories and cosmologies.[49] I analyze Fornander's *An Account of the Polynesian Race* and Tregear's *Aryan Maori* not as authorities on Native Hawaiian or Māori mo'olelo, but as texts revealing the settler colonial logic of possession through whiteness.

Both *An Account of the Polynesian Race* and *The Aryan Maori*'s articulation of a Polynesian Aryanism illustrate how foundational settler colonial narratives about Polynesians' tragic loss of authenticity and seemingly inevitable absorption into whiteness could be projected onto an ancient past. In these narratives, Polynesians' loss of authenticity and purity came from their migration out of India, and their degeneration came from settling in the isolated Pacific Islands. Yet because Polynesians were originally Aryan, just as Europeans were, in Tregear's words, Europeans and Polynesians were "two nations whose ancestors were brothers."⁵⁰ Tregear and Fornander both saw themselves as allies of Māori and Native Hawaiian people. Analyzing their writing is important not to show how settler colonial logic crept in *despite* their "good intentions," but to show how these good intentions actually contribute to their settler colonial understanding of Polynesians as natural white possessions. This analysis therefore highlights the settler colonial violence that is possible through white settler efforts at inclusion of Indigenous peoples and histories into settler societies and imaginaries, rather than only overt, racist exclusion.

### ABRAHAM FORNANDER'S *An Account of the Polynesian Race* (1878)

Müller's approach to Aryanism modeled the kind of mapping that was key to the Polynesian Problem literature, as scholars fixed Polynesians in both an ancient time and a space of origins and migrations that always led back to white Europeans. As an ethnologist, Fornander was deeply influenced by Müller, and precisely understood his work as a kind of living archaeology. He described his research as an intrepid pioneering effort to tame and interpret the "almost impenetrable jungle of traditions, legends, genealogies, and chants" of Native Hawaiians.⁵¹ Yet his specific purpose in collecting and analyzing these moʻolelo was to make an argument about Polynesian racial origins. What Fornander found in that "jungle" of stories convinced him of Polynesians' fundamental descent from the Aryan race, for "their own undoubted folklore, their legends and chants, gave no warrant for stopping there [in Malaysia]. They spoke of continents, and not of islands, as their birthplace."⁵² Like the contemporary Indians in Müller's account, for Fornander, the Polynesian race would almost certainly never regain their former place within the Aryan family. Nevertheless, contemporary Native Hawaiians were important repositories of Aryan knowledge and culture: "Throughout the grosser idolatry and the cruel practices springing from it in subsequent ages, these shreds of a purer culte [*sic*] were still preserved, soiled in appearance and obscured in sense by the contact, it may be, yet standing on the traditional records as heirlooms of the past, as witnesses of a better creed, and as specimens of the archaic simplicity of the language, hardly intelligible to the present Hawaiians."⁵³

In this description, to "the present Hawaiians," the "heirlooms of the past" they hold within their "Polynesian race" are "hardly intelligible." Aryanness was something that was biologically part of Hawaiians, but microscopic and presently inaccessible to them (anticipating, in an important sense, modern understandings of DNA, as further discussed in chapter 5). Their Aryan heritage was thus "soiled" and "obscured" but capable of being rescued by and for Man. Fornander understood his own task in writing his three volumes on Native Hawaiian "antiquities" and "folklore" in exactly these terms.

This understanding of obscure, ancient, civilized "specimens" trapped within Hawaiian language and Hawaiians themselves also endowed an extra significance on the understanding of Polynesians as a "mixed race." Fornander argued that in Polynesian myth, "the body of the first man was made of red earth and the head of white clay," which indicated to him "a lingering reminiscence of a mixed origin, in which the white element occupied a superior position."[54] Note that marking the head as "white," whereas the "body" is red, played directly into notions of the distinction of white men as having "reason" and "self-determination." Thus, in Fornander's reading, Polynesians were originally mentally capable of being white, despite how they appeared as colored bodies. Not incidentally, Fornander was also one of many scholars who argued that Polynesians had not "mixed" or significantly "intermarried" with Papuans. This antiblack stance, which sought to preserve a distinction between the "brown" Polynesian, not destined to be permanently "colored," and the indelibly black Papuan or Melanesian, would remain central to Polynesian Problem literature long after Fornander's writing, as further discussed in chapters 2 and 3. This interpretation of a broad Polynesian origin story also sharply contrasts with Kanaka Maoli interpretations of Kanaka Maoli origin stories, such as the Kumulipo, which relate humans to kalo (taro, a staple food) rather than deploying race, as discussed in chapter 6.

The idea of Indigenous peoples being almost white was not necessarily new or specific to Polynesia, and certainly drew on ideas developed about Native Americans on the American continents. Native Americans are often constructed as the metaphorical and literal ancestors of white people in the United States.[55] Scholars including Yael Ben-zvi, Jenny Reardon, and Kimberly TallBear have analyzed how Native American "redness" has long been understood as genealogically belonging to whiteness.[56] This view on redness contrasts white American views on blackness to the extent that blackness is also understood as the property of whiteness, but never as genealogically related to whiteness. Even when there are literal biological relationships between black and white Americans, they are often denied, whereas many white Americans continue to claim Cherokee princesses as their ancestors.

Whereas with anthropology on the American continent the emphasis was often on white settlers as the metaphorical descendants of American Indians, in Fornander's work the characterization was most frequently that Polynesians as a race had (metaphorical and literal) white ancestry. White settlers in Polynesia did not see themselves as the direct descendants of Polynesians, figuratively speaking, as white settlers in the continental United States might, in the sense of arguing their sense of belonging and ownership of Native American land. Rather, in white settlers' logic, Polynesians *used to be* white, and were thus descended from the same ancient Aryan ancestors as the white settlers of Polynesia. From northern India, the Polynesian branch had simply split out to the East, whereas the European branch had gone West.[57] Fornander saw Polynesians as less civilized and less advanced than white Americans and Europeans. But the emphasis on Polynesians' common Aryan ancestry with white settlers fostered a settler narrative that also held that Polynesian women were racially suitable as (or even destined to be) the sexual partners of white settlers. In this sense, Fornander was arguing not just that Polynesians were destined to evolve into white people, but that this was right and good because whiteness itself was indigenous to Polynesia.

### EDWARD TREGEAR'S *The Aryan Maori* (1885)

Edward Tregear's *The Aryan Maori*, published in 1885, argued in a way very similar to Fornander that Māori were descendants of the Aryan race and thus that they shared ancient ancestors with Europeans. As a British settler in New Zealand, Tregear focused on the Māori "as being the type best known to myself," yet also saw Māori as representative of "the light-coloured branch of the Polynesian islanders."[58] Tregear was writing forty-five years after the signing of the Treaty of Waitangi that established New Zealand as part of the British Empire, and after several decades of intensive white settlement and war against the Māori.[59] He participated in many enterprises central to settler colonialism, from fighting in the New Zealand land wars against Māori in the Tauranga district in 1867, to gold mining and land surveying.[60] Like Fornander's idea of Polynesian folklore as "heirlooms" of a noble Aryan past, Tregear felt that, despite the present "uncivilized" state of Māori people, Māori language and mythology held within it a rich heritage that Europeans should also claim as theirs. Tregear wrote, "These uncivilized brothers of ours have kept embalmed in their simple speech a knowledge of the habits and history of our ancestors, that, in the Sanscrit [*sic*], Greek, Latin, and Teutonic tongues, have been hidden under the dense aftergrowth of literary opulence."⁶¹ In other words, Māori language and folklore, because it was less developed (without "literary opulence"), offered a more direct access to the original Aryan language and folklore. This was valuable, in Tregear's eyes, because—in contrast to the "uncivilized" Māori today—Aryans were noble people and the ancestors of the great civilizations in Europe. Aryans were responsible for the "magnificent temples, the great cities, the wonderful systems of religion and philosophy" of India.⁶² Tregear argued that the Aryans "were the outcome of that tribal intelligence, that vitality of mind and body, which evolved the art of Greece, the strength of Rome, the commerce of Britain."⁶³

Notably, in this logic, Aryans are markedly different from those indigenous to India. Tregear cautioned: "I must impress upon my reader the necessity of remembering that the Aryans, who became the ruling and exclusive people of India, were not the original owners of the soil."⁶⁴ It was the Aryans, "not the work of the first inhabitants of Hindustan," who built the great cities and temples of India, and contributed their intelligence and vitality to the Greek, Roman, and British civilizations.⁶⁵ Thus, part of the greatness of the Aryans, in Tregear's argument, was that they were settlers who had improved India and those who were indigenous to India. Implicitly, Tregear sets up an analogy here between Aryans and British settlers in New Zealand. Though the British/Pākēha settlers are not "the original owners of the soil," they hold the potential (through the prior example of their Aryan ancestors) to create a great civilization in New Zealand. In this way, settler conquest was understood as a form of inevitable greatness, rather than as deadly violence and dispossession for Māori.

There is a complicated and potentially contradictory relationship set up in this logic that differentiates European and Māori claims to a common ancestor, the Aryan race. For in Tregear's analysis, Māori are not truly indigenous to Aotearoa either—they migrated from India about four thousand years ago.⁶⁶ If, in this sense, Māori are also settlers, and they are also the descendants of the Aryans, why would Māori not be able to create a great civilization in New Zealand on their own? For any readers skeptical of the idea that Māori could be Aryan, specifically because they have not demonstrated any "greatness," Tregear notes:

> It may be urged that the Maoris have shown little of that colonizing spirit, of that fire of mind and body, which has caused the Aryan race to be the world's history-makers for the last four thousand years; that he

has not advanced in art or science; that he has no great proof of descent. But, as I read history, the Aryan race has never given birth to magnificent discoveries or triumphs of art and literature save when leavened by a spirit coming from without. Egypt, the civilization of Babylon and other nations, brought light to the nearest Aryans—those of Greece; then, after centuries, through the Greek colonies in Italy, Rome woke to power, and sent out her missionaries, brave road-makers, steady rulers.[67]

Here, Tregear invokes diffusionism, as Lang did before him, and again implicitly valorizes British settlement of Aotearoa, suggesting that the British civilizing influence could precipitate latent Aryan greatness in the Māori, just as Britain had been influenced by the Roman and Greek civilizations, which had, in turn, been previously influenced by Egypt and Babylon. The original Aryans as well as the British needed to be "leavened by a spirit coming from without," Tregear concludes. He later elaborates, "So the turn of each comes, when a leaven from without stirs the Aryan blood. By some arrest of development the Indo-Polynesians have not waked to life—yet."[68] By implication, the British settlement of New Zealand was soon to bring about Māori progress. In this logic, British settlers in New Zealand were performing a benevolent service—a leavening of the Māori spirit in order to help it fulfill its latent Aryan talent.

Thus, Tregear understood British settlement of New Zealand as effectively a "new wave of Aryan migration," rather than the dispossession of Māori from land and culture. Because this discourse emphasized racial similarity between British and Māori rather than simply the racial superiority of the British, Tony Ballantyne argues that we must see Aryanism in Polynesia as more than just a "whitening" discourse "using assimilationist arguments to legitimate colonialism."[69] Rather, Ballantyne demonstrates that Aryanism as applied to Polynesians was an extension of "long-established Orientalist and ethnological traditions that developed out of the British encounter with South Asia."[70] For Ballantyne, historians who assume that Aryanism "naturally legitimized colonization" neglect the ways that "Aryan theories could just as easily subvert colonial authority and racial hierarchies as reinforce them. Tregear himself argued that any European or settler who considered themselves superior to Maori had 'travelled little' and no European should 'blush' to recognize their affinity with the 'Bengalee' or the Maori 'heroes of Orakau.'"[71]

Ballantyne points out here that the discourse of Aryanism in the Pacific was not only or uniformly overtly racist. At times those who wrote about

Aryanism understood their actions as disrupting rather than reinforcing commonly accepted Western racial hierarchies. Similarly, Fornander cannot easily be dismissed as an anti–Native Hawaiian racist. Indeed, he was a longtime editor of the *Polynesian*, a pro–Hawaiian Kingdom government newspaper, and was therefore viewed, at least in some respects, as an ally to Kānaka Maoli.[72]

Yet this particular formulation of an Aryan brotherhood, of being from the same "racial stock," nonetheless did exact racial and colonial violence upon Polynesian people. By emphasizing sameness, Fornander and Tregear erase the presence of racism and settler colonialism, and thus allow these structures to be unquestioningly maintained. These discourses foreshadow more contemporary discourses of the postracial and multicultural, and are in great need of analysis and critique precisely because they appear benign. In effect, Tregear naturalized not (only) the racial superiority of white British settlers in New Zealand, but the entitlement of white settlers to Māori land, resources, and bodies. Repeatedly throughout *The Aryan Maori*, Tregear refers to Māori language and story as "ours," meaning white British New Zealanders.[73] It is clear he is not speaking *as* Māori because he continually distinguishes them as "our brothers." Yet, through his insistence on Māori Aryanism, he naturalizes his use of a British "our" in reference to Māori words and folklore. Rather than concluding from his arguments that Māori were of Aryan stock that the British and Māori were (or should be) equal, Tregear's logic may be paraphrased as, though the Māori are not "us" (that is, British), they are "ours." This is an essential component of the logic of possession through whiteness. The discourse of Polynesian almost whiteness allows for the naturalization of white possession of Polynesia and Polynesians, not the extension of whiteness and its privileges to Polynesians.

That Polynesians were also Aryan made them not true, recognizable kin to the British, but exceptional colonial possessions and potentially valuable investments. Tregear goes to some pains to explain for his presumed British/Pākēha settler audience how different and exceptional the Māori and other "light-coloured Polynesians" are from other Pacific Islanders: "It is no uncommon thing for Europeans not well acquainted with the subject to class all the South Sea Islanders as 'blackfellows,' merging the Maori and Australian, the Samoan and Papuan, in one common term. Even those who have more knowledge on the subject have no definite idea how sharply the line of demarcation is drawn between the Maori race and the Papuan in those islands which they inhabit together."[74]

By arguing that Māori and Sāmoans were not black (in the sense that Australian Aborigines and Papuans were understood to be), Tregear notably reinforces both antiblackness and a racial hierarchy among Indigenous Pacific people. Again, even as he is positively identifying Māori as Aryan and thus relatively capable of civilization, this ideology at once violently includes Polynesians as people who were once and will again be white, and violently excludes other Indigenous Pacific people deemed black from being recognized as human. Overall, Tregear's point to his British settler audience is less about conveying that Māori are deserving of equality and kinship than it is about demonstrating why British settlement of New Zealand holds the potential for greatness—indeed, why Māori were excellent possessions—because of the Māori's exceptional "racial stock." The racial stock was exceptional, he went to great pains to explain to a lay audience, because, despite what may be superficial similarities between Polynesians and Melanesians, Polynesians were not black. Polynesians, he argued, were therefore capable of attaining a relative whiteness through white settlement.

Settler colonialism requires mapping Polynesia not just in space, but also in time. By setting up a now-lost authenticity, a prior whiteness and purity, the settler admiration for Māori would remain limited to the Māori of a mythical past. This distinction between the ancient purity held within the Māori and the contemporary Māori is key to the logic of possession through whiteness. For even as Tregear noted that Europeans "need not blush to own his brotherhood with the beauties of Hawai'i or the heroes of Orakau," he also wrote: "The degraded Natives who hang about our towns have little of the appearance or the character of the true Maori."[75] He conceded that perhaps the true Māori existed outside of the cities, noting that "Among the tribes are noble specimens of the human race."[76] However, even those "noble specimens" do not seem to fulfill Tregear's desire for the ancient, pure Aryan Māori that existed four thousand years ago.

This displacement of time is important because it shows that even as later discourses made much of authenticity, meaning prior to colonial contact, in the broader logic of possession through whiteness, the "authentic," "noble" Polynesian was really one that no European living in the nineteenth century would ever be able to meet. This gives the logic of possession through whiteness its haunting quality: Polynesian whiteness is ghostly, never able to be actualized in the present, but constantly echoing through settler colonial discourses. Given the difficulty of restoring Polynesians to the heights they deserved to reach because of their ancient Aryan ancestry, the colonial justification for European settlement of Polynesia would also be displaced into an indefinite future—a project without an end date. Implicitly in Tregear's logic, Māori were "ours" (British) forever.

Fornander and Tregear ultimately shared the belief that because Polynesian language, myth, and biology contained an Aryan heritage, Polynesian peoples and land were naturally also the heritage of white settlers. In this respect, the Aryan "kinship" established in Fornander's and Tregear's works meant less that Polynesians and Europeans were destined to be equal, and more that white settlers felt they had natural claims to and over Polynesian lands, resources, and people—that Polynesia and Polynesians were their heritage. This was how the seeming attribution of whiteness and shared Aryan ancestors resulted in white settler feelings of possession and entitlement over Polynesians, rather than true brotherhood or kinship with Polynesians.

KALĀKAUA'S TAKE ON POLYNESIAN ORIGINS

Kinship meant something different to Polynesian people themselves. While I have focused largely on close readings of Lang, Fornander, and Tregear in this chapter, in order to analyze the key rhetorical moves made in the logic of possession through whiteness, it is clear that at least some Polynesians were aware of the Polynesian Problem studies and pursued similar research, if with different aims. In the next chapter I will discuss Te Rangihīroa (also known as Peter Buck), a Māori scholar who spent many years in Hawai'i and subscribed to some of these theories about Polynesians being Aryan. From the recent work of Kealani Cook and other Hawaiian studies scholars, we also know that King David Kalākaua, who knew Fornander, was interested in studies of Polynesian racial origins and from 1880 to 1891 directed his own research on genealogy and science under the Hale Nauā—in Cook's words, a "cultural and scientific think tank" that "promoted Native Hawaiian knowledge production as a valid and important national resource."[77] Cook notes that "Kalākaua's personal Hale Nauā notebooks ... included a chart attempting to trace the spread of Indo-European languages in relation to the migrations tracked in the Kumulipo [Hawaiian creation/origins chant], affected no doubt by contemporary theories espoused by Abraham Fornander and others that Polynesians were descended from the Aryans."[78]

Kalākaua's interest in Polynesian racial origins were directly tied to significant political stakes. Kalākaua was negotiating to maintain a Native Hawaiian monarchy that valued and protected Native Hawaiian cultural traditions (he is well known and beloved for bringing back public performances of hula after missionary repression) while also seeking to foster international recognition of Hawai'i as an independent nation on par with Western nations. Thus, Kalākaua not only knew about theories that linked

Polynesians to Aryans, but selectively sought to utilize these theories to build political alliances in Polynesia and elsewhere to support Hawaiian independence and check white European and American power in Hawai'i. Cook describes how Kalākaua engaged these ideas during his worldwide tour in 1881, during which he visited Japan, China, Siam (Thailand), Burma (Myanmar), Malaysia, India, Egypt, and much of Europe and the United States. In Malaysia, for example, Kalākaua discussed theories about Polynesian ancient migrations through Malaysia with the maharajah, Sultan Abu Bakar ibni Daeng Ibrahim, "after which the two spent hours probing for linguistic and cultural similarities."[79] In Japan, Kalākaua became interested in Buddhism and "looked for religious parallels between Buddhism and Christianity, hoping to locate an Asian origin for European religion."[80] Cook argues that he was interested in "the concept of nonwestern knowledge preceding, and even creating western knowledge and practices."[81] If white scholars could project themselves at the center of Polynesian origins, Kalākaua could project Asian and Pacific Islander civilizations into the origins of Europe.

Indeed, though some of Kalākaua's white American advisors had hoped that his voyage would impress upon the king the superiority of the West, the trip had the opposite effect. To Kalākaua, Cook argues, his voyage only confirmed that "his people were better off living as an independent Native people," especially through seeing examples in places like Japan of the retention of older traditions alongside more Western modernization.[82] The trip strengthened his resolve to promote Native Hawaiian cultural nationalism—as his well-known push to revitalize hula and other practices largely came after this trip.[83] The voyage also allowed Kalākaua to float ideas of political alliances between non-Euro/American countries, most of which were similarly dealing with Western imperialism in their homelands. In Japan, he proposed a royal marriage between a Japanese prince and his niece Princess Ka'iulani as well as a "Union and Federation of Asiatic nations and sovereigns" to fortify Hawai'i and Asian nations against Euro/American powers.[84] Later, Kalākaua further argued for Japanese immigration by citing his belief that "Hawaiians and Japanese shared a common bond in both being 'Asiatic' peoples and that because of that bond Japanese immigration would reinvigorate the Hawaiian race."[85] On his visit to Malaysia, he similarly commented "that his own people were Asiatics, and he hoped the Asiatic nations would become powerful and stand by one another."[86] In Honolulu, Kalākaua's own residence, Hale 'Ākala (likely built after his world tour, adjacent to 'Iolani Palace, which was completed in 1883) was a two-story, ten-room, pink-colored house, "designed in the style of a north Indian palace."[87]

Evidently, unlike Müller and other haole theorists of Aryanism who sharply distinguished between ancient Aryans and contemporary, unenlightened Indians, Kalākaua was open to making more direct claims of kinship to contemporary Asian peoples on the basis of theories about Polynesian racial origins in Asia, at least if it would further his political aims. He seems to have been interested in becoming fluent not only in Western forms of civilization but also in Asian ones, in the interest not of assimilating but of furthering Hawaiian independence and nationalism. His overtures in Japan did not amount to much, however, as the Japanese turned down both the proposal of marriage between royal families and the Asian confederation of nations.[88] Antiblackness was also not as evident in Kalākaua's writings as in the Polynesian Problem literature, perhaps because Kalākaua had been subject to racism in the U.S. press, which circulated rumors that his dark skin was proof of African American ancestry.[89]

While this willingness to align with contemporary "Asiatics" was a notable departure from white settler investments in Aryanism, undoubtedly Kalākaua and other Native Hawaiians did internalize many ideas about their own racial superiority. Cook analyzes the beginnings of a confederacy forged between Hawai'i and Sāmoa under Kalākaua, in which Hawaiian delegates to Sāmoa emphasized genealogical ties between Hawaiians and Sāmoans as Polynesian kin. However, the Hawaiians clearly saw themselves as superior to Sāmoans because they believed "that Hawai'i had the greatest na'auao of Polynesian peoples," meaning that they had achieved the most progress in mastering Euro/American political structures.[90] One of the Hawaiian delegates complained about the heat in Sāmoa and worried that he would "degenerate into a Happy 'faa Sāmoa' [Sāmoan]" if he stayed too long.[91]

Just as in the logic of possession through whiteness found in the work of Fornander and Tregear, wherein white people and Polynesians were seen as distantly related but far from equal, Cook argues that Native Hawaiians at this time generally "saw Sāmoans as undeveloped versions of themselves."[92] The confederacy was not fully realized due to the Bayonet Constitution of 1887, in which Kalākaua's power was severely limited by a cadre of white settler plantation owners who forced him to sign a new constitution for the Hawaiian Kingdom that curtailed Kanaka Maoli rights while boosting white male rights.[93] So-called because it was signed under threats from the U.S. Navy, the Bayonet Constitution resulted in the recall of the Sāmoan delegation. Yet it is clear that through a confederacy the Hawaiians wanted to remake Sāmoan government into a centralized system modeled on Hawai'i. This intention was also strongly influenced by white settler ideas about civilizational hierarchies within Polynesia. As Sāmoan historian Malama Meleisea notes, unified monarchies such as Kamehameha I's in Hawai'i and Pomare I's in Tahiti were seen as more advanced by Europeans because powerful individual monarchs could be more easily influenced for colonial goals, or, eventually, overthrown.[94] Sāmoa resisted centralizing authority at least through German colonization in the early 1900s, relying on their traditional "unitary system of dispersed power," which balanced governing between matai (chiefs) and nu'u (polities, villages).[95] Kalākaua's proposed Polynesian confederation could simultaneously be anti-imperialist (against German and American powers) and replicate the structures of Western imperialism between Hawai'i and Sāmoa.[96] For, of course, seeing Sāmoans as potentially valuable but inferior (because they seemed to Hawaiians to be "how we used to be") is precisely how white settlers were viewing Hawaiians. Thus, the logic of possession through whiteness could be deployed by Polynesians against other Polynesians, though their purposes were not exactly the same as those of white settlers.

That Native Hawaiians were engaged in responding to and even deploying such racial logics themselves in the 1880s is significant because it demonstrates two things. First, it shows that Native Hawaiians were not simply victimized by racism imported from the United States beginning with the Hawaiian Kingdom's overthrow in 1893. The logic of possession through whiteness was circulating long before the overthrow and was not dictated only by the racial hierarchies enforced at the time in the United States. Too often, discussions about race in regard to Native Hawaiians begins only with the institution of blood quantum legislation in 1921, as I further discuss in the next chapter. Rather than stemming only from U.S. racial ideologies, the logic of possession through whiteness as developed in the Polynesian Problem literature was a more global logic with a foundation in the Orientalism of Aryanism and European fascination with ancient civilizations including Rome and Greece.

Second, we can see that Native Hawaiians were in many ways fluent in racial discourses about modernity and civilization, and even further, that they often sought to use such discourses to their own advantage. This forces us to see that, even as Native Hawaiians were facing colonial violence from haole settlers, Native Hawaiians responded in complicated ways that sometimes internalized and deployed Western notions about Polynesian proximity to whiteness and progress themselves. Especially in relation to Sāmoans, Kalākaua positioned Hawaiians as the most superior Polynesians, due to their more advanced "progress" in Western norms, even as he sought to ally with Sāmoans against European and American imperialists. While some scholars have suggested that Kalākaua was intrigued but confused about Western ideologies about race, Cook's work demonstrates that he was in fact very knowledgeable about contemporary theories about Polynesian origins because he followed such studies and conducted his own.[97]

Polynesian exceptionalism, as a kind of internalization of settler colonial ideologies about white superiority and a link between Polynesians and whites, would continue to structure many other interactions between Pacific Islanders. Tregear viewed the Māori as the most exceptional example of the noble Polynesian, while Fornander found the highest value in Native Hawaiians. Kalākaua also declared Hawaiians to be the most enlightened Polynesians, especially noting their superiority in becoming fluent in Western culture and norms, in contrast to Sāmoans. In each of these cases, Polynesian exceptionalism was being articulated with some kind of nationalism: Tregear as a Pākēha settler nationalist for New Zealand; Fornander as a white, Swedish-naturalized citizen of the Hawaiian Kingdom and royalist supporter of Kalākaua; and Kalākaua in his own right as a fierce advocate for Kanaka Maoli cultural nationalism. That this logic could be applied in various contexts for various aims shows its flexibility and staying power.

Yet the power Native Hawaiians had or sought through claiming their own superiority over Sāmoans was far from equal to the power wielded by white settlers. Through the Bayonet Constitution and later the overthrow of the Hawaiian Kingdom, white settlers ultimately wielded greater military and economic strength over Hawaiʻi. Still, that Native Hawaiians in some ways became invested in the logic of possession through whiteness themselves, insofar as they valued their greater naʻauao or enlightenment over other Polynesians, demonstrates that whiteness was a fiction that did not require actual European people to uphold. Again, this is why I emphasize that this logic is possession *through* whiteness (not *by* whiteness) because whiteness is not an agent in and of itself. Rather, whiteness is a type of knowledge and power that many invest in for multiple and even conflicting reasons.

---

From the 1830s through the 1880s, white settler scholars mapped complex relationships between ancient Polynesians, Greeks, Romans, Egyptians, and Aryans. Lang, Fornander, and Tregear produced Polynesians as a race bound not only to classical civilizations but also to a particular time: an invented, glorified past that Europeans claimed as their own. To European settlers in New Zealand and Hawaiʻi, their claims to Polynesian heritage trumped the claims of contemporary Māori and Kānaka Maoli because they had degenerated from their former heights and required the leavening effect of settler colonialism to ever glimpse their former glory again. Settler colonialism promised not a return to Polynesian civilizations of old, however, but an improvement upon that prehistory through the folding of Polynesia into the British and American empires, which white scholars saw as the metaphorical and literal outgrowths of ancient Rome and Greece. This conferred a ghostly quality to the production of Polynesians as white: their whiteness was always deferred to either a mythological past or to a future to be determined by white settlers.

In this way, the logic of possession through whiteness had a haunting character, relying strongly on idyllic ancient history, while simultaneously projecting the greatness of past civilizations onto a white settler future. Because Polynesians were degenerated versions of Aryans, white European and American settlement of Polynesia was both predestined and benevolent. White settlers would help elevate Polynesians into the enlightened civilization they were always meant to become. For missionaries, this language was steeped in discourses of Christian salvation and the dangers of remaining or backsliding into savagery. For lay scholars like Fornander and Tregear, Polynesian degeneration made Polynesians valuable curiosities ("heirlooms" in Fornander's words), who held some of the nobility and mystery of the ancient Aryan race in their language and stories. Yet, just as Christian missionaries felt that they were required to bring Polynesians into civilized ways of life, white scholars presumed that they were required to record and decode the latent Aryan nobility in Polynesian folklore before it was lost through assimilation and older Polynesians passing away.

Each of these ideas central to the logic of possession through whiteness will show up again in the chapters that follow: that Polynesia and Polynesians are the natural heritage of Europeans, that Polynesians are settlers too, that Polynesians used to be white, and that in the present day, Polynesians had generally degenerated out of whiteness, but some remained whiter than others. The next chapter follows the thread of Aryanism into the development of eugenics in the early to mid-twentieth century, showing how many of the same concerns that Fornander and Tregear expressed were further pursued by physical anthropologists. These social scientists would move from comparing Polynesian languages and stories to Sanskrit to comparing the physical measurements of Polynesian bodies to white bodies. The logic of possession through whiteness would carry over easily to the new methodologies. In Hawai'i, eugenics and physical anthropology would codify a new racial category in both science and law: the Part Hawaiian.

CHAPTER 2

*Conditionally Caucasian*
Polynesian Racial Classification in Early Twentieth-Century
Eugenics and Physical Anthropology

If then the Polynesian is not to be regarded as a true Caucasian, he is to be regarded as at least a decided step in that direction.
—LOUIS SULLIVAN, 1923

In the early twentieth century, physical anthropologists took up the study of Polynesians and their origins. Like earlier scholars of Polynesian languages and mythology, physical anthropologists also largely approached Polynesians as "nearly Caucasian." Yet they claimed that their supposedly rigorous scientific studies of living Polynesian peoples more definitively proved a biological, racial link between Polynesians and Caucasians. To physical anthropologists, comparative measurements of physical attributes provided hard data on similarities between Polynesians and Caucasians that they believed was far more convincing than Fornander's and Tregear's earlier comparative notes between Polynesian and Sanskrit words and stories. As with the earlier studies however, linking Polynesians to whiteness did not mean that Polynesians and Caucasians should be treated exactly the same. Rather, as noted in the epigraph above, Polynesians would be seen as conditionally Caucasian. Not really "true Caucasians," but "at least a decided step in that direction."

As physical anthropologists like Louis Sullivan, who worked in Hawai'i in the 1920s, conducted their research on the Polynesian race, they were heavily influenced by eugenics. The field of eugenics in the early to mid-twentieth century can be broadly understood as a scientific desire and program for combating degeneration, as discussed in chapter 1, in which the biggest fear was Westerners and the West itself regressing from its civilized heights, or "going native." In contrast to the largely religious and mythological discourses about degeneration discussed in the last chapter, eugenics took degeneration on as a matter of biological fact.[1] Gregory Moore describes the fears of degeneration in Europe at this time as something more significant than simple social paranoia or pessimism. Rather, Moore writes, "This putative deterioration of Western civilisation—manifested in the epidemics of 'social pathologies' such as alcoholism, sexual perversion, crime, insanity, and anarchism ... [was] an empirically demonstrable medical fact, as symptomatic of a more fundamental degenerative process within the European races; it eventually gave rise to the eugenics movement."[2] As anthropologist Jonathan Marks has noted, "the extent to which eugenics was actually a mainstream movement among professional biologists and geneticists" from 1910 to 1930 ..."cannot be overemphasized."[3] In fact, eugenics was a key component of Progressivism.[4] Educational programs for "gifted children" and birth control, for example, both trace their histories back to eugenic science.[5]

In the Pacific, eugenics must similarly be understood as part of a white Progressivism. As analyzed in this chapter, eugenicist views toward Native Hawaiians were not necessarily explicitly anti-Hawaiian or anti-Polynesian. Instead, eugenicists like Uldrick Thompson, a teacher at Kamehameha Schools, could see themselves as champions of Native Hawaiians. Thompson advocated that Native Hawaiians should restore the currently degenerated Hawaiian race back to its ancient purity and nobleness through following the tenets of eugenics in marrying and having children with the right partner. Louis Sullivan similarly saw himself as something of an advocate for Native Hawaiians, especially of "Part Hawaiians." Speaking at the Second International Congress of Eugenics in New York City in 1921, Sullivan remarked that "Hawaiian-whites are looked upon as the negroes are in this country."[6] Here again we see how tightly wound the discourse of almost whiteness in Hawaiʻi and Polynesia was with antiblackness. Sullivan did not necessarily see the racism faced by "negroes" as unjust, but thought "Hawaiian-whites" were unfairly targeted because white Americans did not understand their proper racial classification. In Sullivan's estimation, "the part-Hawaiian is biologically a better individual than the full Hawaiian—more capable of coping with modern conditions of life and civilization."[7] Thus, Sullivan championed mixed-race Native Hawaiians because, in his view, they were not black and were also losing their indigeneity as they assimilated to modernity.

This chapter examines Thompson's and Sullivan's views on racial types and racial purity in relation to Native Hawaiians and Polynesians more broadly. Their stances were markedly different in that Thompson was against "racial mixing" and believed Native Hawaiians should do more to preserve their racial purity, whereas Sullivan lauded the benefits of racial intermixture for assimilating Native Hawaiians into proper white Americans. Yet both men's ideals were shaped by similar assumptions about white supremacy and Indigenous disappearance fostered by the logic of possession through whiteness. What both Thompson and Sullivan valued most about Native Hawaiians and Polynesians was what they saw as their proximity to whiteness, and their relative distance from blackness.

Alongside the analysis of Thompson and Sullivan, this chapter also examines the research and writing of Te Rangihīroa (also known as Sir Peter Henry Buck), a famed Māori doctor, statesman, and physical anthropologist. Te Rangihīroa participated in theorizing about Polynesian origins and racial classification in conversation with white social scientists, though his investments in such research were significantly different from those of his white colleagues. Te Rangihīroa's reverence for Polynesian cultures is evident in his writings, as are his hopes that his research could help promote pride and cultural revitalization among Polynesian peoples. Nevertheless, Te Rangihīroa believed that Polynesians were "Europoid" and properly racially classified as similar to Caucasians. He was insistent that Polynesians did not have black or Negroid roots, in contrast to Melanesians. As with Kalākaua's investment in Hawaiian superiority over Sāmoans, I analyze Te Rangihīroa's investment in Polynesian exceptionalism, with an eye toward understanding how Polynesian people today might challenge our own often unacknowledged investments in whiteness that ultimately support settler colonialism over more sustaining Oceanic relationships.

All three of the men whose writing, teaching, and research I consider in this chapter worked in Honolulu in the early twentieth century, at or in close relation to the Bishop Museum, a center of anthropological research in the Pacific at the time. Though Thompson and, to some extent, Sullivan focused much of their concern on Native Hawaiians, the Bishop Museum was a hub for researchers journeying much farther afield in Oceania. Thus, they were in conversation with others about race and culture across Polynesia as well as Micronesia and Melanesia. Te Rangihīroa conducted research not only in Hawai'i but also in New Zealand and other Pacific nations.

While this chapter deals most directly with U.S. settler colonialism, the many locales that Bishop Museum affiliates studied remind us that the logic of possession through whiteness continued to be developed not only in relation to the United States; it remained significant to other settler nations at this time as well. For example, Christine Winter's work on race and racial mixture in German Sāmoa and Sāmoan diaspora to Germany has shown that Sāmoans were officially classified as Aryan during the Holocaust, meaning they were not subject to concentration camps, even as they were certainly never extended equality on par with white Germans.[8] While this chapter focuses on eugenics in the context of Hawai'i from the 1900s to the 1920s, the development of eugenics and racial classification at the turn of the century would clearly have long-lasting, haunting effects, through the Holocaust and beyond.

## ULDRICK THOMPSON'S EUGENIC HOPES FOR THE HAWAIIAN "REMNANT"

In the early 1900s, eugenics was a key topic of instruction at Kamehameha Schools for Boys. Uldrick Thompson, a teacher at, and later the principal of, Kamehameha Schools, published two manuals on eugenics, one in 1913 and one in 1915, for use in his courses on "sex hygiene."[9] Although he was not a scientist, he kept up with all contemporary eugenics literature, as his manuals demonstrate in recommending texts by well-known eugenicists Charles Davenport and David Starr Jordan for his students' further reading. Originally from New York State, Thompson's long career at Kamehameha Schools allows him to be remembered today as a storied advocate of Native Hawaiians. For example, in 2002, staff and advocates of Kamehameha Schools repeatedly invoked a 1904 address of Thompson's while the school faced its first legal battle over the constitutionality of its Native Hawaiians-first admission policy.[10] Yet the eugenics context of Thompson's advocacy deserves closer examination.

Through eugenics, various concerns about Native Hawaiian "blood" took on more weight as both a metaphor for racial ancestry and a literal genetic measure of that ancestry. Native Hawaiian youth at Kamehameha Schools—particularly boys—were often at the heart of eugenic pedagogy and research in Hawai'i. Kamehameha Schools for Boys, opened in 1887 (with a girls' campus opening in 1894), was a school for Native Hawaiian children set up by the will of a member of the royal Hawaiian family, Bernice Pauahi Bishop. Two years after the opening of Kamehameha Schools for Boys, the Bishop Museum was founded, and would become a home to a large collection of Native Hawaiian and broader Pacific cultural and ethnological artifacts. The Bishop Museum shared a campus with the Kamehameha Schools for Boys from 1889 to 1940, making it particularly easy to pull Native Hawaiian boys into the studies of researchers, like Louis Robert Sullivan, who were based at the Museum.

In the early 1900s, eugenics was understood as a scientific solution to social ills (drunkenness, poverty, etc.), and promised to be more comprehensive than social reforms that focused on environmental conditions. At Kamehameha Schools, Thompson accordingly saw eugenics as a science that could help better the lot of Native Hawaiians. His 1913 manual stresses understanding and abiding by the rules of inheritance to improve the human race. He tells his students that "our ancestors" are "not entirely to blame" for the combination of "good" and "bad" qualities "they gave us, because they did not understand these laws of heredity."[11] Yet, for his students, a "Revolution" has begun: "In six states laws have been passed to regulate heredity. These laws say that certain criminals (murderers, thieves and others) shall not have children. People are getting tired of taking care of such creatures.... In time, only the finest men and women will have children. And the weak, the cowardly, the dishonest, the foolish, the lazy and the diseased will die and disappear."[12]

Thompson's exhortation to his students at Kamehameha Schools is that they can, and indeed must, consciously form reproductive, sexual relationships that will result in children of the finest stock. They were to avoid any unions with biologically and psychologically inferior women who might cause their offspring to fall into that category of "the weak, the cowardly, the dishonest, the foolish, the lazy and the diseased." Not incidentally, though he seems to have held ample hope for the specific, relatively privileged, and (in his eyes) assimilable Native Hawaiian youth he taught, Thompson also felt that other Native Hawaiians should have been subject to medical sterilization. Outside of the classroom, Thompson also worked to pass a policy of medical sterilization in Hawai'i's territorial legislature. His proposed bill would "make it lawful for the people of these Islands to refuse parenthood to those who are plainly unfit to reproduce humans."[13]

On the one hand, Thompson's eugenics lesson would have been commonplace at the time. Historian Robert Osgood, for example, demonstrates that the public education system in Indiana routinely taught eugenics principles, and structured a variety of public policies on eugenics, including the development of both "special education" for students with special needs, and education for so-called gifted students.[14] On the other hand, Thompson's eugenics pedagogy at Kamehameha Schools also differed in significant ways from continental U.S. concerns, which Osgood argues was largely focused on managing the reproduction of working-class white immigrants. Though Thompson often uses the same language of degeneracy and immorality in his manuals, the Hawaiian case held its own specific concerns that fit with the overall mission of Kamehameha Schools at this time, to civilize and domesticate Native Hawaiians.

Though established for Native Hawaiian youth by the trust of a Native Hawaiian aliʻi (a chief or royal leader), Bernice Pauahi Bishop, the Bishop estate trust was first executed by her haole (white, foreigner) husband Charles Bishop, with a board entirely composed of male haole trustees who were all supporters of the overthrow of the Hawaiian monarchy in 1893.[15] Accordingly, as Noelani Goodyear-Kaʻōpua has shown, Kamehameha Schools in its early, formative years operated from the premise that Kānaka Maoli were "a tender and vulnerable race, easily moldable by white educators through a program of manual labor and domestic training."[16] Boys learned manual trades suitable for industry or agriculture, and girls learned to run white American–style households as wives. Thus, as Goodyear-Kaʻōpua persuasively writes, Kamehameha Schools at this time was "in the business of producing a heteronormative middle class that would participate in an industrial, capitalist economy and consent to American political rule."[17]

Part of becoming heteronormative and middle class involved inculcating Kamehameha Schools students with white American racial norms about marriage and reproduction. This is abundantly evident in Thompson's eugenics manual, which notes that the largest sin of Native Hawaiians in Thompson's eyes was that most of the "old time Hawaiians" had "died without having reproduced their kind."[18] By this, Thompson did not necessarily mean that "old time Hawaiians" had had no children at all, but that they had had children with non-Hawaiians, thereby producing Part Hawaiians without any of the admirable qualities of their more noble ancestors—resulting in a degenerate contemporary population. Thompson was far from alone in viewing past generations of Native Hawaiians as noble and strong, but believing contemporary Native Hawaiians to be morally, spiritually, and physically degenerated, in much the same way as Lang, Fornander, and Tregear saw Polynesians as once great and comparable to white civilizations but contemporarily lost and dwindling, as discussed in chapter 1. Degenerate in this sense stems from the Latin verb *degenerare*, meaning "to depart from its race or kind."[19] For example, a 1919 biography of Kamehameha the Great by the American scholar Herbert Gowen described contemporary Native Hawaiians as Kamehameha's "degenerate off-spring," with only "a hundredth part of the manhood possessed and used, mainly for good, by this heroic savage."[20] Thompson thus saw his work as helping reverse the trend of degeneration and believed that under his tutelage, his male Kanaka Maoli students could effectively "rehabilitate" their race and masculinity.

In a special section of the manual, titled "To a Remnant," he addressed the particular eugenic challenges faced by Native Hawaiians.[21] Characterizing "old time Hawaiians" as "gigantic in stature and great in strength," "patient and persevering," "honest and hospitable," and "intelligent," Thompson questions how many of these good qualities were passed on to the contemporary generation of Native Hawaiians, whom he deems "a small remnant."[22] He suggests: "the qualities which made the old-time Hawaiians great, in their time and under their conditions, have been transmitted and are still in the blood. Latent, if you will; but present; and capable of development.... It remains for this remnant of a great people to learn how best to keep and how best to transmit, to their children, the qualities that they are proud to say their ancestors possessed. And they must learn these things and act upon this knowledge before it is everlastingly too late."[23]

While Thompson represents the Hawaiian race with the common eugenics language of degeneration, and also uses the popular images of Hawaiians as dying out and disappearing, he argues overall that eugenics can help reverse such decay and foster a stronger Hawaiian race for the future. This use of eugenics as applied to improving the Native Hawaiian race is a rather surprising repurposing of common eugenics discourses about bettering the white race. Eugenics pedagogy in the United States generally focused on *preventing* reproduction among those considered members of a lower class and inferior race, not encouraging it. Even other eugenicists writing about Hawai'i in the early twentieth century tended to view Native Hawaiians as irreversibly doomed to extinction, and were primarily interested in how the physical and moral characteristics of "pure" Hawaiians would be transmitted into the larger, racially mixed population of Hawai'i.[24] Thus, Thompson's plan for biologically bettering the Hawaiian race, through a careful cultivation of the "qualities which made the old-time Hawaiians great," displayed a unique belief in the reversibility of Native Hawaiians' supposed extinction. He encouraged his Native Hawaiian students to imagine a future in which they could also confidently wield the "the qualities that they are proud to say their ancestors possessed."

The advocacy and power Thompson granted in encouraging his students' belief in a Native Hawaiian future should not be easily dismissed. Yet we also cannot ignore that Thompson understood Hawaiian-ness as fundamentally biological and racial, and argued that it was the "pure," "old time Hawaiians" who were the ideal. For Thompson, modern Part Hawaiians (many of his students included) were clearly distinguishable from (and lesser than) the "old-time Hawaiian," of whom he talks about completely in the past tense. In his eyes, the Part Hawaiian was the true degenerate, and the only way that Native Hawaiians could hope to preserve their "good character" was by pursuing racial purity, as modeled after white racial purity. Thompson simply applies the positive eugenics lessons that eugenicists meant for well-off white populations to his students, the relatively privileged (because they were being privately educated) Native Hawaiian boys at Kamehameha Schools. While this application may seem surprising, as my analysis in chapter 1 has shown, Thompson would have had ample literature to draw on that would have tied Native Hawaiians ancestrally to the white race. Indeed, as Szego, who explores Thompson's "racial ambivalence" toward Native Hawaiians through an analysis of a song Thompson composed, has noted: "A great deal, though certainly not all, of Thompson's appreciation for his contemporaries seems to have stemmed from the ways that Hawaiians fulfilled European American standards and desires, rather than an intrinsic valuation of their indigenous practices."[25] Thus, Thompson envisioned Native Hawaiians as close enough to "European American standards" and the white race to be capable of undergoing a similar positive eugenic project of racial betterment within their own communities.

However, negative eugenics were also implicit in Thompson's eugenics teaching and advocacy. Though he held hope for the best of Native Hawaiian youth, he also clearly felt that some Native Hawaiians were "unfit" and should have been subject to the medical sterilization policies he advocated. Szego remarks on this point: "In short, many haole elite regarded a great many Hawaiians as 'unfit,' though Thompson never said as much. He did not have to."[26] In his manuals, Thompson gives few explicit instructions about what kinds of unions or women would be "unfit" for his male students. Yet his repeated mentions of disease and learning the laws of inheritance touch on two taboos that Western observers perceived Native Hawaiians transgressing—namely, incest and leprosy. Some royal Native Hawaiian families practiced marriage between siblings, for example. Additionally, after the outbreak of leprosy in Hawai'i in the late nineteenth century, Native Hawaiians did not initially follow Western standards of quarantining those with leprosy, or Hansen's disease. These things shocked and mobilized Western missionaries, and similar concerns were translated into scientific literature through eugenics, where breaking such taboos became the cause of Native Hawaiian racial degeneration.[27] Sexual relationships between Native Hawaiians with and without leprosy, and relationships deemed incestuous by Western standards, were both capable of producing children whose "bad qualities" were not always immediately or physically apparent, but seemed to Western observers to always lie just below the surface.

Western fears and fascination about Hawai'i in the late nineteenth and early twentieth centuries in fact pivoted on the fact that both leprosy and racial ancestry were not always superficially obvious. At least in the early stages of Hansen's disease, those infected often appeared perfectly healthy. Thus, fears about disabled and Indigenous bodies passing as able-bodied and white were intertwined. For example, in Jack London's stories about Hawai'i, a repeated theme is of a white person coming to terms with the discovery that the beautiful and sexually desirable appearance of a Native Hawaiian man or woman masked both their diseased nature and their true racial identity—because they appeared to the white viewer to also be white, or at least very nearly white.[28] Like Thompson, London was fascinated by what was latent, "still in the blood" of Native Hawaiians. Here the logic of possession through whiteness operates with a kind of compulsory able-bodiedness that is also always, as Robert McRuer has argued, a compulsory heterosexuality. McRuer demonstrates that the presence of disabled and queer bodies often works not as a challenge but as a supplement to able-bodied and straight people, through a constant demand that "people with disabilities embody for others an affirmative answer to the unspoken question, Yes, but in the end, wouldn't you rather be more like me?"[29] In London's stories, mixed-race Native Hawaiians with Hansen's disease are produced as tragedies, because the assumption is that these people would rather be fully white, able-bodied, and part of a productive heterosexual marriage. More broadly, the logic of possession through whiteness similarly stages Polynesians as nonnormative supplements to whiteness, heterosexuality, and undiseased able-bodiedness, all features that define settler nation-states.

Such fears about disease and race in Hawai'i were important to the white American public of whom many were just being introduced to the idea of Hawai'i becoming part of the United States. The Hawaiian monarchy was overthrown by a cadre of white plantation owners in 1893, and Hawai'i was formally annexed as a territory by the United States in 1898. Scientific and popular interest in Hawai'i burgeoned after these events, yet many balked at the idea of adding a "brown" race to the U.S. populace.[30] The association of leprosy with Native Hawaiians was a particular cause of concern.[31] American writer Prince Morrow, for example, argued that considering "more than ten per cent of the Hawaiian race are affected with leprosy it becomes a serious question as to what will be the effect of the absorption of this tainted population upon the health interests of this country."[32] Morrow went on to detail what was not responsible for the leprosy epidemic among Native Hawaiians: "No unfavorable influence of soil or climate or hardship can be invoked in explanation of the decay and death of the native race. . . . Under the same conditions which have led to the depletion of the Hawaiian race, and which threaten its ultimate extinction, the foreign races that have settled here have flourished and multiplied."[33]

While Morrow does not explicitly explain what was responsible for leprosy among Native Hawaiians, it is clear that he places the blame on Native Hawaiians themselves. Rather than viewing Native Hawaiians as subject to conquest by "a civilized race," as in "the case of the North American Indian," Morrow argues that no struggle or competition between races is present in Hawai'i. Rather, he implies that Native Hawaiians are lazy, for they are facing extinction, despite living in a "land where nature is kindly and bountiful."

Thompson also believed that Native Hawaiians were to blame for their own fate under colonialism. Yet he also believed it was possible, under his direction, for the elite Native Hawaiian male students in his classrooms to "rehabilitate" their race. It is the "young men and young women of Hawaiian blood who are meeting the new conditions and holding their own in the struggle for existence and advancement" in whom Thompson believes the good qualities of old-time Hawaiians are "still in the blood."[34] This approach put the blame for Native Hawaiians' loss of power and land under settler colonialism on Native Hawaiians, and Native Hawaiian women in particular, for betraying the "pure" Hawaiian race and producing degenerate Part Hawaiians. His eugenics pedagogy was specifically aimed at young Native Hawaiian men, who were expected to regain control over their race, and over Native Hawaiian women.

Also significant is that Thompson's plan for reinvigorating the Hawaiian race was premised on "purer" unions between elite Native Hawaiians only, and was implicitly staged against children born of interracial relationships.

In a memoir Thompson published in 1941, he would state even more pessimistically and adamantly: "I do not believe in this MIXING THE RACES. It has been going on since Cain migrated to the land of Nod. And the present population of this earth is the result,—a conglomerate of human beings, degenerates, liars, thieves, parasites, murderers, kidnappers, dope fiends, swindlers. If this mixing of the races could be confined to the mating of the finer women and men of each race, the results would be entirely different."[35]

Thompson was not bothered by the idea of racial mixing as a practice as much as he was concerned about the class and pedigree of those who were mixing. Thompson believed Native Hawaiians' best qualities were their similarities to European Americans; thus, keeping their pedigrees within those of a "finer" nature was the only viable future for Native Hawaiians.[36]

SULLIVAN'S "TWO TYPES" OF POLYNESIANS

By contrast, Louis Robert Sullivan, another eugenicist working in Hawaiʻi in the early twentieth century, argued that "the part-Hawaiian is biologically a better individual than the full Hawaiian,—more capable of coping with modern conditions of life and civilization."[37] A physical anthropologist based at the Bishop Museum, Sullivan believed that racial mixing was a boon to the Native Hawaiian race because he believed in "hybrid vigor," a concept that held that racial mixes were healthier and more well-adjusted than pure Native Hawaiians. While Sullivan and Thompson differed in valuing the Part Hawaiian versus the Pure Hawaiian, they both contributed to constructing the Part Hawaiian as a category distinctly separate from the Pure Hawaiian. For both, the logic of possession through whiteness was important insofar as whiteness remained the measure of value. Thompson felt that Pure Hawaiians were better because their racial purity placed them in closer proximity to white blue-blood families, while Sullivan believed the Part Hawaiian was more capable of assimilating to white society.

Visitors to the Bishop Museum Archives today may readily recognize Louis Sullivan's name from a bountiful resource that he left behind after his visiting affiliation with the Bishop Museum in Honolulu from 1921–25: the Sullivan collection of photographs. These images—over 1,300 photographs total, though this is only a fraction of the nearly 11,000 residents of Hawaiʻi whom Sullivan measured—portray a variety of Hawaiʻi's residents from the 1920s and are frequently used today by visitors conducting genealogical research. Yet few visitors may understand the original purpose of these photographs. In a joint appointment between the American Museum of Natural History in New York City and the Bishop Museum, Sullivan was hired to "undertake a definite investigation of the Polynesian elements in the Hawaiian population." In the words of Clark Wissler, curator in the Department of Anthropology at the American Museum, Sullivan, "a highclass [*sic*] museum man," would provide research desired by the Bishop Museum and in the process also direct the production of a "collection of photographs and plaster casts of living subjects to be used in our exhibition halls."[38]

In addition to taking photographs and commissioning plaster casts of the heads of certain individuals who represented specific racial mixes, Sullivan used anthropometric methods to obtain physical data from Native Hawaiian subjects. These methods included measuring stature (height), span, head length and width, anatomical face height, nasal height and width, physiognomic ear length, height, and breadth. Qualitative characteristics were also observed, including classifications of eye color, presence of an epicanthic eye fold, ear lobe shape, nasal bridge height, slope of the forehead, shape of the lips, hair color and form ("straight, low waved, deep waved, curly, frizzly, wooly"), and skin color (both "exposed and unexposed").[39] In anthropometry—a discipline for which Sullivan even wrote a manual specifying a standardized set of practices (see figure 2.1)—all of these features were compared to the average or common features of other races and used to construct ideal racial types. Sullivan was both fascinated and frustrated by the large variety of physical characteristics Polynesians exhibited—as Warwick Anderson notes, he wrote of his work: "I'm trying to work out a method for isolating race types in a badly mixed population."[40] Despite finding it harder to isolate "race types," as an anthropometrist he soldiered on, meticulously cataloging individuals' physical measurements and racial percentages.

The photographs and plaster casts the American Museum hired Sullivan to produce were seen as vitally important data for the eugenics field. Henry Fairfield Osborn, then president of the American Museum, Clark Wissler, Louis Sullivan, and Herbert Gregory, then director of the Bishop Museum and also affiliated with Yale University, were all members of the Galton Society, the premiere professional eugenics organization of the time. As Warwick Anderson notes: "Collecting 'primitive' types was compelling because [Henry Fairfield] Osborn planned a Polynesian hall at the American Museum; the United States boasted a 'historic connection' with Hawai'i and the evaluation of a racially mixed peoples might offer insight into contemporary social problems on the mainland, including New York."[41]

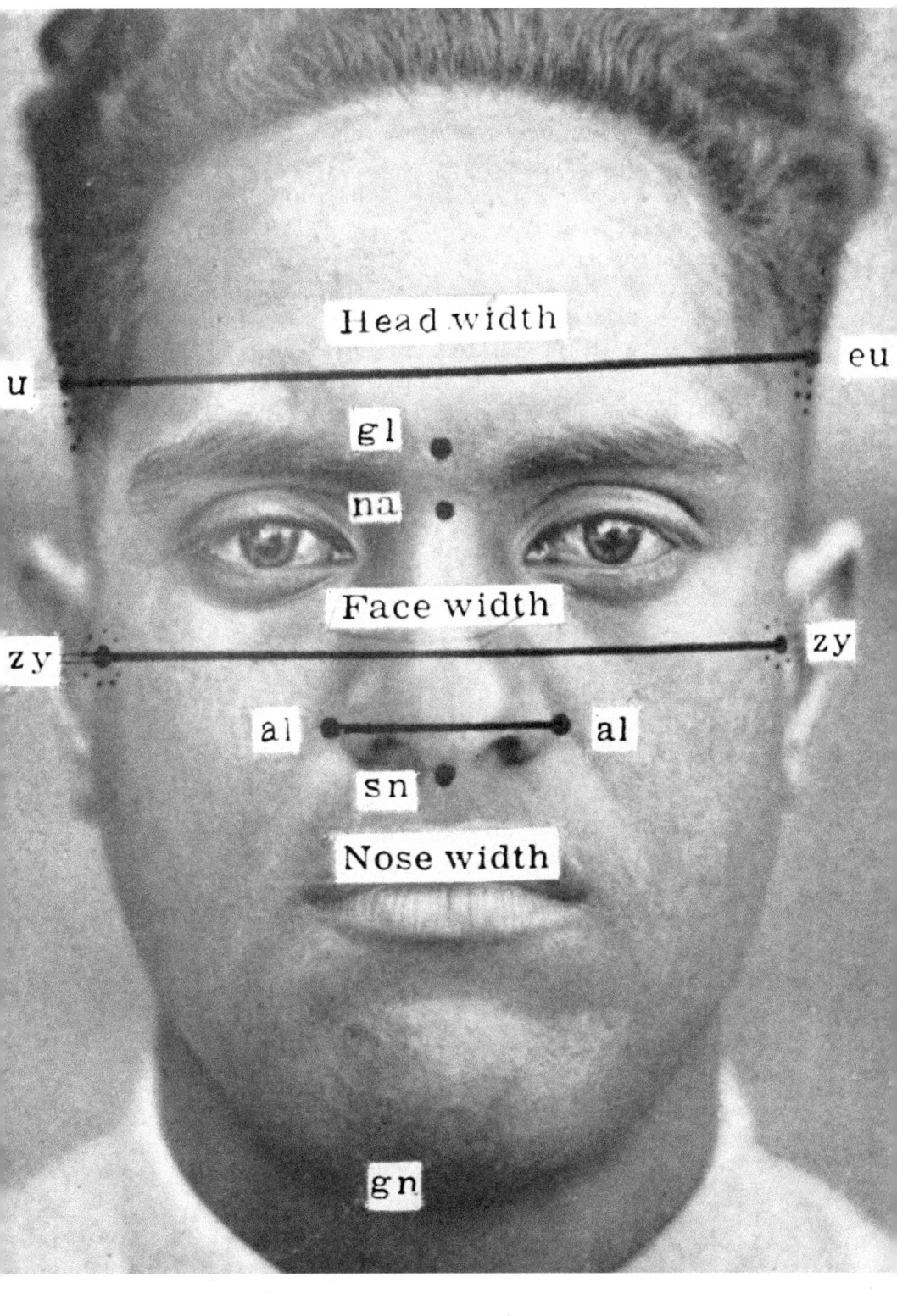

FIGURE 2.1. "The Landmarks and Length and Height Measurements," from Louis R. Sullivan, *Essentials of Anthropometry: A Handbook for Explorers and Museum Collectors* (New York: American Museum of Natural History, 1928).

Anne Maxwell has similarly suggested that white American audiences would have viewed "racial type" photographs such as Sullivan's as a way "to predict what would happen if other racial groups were allowed to mix with [white] Americans, and if reversing the sex of the parents for each racial combination made any difference."[42] This possible future of a racially mixed population was what white visitors would have had in mind while viewing the photographs and casts Sullivan directed as they were displayed at both the American Museum and the 1921 Second International Eugenics Congress in New York City. Each photo and facial cast, made from live subjects, was carefully notated with that person's race. Some were labeled simply "Chinese man," while the Native Hawaiian subjects had much more detailed fractions, allowing viewers to imagine the effects of racial combinations, as Maxwell has noted. Captions inked across the chests of the fifty-four facial casts included, for example: "Hawaiian 6/8 American 2/8," "Hawaiian 3/4, Chinese 1/4," or "Hawaiian 1/4, White 1/4, Chinese 1/2" (figures 2.2, 2.3, and 2.4).

FIGURES 2.2, 2.3, and 2.4. Photos of plaster casts of Harriet Beamer (Hawaiian 1/4, white 3/4), Moses Kamakawiwoole (Hawaiian 7/8, Chinese 1/8), and James Apo (Hawaiian 1/4, white 1/4, Chinese 1/2). Made by George Usborne under the direction of Louis R. Sullivan, 1920–21. One of fifty-four plaster casts prepared for the Second International Congress of Eugenics, October 1921. Bishop Museum Ethnology Collections. Photos by Jesse W. Stephen, copyright Bishop Museum, 2018.

In addition to producing items for the American Museum's Polynesian Hall, Sullivan also understood his work as pursuing a more refined, complex answer to the classic Polynesian Problem. Warwick Anderson has shown that Sullivan's research interests stemmed from his somewhat uneasy mentorship under two famous, and famously opposed, anthropologists: the staunch eugenicist Charles Davenport and one of the first anthropologists to speak against eugenics, Franz Boas.[43] Sullivan had completed his PhD fieldwork on the "Sioux Indians" under Boas, but he was also influenced by, and corresponded with, Davenport because of Davenport's long-established interest in the Polynesian Problem.[44] While Davenport and American Museum president Henry Osborn wanted Sullivan to procure evidence of Hawai'i's various, "pure racial types," Sullivan's training under Boas had also made him "skeptical of racial typologies and fixities," and interested in the physical effects of race mixing.[45] In correspondence with Davenport and Boas, Sullivan emphasized different results; speaking more openly to Boas about his interest in the racially mixed population, while

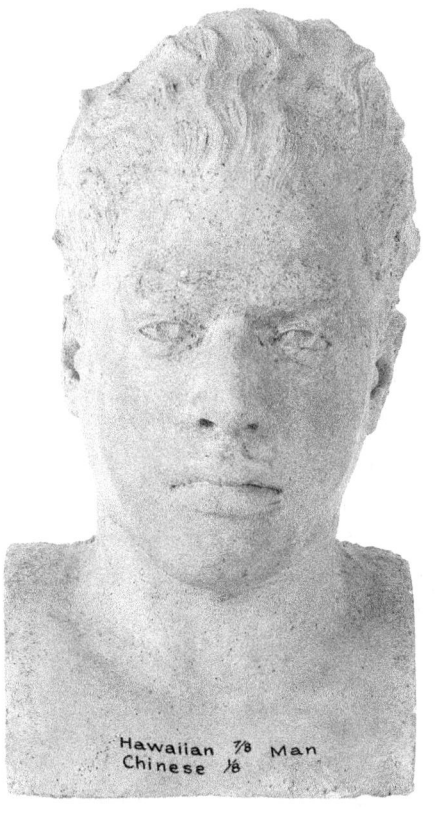

seeming to pursue only "pure" populations in correspondence with Davenport.[46] Anderson goes so far as to argue that Sullivan's health suffered from being pulled between Davenport and Boas.[47]

The tensions of discovering "pure" racial types as well as accepting and studying racially mixed people in Hawai'i are certainly clear in Sullivan's research. A Bishop Museum annual report from 1921 describes Sullivan's interests as pursuing the question: "were there originally only one or several types of physical Hawaiian?"[48] He pursued this question by making measurements of schoolchildren and comparing the "local and foreign-born Hawaiians."[49] Sullivan's mentor Boas had completed similar studies interested in the effects of environment on the physical types of European immigrants to New York City. In applying a similar methodology to the population of Hawai'i, Sullivan was thus working with a model of local-born and foreign-born that centered immigrant experiences: the "local and foreign-born Hawaiians" the report refers to denote recent Asian and European immigrants to Hawai'i as "foreign-born" and "locals" as anyone who was born in Hawai'i, and not only Native Hawaiians. This approach mapped a white American frame onto Hawai'i just as earlier ethnologists had mapped ancient Greece and Rome onto Polynesia, as noted in chapter 1. Sullivan would move away from this model as he became more and more fascinated with the Polynesian race itself. Yet, in some respects, he remained interested in the "immigrant" and "assimilated" aspects of Boas's research, as applied to the Polynesian race itself, insofar as he understood ancient Polynesians as immigrants from Asia and contemporary mixed-race Native Hawaiians as "locals" who were rapidly adjusting to white American culture.

By 1922, Sullivan concluded that there were at least two original Polynesian racial types. He described his preliminary thesis in a professional correspondence with Herbert Gregory: a "primitive type" that was "short, long-headed, wavy-haired, brown skinned," and a second type that was a "tall, short-headed, straight-haired type with lower, broader faces."[50] Most of the remaining research Sullivan would conduct and publish would be centered on these two types of the Polynesian race. Later, Sullivan would describe his two types as the "Polynesians of Polynesia" and the "Indonesians of Polynesia."[51] The Indonesian type corresponded to the first "primitive" and "brown skinned" type he describes above, while the "Polynesian" type corresponded to the "tall, short-headed, straight-haired type." This second type represented to Sullivan the "true" Polynesian.

Antiblackness played an unstated but important role in these distinctions. The "Polynesians of Polynesia" were more authentic because they were not fundamentally "brown skinned," in Sullivan's estimation. In a study published by the Bishop Museum in 1923, Sullivan concluded:

> If then the Polynesian is not to be regarded as a true Caucasian, he is to be regarded as at least a decided step in that direction. The Polynesian, Aino [*sic*], and certain American Indians may egotistically be looked upon as unsuccessful attempts of nature to make a Caucasian. If they are not true Caucasians, they branched off near the stem of the Caucasian type. It was some type closely related and resembling the Polynesian that gave rise to the Caucasoid types. If they are not true Caucasians, there are undoubtedly descendants of this or closely related types in Europe who pass for Caucasians.[52]

Sullivan's writing here is full of conditional clauses ("if they are not true Caucasians") that awkwardly attempt to parse a racial proximity between Polynesians and Caucasians. Polynesians might not be Caucasian, but they are "a decided step in that direction," or "descendants" of Caucasians, perhaps having "branched off near the stem." Here we see the logic of possession through whiteness at work, making a conditional identification between Polynesians and Caucasians that does not attempt to equate Polynesians with "true Caucasians." Rather, Polynesians are seen as "unsuccessful attempts of nature to make a Caucasian." They have some natural potential to become Caucasian, but, it is implied, they will not be able to achieve that status without intervention or guidance from other, truer Caucasians.

Writing for a more popular audience in 1923, in an article titled "New Light on the Races of Polynesia," Sullivan declared the true Polynesian type to be a Caucasoid type. He argued that naming this type Polynesian (of his two acknowledged Polynesian types), though somewhat arbitrary, was fitting because "most of the skeletal material described as Polynesian has been of this type and since the Caucasoid element has been almost exclusively described to the public by London, Stevenson, O'Brien and other writers of South Sea romances."[53] This points to an interesting reliance on popular ideas of Polynesians as well as the linguistic methods and findings of Aryanism, like the earlier Polynesian Problem literature of Lang and Fornander examined in chapter 1. His argument that Polynesians branched off near the stem of the Caucasian type is quite similar to Fornander's argument that Polynesians were "fundamentally Arian [*sic*] of a pre-Vedic type."[54]

To illustrate his points, Sullivan included several photographs with the 1923 article, contrasting two Polynesian men, both dressed in suit and tie (figure 2.5). One photo is marked as the "Indonesian Type" who "Represents the Mongoloid Element with Negroid Characters," and the other shows the "Polynesian Type" in whom "Nature Seems Just to Have Missed Producing a Caucasian."[55] In between, he shows a photograph of a "Hawaiian Fisherman"—whom he notes is of interest to "specialists in language, ethnology and folk-lore," as distinct from his own interests in physical anthropology. Here, we see that Sullivan's creation of one "blacker" type and one "whiter" type of Polynesian clearly echoed long-standing social scientific distinctions between black Melanesians and white Polynesians. Sullivan was arguing that these same black/white distinctions existed within the Polynesian race itself. Conveniently, this perspective allowed Sullivan to acknowledge a diversity of physical characteristics, including seemingly black or "Negroid" traits, within the Polynesian race while also maintaining the existence of the storied "white" Polynesian of "South Sea romances." This was a revision of Fornander's and others' arguments that Polynesians had never mixed with black races—Sullivan was at once acknowledging Polynesian racial diversity and declaring, with visual and physical evidence, that popular views of the Polynesian as a nearly white, noble savage type were still valid.

Sullivan passed away at a young age, in 1925, from pleurisy or complications of tuberculosis.[56] From his papers, it seems that he had not yet reached a satisfying answer to the Polynesian Problem but remained hopeful that more research would confirm his "Polynesian type" as a true Caucasian type.[57] Sullivan, like Thompson before him, took as fact that the Part Hawaiian was the future of both the Native Hawaiian race and Hawai'i overall. They simply disagreed on whether that was a future to look forward to or not. As is clear in a graph from Cold Spring Harbor's eugenics archive (figure 2.6), based on Sullivan's research, breaking the Hawaiian population into Pure and Part categories allowed the evident decline of the Native Hawaiian population to appear much steeper than it actually was. To both, the Pure Hawaiian was passing away. Thompson found this tragic, but the fault of Native Hawaiians themselves, who might reverse this fate only by beginning to value racial purity and marry accordingly. Thompson's view reads as the more overtly racist and obsolete view. Thompson's perspective would go out of favor, at least for a time, because of both Hawaiians' own lack of belief in distinctions between Part and Pure Hawaiians at this time (though, as I discuss in chapter 4, these ideas have been revived at times)

| INDONESIAN TYPE | A HAWAIIAN FISHERMAN | POLYNESIAN TYPE |
|---|---|---|
| He Represents the Mongoloid Element with Negroid Characters | He Attracts Specialists in Language, Ethnology and Folk-Lore | In Him Nature Seems Just to Have Missed Producing a Caucasian |

means certain, however. There may be two short-headed, broad-nosed peoples in Polynesia. The Polynesian type is distributed throughout Polynesia. The distribution of the Indonesian type is not so well known. It occurs in Samoa but not easily recognized. It is so thoroughly mixed up that it is difficult to say just what proportion of the population it forms. In Tonga it is a very important element and less mixed. It is more concentrated in Haano of the Haapai Group than the southern islands of the archipelago. In the Marquesas the sequence varied from island to island. This then is a question for the future.

gists the statement that there is no evidence of the former existence in Polynesia of types of people unlike the present inhabitants. Such a statement now becomes meaningless, since there are living in the islands today at least two distinct peoples. It will be desirable to know which of these two types preceded the other. An immense amount of work will be necessary before any such generalization can be made; for it may very well be that the sequence varied from island to island. This then is a question for the future.

FIGURE 2.5. "Indonesian Type: He Represents the Mongoloid Element with Negroid Characters," "A Hawaiian Fisherman: He Attracts Specialists in Language, Ethnology and Folk-Lore," "Polynesian Type: In Him Nature Seems Just to Have Missed Producing a Caucasian." From Louis R. Sullivan, "New Light on the Races of Polynesia," *Asia*, January 1923.

and the broader sense among white settler men that they were naturally entitled to Native Hawaiian women (as I discuss further in the next chapter).

Though Sullivan's view was more liberal, it was no less dangerous. Sullivan looked much more favorably on the Part Hawaiian because he saw Part Hawaiians as both better suited for what he took as the undoubtedly white future of Hawai'i as part of the United States. It is also likely that he saw the Part Hawaiian as returning to his ideal of the true Polynesian type, that type which was perhaps not "a true Caucasian" but "a decided step in that direction." In Sullivan's scholarship, the Part Hawaiian was almost always a hapa haole. As I will discuss further in chapter 6, *hapa* is a Hawaiian word meaning "portion, fragment, part, fraction, installment; to be partial,

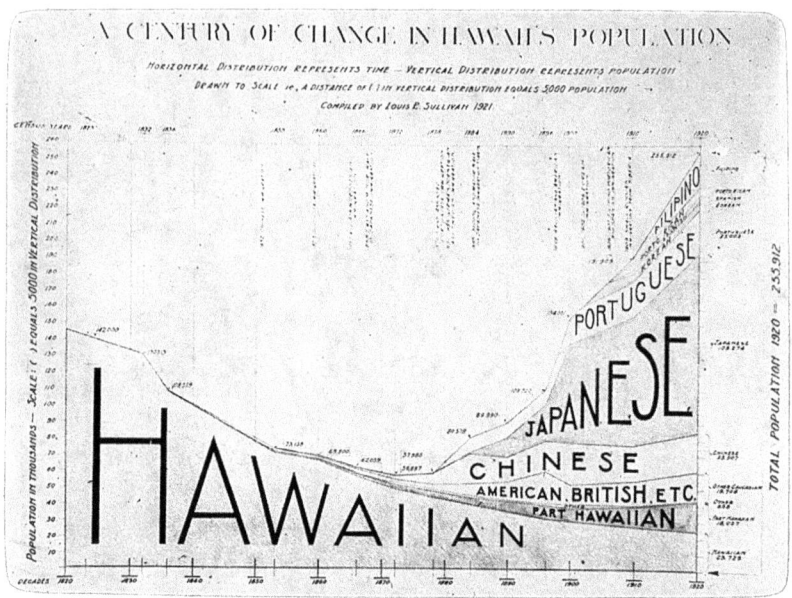

FIGURE 2.6. "A Century of Change in Hawaii's Population." Cold Spring Harbor Image Archive on the American Eugenics Movement, #932. Reprinted with permission from the Harry H. Laughlin Papers, Truman State University, circa 1922.

less," and "of mixed blood."[58] From the late nineteenth century, the term *hapa haole* denoted Native Hawaiians who also had white ancestry, usually individuals who had light skin color and could at times pass as white.[59] Of course, Native Hawaiians "mixed" not only with haoles but also with other Asian immigrant populations. Scientists like Sullivan, however, encouraged the public to understand mixed-race Native Hawaiians as "whitened," no matter what the actual mixture was, a logic I further analyze in the next chapter.

### TE RANGĪHĪROA'S "VIKINGS OF THE PACIFIC"

Te Rangīhiroa, a Māori scholar, understood Polynesians as a noble race of intrepid explorers comparable to the Vikings, cherishing an idyllic view of ancient Polynesia much like those of Thompson, Lang, and Tregear. Though he was also a physical anthropologist and, like Sullivan, believed in the power of precise measurements to solve the Polynesian Problem, Te Rangihīroa, himself of mixed-race heritage, did not put as much stock in blood percentages or "part" identities. While I will focus here on his engagements with the Polynesian Problem literature, his accomplishments are much broader. He served in New Zealand's parliament from 1909 to 1914, served in the Māori Battalion during World War I as a medical officer, and became New Zealand's director of Māori hygiene from 1919 to 1927.[60] His medical practice sparked his further interest in physical anthropology and ethnology. In 1927, he moved to Honolulu to participate in the Bishop Museum's regional survey of Polynesia as an ethnologist conducting fieldwork. He noted that he gave up his post as director of Māori hygiene because the Bishop Museum project "was so appealing to one of Polynesian blood."[61] He later became the director of the Bishop Museum, from 1936 until his death in 1951. In this latter career as an anthropologist, Te Rangihīroa taught at Yale University and the University of Hawai'i at Mānoa, published a number of books and essays, and received numerous honorary doctorates and two knighthoods, from Britain and Sweden.[62]

Te Rangihīroa was a dedicated anthropologist. Alice Te Punga Somerville notes his passion for Polynesian languages and material cultures, and his insistence on active participation in research, for he was "not satisfied that he was able to write about an item until he could construct it himself."[63] As a former medical doctor, he also believed rigorous scientific evidence would at last definitively solve the Polynesian Problem. Like Sullivan, he was critical of prior studies like those of Tregear and Fornander, which relied on analyzing similarities in languages and mythologies. He found such stories to be unreliable sources of biological facts about the racial classification of the Polynesian race, and too steeped in mythical embellishments to aid in determining the historical site of the storied Polynesian ancestral homeland, Hawaiki.[64] He similarly critiqued laymen's explanations of the Polynesian race, such as a mention in a governmental handbook that "the Sāmoans are the purest branch of the Polynesians," strongly cautioning that "No statement as to the manner of men can be accepted by intelligent people unless it is based upon a sufficiently large number of measurements of the physical characters of the human body and careful observations as to the form of hair, eyes, nose, skin colour, and other general features."[65] He found conducting physical measurements of living Polynesian subjects, as he did with Māori in New Zealand and on Mangaia in the Cook Islands, important because, as he wrote, "Until recent years our knowledge of the racial characteristics of the Polynesians was extremely scanty."[66]

Though Te Rangihīroa believed strongly in the importance of ethnology and anthropology, it is also clear from his writing that he experienced this work differently from white social scientists. In his book *Vikings of the Pacific*, he relates an incident at the Otago Medical School during his medical training in which "a fellow Maori student and I first entered the taboo precincts of the Medical School and saw at the top of the stairs a notice offering various prices for Maori skulls, pelves, and complete skeletons. We read it with horror and almost abandoned our quest for western medical knowledge."[67] This anecdote exposes how many parts of his medical and anthropological career entailed difficult confrontations with ongoing colonial violence.

It is evident that Te Rangihīroa's deep reverence and feeling for Polynesian mythologies and genealogies was often misunderstood or not shared by his colleagues. For example, Te Rangihīroa mentions that during his time as a representative in the New Zealand parliament, he was asked to speak in support of a daylight savings bill. Accordingly, he spoke of how "the first practical Daylight Savings Bill in the Pacific had been introduced by the Polynesian demigod Maui."[68] The response in the parliament was, "curiously enough," Te Rangihīroa noted, "what they seemed to regard as a humorous contribution to a dry debate."[69] He concludes, "Of my six years' contribution in Parliament to the welfare of my country, my surviving colleagues seem to remember only my alleged humorous interpretation of Polynesian mythology. I have never confessed until now how really serious I felt at the time."[70] Again, such reflections make it clear that Te Rangihīroa was aware of the different position he inhabited as a Māori politician and scholar, and the belittling attitude many Pākēha statesmen and scholars held toward Māori and Polynesians. Yet that difference seems to have opened up his anthropological research in certain ways that white anthropologists would never be able to access. It is clear in many of the anecdotes he shares in *Vikings of the Sunrise*, as he travels for ethnological research around Polynesia, that his subjects responded to, recognized, and embraced him as Polynesian kin (in contrast to the white researchers).[71]

In addition to his engagement with Polynesian racial origins through Western scholarship on the topic, Te Rangihīroa was also significantly interested in how Polynesians themselves framed their origin stories. Much more than Sullivan or other anthropologists of the time, he took seriously Polynesian stories of Hawaiki, an ancestral homeland spoken of by many different Polynesian peoples. In *The Coming of the Maori*, he detailed the Māori "great migration" or heke from Hawaiki around 1350 AD as a historical event that "ranks in historical and social importance with the Norman Conquest of English history."[72] Te Rangihīroa identified Hawaiki as the Society Islands, or what is now part of French Polynesia, an island group including Tahiti and Bora Bora.[73] Though he acknowledged, as in Western science, that Polynesians likely had ancient origins in India, he also placed importance on Hawaiki as a more recent origin that mattered more to Polynesian people.

Given the different position Te Rangihīroa occupied as a Māori anthropologist of Polynesia, we must understand his contributions to the Polynesian Problem literature as deeply complicated, as again his position in relation to the Polynesian Problem studies was very different from the positions of his white ethnologist colleagues. Without a doubt, however, Te Rangihīroa, like many of the social scientists I have already discussed, subscribed wholeheartedly to the notion that Polynesians were racially Caucasian, or, as he often put it, "Europoid." He based this conclusion on his own interpretation of anthropometric studies of Polynesians. The results of such studies were complicated in the sense that there were different physical "types" evident across Polynesia. As noted above in the discussion of Sullivan's theory about two types of Polynesians, the diversity of physical traits in Polynesian people led to different explanations about the routes of ancient Polynesian migrations as well as the proper racial classification of Polynesians.

Rather than follow Sullivan's "two types" thesis, Te Rangihīroa argued that all Polynesians were Europoid. Instead of intermixture with either Melanesian or "Mongoloid" races, Te Rangihīroa found that Polynesians descended from what he termed the "proto-Polynesians," a branch of "proto-Malayans," people who likely originally migrated from India.[74] These proto-Polynesians, in Te Rangihīroa's account, moved out of Indonesia before they had substantially mixed with "Mongoloids." Their migration out of Indonesia followed a northern route that traveled through Micronesia, avoiding all contact with Melanesia. Te Rangihīroa believed that Micronesia was largely uninhabited when Polynesians passed through the region, and that "the ancestors of the present Micronesians moved in behind the Polynesians."[75]

Te Rangihīroa's take on Polynesian origins and racial classification directly challenged other scholarship that attributed Melanesian ancestry to Polynesians. For example, his emphasis on Hawaiki as a place of origin for the Māori was important partly to demonstrate that Māori did not have Melanesian origins, but Polynesian ones.[76] In particular, he wrote against prior scholarship that attributed the presence of relatively long, narrow (dolichocephalic) heads in Polynesians to Melanesian (then classified as "Negroid") ancestry. Te Rangihīroa argued that "As a result of the studies made on the living in all parts of Polynesia, it is evident that the master mariners of the Pacific must be Europoid for they are not characterized by the woolly hair, black skins, and thin lower legs of the Negroids nor by the flat face, short stature, and drooping inner eyefold of the Mongoloids."[77]

He noted that Māori in particular generally had longer heads in comparison to shorter heads in Hawai'i, Sāmoa, and Tonga. Dispelling common ideas that the longer heads could be attributed to "intermixture with the Negroid population of Melanesia," and the shorter heads to "intercourse with the Mongoloids of Indonesia," he wrote, "it is unlikely that the head form alone should be affected by intermixture and that other physical characters should remain unchanged. If the New Zealanders have a Negroid strain, they should have woollier hair and wider noses than their Mongoloid-infected cousins in central Polynesia, yet the Māoris have the longest noses in Polynesia!"[78]

What were the stakes, to Te Rangihīroa, in having Polynesians classified as Europoid, and as definitively distinct from Melanesians? How were his stakes in such claims different from white anthropologists of the time like Sullivan? Though the answers to these questions are complicated, one way of approaching the questions is by looking at how and why Te Rangihīroa argued that Polynesians were like the Vikings. As the title of his book (*Vikings of the Sunrise*, republished after his death as *Vikings of the Pacific*) suggested, Te Rangihīroa was invested in having Polynesians recognized by the world as great explorers and navigators. In the early pages of *Vikings of the Sunrise*, Te Rangihīroa describes various European explorers' monumental discoveries, including Columbus and Balboa, "the first European to behold the Great Ocean [the Pacific]."[79] He then introduces Polynesians by comparison: "Yet long before Columbus made his great voyage, a stone-age people, in efficient crafts, had crossed the Pacific from continent to continent across its widest part and had colonized every habitable island within its vast interior."[80]

The description of Polynesians as "a stone-age people" here seems unusually pejorative for Te Rangihīroa. Perhaps he was simply describing how he expected Western audiences would perceive ancient Polynesians. Certainly, this language seems to have resonated with mid-twentieth-century American readers. The 1960 second-edition copy of *Vikings of the Pacific* published posthumously by the University of Chicago Press includes a similar blurb on its front cover: "The romantic story of the settlement of Polynesia by a Stone Age people—probably the greatest navigators the world has ever seen."[81]

The intrigue sparked by this blurb was underscored by the cover illustration—an artistic rendering of two brown-skinned women with long black hair, wearing bright pink flowered dresses mirroring the small pink flowers tucked behind their ears. By portraying Polynesians as feminine and dark, the cover shows how even on a book about how Polynesians were really Caucasian, the logic of possession through whiteness haunts through emphasizing racial and gender difference as supplements to whiteness, not ever equal to whiteness. This cover illustration, highlighting the popularity of romantic depictions of Polynesian women, was also at great odds with Te Rangihīroa's intention to highlight the great achievements of Polynesian men, not women, as remarkable explorers of the vast Pacific Ocean (according to some accounts of tradition, Polynesian women were not considered fit to navigate). Perhaps by describing Polynesians as "stone-age," Te Rangihīroa simply meant to emphasize how truly impressive and unrecognized the achievements of a supposedly uncivilized people were.[82] In the book's introduction, Te Rangihīroa describes Polynesians as "surpassing the achievements of the Phoenicians in the Mediterranean and the Vikings of the north Atlantic," since they were the only ones who could "pierce" the vast Pacific horizon.[83] Thus, they had proved they were "a breed of men who not only had an effective form of ocean transport but who had the courage to dare and both the will and the skill to conquer."[84]

Te Rangihīroa therefore sought to have Polynesians recognized by, and on par with, white Americans and Europeans in terms of their bravery, innovation, and overall success in navigating, exploring, and settling all of the isolated islands of Polynesia centuries before Europeans developed the appropriate technology to leave their coastlines behind. In this sense, Te Rangihīroa's engagement with both Polynesian anthropology and Western ideas of exploration and "discovery" is analogous to Kalākaua's engagement with earlier scholarship on the Polynesian Problem. Both enjoyed learning and using Western technologies and knowledge to continue more traditional Polynesian ways of knowing. Both hoped that white settlers would recognize Polynesians as more than capable of mastering "civilized" ways, in part because of the storied feats of their ancestors. Te Rangihīroa wrote, in further explanation of his use of "Vikings" as a descriptor for Polynesians, that "I am hopeful that *Vikings of the Sunrise* will reach my kinsmen in the scattered isles of Polynesia and draw us together in the bond of the spirit. We have new problems before us, but we have a glorious heritage, for we come of the blood that conquered the Pacific with stone-age vessels that sailed ever toward the sunrise."[85]

Thus, it is clear that Te Rangihīroa wrote with a Polynesian audience in mind, to "draw us together" and to face "new problems" with the confidence drawn from "our glorious heritage." In this respect, his stakes differed wildly from those of white anthropologists who argued that Polynesians were ancestrally Caucasian. Te Rangihīroa was not invested in naturalizing white settlement, but in promoting greater pride among Polynesians in their Polynesian heritage and strengthening ties between Polynesian people. Rather than ascertaining an Asian origin for Polynesians, Te Rangihīroa's work centered around Hawaiki, the ancestral homeland spoken of in many Polynesian traditions. As Somerville argues, Te Rangihīroa was interested in such research because he was interested in how Pacific peoples were connected and racialized. Nonetheless, we can hold his investments in supporting research about Pacific peoples in tension with his intense focus on Polynesia as exceptional and distinct from Micronesia and Melanesia. For as Somerville's work demonstrates, it is essential for our own communities to refuse the ways that Micronesians, Melanesians, and Polynesians have been separated in order to truly realize utopic notions by those like Hau'ofa of "our sea of islands." In recognizing and rejecting Polynesian exceptionalism and imposed Western ideals about Polynesians being almost white, Polynesians today can fulfill Te Rangihīroa's work of connecting the Pacific, even if in a different way from what he intended.

Certainly, the question of Polynesian (almost) whiteness would be a much more serious and practical matter to Te Rangihīroa than to his white colleagues, as evident in Te Rangihīroa's denied application for U.S. citizenship. Somerville notes that in the late 1930s, Te Rangihīroa "applied for US citizenship as a gesture of gratitude for the professional opportunities that country had extended to him"—including teaching at Yale University and the University of Hawai'i at Mānoa, and the directorship of the Bishop Museum in Honolulu from 1936 to 1951.[86] However, his U.S. citizenship application was denied, because, as he explained in a letter, in his own words, "I could not become an American citizen under the . . . law for an applicant has to be over 50% Caucasian. The Polynesians are classed as Orientals in spite of anthropological evidence of their Caucasian origin so I could only show 50%."[87] (His father was Irish, and his mother Māori.) This ruling was never reversed despite a resolution in support of his citizenship application from the Hawai'i territorial legislature, which Somerville shows also insisted on Polynesians' Caucasian origins.[88]

Preceding Te Rangihīroa's citizenship application, in 1928, another "Polynesian" had petitioned for U.S. citizenship successfully. Alfred Milner Stephen was a man identified as "three-quarters English and one-quarter Polynesian," who had migrated to Hawai'i from "Neuru Island" (likely Nauru, which is, in fact, classified as Micronesian).[89] In Stephen's case the courts decided that Stephen was sufficiently white to naturalize, perhaps because he was "three-quarters English." Kauanui argues that the "predominance" of Stephen's white "blood" was important, but that his case was also likely successful because of "pervasive notions about the potential for Hawaiians to assimilate and to fulfill the requirements of American citizenship."[90] In her account of the Stephen case, "The judge told the court that it was important to 'consider the fact that the racial admixture which characterizes this applicant is of a very desirable character as the history of Hawai'i and the South Seas has clearly proven.'"[91]

However, by comparing the Stephen case with the case of Te Rangihīroa's denied application for citizenship, it is clear that including Polynesians within whiteness remained conditional and subject to arbitrary and changing standards. Indeed, Te Rangihīroa's case demonstrates that being affiliated with whiteness nonetheless never offered Polynesian peoples any secure, definite access to the rights of whiteness, even for an expert in Polynesian racial origins. The racial indeterminacy of Polynesian whiteness would remain a "problem" for Polynesian peoples themselves, whereas for U.S. law and popular culture, Polynesian proximity to whiteness would authorize white ownership of Polynesia.

---

Though the three scholars I focused on in this chapter differed in many respects, each agreed that the Polynesian race was at least substantially similar to, if not a junior member of, the white race. In arguing for this similarity to whiteness, the so-called Part Hawaiian or Polynesian was key, as the "Part Hawaiian" represented to both Thompson and Sullivan significant possibilities in furthering Polynesian proximity to whiteness. Thompson placed his hope for Native Hawaiians in particular in their ability to preserve the "good qualities" that he felt were "still in the blood." Like Thompson, Sullivan saw two distinct categories among Native Hawaiians, the Pure and the Part Hawaiians, and categorized the subjects in his anthropometric studies accordingly. This distinction was also echoed in his broader work on the Polynesian Problem, in which he argued that there were two separate types of Polynesians—the Polynesian who was "almost Caucasian" and the Polynesian who had "Negroid characters." Sullivan valued both the Part Hawaiian and the "almost Caucasian" Polynesian type for their assumed ability to assimilate into whiteness.

In focusing on the ways that physical anthropologists contributed to the logics that constituted settler colonialism in Hawai'i and the Pacific, my work differs from that of other historians of science. For example, the historian of science Warwick Anderson has focused on how Sullivan and other anthropologists working at this time in the Pacific positively influenced the discipline away from an "older classificatory physical anthropology."[92] Yet closer analysis of Sullivan's work, as I have shown in this chapter, significantly complicates Anderson's conclusion that studies of racial hybridity in the Pacific helped phase out the more biologically grounded aspects of physical anthropology and promote more liberal views about race in science. Anderson holds that Sullivan's era of science in the Pacific was an exceptional, liberal moment, concluding: "While scientists were praising human hybridity, enjoying their modernist biological moment, mainland typologies and classifications gained a foothold on the islands. By the 1970s, when Barack Obama was growing up in Honolulu, the tension between these contrasting racial evaluations would be keenly felt."[93] This argument curiously denies the participation of Sullivan, who was also a member of the eugenic Galton Society, in the perpetuation of racial typologies that allowed blood quantum policies to develop in Hawai'i.

As I discuss further in chapter 4, Sullivan was working at the very same time that the Hawaiian Homes Commission Act established a blood quantum requirement for Native Hawaiians in 1921, namely that they prove they had "no less than half" Native Hawaiian blood to qualify for a Hawaiian homestead (a small, rented parcel of land managed by the territorial and, later, state government). By noting the importation of "mainland typologies" by the 1970s, Anderson implies that Hawai'i did not have race or racism beforehand, and with the reference to Obama, perhaps equates racism with antiblack racism against African Americans (rather than the broader ways that antiblackness structures settler colonialism and racism against Native Hawaiians as well). This chapter shows that what Anderson calls "praising human hybridity" in the work of Sullivan and others was not contrary to the establishment of "mainland typologies and classifications" in Hawai'i, but essential to them.

By contrast, Te Rangihīroa did not necessarily separate the Part and Pure out in the same ways that Thompson and Sullivan did. It is clear that he identified as Māori, for example, not as "Part Māori."[94] However, his writings also evince a sadness for the passing of Polynesian ways of life prior to white settler expansion into the Pacific. He also largely agreed with Sullivan's conclusion about the true Polynesian type being a conditionally Caucasian type. As Te Rangihīroa's case seems to illustrate, Polynesians actually achieving the conditions required to push past the "conditional Caucasian" classification were practically impossible. To actual Polynesians, this conditional state was permanent, despite the various ways the logic of possession through whiteness intimated that Polynesians might transition into real Caucasians through the benevolent influence of white settlers. For the "conditional" designation hid an enduring catch-22: How could Polynesians really prove their whiteness without ceasing to exist as a separate race? The two categories—Polynesian and white, or Hawaiian and white—could not be inhabited simultaneously. Becoming Caucasian, unconditionally, would mean Polynesians ceasing to exist as a separate race, which was, of course, exactly what Thompson and Sullivan were predicting.

Accordingly, though the Polynesian proximity to whiteness seemed to carry a promise, or at least a possibility, of equality for Polynesians to those like Te Rangihīroa, it was clear in practice that there were strict limits to the Polynesian–white comparison on the Polynesian side of the equation. The expression of the "conditional Caucasian" in physical anthropological studies emphasized how much the logic of possession through whiteness was a relentlessly one-way conduit, transferring what was expedient for white settlers to feel at home in Polynesia, while providing little to Polynesians besides the nominal attribution of almost whiteness. The next chapter analyzes related dynamics of "whitening" in the invention of the melting pot ideal in Hawai'i.

CHAPTER 3

## *Hating Hawaiians, Celebrating Hybrid Hawaiian Girls*
Sociology and the Fictions of Racial Mixture

Regrets that she has a quarter Hawaiian—dislikes Hawaiian very much.
—Note by Margaret Lam on an interview with a Chinese Hawaiian woman, 1931

Almost all immigrants were men, who perforce married Hawaiian girls.
—"Hawaiian Medley," *Collier's*, December 11, 1943

"What can Hawai'i teach America about race?" In the summer of 2015, I was invited to respond to this question, contributing to an online forum of various "experts" with something to say about race and Hawai'i. Two prominent media and cultural institutions on the U.S. mainland organized the forum during a summer dominated by ongoing, daily violence against Black people, undocumented immigrants, Muslims, and others. In this context, the forum was directed toward a discussion of what lessons Hawai'i had to teach America about race—presumably because Hawai'i was less racist. Concerned about the instrumental use of Hawai'i as an instructional model (betraying a lack of interest in Hawai'i for its own sake) and the seeming suggestion that Hawai'i was somehow immune to racism and perhaps not really part of the United States, the organizers assured me that my contribution could be critical of the endeavor. I sent in a short piece noting the history of U.S. colonialism in Hawai'i and the ongoing struggles of Kānaka Maoli to revitalize cultural practices and regain rights to land and water. When the piece was finally published, among other edits, I noticed that all instances of the word *colonialism* had been removed.[1]

This inability to acknowledge, much less analyze, colonialism as always intertwined with racism in Hawai'i was deeply frustrating to me, but not at all new. For indeed, the question "What can Hawai'i teach America about race?" is at least a century old, enjoying a prominent place in both the history of social scientific studies about Hawai'i and the securing of Hawai'i's statehood. In the 1920s and 1930s, it was the question at the forefront of the research of Romanzo Adams, a founder of the sociology department at the University of Hawai'i, and it would animate the research of that department and other social scientific studies of Hawai'i for decades to come. Adams, trained by Robert Park at the University of Chicago, saw in Hawai'i the ideal context for studying and modeling Park's theories of assimilation. Adams testified to this effect during federal hearings about the suitability of Hawai'i to become a state, encouraging both residents of Hawai'i and the white American public to view statehood as a natural progression of Hawai'i's exceptional racial harmony. To Adams, Hawai'i fulfilled white American ideals of democracy to an even greater extent than had so far been possible in the continental United States, making it an exceptional model for U.S. race relations.[2] Jonathan Okamura further notes the legacy of Adams's ideas in the persistent image of the "Hawai'i multicultural model," which first emerged in popular and academic literature of 1980s, and continues to be influential today. The repetition of tropes about Hawai'i as "the 'ethnic rainbow,' 'positive example,' and 'melting pot'" in the news media, Okamura argues, has influenced a "countless" audience of people around the world to understand Hawai'i in simplistic, and erroneous, terms.[3]

How has studying Hawai'i for racial lessons so effectively erased the role the United States has played in structuring racial and colonial violence in Hawai'i? Why does colonialism seem necessarily to drop out of discussions about race in Hawai'i? Why has the fiction that Hawai'i has no racism lasted so long? This chapter grapples with these questions in the context of the early to mid-twentieth-century sociological research of Adams and others centered at the University of Hawai'i. Though the sociology of this period largely portrayed Hawai'i as an exceptionally racially harmonious place, there is ample evidence that many people (Native Hawaiian and non-Hawaiian, white and nonwhite, residents of Hawai'i and residents of the continental United States, academics and laymen) found Hawai'i anything but. Historian Christine Manganaro has argued that many Hawai'i residents in this period, even (or especially) those who were themselves in interracial marriages, found Hawai'i to have a great deal of "race prejudice."[4]

In the popular media of the United States in the early 1930s, images of Hawai'i as a "racial nightmare" were in fact splashed over countless newspapers and magazines in response to the so-called Massie affair. The Massie affair involved a series of highly publicized court cases originating from the claims of Thalia Massie, the white wife of a white naval officer stationed at Pearl Harbor, that she had been assaulted and raped by a group of Native Hawaiian and Asian American men in 1931. When these men failed to be convicted due to lack of evidence, enraged white naval personnel engaged in vigilantism. One Japanese American man, Horace Ida, was severely beaten. Further, Massie's husband and mother, with the help of two other naval officers, kidnapped, shot, and killed Joseph Kahahawai—a Native Hawaiian man identified as the "darkest" of the accused. Stopped on their way to dump Kahahawai's body in the ocean, they were caught and arrested. Massie's mother and husband were subsequently convicted of killing Kahahawai, but ultimately, under great pressure from the U.S. Navy and the yellow journalism of the U.S. mainland, the governor of Hawai'i commuted their sentences and they served only an hour under arrest—and not in jail but at tea in the governor's office.[5]

The Massie case was widely reported throughout the United States and the world, shocking readers with depictions of Hawai'i as a terrifying place where "roads go through jungles, and in those remote places bands of degenerate natives lie in wait for white women driving by."[6] Notice again the use of the language of degeneration and degeneracy to describe Native Hawaiians here, an echo of the earlier discourses analyzed in previous chapters. Some have argued that the furor over the Massie case and the racial fears brought on by the widespread media coverage of "degenerate natives" were even responsible for delaying Hawai'i's entry into the country as a state.[7] This new image of Hawai'i as a racial nightmare was completely at odds with the idyllic, carefree image that local government officials of the Territory of Hawai'i wished to promote. It also flew in the face of social scientists' existing views (including Louis Sullivan and his mentor Franz Boas) of the Pacific as a benign and controlled "racial laboratory" for human biology. However, instead of destroying the racial laboratory ideal, after the Massie affair such sociological accounts only gained further importance.

This chapter attempts to understand this seeming paradox: the creation and endurance of the image of Hawai'i as a racial laboratory and racial paradise in the face of ample evidence to the contrary. I focus on the wide gaps between the published research of Romanzo Adams and the unpublished archive of interview data gathered by his graduate student research assistants Margaret Lam and Doris Lorden in the 1930s.[8] In the transcribed interviews, respondents repeatedly share their disgust for Hawaiians and "Hawaiian ways." These negative attitudes contrast with the benefits of racial mixture touted by Adams and more broadly popularized in the image of the hybrid "Hawaiian girl."

Juxtaposing the disregarded sociological evidence of commonplace hatred of Native Hawaiians in Hawai'i with the popularity of pinup-style illustrations of Hawaiian girls and their exotic racial mixes, this chapter shows that the discourse of Hawai'i as melting pot has always been a salable fiction that masks structural racism against Native Hawaiians and others. Thus, in the early to mid-twentieth century, white American men were invited to continue the tradition of racial mixing in Hawai'i that began, as the epigraph notes, with the earliest European immigration to Hawai'i, when "Almost all immigrants were men, who perforce married Hawaiian girls." Overall, this chapter analyzes how hatred and exoticism have intertwined in formations of Native Hawaiian race, gender, and indigeneity, and how these entanglements, like the construction of the almost white Polynesian type examined in the first two chapters, are enabled by the settler logic of possession through whiteness.

REALIZING ROBERT PARK'S DREAM: ROMANZO ADAMS
AND HAWAI'I AS A U.S. RACIAL LABORATORY

Romanzo Adams founded the Sociology Department at the University of Hawai'i in 1919. He was later contracted by Hawai'i territorial officials to head the University of Hawai'i's studies of race relations. Officially titled a Station for Racial Research, it opened in May 1926, with funding from the Rockefeller Foundation. Adams was interested in coming to Hawai'i because of his training in sociology at the University of Chicago under Robert Park. Park and his colleagues predicted that, as Asian immigrants to the United States advanced through the stages of the race relations cycle (contact, conflict, accommodation, and assimilation), they were destined to completely assimilate with white American society. Though they had special interest in Asian American communities in California, in their view, Hawai'i also showed strong evidence of assimilation. As Henry Yu writes, to Park and others from the Chicago School, Hawai'i would become a "fantasy island . . . the ultimate racial laboratory, a place where the formation of the cultural melting pot they had predicted for the West Coast was already taking place."[9] Through the 1970s, sociology at the University of Hawaiʻi would continue to be dominated by those trained in the Chicago School, with many, including Park, conducting research and spending sabbatical years there.[10]

Park and others in the Chicago School had developed many of their approaches first through focusing on issues of European immigrant assimilation and urban African American populations, emphasizing environmental factors rather than inherent ethnic or racial traits as the source of social problems such as urban crime. This antiracist shift, advanced by many Black sociologists who trained under Park, including E. Franklin Frazier and Charles Johnson, was significant to sociology. It pushed social scientists to consider the larger context of so-called black crime as not pathological to Black people but the result of historical and political structures.[11] Yet in the context of Hawaiʻi, Adams applied the Chicago School's structural, environmental approach to glorifying Hawaiʻi as a setting uniquely free of racial, ethnic, or class oppression. While this was an antiracist approach insofar as it similarly argued that racial difference was not the inherent cause of social problems, Adams's investment in seeing Hawaiʻi as a unique, racism-free model did not match reality, while it also made it harder to confront ongoing forms of racism and colonialism in the then U.S. territory. During congressional hearings in 1933 about the suitability of Hawaiʻi to become a state, Adams submitted testimony encouraging the American public to view statehood as a natural progression of Hawaiʻi's exceptional racial harmony and Americanness. Highlighting the relatively high rates of interracial marriage in Hawaiʻi, he summarized: "all races are making a significant contribution toward the creation of the coming Neo-Hawaiian people of Hawaiʻi."[12]

The "Neo-Hawaiian people" Adams projected was an ideal of the future in which everyone living in Hawaiʻi would be multiracial and American. The creation of this imagined new race is illustrated well in a figure from an article describing Romanzo Adams's work published in the *Oakland Tribune* in 1930 (figure 3.1).[13] In this illustration, deeply exoticized and racially typed images of an "Asiatic" and "Polynesian" are symbolically added to the "European," befitting the sociological image of the racial laboratory. Where the Asiatic and Polynesian figures are dressed in stereotypical "primitive" garb (in fact the Polynesian is represented with the image of a Melanesian/Papua New Guinean, emphasizing a "blacker" savagery), the European is dressed plainly in a possibly military uniform, as would have fit the large

FIGURE 3.1. "New Race Growing Up in Pacific," *Oakland Tribune*, 1930.

presence of the U.S. Navy in Hawai'i at this time. The magical result is a "Hawaiian": a dark-haired, mustachioed man in a shirt and tie, his dress also subtly suggesting a military uniform.

The erasure of women from this biological equation is notable and significant. Each figure here is a man, perhaps emphasizing the masculine, objective nature of Adams's social scientific work. Meanwhile, the plus signs obscure yet take for granted that Native Hawaiian and/or Asian American women would eagerly do the reproductive work of producing this "new race" of Hawaiians. Thus, heterosexual reproduction is taken for granted as the mechanism for moving Hawai'i forward into what Tavia Nyong'o has called "the straight time of heterosexuality, wedded to progress" that heralds a "hybrid future" that is also seen as progressing from, and curing, the racism of the past.[14] That the illustration hides from view the details of heterosexual reproduction and/or familial ties growing between Native Hawaiians, Asians, and white settlers in Hawai'i suggests that interracial families remained something of a taboo, unable to be represented (in contrast to the later popular representation of mixed-race women in Hawai'i, as I discuss later in this chapter). In this respect, the illustration operates in a way similar to Civil War–era discourse on racial amalgamation, as analyzed by Nyong'o, in which race mixing was seen as "probable or inevitable," but popular discourse would "stop short of welcoming it as desirable."[15] Here, the outcome—the light-skinned "Hawaiian"—is desirable, but the actual mixing that produces him is simply inevitable, and understood to produce only the mixed-race body, not any other meaningful social or cultural relationships that might threaten whiteness and Americanness in the U.S. territory.

It is telling that the illustration results in a "Hawaiian" rather than simply the multicultural catchall category of "American," which of course is also the underlying suggestion. This is a stark illustration of how settler colonialism required not only the assimilation of Native Hawaiians into the United States but also relied on changing the category of "Hawaiian" into something that white Americans who had settled or aspired to settle in Hawai'i would be able to inhabit, perform, and possess. As the illustration shows, this ideal of multiculturalism was premised on the assimilation of "other" races into the white race. This end-product "Hawaiian" is not a true mix of the other three races but simply a slightly darker version of the European. Indeed, the discourses about racial mixture in Hawai'i were never fixed on the result of an even mix of racial, physical, and moral characteristics. Rather, as Damon Salesa puts it in the context of racial amalgamation policies in colonial New Zealand, "A proper amalgamation did not combine two races into a 'new' race that was substantially mixed or intermediate; rather the process of amalgamation projected, very baldly, the *disappearing* of one race into another."[16] Thus, a racial hierarchy would remain even as such multicultural equations seemed to gesture toward the end of racial distinctions altogether.

Adams, given his strong belief in assimilation as the inevitable and desired end of race relations, took for granted that "pure Polynesians" and "pure Asiatics" were dying out. The Orientalist and tribal markings in the illustration portray Asians and Polynesians as anachronisms, stark contrasts to the neat, modern uniforms of the European and Hawaiian figures. Noticeably, "Polynesian" stands in for "pure Hawaiian," as the most ancient, traditional, or authentic form of the Native Hawaiian. Crucially, describing Hawaiians as Polynesians in this context also transforms the Native Hawaiian into an immigrant (because Native Hawaiians are the descendants of ancient Polynesian voyagers who traveled to Hawai'i from other Polynesian islands). In this way, both the Asiatic and Polynesian figures are represented as equally foreign to modern Hawai'i, but smoothly vanishing into the Hawaiian figure that so resembles the European.

In one sense, Adams and the other Chicago School–trained sociologists who frequented Hawai'i were not directly participating in the Polynesian Problem line of research examined in the previous two chapters. They narrowly focused on race relations in U.S. society and the potential lessons Hawai'i had to offer to the continental United States and had little or no interest in the larger Polynesian or Oceanic regions. Nonetheless, I understand their work as fundamentally grounded in the same logic of possession through whiteness as the earlier Polynesian Problem studies. To Adams, Park, and others, Hawai'i was living proof that whiteness could win out, that whiteness could engulf and dissipate racial difference.[17] Eliminating racial prejudice would ultimately require eliminating racial difference altogether, through assimilation. This disappearance of racial prejudice and difference hinged on the ability of researchers to reason that Native Hawaiians and Asian immigrants to Hawai'i were capable of becoming white, or white enough. This proximity to whiteness for both Native Hawaiians and Asian immigrants to Hawai'i was knowledge enabled by the prior Polynesian Problem studies in both Aryanism and physical anthropology that had demonstrated that whiteness had ancestral roots and branches in Asia and Polynesia.

Early in his career, Adams's research focused specifically on concerns about Japanese assimilation in Hawai'i. White, mainstream American anxieties about whether Japanese immigrants were willing or able to assimilate, or if they would remain loyal to Japan, were referred to as the "Japanese Problem." These concerns were a major potential obstacle raised in hearings during the 1930s about the potential of Hawai'i to become a state.[18] Adams sought to refute the idea that there was any Japanese Problem by illustrating that Hawai'i's Japanese population was not a barrier to Hawai'i's Americanization. Through analyses of demographic shifts, he emphasized that though Japanese residents of Hawai'i were then by far the least likely to intermarry with other races, they would likely follow the example of other Asian groups like the Chinese and eventually intermarry with whites and Native Hawaiians.[19] Adams's scientific view backed up other popular writing about Hawai'i at this time as, in Honolulu minister Albert Palmer's words, "a bridge between Japan and America." Palmer concluded his 1924 book *The Human Side of Hawaii* thus: "After all that is just what Hawaii means—a human bridge of international good will and understanding between East and West!"[20]

Adams would take the idea of "a human bridge" between the East and West rather literally. After his research on the Japanese Problem, for the rest of his career, he would focus on racial intermarriage in Hawaiʻi. This topic was significant to Adams because of the Chicago School's understanding of race relations as primarily about attitudes and feelings, rather than structures. Interracial marriage between East and West was seen as a key bellwether of lessening racial prejudice. For Adams, Hawaiʻi's rates of racial intermarriage were exceptionally high relative to the mainland United States, and thus, race problems seemed to him practically nonexistent there. Hawaiʻi's high rates of racial intermarriage also seemed to uniquely prove the achievement of assimilation (according to the Chicago race relations cycle) into American society. Manganaro argues: "Notably, Chicago sociologists saw interracial sex and marriage as both symbols of closing distance as well as the most efficient actual pathways to assimilation if they produced children. In other words, they were both the cause and effect of assimilation."[21]

Yet interracial marriage did not in fact magically produce assimilation or racial harmony. Since white supremacy and settler colonialism are structural, interpersonal relationships are not sufficient solutions to systemic inequities. Further, couples who marry interracially are not necessarily guaranteed to hold less racist views of other races; often personal exceptions can be made that do not change an individual's overall perception of a race. Instead of reflecting an actually existing racial harmony, the image of Hawaiʻi as melting pot allowed sociologists and representations of Hawaiʻi in popular U.S. media to ignore and trivialize the racism that many in Hawaiʻi did experience, while it also erased the historic and ongoing settler colonial occupation of Hawaiʻi.

### SURVEYING CHINESE HAWAIIANS

Under his direction in 1930–31, Adams's graduate students Margaret Lam and Doris Lorden conducted over two hundred interviews with mixed-race Chinese Hawaiian families in Honolulu, Hilo, and Wailuku, Maui.[22] At the heart of the interviews was an assessment of the interviewee's attitudes toward what the surveyors classified as four separate racial groups, namely Chinese, Hawaiians, "Chinese-Hawaiians," and "Caucasian-Hawaiians." Though it is unclear exactly what questions Lam and Lorden asked those interviewed (the record only reflects the recorded answers under the headings of each racial category), the answers largely reflect whether the interviewee personally had close friends in each of the racial categories.[23] Based on their history of friends since childhood and their current social groups, they would state whether they felt positively or negatively toward each group. This emphasis was in keeping with the Chicago School's emphasis on race relations as a matter of feeling and the absence or presence of prejudice in individuals.

However, multiple aspects of the responses also trouble and exceed the framing the interviewers attempted to impose on these discussions of race. Many interviewees did not agree with the four stated racial categories. Some respondents who stated they primarily identified as Hawaiian also insisted that Chinese Hawaiians and Caucasian Hawaiians were all the same and belonged to one category—simply "Hawaiian." I read this refusal of the imposed hybrid racial categories as a regenerative refusal of the sociologists' questions, in keeping with Native Hawaiian epistemologies that emphasize broad inclusion along ancestral patrilineal and matrilineal lines. This expansive definition of Hawaiian-ness refused the idea that there was such a thing as a part Hawaiian, while it also insisted that Native Hawaiians were still a people and nation distinct from Asians and Americans. Several respondents who identified as primarily Chinese made a similar argument that they took Chinese Hawaiians to be simply Chinese. So too, many brought up other racial groups beyond the scope of these four categories, who were also clearly part of their social lives. These included many of the other racial groups that constituted society in Hawai'i at this time, the most frequently mentioned being Japanese and Portuguese. Yet the survey limited its focus to soliciting opinions about Chinese, Hawaiian, Chinese Hawaiians, and Caucasian Hawaiians.

A striking fact about the interview data is that, of 206 individuals surveyed, over half (114, or 55 percent) of the respondents stated negative or deeply conflicted feelings about "pure" Hawaiians.[24] As I analyze further below, they stated they intensely disliked, "didn't care for," hated, or even feared pure Hawaiians, or made a caveat that some Hawaiians were good, but that other Hawaiians were lazy, dirty troublemakers who possessed supernatural powers of revenge ("kahuna practices").[25] In contrast, attitudes toward both Chinese and Chinese Hawaiian people were overwhelmingly positive. Seventy-five percent (155) of those interviewed admired Chinese business sense, discipline, and other positive attributes, while 68 percent (141) felt similarly about Chinese Hawaiians. Despite these clear trends,

Romanzo Adams's subsequent scholarship commented only on the positive attitudes toward Chinese Hawaiians and mixed-race people more generally. The obvious evidence of widespread hatred toward Hawaiians (held so deeply by those who were Hawaiian themselves) did not change Adams's insistence on Hawai'i as a place of racial harmony because Adams was so deeply invested in his ideal of the neo-Hawaiian race replacing Native Hawaiians. Again, this is the logic of possession through whiteness at work, for Adams took for granted that Native Hawaiians were dying out and/or assimilating into whiteness. Perhaps he felt racism against Native Hawaiians would end as the neo-Hawaiian race replaced Native Hawaiians. Yet the ideal of the neo-Hawaiian race was partially responsible for the racism against Native Hawaiians. Native Hawaiians faced racism related to the fact that they did not always accept assimilating into whiteness, or, as analyzed below, Chinese-ness.

HATING HAWAIIANS

The next two sections analyze the Lam/Lorden interviews. Though there are clear trends in the interview data, analyzing these interviews from a contemporary perspective is no less a fraught endeavor than it was for Adams or his graduate students. Given the lack of information about how the interviews were actually conducted, and the likelihood that no kind of informed consent (as we would recognize it today) was provided to these interviewees, the interviews cannot be viewed as unmediated evidence. The interviews (both the questions and the answers) were shaped in significant ways by the assumptions of sociology at the time and by the specific power relations between the interviewer and interviewee. It appears that Margaret Lam, a Chinese American woman, conducted the bulk of the interviews. Her presence likely had some effect on respondents' generally positive attitude toward Chinese people, and perhaps even some effect on the general negative attitude toward Hawaiian people. At times, for example, her lines of questioning about Hawaiian customary practices seemed to suggest that she found them superstitious and backward, though she also seemed to suggest that families were no longer really Hawaiian if they did not engage in them. Also, there is evidence that she spoke to some interviewees in Chinese, which may have emphasized a common, positive bond in a Chinese American identity.[26] I cannot fully know to what extent the answers given to the interviewers are "true" in the sense that the people who spoke them really believed them, or if their answers were a performance of a dominant script they expected the interviewers wanted to hear. Yet I believe that the performance and discourses that circulated in the interviews are deserving of further analysis regardless, because as performances, they give us a rare insight into the logics of race and settler colonialism at this time as well as today. And it is striking that their negative views about Native Hawaiians did not make it into Adams's published work, suggesting that the interviewees were not performing a dominant script, or at least not one that Adams ultimately wished to hear.

The major trend of the interview data, stated hatred for Hawaiians, ranged from the seemingly innocuous—"they are too talkative," "they gossip too much"—to more serious, explicitly racist tropes. Hawaiians were seen as drunks, troublemakers, liars, lazy, ignorant people who had lost their land by their own fault, and who were potentially dangerous if they practiced "kahuna" (spoken of as akin to voodoo or witchcraft for revenge). The negative opinions shared about Hawaiians tended to acknowledge that some individuals were "good," but that as a race Hawaiians were generally bad. This discourse echoed and sometimes explicitly referenced the antiblackness of the earlier Polynesian Problem literature, such as the work of Louis Sullivan, which separated Polynesians into two types: the whiter, almost Caucasian and the blacker Mongoloid, more akin to the Melanesian. One woman, age twenty, noted in her interview that her mother (who was "pure" Hawaiian) belonged to the "fair type of Hawaiian."[27] She explained: "You know there are three classes of Hawaiians—one is the dark class and other very fair—almost blonde. Some of them have red hair. My mother has straight nose—yes, something like Grecian nose. And my mother has no Hawaiian ways. Really, she has no Hawaiian ways in her. I'm proud of her too because she can read and write. Many of my friends don't believe I'm Chinese-Hawaiian. They all think I'm half-white."[28]

This woman contrasted her mother's type of "fair" Hawaiian to other Hawaiians who were "so funny looking. . . . They have so big flat nose, and they are so black."[29] Again, here we see strong evidence that the logic of possession through whiteness was also always a logic of antiblackness. Those "black" Hawaiians were, in her opinion, "too lazy and they are not ambitious."[30] Others also distinguished between fair and "black" Hawaiians, and noted that pure Hawaiian "mannerisms and appearance" were "repulsive."[31] Many of these stereotypes about "black" Hawaiian male aggression, laziness, and stupidity were, of course, also frequently appearing in social scientific and popular representations of African Americans in this period of the Jim Crow South.

Other interviewees insisted that contemporary Hawaiians were not as good as the ancient Hawaiians. "They are bums and loafers," said one boy, age fifteen, as he explained why his father discouraged him from befriending Hawaiians.[32] "Nowadays, the Hawaiians are not good anyway," he concluded.[33] This echoed Uldrick Thompson's view of the "old time Hawaiians" as the great and noble ones, of whom the contemporary, degenerate Hawaiians were only a "small remnant." Many comments implicitly pointed out the changes wrought by settler colonialism, even as they blamed Hawaiians for not persevering under contemporary conditions. For instance, one woman, age thirty-seven, noted, "Hawaiian people before were hardworking people. They were brought up to be hard working.... They were always working—planting taro, fishing or weaving. Today different—the Hawaiians today won't work like before."[34] Planting taro, fishing, and weaving, of course, were all forms of work and sustainable living that were being eradicated by the imposition of capitalism and the plantation economy. Yet many unquestioningly accepted that it was Hawaiians' own lack of ambition and general bad character that were to blame for their lack of employment. "They never look ahead of them. They never think of the future," one interviewee elaborated.[35]

Indeed, many interviewees so strongly believed that laziness was an inherent trait of Native Hawaiians that they mentioned being glad to have some Chinese ancestry, to which they attributed their industriousness. "I think without my Chinese blood in me I wouldn't care for anything," one man, age twenty-eight, confessed. "You take pure Hawaiian—they don't own nothing, they are not successful in anything. All they are—get a drink, get drunk—and play the guitar. Suppose I'm a thorough-bred Hawaiian, I wouldn't have any ambition."[36] Others went further in their poor characterizations of Native Hawaiians, especially Native Hawaiian men, emphasizing not only their general laziness and lack of intelligence but also insisting that they were violent "troublemakers." "Every time there's a fight you see some Hawaiians," one male teenager explained as to why he didn't care for Hawaiians.[37] Interviewees often noted that their parents "forbade them to mingle freely with Hawaiians."[38] A thirteen-year-old boy stated that he "received rough treatment from his Hawaiian friends" and thus he "does not care to play with them anymore."[39]

Many further emphasized that they distinguished educated Hawaiians from the general, more ignorant population of Hawaiians. Opinions about Hawaiians' intelligence were not limited to their educational status, however, but often reflected deeper understandings of Hawaiians as mentally inferior. One woman noted: "I like Hawaiians, but of course they are slow and they are ignorant. You can't blame them for being so ignorant because they didn't have any education.... The Chinese are strong-minded and the Hawaiians are weak-minded, I think."[40]

The attribution of "weak-minded" here evokes the psychological intelligence testing of this era. In answering one of the standard survey questions under the heading of "education" about whether or not they attended lectures, several interviewees noted that they had recently attended a lecture by Stanley Porteus, a psychologist at the University of Hawai'i, whose research focused on testing the intelligence of different races.[41] Like Sullivan, Adams, and others, Porteus had come to Hawai'i precisely because of its variety of races.[42] Yet nothing he found there apparently disproved his main thesis: that whites were more intelligent than any other race. He negatively characterized most nonwhite races in Hawai'i, but consistently ranked Hawaiians and Filipinos at the bottom of his intelligence scales.[43] Though none of the interview transcripts offer direct opinions about Porteus's findings, interviewees often echoed his arguments about what he called Hawaiians' "educational retardation."

The interviews also demonstrate that this internalized racism against Hawaiians was not complete. Overall, 32 percent stated positive feelings toward Hawaiians, though this was less than half the number of those with positive feelings toward Chinese and Chinese Hawaiians. Many expressed that they felt most at home with Hawaiians, even if they also had negative attitudes about them. For example, one woman, age forty-three, stated: "I like Hawaiian people very much. I like to talk to the old folks especially," though she also noted that she did not like some of their habits and ways. Another male, age sixteen, reported, "Hawaiians, oh they are good. I like them—good time, those guys. They are open-hearted and they treat me good."[44] This comfort with Hawaiians was especially true if the interviewee could speak Hawaiian or practiced Hawaiian cultural traditions such as hula. One woman, age eighteen, stated, "I like Hawaiian and Hawaiian customs very much. Well, I like their dances, the hula and I like the Hawaiian people. I can dance the hula."[45] Another woman, age forty-three, noted: "I like Hawaiians because I understand them and they can talk Hawaiian with me."[46] Notably, when the interviews are analyzed by age group, those who were over age forty were more likely to have positive opinions of Native Hawaiians; for example, in the forty interviews of those between age forty and fifty, 43 percent stated negative views of Hawaiians (significantly less than average), and 43 percent stated positive views. These interviewees were likely of an age in the 1930s to be able to recall the Hawaiian Kingdom, or at least their parents' memories of it, before the overthrow and annexation by the United States.

The minority positive views notwithstanding, the depth of the hatred toward Hawaiians is striking in many interviews, especially when that hatred is self-directed. Several interviewees expressed deep discomfort with having Hawaiian ancestry (while no such feelings were reported for Chinese ancestry). Such comments as noted by the interviewers on the surveys included: "Regrets that she has a quarter Hawaiian—dislikes this group very much";[47] "Does not wish to identify herself with this group. Regrets she has Hawaiian blood";[48] "Hawaiian: Dislikes this group very much. Has gone as far as not to feel at home with own grandparents now."[49] How does this deeply felt anti-Hawaiian self-hatred sit alongside the more positive ideals about Hawaiʻi being a racial paradise, amid the broader social scientific history of Polynesians being relatively white and civilized? And again, why did evidence of such hatred fail to register at all in Adams's scholarship and his overall promotion of Hawaiʻi as an exceptional American melting pot?

Whereas the Polynesian Problem literature was based on a fundamental split between a perceived black Melanesia and white Polynesia, as these broader ideas about race in the Pacific filtered down into specific national contexts, that split was replicated within the Polynesian race itself. Louis Sullivan, as examined in chapter 2, split the Polynesian race into two types of Polynesians: the almost white Polynesian (who was biologically linked to the Caucasian race) and the darker Negroid/Mongoloid type (who may have had Melanesian ancestry). Evident in these interviews is a further split within how Native Hawaiians were perceived in Hawaiʻi, between a whiter, good type and a blacker, bad type. This repeated theme of the two types shows that even as white settlers were using the logic of possession through whiteness to feel at home in Hawaiʻi, this logic, which seemed at one register to promote a relatively positive view of Native Hawaiians as almost white, never eradicated more overtly racist ideals about Native Hawaiians. In fact, this logic was always producing those overtly antiblack and anti-Indigenous ideals about Native Hawaiians alongside a co-constituted ideal of Native Hawaiians (and Native Hawaiian women in particular) as assimilable within whiteness.

The two types, in their multiple iterations and shifting proximities to whiteness and blackness, kept these seemingly opposite but mutually reinforcing racial formations constantly and flexibly at play in social scientific knowledge production about Native Hawaiians and Polynesians. In Hawaiʻi from the early to mid-twentieth century, the whiter type would come to be associated with those with mixed-race ancestries (especially white and/or Chinese), while the blacker type would more commonly be attributed to so-called pure Hawaiians. Those pure Hawaiians were assumed to be dying out, and thus Adams as well as territorial officials could argue that there were no real racial threats in Hawaiʻi. However, as the interviews and widespread evidence of self-hatred of Hawaiian-ness among Chinese Hawaiians shows, the logic of hating Native Hawaiians' darker side was not vanishing and remained a substantial cause for anxiety and conflict in the 1930s. This anxiety about Native Hawaiians' possible proximity to blackness, especially when Adams and other social scientists completely erased it in their scholarship despite having overwhelming evidence, did not stop the logic of possession through whiteness from functioning. Rather, it subtly highlighted the difference between Native Hawaiians and white settlers by emphasizing that though the Polynesian race used to be white, they had degenerated to such an extent that white settlers were the rightful possessors of Hawaiʻi. Again, this logic made whiteness indigenous to Hawaiʻi, while it simultaneously made Native Hawaiians not truly white and not truly Indigenous. This logic was also at least partially internalized by many Native Hawaiians themselves, and was used either as a form of self-hatred or as a kind of exceptionalism, reminiscent of the exceptionalism we saw with Kalākaua's Polynesian confederacy elevating Native Hawaiians over Sāmoans and Te Rangihīroa's insistence on Polynesians as Caucasoid. While these cases demonstrate different ways that Native Hawaiians or Māori were valorized as whiter than other Pacific Islanders, the animating logic of possession through whiteness haunts each context.

VALORIZING CHINESE AND CAUCASIANS

Social scientific discourses about Chinese and Japanese populations in Hawaiʻi also reinforced the settler colonial logic of possession through whiteness. The relative ability of Chinese and other Asian groups to assimilate to white American norms seemed to prove that Hawaiʻi was destined to assimilate. Racial mixture between Chinese and Hawaiians could thus be read as further integrating Hawaiʻi and Native Hawaiians within the boundaries of whiteness. As Ellen Wu has argued, even though the Chinese in Hawaiʻi were not white, they were a model minority who were also definitively not black.[50] If Hawaiʻi was understood as a place mainly of Asian Americans, with Native Hawaiians as a minority who were rapidly amalgamating within either Asian American or white populations, Hawai'i's formal elevation from a territory to a state was benign and free of any racial problems. Wu argues that the racial paradise trope "hinged in part on regenerating the trope of the vanishing native in relation to Asian American 'success.'"[51] This did not mean that Asian Americans in Hawai'i would ever lose the stigma of being foreign, but the construction of Asian Americans as not black and not Native was central to making them safe and similar enough to white Americans.

The logic of possession through whiteness thus incorporated both Asian Americans and Native Hawaiians into a white settler society by placing both in positions proximate to whiteness, though Native Hawaiians also remained simultaneously (due to the "two types" construction) in proximity to blackness. This is also a clear trend in the Lam/Lorden interviews. Views expressed toward both Chinese and Chinese-Hawaiians in the interviews were overwhelmingly positive and affirmed that Chinese Americans were hardworking, intelligent, and good businessmen. Of the 206 interviews, 75 percent stated positive feelings toward Chinese and 68 percent stated positive feelings about Chinese Hawaiians, whereas only 32 percent stated unqualified positive feelings toward Hawaiians and just 27 percent expressed positive feelings about Caucasian Hawaiians.[52] For the majority of respondents with negative feelings toward Hawaiians, Chinese Hawaiians were viewed relatively more positively because of their Chinese blood.[53]

Thus, the moral character and intelligence of Chinese people, especially when compared to perceptions of Native Hawaiians as lazy and stupid, seemed to make the Chinese perfect for and deserving of assimilation into the United States. This social scientific construction was significant to the eventual incorporation of Hawai'i as the fiftieth state. As Wu argues, the "claim that Hawai'i was American enough for admission [as a state], 'that its people had shed their strange ways,' rested in part on proving that its Asiatic population had acculturated to white, middle-class standards, behaviors, and orientations."[54] Adams's research was essential to making these claims. For example, the surveys documented how many Chinese traditions Chinese Hawaiians still practiced, such as "ancestor worship," and largely showed that such practices were on the decline in Hawai'i.

When the interview responses about Caucasian Hawaiians are analyzed, it is even clearer that the construction of Asian Americans as a model minority played an essential role in the construction of Hawai'i as a perfect American melting pot. For arguably, the perception of the Chinese

Hawaiian played a more important role in positive discourses about racial mixture than perceptions about Caucasian Hawaiians, who were on the whole seen by those interviewed in a negative light. Only 27 percent of the interviewees reported positive feelings toward Caucasian Hawaiians, or hapa haoles, as they were more colloquially referred to. Yet notably, the percentage of interviewees reporting strongly negative feelings toward hapa haoles (32 percent) was significantly less than the percentage of negative feelings toward Native Hawaiians (55 percent). In addition, 31 percent of those interviewed stated that they did not know any Caucasian Hawaiians and declined to offer any opinion about them. This large percentage of those who did not know any Caucasian Hawaiians, along with the stated reasons for negative feelings, points toward a class divide between Caucasian Hawaiians and Chinese Hawaiians. Respondents commonly expressed sentiments such as "I feel the hapa-haoles are too fresh, high-brow and too conceited"; "Feels they act 'too high,'"; "They are too stuck-up"; "Hapa-haoles too high for me and I'm too low for them."[55] Some interviewees classified hapa haoles as haoles, and discussed facing discrimination from them. One subject confessed: "They call me poi dog."[56] A note on a different survey says, "Caucasian-Hawaiian: Thinks this group regard him inferior—due to color."[57]

Thus, it was not that there was a common feeling among these surveyed Chinese Hawaiians that white people or hapa haoles were necessarily the best, or that they should be emulated. Chinese and Chinese Hawaiians are viewed most positively overall. But the criticisms of Caucasian Hawaiians are almost entirely about them acting too "high," if the subject knew any at all. This critique suggests that Caucasian Hawaiians were wealthier and had it easier in Hawaiian society at the time. This is not at all the same type of vitriol reserved for Native Hawaiians, who are described with disgust and fear for their low intelligence, laziness, troublemaking, and "kahuna" powers. Overall, the relatively benign negative view of Caucasian Hawaiians suggests that the logic of possession through whiteness did not depend (only) on valorizing white people or hapa haoles in Hawai'i; rather, it could valorize the model minority aspects of Chinese and Chinese Hawaiians as a kind of proxy for whiteness. The valorizing of Chinese people still quite effectively emphasized that Native Hawaiians were, by contrast, of two types: a small minority of "good" and "fair-skinned" Hawaiians, and a hopefully vanishing majority of "bad" and "black" Hawaiians who were a threat. By offering an example of a nonwhite group who seemed to be effectively assimilating into white American norms, the Chinese example deepened the sense that Native Hawaiians' failure to assimilate was due to their own shortcomings and laziness.

Overall, the Lam/Lorden interviews demonstrate that, at the very least, in the lived experiences of many Chinese Hawaiian people, there was no widespread belief that Hawai'i was (or even necessarily should be) free of racism. Instead, account after account expressed both the pain of being subject to racist attitudes and, just as often, strong internalized beliefs in racist stereotypes about Native Hawaiians. Neither was there any indication that interracial marriage in Hawai'i between Chinese and Hawaiian people heralded the coming of a "neo-Hawaiian race," as Adams insisted. Rather, the interviews show that most people identified more strongly with and as a single race, either Chinese or Native Hawaiian. Thus, being multiracial did not automatically mean that people were identifying or inhabiting a new mixed-race category (Chinese Hawaiian); their identifications largely depended on their personal experiences and relationships with Chinese or Hawaiian friends and family members. By ignoring especially the frequent racism directed at Native Hawaiians, Adams helped ensure that Hawai'i was viewed as a serene, tropical asset to the United States, whose land and people should naturally be enjoyed by white settlers. Next, I examine one of the more enduring images that stems from the melting pot ideal of Hawai'i: the mixed-race "Hawaiian girl," fetishized and promised as the entitlement of all white, male settlers.

### HYBRID HAWAIIAN GIRLS

Whereas the 1930 *Oakland Tribune* illustration analyzed earlier presented a magical equation of Polynesian, Asiatic, and European men adding up to a "Hawaiian," later popular media about Hawai'i as melting pot came to focus entirely on Native Hawaiian women. While there is scholarship about the "hula girl" image as the exotic emblem of the tourist industry in Hawai'i, one aspect of this image that has generally been under-theorized is the importance of the so-called hula girl being not just light-skinned but mixed-race.[58] In this final section, I argue that the hula girl image must be understood as generated not only by the tourist industry but within a deeper genealogy of social scientific studies about Native Hawaiians and Polynesians. Specifically, there are direct links between the research of sociologists at the University of Hawai'i in the mid-twentieth century and the dissemination of popular media about "hybrid Hawaiian girls" that fetishized multiracial female identities and bodies in Hawai'i. These women represented not only an enticing lure to white male American tourists and military servicemen stationed in Hawai'i but further, appealing proof that the "neo-Hawaiian" race that Adams predicted was coming to pass.

This mid-century focus on multiracial Hawaiian women was in part a conscious effort to move the popular imagination of Hawai'i away from the presence of Native Hawaiian men. For fears about Native Hawaiian men raping white women were sensationalized across the United States in response to the Massie affair in 1931 (as described in this chapter's introduction). These racial and gendered fears were not entirely new, but can also be found in public debates about the annexation of Hawai'i to the United States. Many white Americans balked at the idea of adding a "brown" race to the U.S. populace before and after its formal annexation in 1898, and newspaper cartoons mocked the deposed and imprisoned Queen Lili'uokalani as a barbarian queen.[59] After the Massie affair, the U.S. government was anxious to dispel such fears. The Department of the Interior published a booklet called *Hawaii and Its Race Problem* in 1932, which sought to reassure the public that "race antagonisms" in the islands were "practically non-existent." The booklet concluded: "There is much apprehension lest groups in Hawai'i based on race should come into political dominance.... It is a part of the beautiful experiment, here in the mid-Pacific, that self-government is to be tried out under conditions and with human material that is new. There is nothing so far to indicate that the experiment will not turn out to be as successful as it is interesting."[60]

The rhetoric of Hawai'i as a racial laboratory or experiment station closely mirrored the sociological work of those like Romanzo Adams, and is deployed in this government document to underline the fact that the United States was in charge of all "experimenting" and that the white population of Hawai'i had the racial masses under control. Seeing Hawai'i as an experiment bound to produce something new also conveniently erased the long-standing history of the Hawaiian Kingdom.

These public policy and sociological stances also shaped popular media about Hawai'i, especially during and after World War II. For example, such rhetoric provided the ideological backbone for a photo essay, titled "Hawaiian Medley," published in 1943 in the popular magazine *Collier's* (figure 3.2).[61] Festooned with Hawaiian prints and flowers, the photographs clearly draw on developing tourist industry tropes about Hawai'i's "hula girls," though it claimed to depict simply a number of typical "Hawaiian girls." The captions of the photographs identify these women primarily by listing their individual racial mixtures, with these lists declared in all capital

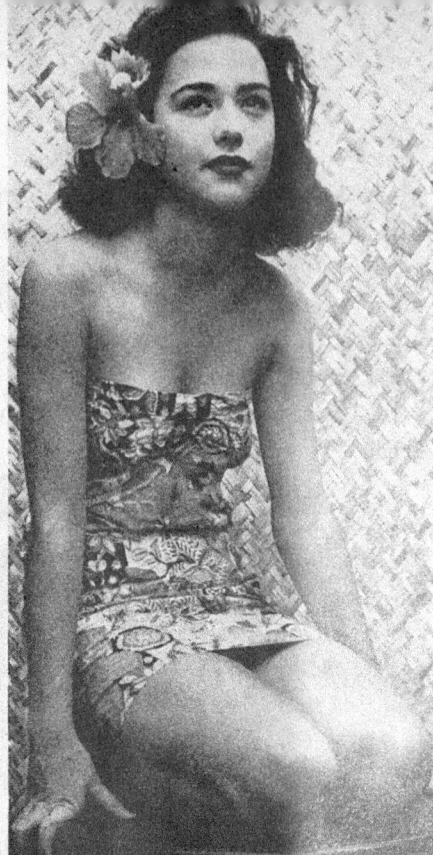

# Hawaiia Medley

PHOTOGRAPHS FOR COLLIER'S

THE girls you see on the product of mixed m greatest melting pot Hawaii. The late Lieutena McClelland Barclay, noted il impressed with their love sketched the ones shown he cific pin-up girls. The ph made by Henry Inn, connois art and architecture, and with his father of the oldest shop in Honolulu.

Name any two countries, are you'll find that they are Hawaiian marriage. Some girls have a most complicate the "League of Nations Gir loha Leong, endowed with Hawaiians, Spaniards, Chi Englishmen, Germans and S

Hawaii outdoes the U.S.A. characteristics. For 150 yea tionalities have been so ble anthropologists consider the laboratory for testing theor

Until its discovery by Cap in 1778, isolated Hawaii's pe one stock, a thousand-year Mongolian and Caucasian r bred. They were fine phy maintaining an orderly, ha which crime and disease were

The coming of the Wes changed this. The developm demanded laborers. The Un the Reciprocity Treaty in 18 ingly after Hawaii became a 1900, brought in a successior under a "desirable citizen" 4,450 Norwegians, Germans, sians and Poles, 16,000 P Spaniards, a few hundred Ita portant numerically was th nese, with Japanese, Korear Puerto Ricans also importa A few Negroes and Hindu complications. Almost all i men, who perforce married

In the beginning, the char ble. Pure Hawaiians had no ropean diseases. Measles death-dealing plague. Tube ism and venereal disease deci lation. In the 100 years fo Cook's arrival, the number ians dropped from 300,000 to

But the new part-Hawa showed great vigor, with mixed marriages holding in and economically, and mai high birth rate, which, ev greatest among all the races.

Nowhere else, anthropol mixed marriages occurred under such favorable conditi racial intermarriage occu among the underprivileged, spring, for reasons having no race, are apt to be inferior.

The offspring of a Europ riage may be equally unacce and in Europe, but in Hawa termarriages united the fines with men who by coming proved their enterprising s you see here are members o lies. They can look forwa careers and happy marriage

Anthropologists decline to cial intermarriage is good or state that a crossing of strai tle, horses or people—often sis or "hybrid vigor." That will be bigger, stronger and the parents. Hawaii seems t point.

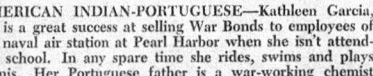

WAIIAN-CHINESE-AMERICAN—Jackie Tatum, 18, he leading dancer in Hawaii's USO troupe of Flander es. She sometimes wears her entire collection of 100 venir military insignia on her trench coat. Maybe you her in a recent newsphoto, dancing with Admiral Nimitz

HAWAIIAN-PORTUGUESE-ENGLISH—Bernice Keala Gomez, 16, is a secretary, a model and an amateur photographer. Like all island girls, she's a fine swimmer. War workers will readily recognize her as the slim little hula dancer who appears often at local entertainments

ERICAN INDIAN-PORTUGUESE—Kathleen Garcia, is a great success at selling War Bonds to employees of naval air station at Pearl Harbor when she isn't attend school. In any spare time she rides, swims and plays nis. Her Portuguese father is a war-working chemist

PORTUGUESE-ENGLISH—One of the most popular USO entertainers in Hawaii is Alyce Lewis, 18-year-old blues singer. She was chosen by one Army outfit as "The Girl You'd Like to Take Home." She is a high-school senior and, naturally, she swims, dances

FIGURE 3.2. "Hawaiian Medley." Photographs by Henry Inn, *Collier's*, December 1943.

letters before their names are even mentioned. The captions accompanying the two leading photographs, for example, read: "HAWAIIAN-CHINESE-AMERICAN—Jackie Tatum, 18, is the leading dancer in Hawaii's USO troupe of Flanderettes" and "HAWAIIAN-PORTUGUESE-ENGLISH—Bernice Keala Gomez, 16, is a secretary, a model, and an amateur photographer. Like all island girls, she's a fine swimmer."[62]

Along with such careful notations of racial mixture and lists of the women's typical "island girl" interests, the *Collier's* article provides a popularized reading of social scientific studies of Hawai'i. In a short, breezy history of Hawai'i, the author explains that the men who immigrated to Hawai'i as part of the plantation economy had no choice but to marry women of other races: "Almost all immigrants were men, who perforce married Hawaiian girls.... In the beginning, the change spelled trouble. Pure Hawaiians had no immunity to European diseases.... But the new part-Hawaiian population showed great vigor, with the children of mixed marriages holding their own socially and economically, and maintaining a very high birth rate, which, even now, is the greatest among the races."[63]

Focusing on the newness and "vigor" of the "part-Hawaiian population," and representing this population so enticingly as glamorous young women in bathing suits, encourages the presumed white, male, American reader to desire both exotic mixed-race women and the Hawai'i that they symbolize. If any lingering doubts about the prospects of interracial marriage remain, the article concludes: "Anthropologists decline to say whether racial intermarriage is good or bad, but they do state that a crossing of strains—in dogs, cattle, horses, or people—often results in heterosis or 'hybrid vigor.' That is, the offspring will be bigger, stronger and more fertile than the parents. Hawaii seems to be proving the point."[64]

The article therefore drives home the desirability of coming to Hawai'i and racially intermarrying, arguing that it is scientifically proven that white American men in creating a "Hawaiian medley" family would ultimately strengthen the human race itself. Not so subtly equating part-Hawaiian women to dogs, cattle, or horses to be bred, the article smooths over any latent defects in their Asian or Native Hawaiian backgrounds by assuring the reader that their children will be "bigger, stronger and more fertile." In this way, the "girls" are presented as evidence of the success of Hawai'i's colonization and its fated future as culturally and racially white. Nyong'o has perceptively written that "heterosexuality has been a preeminent metaphor through which a heterogeneous, mongrel past is recuperated as both a stable racial binary in the present and a possible hybrid utopia in the future."[65] Indeed, the article uses heterosexual reproduction as the mechanism for curing any racial threats in Hawai'i. By focusing on the "possible hybrid utopia," as Nyong'o puts it, especially in its claims of hybrid vigor promising a better race, the article encourages readers not to dwell on the colonial history of Hawai'i or the ongoing circumstances of U.S. presence in Hawai'i. Instead, white settler men are encouraged to think of themselves as experimental breeders, doing their heterosexual reproductive duty for the United States in turning Hawai'i whiter.

My point is that the carefully notated mixed racial backgrounds were actually key to the sexualization (and the attendant construction of race and indigeneity) for these Hawaiian women. Having "AMERICAN" or other presumably white European races like "ENGLISH" appended to the racial identities of these women managed to downplay any potentially off-putting darkness or foreignness in their display as tropical, exotic women by assuring the reader that their foreignness was quickly dwindling along with the "Pure Hawaiian race." Native Hawaiian men were conveniently displaced from the picture altogether, subtly associating the men with the Native Hawaiian race that was disappearing, dying, and vanishing—which meant that Native Hawaiian men were weak, not threatening. This allowed coverage of Hawai'i's hybrid future to distance itself from the "black" side of the Hawaiian race, as evidently so feared and hated in the interviews described earlier in this chapter. This displacement left space for white men to imagine claiming their own "Hawaiian girl."[66] In promoting the mixed-race woman as a "Hawaiian girl," the racial fears spurred by the Massie affair were thus turned into sexual fetish and desirability. The pervasive image of victimized Thalia Massie gradually transformed over the 1930s and 1940s into the "white enough" women of the "Hawaiian Medley"—figures that echo the "almost white" figures of the ancestrally white Polynesian and the Part Hawaiian examined in chapters 1 and 2.

This tempering with whiteness occurred with women who were Native Hawaiian as well as those who were Asian. Yet the racial categories attributed to Native Hawaiians and Asians also importantly tempered each other. By insisting on a mixed-race woman as the symbol of Hawai'i in the midst of World War II, Native Hawaiians and Asians became mutually associated even as they were differently incorporated into U.S. racial hierarchies. Asian women were made more familiar and less threatening through the representation of them as "Hawaiian girls," decorated with appropriated and fetishized tropes of Native Hawaiians. At the same time, Native Hawaiian women—as primarily Native Hawaiian, as an Indigenous people rather than a race—are fixed on a vanishing horizon where their unique cultural and political attributes have been diluted as Native Hawaiian culture and women are portioned out to white and Asian male settler populations of Hawai'i.[67]

This process is even clearer in a coffee-table book published in 1945 by Henry Inn. Inn was the photographer for *Collier's* "Hawaiian Medley," and he included some of the same photographs and many more similarly styled, under the new title *Hawaiian Types*.[68] The cover portrays a smiling Native Hawaiian woman, standing out against, if somewhat haunted by, the specter of a stoic-faced, dark-skinned Native Hawaiian man, who seems to be part of a background the woman stands in front of (figure 3.3). Symbolically, he is shown as her past, not her future. Inside *Hawaiian Types*, the captions to the photographs become entirely limited to their racial mixes. Their names, or any other individual information, are no longer included at all. The book includes forty-seven photographs in all, each taking up a full page, with the facing page remaining blank except for captions such as "English-German-Hawaiian" (figure 3.4). Inn does include some women who are monoracially identified (e.g., Hawaiian, Chinese, Filipino, and a portrait of two women identified as Korean), yet these women are photographed in the most culturally traditional clothes and poses, which make them seem quite old-fashioned or anachronistic amid the other women, who are seen smiling and relaxing in tropical scenes with Hawaiian shirts, bathing suits, hibiscus in their hair, leis around their necks. The more European "types" are the only ones represented in professional settings (as nurses, for example), while all others are in generic tropical or exotic settings. This is despite the fact that all of the women who modeled for this photo shoot were college students at the University of Hawai'i—and thus all relatively educated and upwardly mobile.[69]

Andrew Lind, a sociologist who was also trained at the University of Chicago, wrote the introduction to *Hawaiian Types*. Lind conducted his dissertation research in Hawai'i and became a permanent faculty member at the University of Hawai'i in 1931, constituting with Romanzo Adams the Sociology Department, a department of two.[70] In the *Hawaiian Types* introduction, Lind affirms the U.S. racial laboratory image of Hawai'i, noting changes he describes as not only physical or superficial but of expression and character. The new mixed-race populations of Hawai'i were different from their predecessors even in the utilization of their "facial muscles"— which Lind argued had become more relaxed and expressive, in contrast to the "inflexible facial cast of the Oriental and European immigrant pioneers."[71]

FIGURE 3.3. Cover of *Hawaiian Types*, by Henry Inn (New York: Hastings, 1945).

FIGURE 3.4. "English-German-Hawaiian," in *Hawaiian Types*, by Henry Inn (New York: Hastings, 1945).

This characterization worked not only to minimize the trope of the "inscrutable," "sneaky" Asian but also to put Asian immigrants on par with European immigrants, drawing them both into the category of "typically American" despite the very different histories of immigration. Despite its obvious ties to the pinup girl genre, the inclusion of Lind's introduction allowed Inn's book to maintain a high-art distinction, as it also allowed a presumed white American male audience to understand their gaze as "scientific" rather than purely sexual.

The figure of the mixed-race, hapa haole hula girl continues to represent Hawai'i as a welcoming racial paradise. The hybrid "Hawaiian girl" is nonthreatening because she is welcoming and soft, with a long list of ethnicities rather than a strong identification as Native Hawaiian. Indeed, as Inn's models show, the "Hawaiian girl" did not even have to be Native Hawaiian at all. In this way, mixed-race, young Native Hawaiian women would come to symbolize the possession sought by the logic of possession through whiteness. For, beyond promising a sexual fantasy to the tourist, the hybrid Hawaiian girl signaled, within the ideology of settler colonialism, the inviting means of production of the neo-Hawaiian race.

---

In 2011, a white off-duty federal agent, in town for the Asia-Pacific Economic Cooperation (APEC) summit, shot and killed a young Kanaka Maoli man, Kollin Elderts, in a Waikīkī McDonald's. To many Kānaka Maoli and their allies, this incident echoed the rampant police violence against black men in the continental United States and also recalled the state-sanctioned murder of Joseph Kahahawai under the territorial government in the 1930s.[72] Yet much of the media coverage portrayed this as an isolated incident, with few commentators engaging issues of race and racism. Elderts's death was a sour note that nonetheless went largely overlooked in the overall push for Hawai'i to be the hub that would lead the United States into greater prosperity through increased trade with the Asia-Pacific region. Elderts and other Native Hawaiian men appear to be particular targets of racism because they fail to signify Native Hawaiian assimilation into whiteness. Within the logic of heteropatriarchy, Native Hawaiian men are also unwelcome reminders that white settler men have competition for their supposedly open access to Native Hawaiian women.

Though much of Romanzo Adams's language about his prophesized "neo-Hawaiian race" sounds outdated today, his underlying belief in a multiracial but whitening Hawai'i continues to dominate mainstream ideals about Hawai'i, both locally and nationally. Hawai'i is still revered as a model of harmonious race relations, and addressing racism, much less settler colonialism, in mainstream forums continues to be unusual at best, as I noted in the introduction to this chapter through my experience with an online forum about what Hawai'i could teach the United States about race. Adams's construction of the neo-Hawaiian race, so tellingly drawn in the *Oakland Tribune* illustration of adding up Polynesian, Asiatic, and European to create a Hawaiian, is in many ways the epitome of the logic of possession through whiteness. Again, it is not just that white settlers have instituted white supremacy in Hawai'i through the history of missionizing and the later plantation economy, where Native Hawaiians are at the bottom of a racial hierarchy (though this is also true). More insidiously, possession through whiteness has also erased the existence of an obvious racial hierarchy by insisting on the apparently universally multicultural and multiracial population of Hawai'i. The ideal of Hawai'i as model melting pot has made it nearly impossible to name the way that white settlers have come to possess and inhabit the identity of "Hawaiian," while diminishing, through blood quantum policies and the representation of pure Hawaiians as nearly extinct, the ongoing lives of Kānaka Maoli. White settlers not only replace Native Hawaiians, then, but more fundamentally, in prevailing social scientific and popular cultural texts, whiteness becomes Indigenous, while Native Hawaiians become displaced and dispossessed.

While it may seem more contemporary than the other aspects of possession through whiteness examined in chapters 1 and 2, the neo-Hawaiian race ideal is intimately tied to the earlier ideals of Polynesians as "heirlooms of the Aryan race" and as "conditionally Caucasian." Adams's work built on these social scientific understandings of Polynesians as capable of whiteness, because of their ancestral links and racial proximity to the white race. By analyzing Adams in relation to those like Tregear, Fornander, and Sullivan, I seek to place Adams in the long line of Polynesian Problem researchers because, in many respects, Adams's work would popularize their conclusions to such an extent that it would become a ruling episteme. More than any of his predecessors, perhaps, Adams took for granted that the Polynesian Problem was solved: Polynesians were almost white. Where Adams differed from his predecessors was that he ceased to find Polynesians of much interest, because he believed so strongly in their extinction and the growing similarity between Natives and white settlers in Hawai'i. Part of the lasting damage of Adams's research is that he successfully represented Hawai'i as a natural extension of the United States. In doing so, he encouraged a local and national public to cease viewing Hawai'i as part of a broader Polynesia, as well as to stop understanding Native Hawaiians as Polynesians and as Indigenous. This does not mean that the questions animating the Polynesian Problem literature ever died. Yet increasingly, after Adams, contemporary Polynesian people and societies would be oddly outside the scope of the Polynesian Problem because of their perceived lack of purity and authenticity. Rather, the search for Polynesian origins would continue through archaeology and, as I show in chapter 5, genomic technologies for tracing ancient populations' migrations. More broadly, the following chapters of part II show how Native Hawaiians and Polynesians continue to refuse the logic of possession through whiteness and settler colonial ideologies about race, gender, and sexuality.

PART II

# *Regenerative Refusals*

## Confronting Contemporary Legacies of the Polynesian Problem in Hawai'i and Oceania

---

Race mixture has had a field day in Hawaii.... There is no colour bar in Hawaii and no legal disability based on race, although contact between the same races elsewhere has given rise to them. Why, one might ask, has Hawaii become the seat of such an amicable arrangement?
—HARRY SHAPIRO, *Race Mixture*, 1953

---

Native Hawaiian is inclusive hundred percent to one percent Hawaiian blood quantum. The limitation of the Hawaiian Homes [Commission] Act of fifty percent must be redone.
—WILMA NOELANI JOY, testimony at Department of the Interior public hearing on federal recognition, Kaunakakai, Moloka'i, 2014

---

The idea of Hawai'i as a unique American melting pot, perpetuated by the work of Romanzo Adams and others, continues to haunt discourses about race in Hawai'i. Social scientists who came after Adams further invested in ideas about the unique nature of racial mixture in Hawai'i and Polynesia, promoting the region as a potential model for the world. Harry Shapiro, an anthropologist who was Louis Sullivan's successor at the Bishop Museum, saw Hawai'i as a potential model of harmonious race relations, because of its mixed-race population who faced "no legal disability based on race."

Shapiro's writing on race mixture in Hawai'i was included in essays published by UNESCO about race after World War II, like the *What Is Race?* booklet examined in the introduction. Shapiro's account, like Adams before him, actively erased experiences of racism faced by Native Hawaiians, Asian Americans, and others in Hawai'i.

In a different register, Shapiro's comments about the lack of any "legal disability based on race" also erased the existence of a deeply divisive and damaging law that certainly did impose legal dispossession based on race, namely the Hawaiian Homes Commission Act, enacted in 1921. This act mandated a blood quantum policy for Native Hawaiians, requiring "at least one-half part" Native Hawaiian "blood" to be eligible to lease a homestead (a small parcel of land meant to "rehabilitate" Native Hawaiians into white American ways of life). Native Hawaiians today still live with the 50 percent blood quantum restriction, though it is challenged by many, like Wilma Noelani Joy, who declared at public hearings in 2014 that the 50 percent blood quantum must be undone and made inclusive "one hundred to one percent." As further discussed in chapter 4, while many Native Hawaiians are proud of their multiracial ancestries and multiethnic upbringings, Joy's comments point out that Native Hawaiian identity can be thought of as expansive and inclusive rather than always diminishing and fractional. Further, it is unjust that Native Hawaiians are subject to legal restrictions on their eligibility for access to land based on the purity of their "blood." The 50 percent blood quantum rule also circulates beyond the legal eligibility for Hawaiian homes, influencing how Native Hawaiian membership and authenticity are perceived by those both within and outside of Native Hawaiian communities. The difficulties that Native Hawaiians face in respect to blood quantum also puncture Adams and Shapiro's ideals of Hawai'i as an extraordinary, amicable place of racial mixture.

Part II centrally considers how universalizing narratives about racial mixture in Hawai'i and Polynesia continue to be foundationally haunted by and based on the idea that Polynesians are natural possessions of whiteness. Whereas part I focused on the history of Western social scientific thought about race in relation to Polynesians, and Native Hawaiians more specifically, part II emphasizes how contemporary Native Hawaiians and Polynesians contend with discourses about blood quantum, mixed-race identity, and more recent technologies that make claims about "genetic ancestry" in complex ways. In contemporary arenas including art, law, and science, the same logics of the Polynesian Problem literature continue to place Polynesian people in proximity to whiteness in order to naturalize settler claims to Polynesia. Yet Polynesian artists, activists, and scholars are also continuously challenging such claims, refusing the idea that indigeneity vanishes into whiteness and unsettling notions of Hawaiʻi and other parts of Polynesia as a "hybrid future" convenient for white settlers. Thus, Polynesians participate in multifaceted attempts to remap the Pacific Islands within Indigenous space-time and regenerate the genealogies between us that continue to be haunted by colonial, racial discourses that were always meant to divide us. Part II examines how, in various examples of representations of racial mixture, the logic of possession through whiteness remains a significant influence that Polynesian people alternately challenge and co-opt as they move toward decolonization.

## "SIGNIFYING OTHERWISE": RACIAL MIXTURE AS SOLUTION AND THREAT

Hawaiʻi was by no means the only model of a racial melting pot that social scientists waxed eloquent over in the early twentieth century. The Caribbean and Latin America, in addition to the Pacific, also were frequently praised as examples of supposedly racially harmonious populations with high rates of racial intermarriage. Denise Ferreira da Silva has described the writing of the Brazilian national subject precisely along the lines of Hawaiʻi, as a model site of racial mixture and harmony.[1] Antiblackness as a key component of the melting pot ideal is more evident in the Brazilian case, making it an instructive comparison in relation to the Hawaiian and Polynesian cases, where antiblackness is also key, though often in more subtle ways. Silva makes plain that the insistence on Brazil's supposedly unique "racial democracy" and destined "whitening" in social scientific accounts reflected an investment in the production of a "tropical civilization" under the domain of a "slightly tanned" but fundamentally European male, national subject.[2] Despite the widespread presence of antiblack violence, Brazil is not understood as a place where racism (configured in social science as racial exclusion) exists, because racial difference is officially accepted, often even selectively appropriated and celebrated. Racial difference is accepted because it has already been resolved in the "interiority" of the mixed-race Brazilian subject, the product of miscegenation. Silva concludes that miscegenation in the Brazilian national account has been recuperated as a "process and index of the obliteration of racial difference," rather than evidence of racial difference (as in the "one drop rule" regarding blackness in the United States). This echoes the case in Hawaiʻi, as discussed in chapter 3, where the presence of multiracial people is used as evidence of a supposedly inevitable end of racial distinctions altogether.

This "post-racial" perspective on racial mixture is deeply structured by heteropatriarchy. Silva emphasizes that it is through patriarchy that racial difference is obliterated and recuperated as cultural difference. She reads the logic of anthropologist Gilberto Freyre's influential studies of Brazil as rewriting Brazilian miscegenation as the creation of a "colonial family." Silva points out that the "successful version of the Brazilian subject had a price," namely, "precisely because the appropriation of the black female body was also premised on the idea that only whiteness signifies the transparent I, the blackness and Africanness the woman's offspring inherit from her remain as dangerous signifiers of a subject of affectability who cannot but signify Brazil's unstable placing at the outskirts of the modern global configuration."[3] In other words, because the Brazilian national subject has successfully been constructed as fundamentally white, those Brazilians who fail to signify whiteness are seen as dangerous to the nation. That danger is inherited through black Brazilian female ancestors who were assumed to be, with white European males, the progenitors of the country. This explains for Silva why violence against contemporary "generations of black and brown Brazilians" causes no moral outrage—because it is "but the latest manifestation of the national desire to obliterate the Brazilian people who, regardless of its elites' desire for whiteness, insist on signifying otherwise."[4] Similarly, in the Polynesian context, this helps explain why racist and colonial violence against Native Hawaiians and other Polynesian peoples causes no moral outrage, when after centuries of the discourse of Polynesian whiteness, Polynesian people "insist on signifying otherwise," especially through insisting on indigeneity and sovereignty.

Harry Shapiro's *Race Mixture*, which emphasizes, as noted in the epigraph above, that "Race mixture has had a field day in Hawai'i," demonstrates many of the above points about the erasure of racial difference through a patriarchal celebration of diversity. A major theme of Shapiro's essay, which is also echoed throughout the UNESCO pamphlets, is of the especially unjust mistreatment of mixed-race people. He noted: "The great injustice, after all, that has been placed on the mixed-blood is that he is judged, not as an individual, an elementary right to which he is entitled, but as a member of a group about which there is much prejudice and little understanding."[5] Thus, Shapiro was interested in championing mixed-race people because he felt they were especially unfairly classified (in contrast to the "prejudice" displayed against "purer" racial types). Notice here that antiblackness can remain intact in this view of mixed-race people, as Shapiro's championing of mixed-race people depends on distancing them from purer, and presumably blacker, more Indigenous types. As a long-established researcher of Indigenous Pacific Islanders, Shapiro implies that mixed-race people of the Pacific were especially undeserving of racial discrimination because, despite the physical or cultural traits which might, in Silva's words, "insist on signifying otherwise," they were fundamentally (part) white.

Despite the repeated claims of Polynesians' fundamental whiteness, and certain mixed-race Polynesians' even more ascendant whiteness, such claims were never incompatible with the Polynesian race's obliteration or extinction. Indeed, the expression of their latent whiteness signaled the obliteration of Polynesians as a distinct race. Though measuring people by designations such as "half-bloods" was ostensibly invalidated by Mendelian genetics, as the UNESCO documents go to great pains to explain, Native Hawaiians would still be subject to blood quantum measurements that set their racial membership at 50 percent. Though seemingly contrary to the rules of dominant and recessive genes in which some traits associated with white people (for example, blue eyes) are recessive, both science and law dictated that white "superiority," or European consciousness, would nonetheless win out in mixed-race Native Hawaiians and other Polynesians. This analysis suggests that contemporary uses of discourses proclaiming "we are all mixed-race," though formulated in a post–World War II articulation of antiracism, are embedded in a definition of the human that is tied to an antiblack, anti-Indigenous, white ideal of Man stemming from the European Enlightenment. In seeking decolonization in Polynesia and elsewhere, then, we must look to craft different definitions not just of race and racial mixture as they relate to Indigenous forms of kinship and belonging, but also different definitions of humanity itself.

REGENERATIVE REFUSALS

Whereas part I focused on the history of scientific studies of the Polynesian Problem and the Hawaiian melting pot, part II offers an interdisciplinary and contemporary approach to issues of race, gender, and indigeneity in the Pacific. In the next three chapters, I look at several contemporary examples of how the logic of possession through whiteness structures how white Americans continue to see and value Native Hawaiians and other Indigenous Pacific Islanders. Throughout part II, I analyze what I call regenerative refusals in Indigenous Pacific efforts in the realms of law, art, and genomic science. Regenerative refusals are actions that seek to restore balance and life to Indigenous communities that continue to live with structures of settler colonialism. In dialogue with the theories of other Indigenous feminist scholars including Leanne Simpson, Audra Simpson, and Lani Teves, regenerative refusals are, in my framing, concerned with divesting our communities from racialized and gendered hierarchies.[6] Indigenous feminisms seek to draw attention to how settler colonialism is fundamentally a gendered process that relies on the instillation of heteropatriarchy to destroy colonized communities' connections to their bodies, to each other, and to the land. Regenerative refusals seek to restore these connections, often through the clear rejection of ongoing colonial ideologies both imposed upon and sometimes deeply internalized within Indigenous communities. Regenerative refusals in my usage are not about return to exactly what things were like before; they are an ongoing reckoning with settler colonialism, rather than a denial of it.

Regenerative refusals further offer a lens through which to understand some of the tensions between competing visions of identity, membership, and justice among Indigenous communities. In this approach, my theory of regenerative refusals is in harmony with Lani Teves's theory of "defiant indigeneity," a method of Indigenous performance that "challenges, resists and reorganizes the conditions and limits prescribed by the colonial order, materializing heterogeneous possibilities of Kanaka Maoli being."[7] Concerned with what is lost when Native Hawaiians who are queer or perform hip-hop are labeled as too white or too black by their own community, defiant indigeneity signals not only a resistance to the state, but a resistance to the ways that notions of authenticity and tradition, when rigidly internalized, can be stultifying and damaging to the diversity of Indigenous communities. For many Polynesian artists and activists, decolonization is not truly decolonization unless it structurally overturns Western hierarchies of race, gender and sexuality, and attendant notions of the "real Native." Nonetheless, others become invested in state-recognized forms of authenticity, and willingly collaborate with settler colonial state governments in the name of receiving their due, or at least "taking the best we can get." Those who reject such moderate offers from the settler colonial governments or industries are often depicted as "crazy," hostile, or ignorant—as the mainstream media described Native Hawaiians who testified against federal recognition in 2014, for example, as I analyze in chapter 4. However, if we analyze such refusals through a framework of regenerative refusals, there is space to recognize that such rejections are not merely empty, negative challenges to settler colonialism but also positive, future-oriented acts aiming to realize a different way of being in and relating to the world.

Chapter 4, "Still in the Blood: Blood Quantum and Self-Determination in *Day v. Apoliona* and Federal Recognition," begins theorizing regenerative refusals by analyzing two contemporary public debates about the boundaries of Native Hawaiian membership and how Native Hawaiians should be recognized by the state. I juxtapose the claims of Native Hawaiian plaintiffs in the case of *Day v. Apoliona* (2009) that the state has failed to enforce the definition of Native Hawaiians as those with "no less than one-half part blood," against many Native Hawaiians who testified against this blood quantum restriction at public hearings about federal recognition in 2014. The intergenerational testimonies about the importance of refusing to comply with the definitions of indigeneity imposed by the U.S. Department of the Interior demonstrate how powerful refusals in the face of unequal power can be.

Chapter 5, "The Value of Polynesian DNA: Genomic Solutions to the Polynesian Problem," returns to the domain of science, specifically genetics and genomics. New genetic technologies have revived many of the same questions as the original Polynesian Problem, as discussed in part I of this book, over where Polynesians really originated and how to properly racially classify them. This chapter examines how a number of studies and technologies including genomic mapping, genetic ancestry testing, and biobanking impact Polynesian communities. I look at how Indigenous Pacific activists and scholars have refused to participate in or accede to Western forms of knowledge, in ways that echo and amplify the regenerative refusals analyzed in chapter 4.

The final chapter extends my theorizing of regenerative refusals through a focus on contemporary Indigenous art of the Pacific. In chapter 6, "Regenerating Indigeneity: Challenging Possessive Whiteness in Contemporary Pacific Art," I look at the work of Yuki Kihara (Sāmoan), and Adrienne Keahi Pao (Kanaka Maoli), and the strategies they each use to critique the Western ethnographic gaze long directed at Indigenous peoples. Both of these artists are Indigenous and mixed-race, and yet their work insists on indigeneity as a category and analytic that cannot be diminished by racial discourses. I compare the strength of their work to Chinese American artist Kip Fulbeck's work, which also focuses on mixed-race identity but tends to universalize the mixed-race experience and erase indigeneity. Kihara's and Pao's works also do more than provide powerful critiques. They offer new visions of Indigenous futures, futures not untouched by settler colonialism but not constrained by it either.

Throughout part II, my analysis is interdisciplinary and contemporary, with examples largely drawn from the first two decades of the 2000s. In jumping to this time period from the 1950s, where chapter 3 ends, I am skipping an enormous amount of significant history that occurred in the interim. Hawai'i officially became a state in 1959, and soon statehood celebrations gave way to the rise of the Hawaiian Renaissance of the late 1960s and 1970s, which was a watershed period for Native Hawaiian activism, especially around land rights, environmental protection, cultural revitalization, and the growth of political organizing for sovereignty.[8] In this, Kānaka Maoli acted in concert with many other decolonial movements happening around the world, including within the Pacific Islands. Like Kānaka Maoli, Māori in Aotearoa organized in the 1960s and 1970s around issues of land rights and urban poverty.[9] Māori also formed alliances with Polynesian immigrants to New Zealand, resulting in groups such as the Polynesian Panthers, who were explicitly modeled after the Black Panthers.[10]

Elsewhere in the Pacific, formal decolonization was achieved. In 1962, Sāmoa became the first Pacific nation to officially gain independence from its former colonizer (New Zealand) after decades of nonviolent actions organized by the Mau Movement. Fiji, Papua New Guinea, the Solomon Islands, and Kiribati all achieved formal independence in the 1970s, while Vanuatu, the Marshall Islands, the Federated States of Micronesia, and the Cook Islands followed in the 1980s.[11] In practice, independence did not result in complete freedom from imperial powers, but it did allow for important changes in leadership and decison making that were meaningful to Indigenous Pacific peoples and should not be easily dismissed. Many other Pacific nations continue to seek independence from their settler colonial powers, such as French Polynesia, where the Mā'ohi have consistently protested the use of their islands for nuclear testing by the French.[12] In more recent decades, broad alliances for a demilitarized and nuclear-free Pacific have flourished across contexts as varied as Palau, the Marshall Islands, Guam, Hawai'i, and Okinawa, all haunted by past and ongoing U.S. military actions that have wrought violence on Indigenous peoples and lands.[13] As in part I, part II of this book is attentive to this broader context of varied forms and struggles for decolonization across Polynesia, but focuses most closely on such efforts in Hawai'i. Yet I also still seek to show how interconnected Kanaka Maoli actions to challenge settler colonialism are with similar efforts across Polynesia, for example, through links to the Tongan Genome Project in chapter 5 and Yuki Kihara's (Sāmoan) art in chapter 6.

I jump in time from the mid-twentieth century to the early twenty-first not because the interim history is unimportant, but because I find it urgent to demonstrate how deeply our present moment is shaped by the logic of possession through whiteness that is too easily relegated to distant history. Struggles for decolonization continue, and continue to remap the Pacific Islands in ways that complicate and flout racial divisions including the Polynesian, Melanesian, and Micronesian designations and the 50 percent blood quantum legislation in the Hawaiian context. In the next chapters, I critically analyze a broad archive, including contemporary political debates about the future of the lāhui, contemporary Indigenous art, and the meanings assigned to a "Hawaiian genome" and other forms of "genetic ancestry" through the use of genetic technologies. What links these different visual, ethnographic, and cultural archives together for me is the resonance in the strategies, which I call regenerative refusals, that Polynesians use to challenge the logic of possession through whiteness, which continues to animate settler colonialism. Throughout these chapters, I seek to recognize the significance of the work of Indigenous Pacific artists, activists, and scholars who critique and confound the logic of possession through whiteness in creative and profound ways. In doing so, I hope to amplify and strengthen their desires and visions of different Indigenous futures, not determined by colonial and scientific damage.

CHAPTER 4

*Still in the Blood*
Blood Quantum and Self-Determination in
*Day v. Apoliona* and Federal Recognition

---

Article XI, Section 6 clearly states that the income and proceeds from the §5(f) trust must be used solely for native Hawaiians not native Hawaiians and Hawaiians.
—Appellant's opening brief, *Day v. Apoliona*, 2008

---

We need small "n" [native Hawaiian] to swallow the big "N" [Native Hawaiian] and put people on the land.
—GENE ROSS DAVIS, public hearing on federal recognition, Kaunakakai, Moloka'i, June 28, 2014

---

Eugenics of the early twentieth century, as discussed in chapter 2, may seem outrageously outdated to a contemporary audience. Yet the Hawaiian Homes Commission Act's (HHCA) definition of "native Hawaiian," created in 1920 and still on the books with minor revisions today, continues to be steeped in the same white supremacist and patriarchal ideological context. In the logic of blood quantum, there are "pure" Hawaiians, quickly dying out, and "part" Hawaiians, quickly becoming white Americans. Like the valorizing of the "Part Hawaiian" by anthropologist Louis Sullivan, the HHCA ostensibly saw more value in Part Hawaiians because they were more Americanized and thus did not need the additional pedagogical instruction of a homestead (including paying rent and maintaining a nuclear family home) in order to be civilized American citizens. Despite the differences in value judgment, however, the HHCA would permanently embed Kamehameha Schools' eugenics teacher Uldrick Thompson's advice to "develop" the great qualities of the "old-time Hawaiians," which are "still in the blood" within Native Hawaiian communities. To be able to ensure the next generation's rights to lease or inherit a homestead, Native Hawaiians necessarily must engage with the complex calculus of blood, whether they agree with it or not.

In recent years, Native Hawaiians have, in a variety of ways, contested the terms of recognition imposed by the state government of Hawai'i and by the federal government. This chapter examines various battles over codifying Native Hawaiian identity in law, where Native Hawaiians have rejected the authority of the state to determine Native Hawaiian identity, while sometimes seeking simultaneously to gain stronger recognition from state and federal law for Native Hawaiian rights to land and political sovereignty. While simultaneously rejecting and seeking state authority may seem impossibly contradictory, this is often the position Indigenous peoples are forced into. For example, in 2005, five Native Hawaiian men sued the Office of Hawaiian Affairs for failing to restrict several of their social programs to the definition of "native Hawaiians" as being "of not less than one-half part blood." The case, *Day v. Apoliona*, would reach the federal Ninth Circuit Court of Appeals four years later. Superficially, the only difference between "native Hawaiians" and "Native Hawaiians" is a matter of capitalization; yet state and federal law distinctly distinguishes the two. The *Day* plaintiffs, Virgil Day, Mel Ho'omanawanui, Josiah Ho'ohuli, Patrick Kahawaiola'a, and Samuel Kealoha, argued that the Office of Hawaiian Affairs (OHA) was obligated to enforce the legal definition of "native Hawaiian" as first stipulated in the 1921 Hawaiian Homes Commission Act (subsequently reinforced in the 1959 State Admission Act) as a person having at least 50 percent "blood." As noted in their distinction between "native Hawaiians" and just plain "Hawaiians" in the epigraph above, the plaintiffs saw "native Hawaiians" as the only recognizable Indigenes in law.

Part of what was at stake for the *Day* plaintiffs was the potential formation of a new Native Hawaiian "governing entity" that would allow both "native Hawaiians" and "Native Hawaiians" to enroll as citizens. The *Day* plaintiffs were responding to the so-called Akaka Bill, a federal legislative effort beginning around 2000, spearheaded by U.S. Senator Daniel Akaka, to have Native Hawaiians be "federally recognized" in a manner analogous to certain Native American tribes. As I explain further below, the Akaka Bill never succeeded in passing Congress, due in large part to Republican opposition to the idea of creating a new "race-based" government for Native Hawaiians. The Akaka Bill was contested among the Native Hawaiian community for quite different reasons. Broadly, the debate locally centered around the terms of the analogy being made between Native American tribes and Native Hawaiians. Chiefly, the legislation made no concessions of land rights to Native Hawaiians and limited the exercise of Hawaiian sovereignty to the status of a "domestic dependent nation" (as established in federal Indian law) rather than an independent nation. When the Akaka Bill stalled and was effectively defeated in Congress after several reintroductions of the legislation, advocates of federal recognition pursued alternate routes, including recognition from the state of Hawai'i and the Department of the Interior (the agency that manages federal relations with Native American tribes).

While blood quantum is not the only contested issue in the larger debates over state and federal recognition, certainly questions of Native Hawaiian identity (often reduced to "blood") and biologically "building" the nation are central to how arguments both for and against state and federal recognition are articulated. For example, the Office of Hawaiian Affairs, a key proponent of both state and federal recognition, has titled their so-called nation building initiative Ho'oulu Lāhui: Rise, Be Heard. Ho'oulu Lāhui was the motto of King Kalākaua, meaning "to increase, reinvigorate, revitalize the Hawaiian people." The irony of OHA's use of this motto to many is that where OHA's efforts appear designed to better include Native Hawaiians within the United States, Kalākaua's efforts to ho'oulu lāhui focused on revitalizing traditional arts and language, challenging settler colonialism, and maintaining the Hawaiian Kingdom's political and cultural independence from the United States.[1]

This chapter begins by providing further context to the history of efforts to recognize Native Hawaiians at the state and federal levels. I then turn to analysis of the *Day v. Apoliona* case with an eye toward understanding why these Native Hawaiian men sought to reinforce divisive blood quantum definitions and why they turned to the settler state's law to do so. I end by contrasting the claims of the *Day* plaintiffs with the quite different claims levied at the Department of the Interior in 2014 by Native Hawaiians wholly rejecting the authority of the United States to recognize them. These refusals during public hearings over the Department of the Interior's proposal to recognize Native Hawaiians as analogous to Native Americans provide an important foundation for theorizing refusal as regeneration, a theme that develops across each chapter in part II.

## THE HISTORICAL CONTEXT OF FEDERAL AND STATE RECOGNITION FOR NATIVE HAWAIIANS

Since at least the late 1990s, moderate Native Hawaiian organizations like the Council for Native Hawaiian Advancement (CNHA) have advocated for federal recognition of Native Hawaiians, seeking to formalize the status of Native Hawaiians as analogous to federally recognized Native American tribes and Alaska Native villages. At stake in this analogy for CNHA is the potential available legal and financial benefits that federal recognition might offer to Native Hawaiians.[2] For many years, CNHA was a driving force behind the Akaka Bill, federal legislation that would have officially recognized Native Hawaiians as Native people. This legislation was in part the legacy of the 1993 Apology Bill signed by President Bill Clinton, a nonbinding bill that recognized the unjust participation of the United States in the illegal overthrow of the Hawaiian Kingdom. Yet the Akaka Bill's provisions for actual rights to be extended to Native Hawaiians were watered down, to say the least—while providing steps toward creating a Native Hawaiian government, no rights to land were included. The absence of land rights, which many Native Hawaiians saw as the most important foundation for nation building, meant that many Native Hawaiians outside of CNHA and the state Office of Hawaiian Affairs could not support the Akaka Bill.

The Akaka Bill never passed Congress due to Republican opposition. However, in 2014, due in part to lobbying by CNHA and OHA, the Department of the Interior (DOI) opened a new avenue toward federal recognition, proposing a federal rule change that would formally recognize Native Hawaiians as under the DOI's purview in a manner analogous to how Native American political affairs are managed at the federal level by the DOI. As I will discuss later in this chapter, Native Hawaiian opposition to this rule change was widespread, though ultimately ignored by the DOI, which formalized the rule change in September 2016. Yet it is important to note that this opposition drew on several decades of open skepticism about, and opposition to, federal recognition within the Native Hawaiian community, and is likely to continue despite the 2016 rule change. I briefly describe the history of federal and state recognition initiatives and their reception within the Native Hawaiian community in order to better contextualize the legal battle fought by the plaintiffs in *Day v. Apoliona* and the opposition to the DOI rule change in 2014, each detailed later in this chapter.

Part of the problem is that the federal recognition process fits poorly with the Native Hawaiian context. Federal recognition is a legal process developed, rather recently, for Native American tribes that had either never been recognized by the federal government or had been terminated.[3] A formal process for federal recognition was only solidified in 1978.[4] This was precipitated after the era of termination and relocation, in which many tribes that had formally been recognized were considered officially "assimilated." In response to these terminations, political organizing on the part of terminated tribes and other tribes that had never been federally recognized forced the government to formalize procedures for federal recognition. Part of the complicated calculus that leads a Native American tribe to seek federal recognition includes the fact that, as Brian Klopotek notes, a tribe "must be federally recognized to exercise legal jurisdiction over their own land, be exempt from state taxes, or operate high-stakes gaming facilities."[5] In addition, a stigma exists within Indian Country against tribes that lack federal recognition, which Klopotek argues can potentially have a significant negative psychological impact on a tribe's well-being.[6]

Federally unrecognized Native American tribes therefore seek federal recognition for a variety of reasons that both overlap with and differ from the Native Hawaiian case. Supporters of federal recognition for Native Hawaiians, including OHA, assert that federal recognition will reaffirm "that Native Hawaiians are a political (not racial) community that has a special legal and political status. Such reaffirmation would strengthen protections against legal threats to programs and entitlements that benefit Native Hawaiians."[7] This references a desire for better legal protection of Native Hawaiian institutions from so-called reverse discrimination lawsuits such as *Rice v. Cayetano* (1996–2000) and *John Doe v. Kamehameha Schools* (2003–6), as discussed further later in this chapter.[8] Federal recognition advocates therefore support the process in order to have recognized a "Native Hawaiian governing entity," which might allow institutions including the Office of Hawaiian Affairs and Kamehameha Schools to legally serve Native Hawaiians only.

The federal legislation to set up this governing entity, introduced in the U.S. Congress in various forms since 2000, was officially titled the Native Hawaiian Government Reorganization Act, but became more popularly known as the Akaka Bill, as mentioned above. However, the Akaka Bill lacked almost all of the benefits that federal recognition purportedly grants recognized tribes. The Akaka Bill explicitly prohibited gaming rights (because Hawai'i state law prohibits casinos) and offered no provisions for land.[9] Many Native Hawaiians, including respected leader Haunani-Kay Trask, staunchly opposed the Akaka Bill precisely because it did not provide land rights.[10] Trask and others who were part of the group Ka Lāhui Hawai'i initially supported federal recognition and advocated for it as a next step after the 1993 Apology Bill, which acknowledged the role of the United States in the illegal overthrow of the Hawaiian Kingdom.[11]

Today, it is more than just the absence of explicit land rights that upsets opponents of federal recognition. Though the Akaka Bill made no explicit provisions for land, there is a sense among many Native Hawaiians that OHA and other proponents of the Akaka Bill (and state recognition legislation) are seeking an avenue to claim authority over, and potentially sell for profit, the ceded lands of the Hawaiian Kingdom. "Ceded lands" refers to lands formerly belonging to the Hawaiian monarchy, both the lands owned by them personally (the "Crown Lands") and those not used for their own private purposes but for the good of the people of Hawai'i (the "Government Lands").[12] At the time of annexation, the provisional government that had overthrown the Hawaiian monarchy comingled the Crown and Government Lands and "ceded" them to the U.S. federal government, but maintained that they were to be "held in trust for the people of Hawai'i." Subsequently, at the time of statehood in 1959, the federal government transferred "about 1.4 million acres of these lands in trust to the new state of Hawai'i but retained the remaining 373,720 acres."[13] Because no Native Hawaiian "governing entity" currently exists to resume the care and management of the ceded lands, the state of Hawai'i continues to hold them in trust.[14] Many see the ceded lands as a potential land base for the future Native Hawaiian government, but given the lack of trust and respect many Native Hawaiians have for OHA, they fear federal recognition will give these lands over to leaders who may choose to develop (e.g., build hotels, resorts, golf courses) or sell the land rather than use it in ways that would be meaningful to the community.

This distrust is partly due to the championing of the Alaska Native model as a potential model for Native Hawaiian governance. Though not included within the text of the Akaka Bill itself, from the positions of its main Native Hawaiian advocates, CNHA, it is likely that the bill would reorganize Native Hawaiians in a manner similar to that of Alaska Natives. Many Alaska Native tribes were officially reorganized into corporations, with ownership over oil resources, after the Alaska Native Claims Settlement

Act in 1971. CNHA appears to champion the model of the Alaska Native corporations, so that Native Hawaiians (even if not officially reorganized as corporations) would gain a greater share of Hawai'i's tourism and military economies.[15] This stance is incredibly contested because for many Native Hawaiians, the goal of decolonization is the liberation of Hawai'i from its dependence on tourism and its occupation by the U.S. military.

In 2011, after more than a decade of the Akaka Bill failing to pass Congress, a group of Native Hawaiian state senators introduced similar recognition legislation at the Hawai'i state level. This legislation, known as Act 195, passed with the support of recently elected Democratic governor Neil Abercrombie. Act 195 recognized "the Native Hawaiian people" "as the only indigenous, aboriginal, maoli [Hawaiian word for 'native,' 'real,' 'true'] of Hawai'i."[16] It referred to the passage of federal recognition legislation as an inevitability ("recognizing the likelihood of a reorganized Native Hawaiian governing entity") that this state legislation was simply providing better support for. It then proceeded to describe the establishment of the "Native Hawaiian roll commission" which will be responsible for "(1) Preparing and maintaining a roll of qualified Native Hawaiians; and (2) Certifying that the individuals on the roll of qualified Native Hawaiians meet the definition of qualified Native Hawaiians."[17] This Native Hawaiian roll commission was established and recognized by its Hawaiian language name: Kana'iolowalu.

As with federal recognition, Hawai'i state recognition for Native Hawaiians is also influenced by similar legislation for Native Americans in other states, but its benefits also differ in many respects. Approximately sixty-one tribes have state recognition across fifteen states.[18] As Alexa Koenig and Jonathan Stein have noted, in recent years, "states and tribes have increasingly realized that state recognition can serve as an important, albeit limited, alternative to federal recognition."[19] They describe tribes including the Gabrieleño Tongva in California and the Shinnecock in New York as relying on state recognition, at times as a potential stepping-stone to federal recognition, or as a sort of backup when the hefty evidence required to secure federal recognition proves impossible to obtain. State recognition sometimes affords reservation lands, as in the case of three Connecticut state-recognized tribes.[20] However, Koenig and Stein further note that the kinds of benefits that state recognition allows vary widely, from "powers of self-government such as the right to operate a police force, to exemptions from paying state and local taxes, to primarily symbolic acknowledgment of a tribe's longstanding presence within a state."[21]

In the Native Hawaiian case, state recognition is largely symbolic in that it brings no explicit new benefits to Native Hawaiians, and is largely meant to hasten federal recognition through the establishment of the proper membership of the future, federally recognized Native Hawaiian government. This membership is articulated as a "roll." Though the text of Act 195 does not explicitly refer to it, the establishment of a Native Hawaiian roll is only thinkable in reference to the historical use of rolls to determine the membership of Native American tribes. The earliest tribal rolls were established by the federal government between the 1880s and 1920s, "pursuant to a general policy of allotting Indian tribal property to individuals" at that time.[22] Historian Alexandra Harmon argues that "many tribal rolls were the result of dialogues in which Indians partly yielded to and partly gave their own meanings to US law," as tribal leaders mediated the standards of membership the federal government attempted to impose (including preponderance of "Indian blood" and recognizable "tribal relations") according to their own understandings and needs.[23] The processes followed to establish tribal rolls varied according to tribe and location. A single tribe often went through the process more than once, producing different rolls, but the roll "chosen as definitive for later citizenship determinations is known as the 'base roll.'"[24] Native American tribes that have relatively recently gained federal recognition, in the absence of historically established base rolls, at times use census data instead.[25]

The processes of genealogical verification used by the Native Hawaiian Roll Commission are unclear. Yet the act that created the commission specifies that those eligible to enroll include individuals who are descendants of "the aboriginal peoples who, prior to 1778, occupied and exercised sovereignty in the Hawaiian islands, the area that now constitutes the state of Hawai'i," or "an individual who is one of the indigenous, native people of Hawai'i and who was eligible in 1921 for the programs authorized by the Hawaiian Homes Commission Act, 1920, or a direct lineal descendant of that individual" and who has "maintained a significant cultural, social, or civic connection to the Native Hawaiian community and wishes to participate in the organization of the Native Hawaiian governing entity."[26] While these requirements are not overtly structured by blood quantum standards (i.e., a requirement that a person enrolling must have one-half, one-fourth, or some other specific percentage of Native Hawaiian "blood"), the reference to those who were "eligible in 1921 for the programs authorized by the Hawaiian Homes Commission Act" does bring blood quantum in, as that law required individuals to demonstrate that they were "of no less than one-half part" Native Hawaiian "blood" to be eligible for a homestead.

On the one hand, OHA has stated that this roll will only begin the process of constructing a Native Hawaiian governing entity, and "OHA will not undermine the future Governing Entity's inherent right to determine its membership criteria." Thus, they gesture toward the possibility that the future Native Hawaiian government can do away with the roll established by Kana'iolowalu as well as the blood quantum requirements of the Hawaiian Homes Commission Act and instate different membership requirements. On the other hand, OHA has emphasized the danger in "being left out" if individuals choose not to enroll. A 2013 advertisement explicitly references other cases in which Native Americans and Alaska Natives were left out at the time of the constitution of the Cherokee rolls through the Dawes Act and the Koniag (Alaska Native) base roll established in 1971, making each of these cautionary tales for Native Hawaiians who do not sign up for Kana'iolowalu. With the Koniag example, the risk is made explicitly monetary: the Koniag corporation posted a net income of $6.1 billion in 2012. Thus, considering these references to other tribal rolls and the continuing significance of tribal rolls for many federally recognized Native American tribes, OHA's gesture toward a future obsolescence of the Kana'iolowalu roll is another statement that rings false, supporting the exclusion of many while seeming to remain "neutral."

## CALLING THE LAW ON OURSELVES: *Day v. Apoliona*

With the broader context around federal and state recognition sketched out, I now turn to a specific legal case, *Day v. Apoliona*, as one example of how the logic of possession through whiteness continues to haunt contemporary struggles over the terms of blood quantum, membership, and Native Hawaiian political sovereignty. My critical entry into the *Day v. Apoliona* case is through a focus on how law and science are activated by the Native Hawaiian plaintiffs and the judges in the audio recording of the final hearing of *Day v. Apoliona* in the Ninth Circuit Court in 2009, and the resulting written decision in 2010. As is especially evident in the audio recording, there is much confusion and contention over how boundaries can be drawn and maintained between "native Hawaiians" and "Native Hawaiians." In the face of this confusion, how and why do the *Day* plaintiffs maintain such boundaries? In valorizing blood quantum policies and insisting on the 50 percent definition of native Hawaiian, the *Day* plaintiffs simultaneously "call the law on the law" and "call the law on themselves." They call the law on the law in the sense that they insist that OHA (a state agency) is neglecting state blood quantum laws. Yet in the process they also call the law on themselves by insisting that legal and scientific distinctions must be drawn in their own communities between native Hawaiians and Native Hawaiians.

These ideas about "calling the law" stem from a conference on law, violence, and the state that I attended at the University of Southern California in September 2010, specifically two talks given by scholars Sora Han and Fred Moten.[27] Moten in particular questioned how we could escape using the law to police ourselves and our communities, deploying antiblackness against black lovers and reinforcing the legal sovereignty of whiteness. He asked the audience of largely critical ethnic studies and American studies scholars to think about "how not to want this shit," "this shit" being, in my reading, the same status or recognition for any nonwhite community as enjoyed by whiteness in law.[28] This desire for legal protection and sanctioned violence against our own kin and communities is both antiblack and anti-Indigenous (among other things), as it upholds the foundational structure of the nation and society as antiblack and settler colonial.

Incited by Moten's question, I argue that the Native Hawaiian plaintiffs of *Day v. Apoliona* also "called the law on themselves" in order to have Native Hawaiian indigeneity formally recognized in law with a similar, if never quite the same, weight of whiteness. In part, the case can be understood as an example of a legal counterclaim of sorts within the larger context of legal challenges to Native Hawaiian–only programs that have proliferated in the last few decades. For example, in *Rice v. Cayetano* (2000), the U.S. Supreme Court ruled in favor of Harold F. Rice, a white resident of Hawai'i who had claimed that the policy of allowing only Native Hawaiians to vote for the trustees of OHA violated the racial discrimination clauses of the U.S. Constitution. In another example, the private Kamehameha Schools' policy of admitting Native Hawaiian students first has been repeatedly challenged in lawsuits by non–Native Hawaiian plaintiffs who charge that Kamehameha Schools' policy is unconstitutional and racially discriminatory.[29] This context mirrors in some ways the conflicts over blood quantum and enrollment for Native American tribes with gaming rights, as the resource-rich Kamehameha Schools and other Native Hawaiian programs are seen by white conservative groups as "special treatment" that results in a Hawaiian version of the "welfare queen" or "rich Indian," noticeably bringing antiblack and anti-Indigenous sentiments to the fore.[30] Such lawsuits are also part of the trend of anti–affirmative action legislation that has dismantled hiring and school admissions policies that attempt to recruit people of color.[31] Though the Native Hawaiian plaintiffs also chose to sue OHA, *Day v. Apoliona* could be understood as an attempted reversal of legal attacks on Native Hawaiian programs. The *Day* plaintiffs were seeking to regain some of the power Native Hawaiians may have lost over their own resources through such lawsuits. Yet in doing so, the plaintiffs reinforced U.S. colonial definitions of Native Hawaiians as a race whose authenticity is measurable through blood percentages, as they advocated limiting Native Hawaiian programs to an even smaller membership of Native Hawaiians with the proper blood quantum.

While I heartily agree with many Indigenous studies scholars that such efforts toward recognition and formal, legal equality are misguided and incomplete at best, as they often strengthen the sovereignty of the colonial nation-state at the expense of Native nations, I remain haunted by Moten's words. In practical terms, how exactly do we (and our diverse communities, with many for whom legal recognition is not so easily dismissed) go about *not wanting* this shit?[32] For indeed, in the face of scarce and endangered resources and rights, how could Native Hawaiians *not* desire stronger protections under the law? Gayatri Spivak and Wendy Brown have similarly pondered the rights of liberalism as "that which we cannot not want," even when we know the dangers of participating in systems that were never meant to save us.[33] How might such desires for rights, then, be viewed with complexity, even with one eye always on the overarching settler colonial structures that shape our desires and identities? How can we acknowledge and divest from the ways that the logic of possession through whiteness continues to haunt Native Hawaiians today, despite the history of the Polynesian Problem literature seeming to remain so distant?

In approaching *Day v. Apoliona* this way, I find that perhaps the most productive line of inquiry raised by the case is not a question I nonetheless still deeply feel: How could they? That is, how could these Native Hawaiian men defend and actually seek to extend the reach of the 50 percent blood quantum definition? Rather, I ask: Why did they choose to use blood quantum to gain greater resources and recognition, blood quantum being a technology "not of our own making" but nonetheless one that has become an undeniable part of many Native nations?[34] Why did they think this suit could be successful, and what did they hope to actually have recognized? In denying their claim, what was the motivation of the state and federal governments, and why did they stop short of striking down blood quantum policies for Native Hawaiian altogether? To be clear, framing my questions in this manner is not meant to sanction the *Day* plaintiffs' actions but rather to more deeply understand them and their part in shaping dominant forms of Native Hawaiian identity and recognition, especially this clearly heteropatriarchal and colonial, but nonetheless persistent, desire to have "no less than one-half part blood," a desire circulated both by the state and among Native Hawaiians. Overall, my approach fleshes out Moten's provocations about calling the law from an Indigenous feminist standpoint that critiques the ways heteropatriarchy structures settler colonialism, which I will detail further below.

### DILUTION INTERESTS: SITUATING *Day v. Apoliona* WITHIN DEBATES ABOUT NATIVE HAWAIIAN RACE AND GENDER

The *Day* claims against OHA were described as "dilution interest" claims, "referring to their assertion of an interest in preventing the dilution of benefits to Native Hawaiians by limiting eligibility to native Hawaiians only."[35] In suing the trustees of the Office of Hawaiian Affairs for failing to use state trust monies for the sole benefit of "native Hawaiians," the plaintiffs based their claims on the §5(f) clause of the Admission Act (the act that facilitated the admission of Hawai'i as the fiftieth state of the union). This clause, they argued, restricted the use of state monies given to OHA from the revenue of "ceded lands" (amounting to approximately 20 percent of OHA's total funds) to the "betterment of the condition of native Hawaiians."[36] As noted earlier in the discussion of the Akaka Bill, ceded lands refers to the lands formerly belonging to the Hawaiian Kingdom, which were seized by the white plantation-owning oligarchy who overthrew Queen Lili'uokalani in 1893, and were later ceded to the U.S. government to be held "in public trust" after statehood.[37] The *Day* plaintiffs alleged that OHA failed to follow this mandate for the use of ceded lands money specifically in their funding of four items: lobbying for the Akaka Bill and support of three social welfare-type programs.[38]

In Hawai'i District Court, the OHA trustees, as the defendants, repeatedly filed for summary judgment (i.e., a ruling in their favor without a full trial), arguing that their expenditures from the §5(f) trust funds were not legally limited solely to "the betterment of native Hawaiians," as stipulated in the Admission Act, but instead could be extended to the more broadly defined Native Hawaiian public. The district court granted summary judgment in 2008.[39] Plaintiffs appealed to the Ninth Circuit Federal Appeals Court. In 2009, the Ninth Circuit definitively ruled that federal law does not require OHA to use the §5(f) trust funds solely for native Hawaiians.[40] Though the suit was ultimately unsuccessful for the plaintiffs, and thus did not change any laws or policies regarding the use of blood quantum for Native Hawaiians, this case showcases well the ongoing legacies of eugenic thinking about blood and racial betterment, as well as the difficulties Native Hawaiians face in asserting any kind of self-determination over their racial recognition.[41] For the five plaintiffs in this case, "native Hawaiians," those "of not less than one-half part blood quantum," are a distinct group, clearly separate from and, indeed, "more oppressed" and thus "more entitled" to state money than Native Hawaiians.

Indigenous feminist activists and scholars, including Native Hawaiian feminists, have long noted that blood quantum laws—state, federal, and/or tribal legislation that imposes the requirement of a certain amount of Native "blood" (e.g., one-half or one-fourth) for legal recognition or tribal enrollment—are a pressing feminist issue.[42] Such laws create a social and political pressure for Native women to have children with Native men of high blood quantum in order to preserve rather than diminish a community's identity and authenticity. In some cases, Native women are explicitly disenrolled from a tribe if they marry a non-Native man, whereas Native men who marry non-Native women are not subject to the same rule.[43] Native women are therefore called on to "save the race" in a way that Native men are not. Indigenous feminists have advanced important critiques of blood quantum laws while also highlighting alternative modes of recognizing and regenerating Native communities that do not shame or penalize Native women for the sexual and reproductive choices they make.[44]

For Native Hawaiians, the treasured promise of a Hawaiian homestead still requires maximizing one's percentage of Hawaiian blood—and thus, pressure remains on Native Hawaiian men to regain control of their race and encourage Native Hawaiian women to "save the race." If Native Hawaiian women do not have children with Native Hawaiian men (of the appropriate blood quantum), one view is that they are "diluting" Native Hawaiian claims to land. This is a form of compulsory heterosexuality and is a product of settler colonialism, not a "traditional" value, though it is sometimes promoted as such. Native Hawaiian epistemologies dating to precontact times included valued positions for mahu (queer men and/or transgender women) and other sexualities and genders. Thus, when Native Hawaiian men claim that Native Hawaiian women are "betraying their race" by not having "pure" children with Native Hawaiian men, this is an internalized form of colonialism and sexism.

While blood quantum is at the heart of many Kanaka Maoli feminist critiques because of the specific legal context of the Hawaiian Homes Commission Act, other Polynesian feminist work critiques different systems of law, popular representations, and settler colonial violence. To my knowledge, Hawaiʻi is the only context in Polynesia that legislates Indigenous recognition via the specific language of blood percentages. Yet, as I discuss further in the next chapter, other Polynesians are increasingly subject to such language about blood or "genetic ancestry" through the popularization of genetic ancestry tests that provide users with percentages of their ethnic ancestry. Additionally, other Indigenous feminist concerns span Polynesia, including issues of domestic and sexual violence, discourses of compulsory heterosexuality from both the settler state and Indigenous claims about "traditional culture," and restoring gender balance after centuries of heteropatriarchal colonialism.[45]

Some Native women, notably including Haunani-Kay Trask, have distanced themselves from the feminist label because of mainstream feminism's overwhelming whiteness and concern with rights and equity rather than with Indigenous nation-building and decolonization.[46] Others prefer different terms or concepts, such as mana wahine, defined by kuʻualoha hoʻomanawanui as "the physical, intellectual, and spiritual (or intuitive) power of women" that is "individually embodied, but often employs collaborative strategies with other women for the benefit of the ʻohana [family] or Lāhui [nation], where women are the source of knowledge."[47] However, many contemporary scholars and activists value such culturally specific understandings while maintaining a claim to redefining feminism in ways that refuse to cede feminism to white women. At heart, Indigenous feminist theories simply address how "settler colonialism has been and continues to be a gendered process," in the face of much conventional scholarship and activism that has ignored the centrality of gender to colonization, or treated gender as a secondary or tertiary issue at best.[48] Indigenous feminist theories also refuse to split Native nations up in a simple opposition between Native men and women: "Native men are not the root cause of Native women's problems; rather, Native women's critiques implicate the historical and ongoing imposition of colonial, heteropatriarchal structures onto their societies."[49]

Similarly, the *Day* plaintiffs are not the root cause of the problematic ways that race and gender have been shaped for Native Hawaiians; that blame lies with the structures of heteropatriarchy and settler colonialism that govern the U.S. occupation of Hawai'i. Nonetheless, the case can be viewed as a flashpoint in contemporary debates and struggles within the Native Hawaiian community that have often broken along gendered lines. Of these rifts, Ty Kāwika Tengan notes that Native Hawaiian women have at times discounted Native Hawaiian's men's leadership in cultural and political movements, and that in response there has been a sense of "resentment brewing" on the part of Native Hawaiian men.[50] Tengan describes anecdotal experiences of times "when men have made statements such as 'Wāhine need to step aside.'"[51] Noting such sentiments as a "cause for concern," Tengan cautions us against understanding male and female leadership as competing and mutually exclusive.[52] Similarly, Hōkūlani Aikau has used Hawaiian cosmology and the tradition of the double-hulled canoe to argue that "gender complementarity" is a core concept of Hawaiian culture, and is seen to produce "pono," or, in her definition, "appropriate behaviors or codes intended to create balance."[53]

These analyses of the gendered conflicts among Native Hawaiians are especially important because they remind us that such tensions are not natural or inevitable within the community but exist precisely because colonial heteropatriarchy continues to haunt contemporary Native Hawaiian gender and sexual relations. Decolonizing efforts must address the ways that colonialism has structurally divided Native Hawaiian men and women, rather than viewing Native Hawaiian men as the oppressors of Native Hawaiian women or Native Hawaiian female leaders as necessarily emasculating Native Hawaiian men. Native Hawaiian feminists pursue this work by remapping the relationships within our lāhui and beyond it away from the strictures placed on them by settler colonialism and toward more expansive forms of connection.

CALLING THE LAW ON THE LAW:
THE FINAL *Day v. Apoliona* HEARING

The structural, gendered barriers to justice are clear in a closer examination of the final *Day v. Apoliona* hearing in the Ninth Circuit Court of Appeals in October 2009. Overall, the *Day* plaintiffs framed their claims as a problem of neglect, of OHA's failure to "better the condition of native Hawaiians," as the plaintiffs argued was their duty according to the Admission Act. Yet the plaintiffs also constantly challenged the legal authority of the state and federal government. They gestured toward the view of native

Hawaiians as a dispossessed and colonized people, even while they carefully insisted that their argument was solely about enforcing the blood quantum definition enshrined in state and federal law. For example, in his opening address, Walter Schoettle, the plaintiffs' attorney, attempted to demonstrate for the court what he called "the big picture."[54] He stated that the Kingdom of Hawai'i dispossessed native Hawaiians from their lands (referring, as he clarified in his opening brief, to the division and privatization of lands in the Great Māhele of 1848, prior even to the 1893 overthrow of the Hawaiian Kingdom) just as the Native Americans were dispossessed by the United States. In response to this claim, a judge interrupted to say, "Now that we're a statehood, and it went to a popular vote of the people, I take it that it's part of the union.... Let's take it as is."[55] Even though it was the Kingdom of Hawai'i that Schoettle identified as the dispossessor, not the United States, the judge was eager to foreclose any further discussion that Schoettle might have been setting up—such as Native Hawaiians' inherent sovereignty over the whole of Hawai'i—which he saw as far outside the scope of his court and long settled. Schoettle responded, "I'm not ... [laugh] I'm not challenging annexation. I'm just stating the fact."[56] The judge intervened again: "Let's take it like it is. And in the course of becoming a state, certain agreements were entered into between the Kingdom and the United States government, approved by the Senate. That's what we're looking at isn't it?"[57] This was a gross misrepresentation of history, since the agreement to annexation was brokered by the Republic of Hawaii, the government formed by white settlers after the Hawaiian Kingdom's overthrow, not the Hawaiian Kingdom itself. Nonetheless, Schoettle responded, "That's what I'm getting to, your honor, and I'd like to see those agreements enforced."[58] Thus, Schoettle quickly abandoned the language of dispossession—not even challenging the judge's erasure of the history of the Hawaiian Kingdom's illegal overthrow and annexation. He returned to the language of neglect, insisting on the duty of the state to "better" native Hawaiians: "My point is ... that even though this court has indicated on several occasions that 5(f) by itself doesn't require the state to do anything in particular for native Hawaiians ... if you look at 5(f) in connection with 5(b) and section 4.... The state has to do something to better the ... condition of native Hawaiians ... and that is to implement the Hawaiian Homes Commission Act. That is what Congress said in 1959."[59]

The judges responded to Schoettle's claims with two main lines of inquiry—the blood quantum definition and accounting in accordance with the §5(f) trust. Judge Graber brought up blood quantum twice in the hearing. As Schoettle explained the details of the foundation of the OHA and its negligence in serving native Hawaiians, Graber interrupted to ask, "So your complaint has to do with the definition of Native Hawaiian, at bottom?"[60] Schoettle emphatically responded, "My complaint has to do with the fact that OHA has been *ignoring* the definition of native Hawaiians."[61] This again emphasizes the fact that it was the state and federal definition of native Hawaiian that Schoettle and his plaintiffs were attempting to enforce, simply as a matter of law. Graber brought up blood quantum later in the hearing as well, however, as Schoettle emphasized that his plaintiffs' challenges were grounded in the fact that the use of §5(f) trust funds for the Native Hawaiian Legal Corporation, Na Pua, and Alu Like, all programs that provided services without reference to blood quantum, was illegal. They had a heated exchange about blood quantum:

GRABER: That's what caused me to ask you the question I asked you much earlier. Isn't this an argument about blood quantum and the definition of who's sufficiently Hawaiian to receive this money?

WS: Yes, that's what the whole case is all about, is the blood quantum.

GRABER: But anyone who can . . . anyone who meets the definition that you want also meets the definition for these entities, do they not?

WS: No . . . all these entities provide services to Hawaiians without regard to blood quantum.

GRABER: Right, so people with more blood quantum by definition . . .

WS: With less, less . . . I represent Hawaiians that have the blood quantum . . . that are not less than one-half part . . .

GRABER: If there is a .001 bottom, that people who are 50 percent or above by definition are within that group, are they not?

WS: Yes.

GRABER: Okay.[62]

At this point another judge redirected the discussion by questioning whether the case was primarily a problem of accounting—of OHA failing to properly record how their funds specifically impacted native Hawaiians (as distinct from Native Hawaiians more broadly). Schoettle agreed that this was a central part of the plaintiffs' claims—"That's the objection we're making. There is no accounting."⁶³ The judge went on:

JUDGE: Have they received any benefit?

WS: Who?

JUDGE: Native Hawaiians.⁶⁴ Are you saying no native Hawaiian has received any money from the trust?

WS: I don't know. All I know is, from this record, that they have given trust money to three entities that provide benefits to non-beneficiaries as well as beneficiaries . . . and what the entities have done with it . . . they could have spent all the money on native Hawaiians, they could have spent the money on non-native, I mean Hawaiians with less than one-half part . . . they could have spent some of it on one and some of it on the other . . . we do not know. . . . I am saying that by giving the money to an entity that is not restricted to the blood quantum, they have breached the trust because there is no accounting.⁶⁵

The confusion about which type of Native Hawaiians the attorneys and justices were referring to is as palpable in this section as it is in the more heated exchange between Schoettle and Graber about the blood quantum definition. Though Schoettle's argument was that native Hawaiians (of no less than one-half part blood) such as his plaintiffs were the authentic native Hawaiian population that was in most need of "betterment," even he hesitated and stumbled over his words in his explanations. He started to refer to the broader Native Hawaiian population as "non-native" before clarifying, "I mean Hawaiians with less than one-half part." He also began to rely on the language of accounting in describing his clients and native Hawaiians as "beneficiaries," in contrast to the Native Hawaiian "non-beneficiaries."

As the judges moved toward the particular challenge to OHA's support for the Akaka Bill, in contrast to the challenges of funding for the Native Hawaiian Legal Corporation, Na Pua, and Alu Like, Schoettle created an even stronger divide between native Hawaiians and Native Hawaiians. He repeatedly referred to the Akaka Bill as a project of "Native Hawaiians with a capital N," explaining: "They are trying to establish a government for Native Hawaiians without regard to blood quantum. This is not a benefit to the small number of actual beneficiaries. . . . This is a benefit that goes to all

Hawaiians. There are 400,000 Hawaiians. There are only at most 80,000 native Hawaiians."[66]

Schoettle went on to proclaim that "without blood quantum, *everyone* will be Native Hawaiian," as the Akaka Bill as drafted had no blood quantum requirement. This concern about protecting Native Hawaiian identity as separate from other residents of Hawai'i can be understood in part in the context of the still popular ideology of Hawai'i as a racial melting pot, as discussed in regard to sociologist Romanzo Adams in chapter 3. Here we can see that one consequence of the melting pot ideology and its erasure of the distinct identities, relationships, and political status of Native Hawaiians in Hawai'i is that some Native Hawaiians have become more invested in blood quantum ideals in order to prove their distinction from other racial groups or racially mixed people in Hawai'i. For these reasons, Schoettle claimed that the Akaka Bill was "of no benefit" to native Hawaiians as it was basically a way to "deprive" them of their lands.

Schoettle further asserted that the Akaka Bill would be held unconstitutional in any case because "without a blood quantum," it would be a violation of the Fourteenth Amendment to the U.S. Constitution—specifically the equal protection clause. "Racial classification without blood quantum is unconstitutional," Schoettle insisted. He goes on to paraphrase the opinion of Justice Breyer in the *Rice v. Cayetano* case, that he had "never heard of an Indian tribe without a blood quantum."[67] Justice Breyer in his *Rice* opinion further wrote: "Of course a Native American tribe has broad authority to define its membership.... There must, however, be some limit on what is reasonable.... And to define that membership in terms of 1 possible ancestor out of 500, thereby creating a vast and unknowable body of potential members ... goes well beyond any reasonable limit."[68] Using Breyer's argument, Schoettle insisted that his clients' native Hawaiian-ness was not reducible to a racial classification but was instead a properly, "reasonably," defined Indigenous classification—that is, one that was based on a native Hawaiian sovereign right to decide its own membership, but that did not exceed, or even approach, that specter of the "vast and unknowable body of potential members" that so threatened Justice Breyer's sense of order in the *Rice* case. "We would have no objection to governance similar to a Native American tribe," Schoettle explains.[69]

The point of contention for the *Day* plaintiffs was that the "governing entity" that the Akaka Bill would establish started with the full Native Hawaiian population as a base, instead of the smaller and more "in need" native Hawaiian population. He concluded:

> It's up to the tribes to determine the blood quantum ... on their own. And what they [Native Hawaiians with a capital N] want to do is to have this entity establish a blood quantum ... which they won't ... if you start out with no blood quantum, there won't be a blood quantum....
>
> This bill is trying to deprive native Hawaiians of their lands ... it is of no benefit to native Hawaiians.[70]

In a generous reading, the plaintiffs were trying to mark n/Native Hawaiians as a sovereign, Indigenous people—a people "deprived" of "their lands," not just a race. Yet the only way this could be "reasoned" in the law was through the enforcement of a restrictive blood quantum, which was, in practice, undeniably *racial* and thus must be limited to native Hawaiians only. Their arguments ultimately rested, then, on what can be characterized as "calling the law on the law"—on an insistence that the state and federal governments were failing to follow their own laws and agreements with native Hawaiians. Yet this also required "calling the law on themselves"—on dividing communities and families into native Hawaiians as opposed to Native Hawaiians. Like Justice Breyer's remark that an Indigenous population with "a vast and unknowable body of potential members" is "well beyond any reasonable limit," the *Day* plaintiffs were accepting that their potential status as the "real" native Hawaiians, and thus any sovereignty associated with that status, was entirely dependent on state and federal limits.

As for the OHA trustees, the defendants in the case, their claims were limited as well. They did not explicitly contest the formal definition of native Hawaiian as referring only to those of "no less than one-half part." In part, this reluctance to explicitly challenge the blood quantum is a careful stance—OHA had previously supported a referendum to assess and potentially change the blood quantum requirement, and this referendum was also legally challenged by some of the very same plaintiffs as in the *Day* case.[71] OHA's defense in the final hearing simply argued that their programs did benefit both native Hawaiians and Native Hawaiians more broadly, and that the §5(f) clause did not stipulate any strict accounting measures that required proof that their programs would primarily benefit native Hawaiians only.[72]

In the end, the 2010 published decision from the Ninth Circuit's hearing of *Day v. Apoliona* found that OHA had not breached §5(f) in their use of funds for any of the challenged programs.[73] The judges ultimately decided that Congress had given the state of Hawai'i wide latitude in deciding how to manage the §5(f) funds and that OHA was not limited to spending their money solely on "the betterment of native Hawaiians."[74] The *Day* plaintiffs lost, and OHA won. What did the case mean for other Native Hawaiians? The strategy of the plaintiffs in suing the state to limit resources to Native Hawaiians with the proper blood quantum is not representative of the larger, multifaceted landscape of the Native Hawaiian sovereignty movement. Many Native Hawaiians do not buy into any sort of blood quantum thinking or Western definitions of race, gender, and justice, and many also absolutely refuse to acknowledge the authority of the United States or the state of Hawaiʻi over their own affairs.

Further, many insist that Native Hawaiians are not a race, but the political subjects of the Hawaiian Kingdom, which was multiracial. The political group Movement for Aloha No Ka ʻĀina, for example, is vocal in its stance that the vision of an independent Hawaiʻi will be a multicultural, diverse, and inclusive one. Their "platform of unity" stresses the need to respect and honor Kanaka Maoli ways of knowing and living, but also notes: "We will build unity and solidarity with all who share our values and principles."[75] This is but one of many visions of *ea*, a complex Hawaiian word meaning political independence or sovereignty but also, as Noelani Goodyear-Kaʻōpua has written, interdependence and the active state of being, living, and breathing.[76]

Thus, certainly, Native Hawaiians often divest from settler colonial structures and terminologies that foreclose decolonial justice at their very roots. Native Hawaiians, especially in the last few decades, have made tremendous strides in revitalizing the Hawaiian language and cultural practices such as seafaring and kalo (taro) terracing.[77] The importance of such reclamations can hardly be overstated; they provide part of an answer to Fred Moten's beautiful provocation: "How do we not want this shit?" and how do we stop "calling the law on ourselves"? We start not wanting the (settler colonial) law to structure our lives when we build different institutions and different laws that reflect our own visions of justice. What my analysis of *Day v. Apoliona* suggests, and why it deserves critical attention alongside other Native Hawaiian political actions, is that another essential first step toward ending "calling the law on ourselves" may be to remember that Native Hawaiian (and native Hawaiian) identity is a site of conflict that is deeply structured by colonialism—and not, as some would (perhaps understandably) like to see it, as a pure site of culture, resistance, or revitalization. Native scholar Scott Lyons reminds us that, "on top of blood, enrollment, and behavior . . . another material used for the intersubjective construction of Indian identity [is]: the historical fact of American participation."[78] My analysis has shown that blood itself is also an idea and material object that is constructed through American participation. Keeping our fingers on precisely this pulse—"the historical fact of American participation" in the construction of Indigenous identity generally and the perpetuation of blood quantum in particular—is important because it is necessary to remember that it is not the *Day* plaintiffs who created the blood quantum laws. Blood quantum laws are a state and federal creation, and it will require further effort in and beyond the courts in order to change them.

Yet, as Moten also recognizes, it is never as easy as simply recognizing and then discarding "the historical fact of American participation" in Black and Indigenous identities. This fact is never easily discarded or excised; it is too deeply embedded in individual and community ideals. The distinctions Schoettle is eager to create and maintain between "Native Hawaiians with a capital N" and "native Hawaiians of not less than one-half part," are dependent on biological, heteropatriarchal definitions of native Hawaiians. Native Hawaiian women (and native Hawaiian women) are required to biologically reproduce and maintain communities of native Hawaiians of not less than one-half part—crucially with native Hawaiian men who are also of not less than one-half part. That none of the plaintiffs, the defendants, or the judges ever mentioned the difficulties in maintaining a distinct native Hawaiian population seems shocking—and yet it is also fitting because the blood quantum law (which was not being contested in itself—only its proper application) is entirely dependent on heteropatriarchal definitions. The next section turns to a different example of Native Hawaiian political action that does contest the divisions imposed between Native Hawaiians with a capital N and native Hawaiians of not less than one-half part. As part of public hearings about federal recognition through the Department of the Interior, many Native Hawaiians who were legally "native Hawaiian" and living on Hawaiian homesteads testified powerfully against blood quantum restrictions on Native Hawaiian identity and access to land. Most also rejected the authority of the Department of the Interior to recognize Native Hawaiians, calling for a regeneration of the Hawaiian Kingdom, rooted in the authority of the ancestors who had resisted the overthrow and annexation.

## REGENERATIVE REFUSALS TO THE DEPARTMENT OF THE INTERIOR AND BLOOD QUANTUM DIVISIONS

In the summer of 2014, with very little advance notice, the Department of the Interior held a series of public hearings in Hawaiʻi about a proposed rule change under consideration that would potentially federally acknowledge Native Hawaiians. As noted above, federal recognition for Native Hawaiians had long been contested, though until this point the conflict had centered around the Akaka Bill, federal legislation that had failed to pass Congress. The Department of the Interior was proposing a kind of workaround to achieve federal recognition or "acknowledgment" without the Akaka Bill. Instead of requiring congressional approval, the Department of the Interior (DOI) would formally declare their jurisdiction over Native Hawaiians in a manner analogous to the DOI's jurisdiction over Native Americans. More importantly, if this rule change occurred, DOI would work to support the creation of a Native Hawaiian governing entity by Native Hawaiians, an entity meant to be analogous to Native American tribal governments and able to resume a "government-to-government" relationship with the United States.

Native Hawaiian and allied communities packed the school cafeterias and gymnasiums where the hearings took place. After a brief explanation of the proposed rule change, a small panel of DOI representatives asked community members to share their responses to a series of questions related to the possibility of the DOI facilitating the "reestablishment of a government-to-government relationship with the Native Hawaiian community."[79] The questions sketched the intentions of the DOI—they hoped to assist in "reorganizing" a Native Hawaiian government and "reestablishing" a formal political relationship between that new government and the federal government. The Native Hawaiian community largely met these intentions with skepticism, annoyance at their formality and unclear terminology, or outright rejection. When the DOI panel opened the hearings to public comment, community members were limited to two minutes each. Over and over again, Native Hawaiians stepped up to the microphone and defiantly answered no or aʻole (no in ʻōlelo Hawaiʻi, Hawaiian language).

The "no" answers formed a clear majority of the statements in every one of the fifteen public hearings held in Hawaiʻi. Despite this fact, and citing the need to weigh public testimony with comments submitted online, the DOI eventually formalized the rule change in September 2016, effectively beginning a process to create a new Native Hawaiian government that the

DOI would officially recognize. This section analyzes how those statements used refusal as a regenerative action, reorienting the terms of the hearings away from those prescribed by the federal government. Instead, speakers highlighted the relatively recent history of the overthrow of the Hawaiian Kingdom, memories passed down through families of the kingdom and especially Queen Liliʻuokalani, and the ongoing legacies of the overthrow and settler colonialism. Native Hawaiians, testifying in both English and ʻōlelo Hawaiʻi, clearly and confidently stated their desires and faith in a restored, independent Hawaiʻi, separate from the United States rather than recognized as a nation within the United States.

Unfortunately, much of the mainstream reporting about these hearings at the time described Native Hawaiians as rude or hostile to the DOI panel, without significant attention to the content of the testimony or the settler colonial context shaping the emotion on display. As Lani Teves and I argued at the time, these descriptions of how angry and unwelcoming Native Hawaiians were at the hearings were shaped in significant ways by settler colonial ideologies of Native Hawaiians as barbaric and uncivilized, on the one hand, and as passive and friendly hosts who should be grateful to the United States, on the other.[80]

As other Native Hawaiian scholars including Noelani Goodyear-Kaʻōpua have argued, the statements deserve a much deeper analysis.[81] Below, I analyze some of the major themes of the statements, including the rejection of race as a criterion for membership in a new Hawaiian nation. Overall, the statements provide an important contrast to the actions of the *Day* plaintiffs as discussed above. Like the charges brought by the *Day* plaintiffs, the testimony at the public hearings was largely dismissed by the authority of the federal government. Yet, in contrast to the *Day* plaintiffs' actions, the testimony succeeded in creating a potentially more expansive vision of the future of the Hawaiian lāhui than the one put forward by the *Day* plaintiffs. The statements also came from a broader range of Native Hawaiians, including men, women, mahu and transgender peoples, children, kupuna (elders), as well as non-Hawaiian allies (and a few non-Hawaiians in opposition). In addition to providing a contrast to the claims of the *Day* plaintiffs, these statements can be read in direct contrast to the interviews analyzed in the last chapter, where sociological interpretation of Hawaiʻi as a racial melting pot encouraged Native Hawaiians to dis-identify and hate being Native Hawaiian. Instead, these testimonies centered and valued Native Hawaiian identity and indigeneity while critiquing blood quantum restrictions and refusing the authority of the state to decide Hawaiian futures.

## A'OLE AS INTERGENERATIONAL REGENERATION

In a space of ongoing violent misrecognition and denial of settler colonialism, Native Hawaiians testifying in front of the DOI panels shared moving remembrances of the Hawaiian Kingdom, orally passed down through the generations, strong demonstrations of ongoing political and cultural sovereignty, and rousing calls to action that decentered federal recognition as the only pathway toward justice. While no or a'ole was repeated over and over again, the rejections of the proposed rule change were not simple or flippant. Rather, they were grounded very clearly and strongly in a Kanaka Maoli nationalism that repeatedly recentered the conversation on the Hawaiian Kingdom, its illegal overthrow and later annexation by the United States, and the ongoing cultural and political work most meaningful to Kanaka Maoli communities. These statements were also consistently intergenerational, making reference both to ancestors and to past struggles of Kānaka Maoli, as well as to children (who were often present and testifying themselves) and future generations.

This constant recentering of the conversation away from federal recognition and toward frank discussions of past and present settler colonialism was impressive, especially given the time constraints imposed. Analyzing the statements in further depth, I argue below that these statements of refusal performed a regeneration. Regeneration in this instance signaled a persistent belief in a genealogy of Kanaka Maoli resistance linking past struggles such as the Kū'e Petitions to the present struggle against U.S. occupation. Based on these past struggles, Kānaka Maoli also projected a belief in a not-yet-realized but achievable decolonized future. The statements fostered pride in Kanaka Maoli ancestors for their brave actions, and pride in the Kānaka Maoli actually in the room for standing up and not being afraid to object to the proceedings and reject federal recognition. By speaking to the DOI but in front of each other and on video streaming to many other Kānaka Maoli in Hawai'i and beyond, the refusals resonated widely, sparking lively discussion of multivalent desires for a future independent nation and lāhui. In this sense, the refusals at the DOI hearings regenerated hope, pride, and desire for more than the pittance the federal government seemed to be offering.

"These questions are irrelevant," said Kanoelani Davis at the Moloka'i hearing held June 28, 2014.[82] Davis was repeating a common stance echoed by many at this and other hearings. "You must go back and tell your bosses that the questions are irrelevant that you have brought to Kānaka Maoli," stated Richard Kealoha Ho'opi'i Sr. at the same hearing.[83] Even as Kānaka Maoli answered "no" to the questions, they also insisted that the questions as asked were wrongheaded and offensive. Davis's comment about the questions' irrelevance was framed thus:

> The biggest thing is we need to have is clarity, we need to make right decisions for ourselves and our future. [The proposed rule change is] ... like settling for the crumbs when we actually own the whole cookie. How do we establish [a] government-to-government [relationship] when we are our own nation? There's so much confusion and laziness that's instilled in us, so we cannot even decipher what is right and what is wrong. The next generation is growing up to understand, to clear the muddy waters, our generation is still tryin' figure it out. These questions are irrelevant, we own the cookie, that's ours.[84]

After establishing that the DOI's questions were irrelevant to the larger project of nation-building and the future of the lāhui, which Kānaka Maoli must decide "for ourselves," Davis parlayed her refusal to acknowledge the authority of the DOI to a deep faith and pride in the "next generation." After her testimony, she turned part of her two minutes over to her young daughter. Her daughter, shy and holding her hands over her face, handed Davis her written testimony, which Davis then shared in 'ōlelo Hawai'i (Hawaiian language). Punctuated by five clear statements of "a'ole" in response to the five questions, her daughter's testimony signaled an intergenerational refusal and evidence of intergenerational change promising an ongoing life for the Hawaiian language and nation. Davis concluded their testimony by stating: "This land is for my children, this land is my land, this land is for the kūpuna. Return the land to the center."[85]

Indeed, as much as those testifying referenced the next generation and the future of the land and the lāhui, equally important were references to our kūpuna (elders, ancestors). Many shared their own stories of resistance or memories of the Hawaiian Kingdom passed down through their families. Many wore red ribbons, which they stated symbolized their support for Queen Lili'uokalani and an ongoing effort to keep alive the memory of the injustice of her overthrow and the continuing belief in a Hawaiian Kingdom. Speakers also repeatedly shared writing from previous eras of Kanaka Maoli resistance. This "writing from our kūpuna," as one speaker put it, most frequently drew from the mass organization in the late 1890s against the U.S. annexation of Hawai'i, which resulted in what is now known as the Kūʻe Petitions. With over 38,000 signatures of Kānaka Maoli against becoming an official territory of the United States, these petitions and the organization around them (brought to light by the research of Noenoe Silva as documented in her book *Aloha Betrayed*) were grounded in aloha ʻāina (love of the land and nation).[86]

For example, Wendy Espanola, also at the Molokaʻi hearing, testified, citing an article about the Kūʻe Petitions published in a San Francisco newspaper in 1897. After stating, "I say no to every single question that you ask," she read a quote included in the article by Emma Nāwahī, a respected Kanaka Maoli leader and organizer of the Kūʻe Petitions: "We Hawaiians have no power unless we stand together.... Let us show them ... we love our country and pray they do not take it from us. Shoulder to shoulder, heart to heart ... surely that country [the United States] will hear our cry. They must hear us."[87] Noting that there are many other quotes like this, Espanola went on to say, "the people are saying many of the things like we are saying today: tell America I don't want annexation, I want my Queen."[88] By linking the contemporary Kanaka Maoli resistance to U.S. settler colonialism to the prior resistance evident in the Kūʻe Petitions, Espanola and others educated the DOI panelists on the significant legacies of opposition to the federal government. In doing so, Espanola successfully reframed the discussion from a matter of federal recognition to an ongoing practice of aloha ʻāina that must refuse to accede to any actions that would take our country from us. The quote Espanola reads, citing Nāwahī's belief that the United States "will hear our cry" for justice, appeals to a higher morality to critique the unjust actions of the federal government in Hawaiʻi, both past and present.

Other statements launched from answering no to all the DOI's questions into more specific critiques of how the state limits Native Hawaiian access to land through blood quantum laws and other static commodification of Native Hawaiian membership, such as the Native Hawaiian roll (Kanaʻiolowalu), modeled after tribal rolls, which was created through the achievement of state recognition in 2011. Directly contradicting much of what was argued by the plaintiffs in *Day v. Apoliona*, as discussed earlier in this chapter, many Kānaka Maoli testified strongly against blood quantum policies, arguing that all Native Hawaiians should have rights to land, not only those with 50 percent and who thus have enough to qualify for a Hawaiian homestead. Notably, in the rule change that was eventually passed in 2016, the DOI maintains a very clear distinction between Native Hawaiians who are HHCA beneficiaries (i.e., those that have met blood quantum requirements and live on Hawaiian homesteads) and those who are not, with the stated intention of maintaining those beneficiaries' rights under the HHCA. While the newly formed Native Hawaiian government would not necessarily have a blood quantum requirement, then, the blood quantum requirement for Hawaiian homes would remain intact (unless overturned by other legislation).[89]

Some of the public hearings took place directly in Hawaiian homestead communities. While some expressed concern over the effect of federal recognition on their distinct status as homesteaders, many, including homesteaders, worried about their ability to pass their lots on to future generations, testified strongly against blood quantum policies, arguing that all Native Hawaiians should have rights to land, not just those who have enough "blood" to qualify for a Hawaiian homestead. For example, George Laiʻohi on Molokaʻi stated, "I speak on the behalf of my kupuna, my grandmother . . . 90 years so far holding to the homestead. I worried about that, you know. I have homestead too, I worried about that too. Because you know what, there never should have been a blood quantum, none. Hawaiian is Hawaiian is Hawaiian."[90]

Even the minority of Native Hawaiians who supported the rule change offered similar critiques of the blood quantum, such as Wilma Noelani Joy, also on Molokaʻi, who stated that her support of a new Native Hawaiian governing entity was conditional on whether "Native Hawaiian is inclusive hundred percent to one percent Hawaiian blood quantum. The limitation of the Hawaiian Homes Act of 50 percent must be redone."[91] Phyllis Uʻilani Kaʻahanui Cologne similarly testified: "My Native roots date back several generations before Captain Cook. . . . My concerns are as follows . . . there needs to be established a federal recognition to recognize us as Hawaiians. . . . I have multi-generations in my family, and I would like to keep my homestead within my family's confines. Lower the Department of Hawaiian Homelands' blood quantum and support the government, support our government, the Hawaiian nation government, and assist in all that is Hawaiian."[92] Like Joy, Cologne's support of federal recognition is conditional or dependent on the sense that with federal recognition there might be the ability to change the blood quantum requirement of the Hawaiian Homestead Commission Act.

Gene Ross Davis, who also identified as "a product of the homestead project," testified at the same meeting on Molokaʻi against federal recognition. In reference to the blood quantum, he stated, "We need small 'n' to swallow the big 'N' and put people on the land."[93] This reference about the "small n" and "big N" referred, of course, as discussed in connection with *Day v. Apoliona* above, to the legal distinction between Native Hawaiians with less than 50 percent blood and native Hawaiians who can prove they have more than 50 percent and are thus eligible for a homestead. Notably, the official transcriber of the hearings, who could not record Hawaiian language (in the transcripts there is simply a bracket stating "[speaking Hawaiian]" for all of the rich statements given in 'ōlelo Hawai'i), also misunderstood what Davis was saying here. The official transcript reads: "We need small ants to swallow the big ants and put people on the land."[94] Such errors and elisions allowed the DOI to ignore such testimony. For Davis, every person with Native Hawaiian ancestry should qualify as a "small 'n'" Hawaiian and have access to land in Hawai'i. In Davis's testimony, like the others described above, there is a strong rejection of the sense that those who already qualify for homesteads should defend their eligibility from potential "dilution claims," as the *Day* plaintiffs alleged. Davis and others demonstrated that native Hawaiians have important relationships among those with less than 50 percent "blood." Literally, many families with homesteads are concerned that they won't be able to pass them down to their children or grandchildren who may not meet the blood quantum requirements. More broadly, the statements point to a general sense that these divisions are damaging and unnatural for Native Hawaiians: "Hawaiian is Hawaiian is Hawaiian." Further, for at least a few of those testifying, blood quantum was beside the point because they argued that the lāhui should not consist of only Native Hawaiians, but should be a multiracial nation, just as the Hawaiian Kingdom was before the overthrow.

Another key aspect of the testimony at the DOI hearings was the way that Native Hawaiians engaged the analogy that the DOI was constructing between Native Hawaiians and Native Americans. Many commented on Native Americans during their statements, in both problematic and potentially constructive ways. There was a general desire to have the DOI representatives acknowledge that Native Americans and Native Hawaiians were significantly different, in large part because of the sense that the DOI was trying to mold Native Hawaiians to fit within the boxes the DOI uses to manage Native American affairs.[95] For example, Gene Ross Davis noted, "I give respect to my Native American brothers, but we should be classified differently."[96] For many the difference that they wanted the DOI to acknowledge between Native Hawaiians and Native Americans was the unique history of the Hawaiian Kingdom and its overthrow, annexation, and ongoing occupation by the United States. Some statements linked the injustices wrought by the United States on Indigenous peoples in both Hawai'i and in what is now the continental United States. Others seemed to suggest that Native Americans had been even more oppressed because they were subject to the DOI. For example, Sam Kealoha O'Hara noted in his testimony against federal recognition that "we are Native Hawaiians. We are not Indians.... We see how you treat Indians."[97] Kekane Pa at the Waimea, Kaua'i, hearing noted the potential for Native Hawaiian federal recognition to be modeled after the Alaska Native corporation model established by the 1971 Alaska Native Claims Settlement Act (ANCSA), as is indeed advocated by federal recognition supporters like Robin Danner. Pa argued that the "true purpose" of past and present federal recognition efforts was "to extinguish the aboriginal land title ownership of my people, the Native Hawaiians, and their national lands ... the Hawaiian people would receive a cash compensation for extinguishing of your aboriginal land title ownership that provided to the Alaskan settlement.... Same as the Native American Indians, people. They will give you a federal recognition without telling you you're giving up your land, and there goes it. Refuse federal recognition."[98] Pa thus evoked the long histories of land dispossession among Native Americans and Alaska Natives through treaties and ANCSA, in order to argue how hollow federal recognition would be for Native Hawaiians, especially because it could further dispossess Native Hawaiians of land.

While testimonies like Pa's generally pointed out the ways that Native Americans had been unjustly treated and implied that they deserved better, other comments in this vein were explicitly anti-Indian. In at least one of the hearings, one of the DOI representatives, Venus Prince, a member of the Poarch Band of Creek Indians, was disparagingly called "Pocahontas." Prince often talked at the beginning of the hearings about the benefits of federal recognition as she had experienced them in her tribe, which gained federal recognition in 1984.[99] Such disparaging comments were made in the context of apparent exasperation at the DOI representatives, who often seemed impassive or flustered by the repeated, passionate calls for independence for Hawai'i rather than federal recognition. Many Native Hawaiians told the representatives to "go home," because their questions were irrelevant. Many said the DOI was the wrong agency to be speaking to them, and that the DOI representatives should return to Washington, DC, and send back the State Department, which would be more appropriate to handling Hawai'i given their purview over international (rather than domestic) affairs.

Calling Prince "Pocahontas" obviously stemmed from this intense frustration with the DOI representatives for refusing to substantially discuss independence with the speakers. Nonetheless, these comments were upsetting to many because they indicated an internalization of settler colonial, racist, and sexist ideas about Native Americans that have been perpetuated through U.S. government policies, miseducation about Indigenous issues in most schools, and mainstream popular culture's sexualization of Native American women. As an epithet, "Pocahontas" could raise accusations of a Native woman's betrayal of her people (because the Pocahontas story generally romanticizes her relationship with the settler John Smith) or more broadly the sexualization of Native American women (the real Pocahontas is reported to have been twelve years old when she met John Smith).[100] Calling Prince Pocahontas in this context demeaned her expertise in American Indian policy by associating her with a sexualized fantasy, and more broadly rejected potential solidarity with Native Americans, whether they are federally recognized or not.

While most of the statements at the 2014 public hearings demonstrated a counterbalance to the *Day v. Apoliona* plaintiffs' attachment to restrictive ideas about blood quantum and the attendant pressure such policies place on Native Hawaiian women to marry and give birth to children with the proper blood quantum, the Pocahontas comment is one example of where these two examples are in closer alignment. The *Day* plaintiffs were also strongly against federal recognition, then in the form of the Akaka Bill, because it threatened to open up the membership of Native Hawaiians who might become part of a newly recognized Native Hawaiian government to anyone with Native Hawaiian ancestry, rather than only those with 50 percent blood. The *Day* plaintiffs thus sought to keep Native Hawaiian membership exclusive and tied to settler colonial ideas about blood quantum. The Pocahontas comment similarly reified divisions between Native Hawaiians and Native Americans and acceded to settler colonial ideas about Native Americans that many Native Hawaiians know are just as harmful and false as the settler colonial ideas perpetuated against Native Hawaiians. Fortunately, many other Native Hawaiians who testified demonstrated strong relationships with Native Americans and even evinced concern about how federal recognition for Native Hawaiians might impact Native American tribes. For example, one woman asked at the Moloka'i hearing: "It sounds to me like monies from the federal government coming down... into this one big pot.... We will be receiving monies like the Native... American Indians? I just want to make sure if it does happen... I just want to make sure that that these monies will not cause... any monies taking away from American Indians, that we will be fighting with one another, two nations facing nations."[101]

The DOI representatives explained that this was one reason why there would also be public hearings held with Native American tribes on the continent, but also that in general, Native American tribes would not be impacted by a new Native Hawaiian government because there would be separate funding sources. Later, another man asked, "How you going protect Native Hawaiians from disenrollment? They being disenrolled, guys, the leaders got power to disenroll from the tribe. How you going protect the Native Indians from what's going on already?"[102] His question similarly indexed a concern for Native Americans and what the federal government has put them through, while also acknowledging that a major problem facing tribes today—disenrollment—could be a shared problem under a new Native Hawaiian government.

---

In the end, the Department of the Interior dismissed these powerful statements and argued that the online comments they received from Native Hawaiians were largely in support of federal recognition. The DOI passed the rule change in September 2016, and will be facilitating a process to create a new Native Hawaiian government that the DOI will formally recognize. Despite this outcome, the statements demonstrated a significant rebuke to the federal government and the ongoing structure of settler colonialism in Hawai'i. Noelani Goodyear-Ka'ōpua writes of the statements: "If you are not moved by them, you are not listening closely enough."[103] My analysis of the statements in this chapter is motivated by a similar conviction that they represent an important resource and a unique archive that indexes a part of Native Hawaiian understandings about the future of the governance of the lāhui. In particular, they offer insight into the possible changes community members would like to see in issues such as blood quantum restrictions and land rights, and the kinds of coalitions that may be desired with Native Americans, other Indigenous peoples, and non-Indigenous allies.

In both the *Day v. Apoliona* case and the DOI rule change, each of these decisions (about the scope of the application of the 50 percent blood quantum rule and federal recognition, respectively) reaffirmed the authority of the state to determine the terms and membership of a Hawaiian nation. That the DOI ultimately ignored the majority of the statements that rejected federal recognition is similar to the Ninth Circuit Court of Appeals dismissing Native Hawaiian attempts to exert more authority over the terms of blood quantum legislation, even as the politics of these cases differ. Both the *Day* plaintiffs and the Native Hawaiians who testified at the public hearings sought some modicum of self-determination over their own affairs. In both cases, they were denied. What I have sought to highlight in this chapter is the significance of the difference in strategy and political positions of the *Day* plaintiffs and the speakers at the public hearings, and what each position opens or forecloses in terms of the future for Native Hawaiians.

Read in contrast to the *Day* plaintiffs, the statements at the DOI hearings offer a significantly different kind of refusal in the face of settler colonial state power. The *Day* plaintiffs sought more power before the law by, in effect, seeking to define Native Hawaiian identity through purity of blood, thereby acceding to the logic of possession through whiteness by reinforcing the eugenic idea that there are "pure" Native Hawaiians and "part" Native Hawaiians who are vanishing into whiteness. The DOI statements largely rejected this imposed division, as Native Hawaiians (largely ones who were homesteaders and thus did have at least 50 percent "blood") repeatedly stated that the 50 percent rule must be done away with and that "Hawaiians are Hawaiians are Hawaiians." Thus, the statements effectively showcased a move away from the kind of regeneration advocated by the *Day* plaintiffs—a regeneration that was in line with earlier eugenic notions of regeneration as staving off racial degeneration. Rather, the statements performed regeneration through refusal of both blood quantum logics and the authority of the Department of the Interior to determine the shape and boundaries of the lāhui. This regenerative refusal was consistently intergenerational and expansive, with an eye on both the strength of our ancestors and the importance of future generations. This kind of regenerative refusal is the kind of regeneration most productive in unsettling the logic of possession through whiteness animating the past and present of settler colonialism in Hawai'i and Polynesia. In the following chapters, I return to these ideas about regeneration and refusal as demonstrated in the work of other contemporary Native Hawaiian and Polynesian artists and activists.

CHAPTER 5

*The Value of Polynesian DNA*
Genomic Solutions to the Polynesian Problem

In October 2015, the Department of Hawaiian Home Lands (DHHL) announced a proposed rule change to allow the use of DNA testing to determine an applicant's eligibility in meeting the 50 percent blood quantum requirement required to lease a homestead. Announced prior to "beneficiary consultations" with homestead communities across the state in November and December of 2015, the proposed rule change was heralded as "Genetic Testing: Proposes DHHL accept DNA tests to establish family ties in order to qualify for the Hawaiian Home Lands program."[1] As discussed in chapter 4, the 50 percent blood quantum requirement is deeply divisive among Native Hawaiian communities. Thus, the announcement was met with a mix of suspicion but also, for some, hope. For those lacking proper documentation recognized by DHHL, this rule change could potentially rectify their status and allow them to qualify for a homestead. The substance of the rule change was limited to the use of paternity (and analogous) tests to determine direct relatives of people whose blood quantum was already properly documented. However, the generic language of "genetic testing" used in the announcement raised larger questions about what genetic ancestry tests can actually tell consumers and if such tests might qualify for establishing DHHL eligibility in the future.

In the nineteenth and twentieth centuries, the Polynesian Problem literature used linguistics, ethnology, and physical anthropology to formulate the relationship between Polynesians and Man. In the twenty-first century, this relationship is now often investigated through genetics and genomics. Jenny Reardon and Kimberly TallBear remark on the echoes of earlier social scientific inquiries regarding Indigenous peoples in contemporary genomics in their article, "Your DNA Is Our History." They note that anthropologist Henry Morgan understood Native Americans as representing an earlier stage of human civilization, and thus in his view, Native Americans and all their resources were the true inheritance of (white) Americans and indeed all (white) humanity. Reardon and TallBear argue this view of Native people as a natural heritage and resource of white people continues in new ways via genomics: "In recent decades, Native American DNA has emerged as a new natural resource that Native peoples possess but that the modern subject—the self-identified European—has the desire and ability to develop into knowledge that is of value and use to all humans."[2] TallBear has further written about Native American DNA as a rather recently invented, but highly desired and fetishized, "object of knowledge." She critiques the scientific construction of Native American DNA as a kind of "molecule-made-transcendent" for further confusing the often already poorly understood historical and political complexities of Native American tribal belonging.[3]

In the context of Polynesia, indigenous DNA has similarly been a much desired and sought-after "object of knowledge" in recent years. This chapter examines three linked areas of genetic and genomic research that impact or involve Polynesian people today: genomic mapping of ancient human migrations, genetic ancestry tests, and proposed genome biobanking projects.[4] Such research and direct-to-consumer testing are flashpoints for contemporary discussions of and debates over indigeneity and race in the Pacific. Genomic mapping research in particular has revived many of the same concerns of the late nineteenth-century Polynesian Problem literature examined in chapter 1, investigating where the Polynesian race originated and what routes they took as they expanded into the Pacific Islands. Genetic ancestry tests (which are based on studies involving genomic mapping of ancient human migrations) seem to offer hard evidence of individuals' ancestral origins, which appeals to many who for various reasons cannot prove their indigeneity to the state. Yet the tests also further codify indigeneity according to racial percentages, based on partial knowledge of a small number of a person's ancestors from tens of thousands of years ago. These percentages are then often approached as if they are evidence of blood quantum, as discussed in chapter 4, bringing new complications to already fraught meanings of Indigenous identity and legal recognition. Proposed genome biobanking projects in Hawai'i and Tonga have further triggered long-standing concerns about the monetization of Indigenous genetic material by scientific corporations and national governments.

Overall, this chapter traces the contemporary perpetuation of and resistance to the logic of possession through whiteness in genomics research and related technologies. The first section examines genomic mapping and critiques a common narrative that arises from this research from both genetic scientists and science writers—namely, that the extraordinary amount of genetic racial mixture in Hawai'i makes it a global example for the end of race and racism. I show how assumptions about both racial and gendered difference in science writing about Hawai'i are informed by settler colonial logics, and why it is important to carefully parse genetic narratives that make universal claims about humanity and its connectedness. The second section analyzes several ways in which direct-to-consumer genetic ancestry tests raise new challenges for how Native Hawaiian and other Polynesian individuals personally understand their identities and indigeneity, as well as how the state assesses and recognizes individuals' blood quantum for eligibility for a Hawaiian homestead. Finally, this chapter focuses on Kanaka Maoli regenerative refusals of the proposed Hawaiian Genome Project and how those refusals opened up possibilities for an anticolonial and antiracist critique that did not depend on a narrative of our common humanity. Instead, these refusals rerouted dominant ideas of race, gender, and indigeneity toward a more just definition of humanity itself. In the face of some of the threats that genomics newly poses, Indigenous peoples have acted in important, regenerative ways to protect their rights to self-determination, and in doing so demonstrate creative methods toward undoing the colonial, scientific foundations of Man.

## "HAWAI'I'S GENETIC MIXTURE GIVES THE WORLD A MODEL TO END RACE AND RACISM"

Today, dramatic headlines reporting on genomic and other scientific studies regularly proclaim new, seemingly definitive answers to ancient Polynesian origins: "Ancient Chicken DNA Reveals Philippines Home to Polynesians," "Polynesians Descended from Taiwanese, Other East Asians," and "'Polynesians Are All Sāmoans,' Says Captain of Voyaging Canoe Hokule'a."[5]

Such claims are enabled by scientists studying ancient human history through the identification of genetic markers specific to certain geographic populations. Such headlines must be understood within the longer history of the Polynesian Problem, with a critical analysis of what kinds of claims to indigeneity are being made, or being undercut, within various regional political contexts. For example, Indigenous groups in Taiwan sometimes promote studies that show Polynesian origins in Taiwan to strengthen their claims to a Pacific-oriented indigeneity separate from the Taiwanese nation-state.[6] At the same time, the Taiwanese government promotes the image of Indigenous Taiwanese peoples (though they are minority populations living with ongoing legacies of colonialism by the Taiwanese state) to strengthen their distinction from the Chinese mainland. Overall, narratives about Taiwan as a Polynesian homeland can be problematic for both Polynesians and Indigenous Taiwanese peoples. For Polynesians, these narratives can be used to represent Polynesians as immigrants from Taiwan to their native lands and therefore positioned equivalently to other immigrant citizens of settler states like New Zealand. For Indigenous Taiwanese, these narratives can sometimes portray them as merely genetic repositories for Polynesians.[7] Thus, for all such claims to genetic ancestral ties, it is essential to parse who is making these claims and why. Genomic evidence is increasingly used to bolster specific political agendas and identity claims, despite the fact that modern-day identities based in nation-states and races or ethnicities are being mapped onto ancient human populations and their migrations in time periods when Polynesia, Taiwan, and Sāmoa as we know them today did not exist.

More broadly, common narratives told by genomic scientists, in justifying the value of their work, as well as by popular media reports on genomics research tend to promote grand, ahistorical, and universalizing narratives about humanity, about who "we" all are and how we are related. This rhetoric mirrors other universalist tropes about humanity that enable dispossession of Indigenous peoples and others through nominal inclusion within Man (as conceptualized by the European Enlightenment), as I have discussed throughout this book. TallBear similarly analyzes such narratives in her book *Native American DNA*, skewering popular notions including "we are all African," "genetic science will end racism," "we are all related," "Native people are vanishing," and more. Despite seeming like stories that are "hopeful or inevitable ... multicultural and democratic," as TallBear points out, "These are not simply feel-good stories. They are not possible without histories of violence, and a critical reading from a standpoint that is in part indigenous makes that abundantly clear."[8] Showing how these narratives easily play into contemporary discourses of multiculturalism while maintaining older, problematic ideas about race, she persuasively argues that such science "does not undermine race and thus racism, but it helps reconfigure both race and indigeneity as genetic categories."[9]

One of many popular science books about genomics, Steve Olson's *Mapping Human History* draws on genomic studies about ancient human migrations to tell a universal story about who "we" are today. Olson's aim is to tell a grand new narrative about humanity's history from the findings of genomic studies. He frames his text with a common claim: genomics demonstrates that all humans, of all races, are genetically very similar; thus, genomic science will help end racism by proving there is no biological or genetic basis to race. He cites Himla Soodyall, an Indian South African geneticist with firsthand experience of the damaging effects of apartheid, as one voice of this common refrain. Soodyall says of her work on mitochondrial DNA, "These data have the potential to abolish racism.... Race is purely circumstantial. It establishes a social hierarchy that people can use to exploit others. But that hierarchy has no basis in biology."[10] Based on this knowledge, Olson and many others argue that if more people simply understood that race is not scientifically "true," then they would cease to be racist. With such claims, Olson echoes the rhetoric of the *What Is Race?* UNESCO pamphlet discussed in the introduction, which purported to educate the public about the scientific basis of race in order to eliminate racism, with similarly problematic results. Like the UNESCO publications, this rhetoric about genetic studies disproving the accuracy of racist views maintains the necessity of studying human genetics using race as a valid category.

This assumption that disproving the genetic basis of race will end racism is especially reminiscent of Romanzo Adams's belief, as examined in chapter 3, that racial intermarriage will end racism. In both cases, Olson's and Adams's assumptions are not only wrong, but actually contribute to erasing the ongoing structural violence of white supremacy and settler colonialism by making racism a matter of individual prejudice. As part I of this book has shown, far from being distanced from racism, biological and social sciences have been important sites of knowledge production about race that have unquestionably fueled racism.[11] This history is far from over, and it is naïve at best for contemporary scientists to ignore science's role in instituting settler colonial knowledge as fact. It is also clear from the history of the Polynesian Problem literature that the grand, universal humanity that is the subject of Olson's arguments deserves a deeper analysis. Indeed, very similar claims about Polynesia as the heritage of humanity allowed for the discursive construction of the Polynesian race as the natural possessions of whiteness, as noted in chapter 1.[12] Certainly, the idea of Polynesians being related to white people has never stopped scientific interest in studying difference in regard to the Polynesian race, and fears about Polynesians' possible proximity to blackness as well. Tregear's *Aryan Maori* emphasized the fraternal nature of Māori and white settlers, as analyzed in chapter 2, but this relationship was described consistently as a top-down, paternalistic view of Māori. The "familial" connection justified white settlement and possession over Indigenous resources, but also fueled social scientific inquiry that would calculate and commodify Indigenous difference.

Indeed, there is a certain fetish attached to Polynesia and Polynesians, more readily associated with romantic and touristic ideas of the region and its people, that also continues to circulate in scientific accounts. To return to Olson's *Mapping Human History*, this fetish is abundantly clear in his lavish account of Hawai'i. He writes: "Today visitors to Maui land on a runway just downwind from the shore where Captain Cook battled the surf eleven generations ago. Once out of the airport, they encounter what is probably the most genetically mixed population in the world. To the genes of Captain Cook's sailors and the native Polynesians has been added the DNA of European missionaries, Mexican cowboys, African-American soldiers, and plantation workers from throughout Asia and Europe. This intense mixing of DNA has produced a population of strikingly beautiful people."[13]

In this retelling, Captain Cook's "battle" is not with Native Hawaiians but more passively with "the surf" off Maui. This move displaces conflict between people to a conflict between "man" and nature. It further allows Olson to focus on the seemingly benign "mixing" between everyone in the long, diverse list. Notably, besides the "native Polynesians," all those in Olson's list are presumably men, because they are described in the form of traditionally masculine labor: sailors, cowboys, soldiers, and plantation workers. By contrast, Olson's primary examples of Hawai'i's "strikingly beautiful people" are tellingly feminine. He illustrates Hawai'i's "mixing" by noting, "Miss Universe of 1997 and Miss America of 2001 were both from Hawaii. The former, Brook Mahealani Lee, is a classic Hawaiian blend. Her ancestors are Korean and Hawaiian, Chinese and European."[14] Hawai'i and its racial mixture are represented here by literal beauty queens. Olson's choice of representatives, as well as his detailed list of Lee's racial makeup, strongly echoes the portrayal of mixed-race women from Hawai'i in Henry Inn's *Hawaiian Types*, as discussed in chapter 3. Like the portrayal of young mixed-race women as both the product and promise of a white settler possession of Hawai'i in the 1940s, Olson's association of genetic mixture with "beautiful people" is structured by a heteropatriarchal male settler gaze. This is again also structured by antiblackness in that the image of the racially mixed future is portrayed as a number of light-skinned, non-black women.

Studies of genetic ancestry, and the narratives popularized about these studies, are bound up in problematic assumptions not only about race, but also about gender and sexuality. Catherine Nash argues that while geneticists have been forced to reckon, at least minimally, with issues of race, "sex and sexual difference remain relatively unproblematized concepts within the field."[15] In studies of gendered migration patterns and other gender-related genomic mapping issues, Nash notes, "There is a sense in these accounts of a relaxed release from the political controversies about race that dog the subject. The pleasures of risqué science replace the risk and threat of race."[16] Olson demonstrates a similar "risqué" pleasure in writing about the gendered dynamics of the "intense mixing of DNA" in Hawai'i. This continues throughout the chapter on Hawai'i, far beyond the example of beauty queens as symbols of Hawai'i and its genetic mixture. In Olson's telling of Hawaiian history, for the "Polynesian inhabitants" of Hawai'i, the arrival of Cook's ship *Resolution* in November 1778 "must have looked as strange to them as a spaceship from another planet. Yet they responded without hesitation. They boarded canoes and paddled to the ship. From atop the rolling swells they offered the sailors food, water, and, in the case of the women, themselves."[17] In this breezy account of first contact, reminiscent of the American myth of the first Thanksgiving between Native Americans and the Pilgrims, the subsequent violence of Hawai'i's colonial history is erased. Olson focuses instead on Native Hawaiian women's innocence, openness, friendliness, and sexual promiscuity. In his telling, "lower-class" Polynesian women seeking a "rise in status" routinely traded "sexual favors for a tool, a piece of cloth, or an iron nail."[18] It is critical to challenge such accounts because they encourage an erroneous view of Polynesians—a sexualized white, male perspective of Polynesian women that is shaped by the settler colonial logic of possession through whiteness, though it is presented by Olson as neutral and "scientific."

When it comes to further explaining the promise of Hawai'i's genetic mixture, Olson's argument begins to run in contradictory directions. On the one hand, he insists on the near-magical effects of Hawai'i's high rates of racial intermarriage.[19] On the other hand, he later tempers the rapidity of this "clean slate" of human physical difference, noting that, "Of course, ethnic and even 'racial' groups still exist in Hawaiʻi, and they will for a long time. Despite the rapid growth of intermarriage in Hawaiʻi and elsewhere, the mixing of peoples takes generations, not a few years or even decades.... Five hundred years from now, unless human societies undergo drastic changes, Asians, Africans, and Europeans still will be physically distinguishable."[20]

In arguing both sides of this question, that "physical distinctions" will be, on the one hand, "wiped clean with a few generations of intermarriage" but on the other, that "the mixing of peoples" will not be complete even in the next "five hundred years," Olson effectively contradicts himself. Yet this contradiction allows a romantic image of Hawaiʻi's "strikingly beautiful" genetically mixed people to stand as an isolated case that he believes the world should aspire to. As with Adams and the Chicago School, Hawaiʻi remains a model and "experiment station" for the United States and the world, but isolated at a safe distance from it.[21]

Olson's perspective on Hawaiʻi's "beautiful" racial mixture and Polynesian women as primarily the sexual objects of male settlers also echoes the post–World War II discourses about racial mixture discussed in chapter 3 in significant ways. This is particularly true in terms of how Olson uses his descriptions of racial mixture in Hawaiʻi to suggest a grander vision of the "end of race" for all humanity. Not only is racial mixture in Hawaiʻi made representative of a potential global racial harmony, but also white settler men (specifically, Captain Cook and his men in Olson's account) are implicitly constructed as, in Silva's terms, the productive colonial force that creates the "strikingly beautiful" mixed-race Hawaiian subject, while discarding the darker-skinned female progenitors of this new race.[22] Olson, like Shapiro and others who wrote for UNESCO after World War II, argue that the simple fact of relatively large numbers of people of mixed-race heritage *existing* means that race will become less important. Yet, like the idea that proving there is no scientific basis to race will herald the end of racism, the fact of mixed-race people does not necessarily have any relation to changing ideas about race, as demonstrated in chapter 3. Further, as part I of this book shows, studies of mixed-race people have been directly implicated in scientific knowledge production that has strengthened racist and settler colonial ideas and material practices, such as the notion that mixed-race Hawaiians are already assimilated into white American society that helped institute the 50 percent blood quantum requirement for Hawaiian homes. Therefore, the story that mixed-race people herald the end of race is effectively a non sequitur that has for too long stood as a substantial argument because of the settler colonial logic of possession through whiteness.

Olson concludes his chapter with a final meditation on Hawai'i's example for humanity's future: "Ethnicity is not yet *entirely* voluntary in Hawaii, but in many respects the islands are headed in that direction.... When we look at another person, we won't think Asian, black, or white. We'll just think: person."[23] Through such a reading of genetic history, Olson's spin on the Polynesian Problem is effectively to declare race not dead but complexly related to one's microscopic genetic material, which science is destined to decode. This logic is key to keeping the Polynesian Problem open, despite the fact that the mapping of human history through genomics has confirmed that Micronesians and Polynesians are of "Island Southeast Asian origin," and followed "a colonization route along the north coast of New Guinea."[24] The question of who Polynesians really are both biologically and politically—that is, should a Polynesian identity really be biologically determined or, as Olson wishes, should everyone be free to choose—is still just indeterminate enough to justify both continuing the study of Polynesian genes and validating non-Indigenous claims to ownership of Polynesian lands and resources. In the end, Olson is convinced that while biological race may, unfortunately, always exist (at least in the sense that human populations can be differentiated by distinct haplotypes), the ways that societies interpret a person's "ethnicity" are beginning to be divorced from their biology. Indeed, this divorce seems to define the difference between "race"—a biological and usually visible marker—and "ethnicity"—the social and cultural distinctions between human populations, which he believes should not require any biological component.

For all his excitement about Hawai'i's genetic mixture, Olson envisions Hawai'i as a global model not of the end of race, but the end of race-based ethnicity. In the particular case of Native Hawaiians, he sees this as particularly desirable: for a Native Hawaiian to be defined in state law not by biology but as "instead a cultural, political, or historical distinction." In a way, this is what many (though not all) Native Hawaiians advocate themselves—as Native Hawaiians have long understood themselves as members of an overthrown independent nation, or at least as a historically (and contemporary) colonized people. Yet for Native Hawaiians, these distinctions are not about ethnicity; they are about indigeneity—about honoring one's ancestral and familial relationships and responsibilities to land and people. Further, Olson is misguided at best in his claim that "State law, for example, is gradually coming to define a Native Hawaiian as anyone with a single

Native Hawaiian ancestor." The 50 percent blood quantum requirement remains in full effect in order to qualify for a Hawaiian homestead, with little likelihood of that changing at all in the future. So too the use of a tribal roll, as I discussed in chapter 4, for the state and future federally recognized Native Hawaiian government complicates the ability of "anyone with a single Native Hawaiian ancestor" to qualify for official recognition, as it requires individuals to agree to the ways the state delineates how Native Hawaiians can be recognized.

Overall, though the genomics narrative that racial mixture in Hawai'i offers the world a model of how to end race and racism may make certain people feel good, my analysis shows that this story is just as unsupportable with seemingly more definitive genetic evidence as it was in the sociological work of Romanzo Adams. This story assumes that mapping human "connectedness" and projecting a new raceless future is self-evidently positive, in part by remaining ignorant of how very similar claims have long circulated from scientific knowledge production about Hawai'i and Polynesia. These claims explicitly supported settler colonial ideologies about "two types" of Polynesians, the blacker type destined to vanish and the whiter type becoming the basis of a new race. Beyond codifying racial difference, this narrative also depends on naturalizing settler colonial assumptions about gender, specifically in how Native Hawaiian women are made to represent the face of racial mixture and the new raceless future.

GENETIC ANCESTRY TESTS: NEW EVIDENCE
FOR STATE-RECOGNIZED INDIGENEITY?

While genomic studies of ancient human populations look at distant time periods in which modern-day identities would not have existed, many direct-to-consumer testing companies use such studies to exploit people's desires for quantifiable racial, ethnic, and/or indigenous origins. Lana Lopesi, a Sāmoan journalist, has written about her experience taking such a test from the company EasyDNA for *E-Tangata*, an online news journal directed toward Māori and Pasifika audiences in New Zealand. The DNA results found her to be, as she put it, "whiter than the milkman."[25] The test returned evidence of her mother's European ancestry, but none of her Sāmoan ancestry.[26] She responded: "the results are absurd. There was no trace at all of my Sāmoan father's bloodline."[27] She reviews the work of scholars like Deborah Bolnick who explain that such tests can only provide information about approximately 1 percent of one's entire genealogy.

Initially, Lopesi expressed fear about finding out that she's "over 50 percent European" because "being white will change completely who I claim I am: a Pacific woman."[28] Yet, having received the results, she finds the notion that her ancestral "regional affiliation" is "northern and southern Europe" laughable. Accordingly, she concludes that the test could not accurately explain her genealogy and identity, and that "the idea that I could have learned who I really am through DNA testing was nonsense."[29] She advises her readers not to waste their money on the $500 test.

Lopesi's account is refreshing in its open acknowledgment of the anxieties such tests often raise for Indigenous people, as well as its strong critique of how little meaning the tests ultimately hold about one's identity and relationships to people and land. This is a regenerative refusal in the sense that, though she tried the DNA test, she refuses to let the results determine how she thinks about her Indigenous identity and encourages others to do the same. Her take is in stark contrast to other popular writings that do attempt to craft narratives about humanity from the results of genomics studies. In many popular accounts, the ancient populations that scientists have identified through certain genetic mutations roughly correspond to today's major races.[30] Yet the ways that discourses of race overlay population genomics depends in large part on a common collapsing of popular understandings of race and population. Weiss reminds us that a strict differentiation must be made between race and the geographically based populations that genomics divines: "Nothing in genetic data suggests categorical 'race' divisions. It is obvious that individuals from the same geographic area are far from identical."[31] Writing with Jeffrey Long, Weiss has further argued for revising the assumptions of commonly used analytical software that abstract "distinct and independently evolved populations" ("pure" parental populations) out of which all of the people living today are admixtures.[32] Weiss and Long note that this admixture is often connoted to "mate exchange" during "colonial era migrations," as if no population movement or admixture occurred previously.[33] Expressing special concern about "'recreational' genetic ancestry analysis," which is always "approximate at best," they caution: "Genotypic affinity is related to, but not identical with, genetic or demographic ancestry. Genotypes may predict an individual's broad geographic ancestral homeland(s), but the homeland does not predict his genotype. Above all, a present-day population is not a literal ancestor!"[34]

Part of the confusion about genetic ancestry tests stems from the different types of tests that are available. Each differs from the others, at times enormously, though companies and popular television shows promoting such tests (such as NBC and the BBC's *Who Do You Think You Are?*) are often vague about which type of service is actually being used in any given test.[35] In short, direct-to-consumer (DTC) genetic ancestry tests are all quite blunt tools, ill-matched for the types of affiliations and histories that are indexed in contemporary forms of racial, ethnic, and Indigenous identities. Alondra Nelson concludes that they all provide "at best, a very approximate subcontinental origin at a point of time with very large uncertainty, typically somewhere between 5,000 and 40,000 years ago."[36] Also, these tests provide a window into only a very small part of any one person's genealogy—Y-DNA and mtDNA tests, for example, can only test one branch of paternal or maternal lineage, which is a fraction of a person's entire "family tree." While this does not necessarily mean that such tests are effectively meaningless for everyone, it does mean that such technologies do not provide self-evident, simple truths despite the contemporary tendency to view DNA as a kind of "molecule-made-transcendent."[37] These technologies are subjective (and often secret and proprietary to the specific genetic ancestry company) interpretations of a small and distant portion of one's ancient ancestry.

For some, genetic genealogy does allow for the recuperation of ancestry and identity lost through colonialism and slavery. Nelson shows that African Americans and others are increasingly using genetic technologies in service of powerful projects of social justice and reconciliation.[38] Direct-to-consumer companies such as African Ancestry offer users, among other services, genetic connections to specific ethnic groups in Africa, allowing them a modicum of personal genealogy that has otherwise been irretrievably lost through the history of the transatlantic slave trade. Companies like African Ancestry can be seen as exploitative in the sense that they generate profit from the desires of African Americans to recover the familial connections lost through the history of African slavery.[39] Yet Nelson also demonstrates through her ethnographic study of users of such tests that such consumers are largely not simply dupes who reorient their entire identity according to test results, despite the tendency of companies and television shows to hype the performance of a shocking "reveal." Rather, people often contextualize and make conscious choices about which parts of the test results to value within broader personal meaning-making projects related to their racial, familial, and national identities. Thus, many of the subjects in Nelson's study echo the sentiments of Lana Lopesi described above, in acknowledging that genetic ancestry test results cannot completely determine one's identity and genealogy.

Whatever opinion one has about DTC genetic ancestry tests, genetics researchers, including many who would identify as liberal and antiracist, often seem naïve at best about the reasons African Americans might turn to these tests to recover ancestral ties to Africa or why Indigenous peoples might require quantification and verification of their Indigenous ancestry for state or tribal forms of recognition. In *Mapping Human History*, Olson interviews Rebecca Cann, a genetics professor at the University of Hawaiʻi at Mānoa, who was involved as a graduate student in identifying "mitochondrial Eve" and has more recently focused her work on identifying genetic lineages in Polynesians and Micronesians.[40] Cann notes: "I get people coming up to me all the time and saying, 'Can you prove that I'm a Hawaiian?'"[41] Cann finds the question unsettling, concluding, "I get nervous when people start talking about using genetic markers to prove ethnicity. . . . I don't believe that biology is destiny. Allowing yourself to be defined personally by whatever your DNA sequence is, that's insane. But that's exactly what some people are going to be tempted to do."[42]

It is understandable that Cann would distance herself from the complicated business of determining Hawaiian-ness, which she is wholly unqualified for. Yet her response is ignorant of the ways that Native Hawaiians must demonstrate proof of their identity and difference in general ways (to distinguish themselves from the idea that "everyone is Hawaiian at heart," for example) and to meet specific legal requirements (i.e., providing documentation of 50 percent "blood" to qualify for a homestead). Cann instead characterizes the verification of Hawaiian-ness as a personal, and perhaps trivial, issue—one that some "insane" people might pursue—rather than an institutional problem created by state and federal governance and the larger structure of settler colonialism, which DTC genetic ancestry companies capitalize on.

To return to the example of the proposed rule change that would allow genetic testing to be used to determine eligibility for a Hawaiian homestead, as mentioned in the opening of this chapter, there are many who, for various reasons, lack the proper documentation to be recognized as Indigenous. The desire to use genetic technologies to fill in the gaps is understandable, even as there are indeed many reasons to be cautious about how science is being used in such cases. As reported by the *Honolulu Star-Advertiser*, the proposed rule change was sparked by the case of Leighton Pang Kee, a Native Hawaiian man who was initially denied eligibility for a homestead because he was adopted and his birth certificate did not include the name of his father.[43] Pang Kee sued DHHL in 2012 to be allowed to use a DNA test to determine a biological relationship to his late father's brother, which would then demonstrate that he had the proper blood quantum to be eligible. The DHHL eventually settled with Pang Kee, placing him on the waiting list for a homestead, and also decided to propose this larger rule change for others in similar situations.

While the case that sparked the proposed rule change was related to paternity testing (itself a type of identification that is implicated in heteropatriarchal norms that value authenticity through verification of legitimate fathers), the vague language of "genetic testing" raised larger questions. Would the DHHL begin accepting the results of genetic ancestry testing companies such as 23andMe, which purport to give consumers percentages of their racial backgrounds? DHHL spokespeople sought to reassure Native Hawaiians that such genetic ancestry tests would not be accepted to prove eligibility. As the *Star-Advertiser* reported, "The idea of using DNA to prove ancestry conjures up commercials advertising DNA testing kits. But those tests can't prove someone has Hawaiian ancestry, just that someone has general Polynesian ancestry."[44] Camille Kalama, a lawyer at the Native Hawaiian Legal Corporation, noted: "The testing to prove Hawaiian ancestry is more like a paternity test."[45]

However, such tests to determine paternity have been offered by DTC genetic ancestry companies, alongside their suite of other tests. Thus, the line between the types of genetic ancestry services discussed above and DNA paternity tests is considerably more blurred than Kalama suggests. Kim TallBear discusses such tests to determine immediate biological relationships (that is, links between one or two generations, rather than tens of thousands of years), which are alternately called DNA profiles, DNA fingerprints, or DNA parentage tests. Some Native American tribes use these tests to determine eligibility for tribal membership. TallBear clearly states that a "tribe is not, strictly speaking, a genetic population. It is at once a social, legal, and biological formation, with those respective parameters shifting in relation to one another."[46] Yet she finds that some tribes employ DNA parentage tests precisely because they can fit with notions of tribes as genealogically tied, which differs from seeking out DNA tests to simply verify the presence of generic "Indian blood."[47] Nonetheless, TallBear also shows that there is often a lot of confusion among tribal members about the difference between these DNA profile tests to determine genealogical connection and other genetic ancestry products that provide racial percentages, and sometimes in how companies market the tests as well.[48]

For DHHL, the rule change process could take years, and it remains unclear if such testing will be systematically accepted or which companies will be approved to provide such tests. As of this writing, the DHHL website states: "DHHL does not currently allow the use of DNA testing for the purposes of verifying blood quantum eligibility. However, the Department is examining the matter closely."[49] Despite the efforts of DHHL-affiliated spokespeople to differentiate between paternity-like testing and other genetic tests, the anxiety about genetic testing determining Native Hawaiian identity and eligibility for land leases will likely persist. For other Polynesians, blood quantum verification may not be as relevant, given the lack of laws like the Hawaiian Homes Commission Act that requires 50 percent blood, but as Lopesi's account above indicates, the logic of racial percentages being determined by genetic science has a much wider reach. For, as genetic ancestry testing technologies proliferate, it is often unclear to the public how DNA tests to determine paternity differ from other tests that provide information about a person's ancestry on the scale of thousands of years ago (often calculated through comparing a consumer's DNA sample to proprietary databases). Alondra Nelson has referred to the slippages between distinct genetic testing technologies as "DNA spillover," which "occurs when an individual's experience with one domain of genetic analysis informs his or her understanding of other forms of it or authorizes its use in another domain."[50] Genetic ancestry companies often seem to depend on this DNA spillover in getting their customers to buy into their services and trust that the results they receive are, as Nelson notes, as unassailable as the use of DNA in criminal forensics. Next, I discuss a final area of genomics that impacts Native Hawaiians and Polynesians: genome biobanking. In this case, DNA spillover did not function in favor of a proposed Hawaiian Genome Project, as Native Hawaiians did not find the project's promise of potential genetic answers to their medical problems sufficient cause to allow their DNA to be "banked" by researchers.

REGENERATING KANAKA MAOLI CONCEPTS OF HUMANITY
AFTER THE HAWAIIAN GENOME PROJECT

Almost daily it seems there is a news article proclaiming new discoveries about the Māori having a "warrior gene," or Pacific Islanders being genetically destined to be football players.[51] Such discourses combine with sobering statistics about Polynesians' genetic susceptibility to obesity and diseases such as diabetes to propagate rather fatalistic community understandings of what it means to be Polynesian. As Lena Rodriguez and James Rimumutu George argue in their sociological study of Polynesian communities living in Australia, the common language of "high risk" in relation to diabetes has "contributed to an idea pervasive among Polynesians that such ailments are genetically 'inevitable.'"[52] Diabetes should not be a fatal disease, as it has been shown to be treatable through proper management of diet and exercise.[53] Yet, Rodriguez and George argue, because of lack of access to proper care and education, as well as because treatment for diabetes is often described as a project of individual care that contravenes the communal nature of meals for many Polynesians, combined with the sense of genetic "inevitability," many Polynesians do die from diabetes.

Nonetheless, genomics continues to be promoted to Polynesian communities as holding potential answers to diabetes and other diseases. Below, I focus on the proposed Hawaiian Genome Project (HGP) and the largely negative response it elicited from Native Hawaiians. Yet it is important to point out from the outset that there is no singular response from the Native Hawaiian community toward genomic projects targeting Native Hawaiians, just as there is no singular response to the 50 percent blood quantum rule or the issue of federal recognition, as discussed in chapter 4. Some Native Hawaiians are in favor of genomic projects, as long as they conform to certain guidelines that ensure Native Hawaiians can exercise free, prior, informed consent and that there is some form of governance and continued information about the ways in which their genetic samples are used. A study by Maile Tauali'i and colleagues, for example, showed that among ninety-two participants in focus groups throughout Hawai'i, all of them theoretically supported biobanking because of the potential "benefits of medical research and how it led to advancements in preventing, diagnosing, and treating disease."[54] Further, the study showed that many of the participants "noted that participating in research operationalized the Native Hawaiian value of helping others and contributing to the common good."[55]

Following the critiques made in the previous two sections, my analysis here is interested in how Native Hawaiians, and other Polynesian and Indigenous peoples, might effectively refuse not (just) genomic studies per se but the broader rhetoric of "helping others" and contributing to the "common good" when such discourses are used to further settler colonial aims. Tauali'i and colleagues, along with many other scholars, including TallBear and Reardon, have written productive critiques suggesting a variety of ways to ethically engage Indigenous communities in genomic research—from rigorous standards of free, prior, informed consent (and re-consent) and approvals by both university and Indigenous nations' institutional review boards to innovating new methodologies to incorporate cultural protocols, or understanding Indigenous DNA samples as "on loan" and to be returned to the Indigenous community along with the results of the study after its completion.[56] Such critical work is undeniably essential to protecting Indigenous peoples' rights. Though indebted to such productive scholarship, my analysis is a more structural critique, directed at unsettling the rhetoric of "common good" that genomic studies so often deploy, which I argue are grounded in the deeply exploitative, settler colonial underpinnings that work to incorporate Indigenous peoples into a Western ideal of Man, often with dire consequences for Indigenous peoples.

During the Cold War, the United States tested nuclear weapons in the Marshall Islands, arguing that these tests were vital "for the good of mankind." The nuclear tests rendered some islands uninhabitable and caused thyroid cancer and miscarriages among the Marshallese people. Thus, the rhetoric of scientific studies for the common good, which produce violence against Indigenous peoples and lands, is far from new in the Pacific Islands. Saying no to scientific research may require repositioning all people within Indigenous conceptions of the human and liberating us all from the Western ideal of Man as the individual, transcendent subject. Indeed, in response to the Hawaiian Genome Project, some Native Hawaiians repositioned themselves within a Native Hawaiian understanding of humanity, rather than a European one. I believe this example hints at what Indigenous peoples and their allies might do to effectively decolonize the relationships between science and settler colonialism, beyond simply making science more culturally competent or including better consent (though these should indeed be necessary prerequisites to any scientific project). Below, I offer the context of the HGP before discussing some Native Hawaiian responses.

Charles Boyd, a professor at the Pacific Biomedical Research Center at the University of Hawai'i at Mānoa, proposed the Hawaiian Genome Project in 2003. The HGP was proposed as a type of gene bank, which can be defined as "a stored collection of genetic samples in the form of blood or tissue, that can be linked with medical and genealogical or lifestyle information from a specific population, gathered using a process of generalized consent."[57] The most famous gene bank is the deCODE project, run by a U.S.-based company but located in Iceland. DeCODE was authorized by the Icelandic parliament in 1998 and heralded the potential to map the genome of the Icelandic people, in the interest of discovering possible genetic causes (and remedies) of diseases.[58] This was conducted through analysis of the health records of all Icelandic people, which Iceland's government licensed to deCODE, along with blood samples volunteered from about 50 percent of the country's citizens, from which DNA information was extracted. DeCODE was interested in the Icelandic population because it was relatively homogeneous, given its isolated island location as well as having experienced several historic catastrophes (bubonic plague in the 1440s, and smallpox as well as a devastating volcanic eruption in the 1700s). These catastrophes resulted in "genetic bottlenecks"—in other words, the deaths of large percentages of the population reduced the population's available genetic material. Those who survived these catastrophes in isolated locations become a relatively small group of "founders" for the following generations, resulting in a significant narrowing of the population's genetic diversity.

The genetic homogeneity of Iceland and the overall importance of genetic studies focused on populations shaped by "founder effects" are both contested.[59] Yet the common reasoning given for why genetic homogeneity is important is that genomics studies on disease depend on uncovering genetic causes (different genetic mutations) in a population for a certain disease by comparing that population's genetic data to a "healthy" population. A genetically heterogeneous population presents a less reliable data set for this purpose because greater genetic diversity overall makes the differences between healthy and unhealthy populations less apparent. Somewhat ironically, given Hawaiʻi's constant praise today as a diverse melting pot, it was precisely the Native Hawaiian population's perceived genetic homogeneity that interested Boyd and colleagues in sequencing a "Hawaiian genome." As Lindsey Singeo describes it: "Already an isolated society, the Hawaiian population became even more homogeneous as a result of massive epidemics and population reduction during the mid-1880s. During this time, foreigners introduced previously unknown diseases to Native Hawaiians, including measles, whooping cough, mumps, and smallpox. Unlike the foreigners, Native Hawaiians lacked the immune system resistance and suffered significantly high mortality rates."[60]

Thus, in a strange (or perhaps only fitting) way, it was precisely the effects of colonialism—depoliticized in the rhetoric of the project's proposers as the natural if tragic impact of measles, whooping cough, mumps, and smallpox—that made the Native Hawaiian population genetically homogeneous and particularly attractive to genomics researchers. Yet the project obliquely proposed to compensate for the contemporary legacies of colonialism—namely, health disparities faced by the Native Hawaiian community—by potentially providing genetic information to explain Native Hawaiians' higher risk for diseases including diabetes, hypertension, and renal disease.[61]

If the "Hawaiian genome" proved fruitful, it could also potentially be licensed to the UH researchers by the Native Hawaiian community (after the Icelandic model) for a certain monetary amount. This possibility is reminiscent of the corporation model of some Alaska Native tribes that some would like to emulate in a potential federal recognition for Native Hawaiians, as discussed in chapter 4. Like that model, promoting the HGP as a matter of financial benefit sidestepped the matter of self-determination and what Native Hawaiians might actually want, besides money, from such research. A University of Hawai'i magazine article announced the project by advertising its potential to provide medical and financial benefits to the Native Hawaiian community, claiming, "It's a potentially lucrative market—Roche pharmaceutical company paid $200 million outright for rights to the Icelandic genome, which underwent a similar bottleneck."[62] In any case, how much commercialization the Hawaiian Genome Project might involve was quite unclear at the time the magazine article was published.

There are other models that the HGP could have drawn from that would not have any corporate involvement or would limit such involvement instead of granting companies exclusive rights.[63] Yet there had also recently been a gene bank project proposed in Tonga in 2000 by Autogen, an Australian biotechnology company, which did closely follow the Icelandic model. In this proposed study, the Kingdom of Tonga's Ministry of Health signed an agreement with Autogen to build a private database of all Tongan citizens' genetic information. Reportedly, this database would have been owned by the Kingdom of Tonga, not Autogen, but Autogen would receive exclusive access to the database to pursue disease-related drug research.[64] In exchange, Autogen promised funding to the Tongan Ministry of Health, royalties on future drug patents developed from the database, and access to any such drugs for free.[65] While, initially, the Tongan government claimed that there were no concerns registered among Tongans, the project was never carried out due to local opposition, especially from church groups, who, as Austin and colleagues report, "objected to the 'conversion of God created life-forms, their molecules or parts into corporate property through patent monopolies.'"[66] There were also likely concerns about the government owning the people's genetic information in perpetuity.

The Native Hawaiian community also strongly objected to the proposed HGP. As with the Tongan project, licensing a "Hawaiian genome" to the university violated a number of cultural and religious beliefs. Further, the HGP seemed to many Native Hawaiians to be both an obvious extension of historic and ongoing colonial expropriation of Native Hawaiian lands and resources, and a potential replication of other seemingly exploitative genetic studies such as the patenting of a cell line of an Indigenous Hagahai man from Papua New Guinea by the U.S. National Institutes of Health.[67] In November 2003, the Association of Hawaiian Civic Clubs issued a resolution "Urging the University of Hawai'i to Cease Development of the Hawaiian Genome Project or Other Patenting or Licensing of Native Hawaiian Genetic Material Until Such Time as the Native Hawaiian People Have Been Consulted and Given Their Full, Prior and Informed Consent to Such Project."[68] This resolution made explicit reference to the modeling of the HGP after Icelandic deCODE project, and asserted that such licensing of Native Hawaiian genetic material and the mapping of a Hawaiian genome would require the prior, informed consent of all Native Hawaiian people, since "the Hawaiian genome represents the genetic heritage of our ancestors and is the collective property of the Native Hawaiian people."[69] The resolution further drew comparisons to the activism of other global Indigenous peoples, arguing that "other Indigenous peoples globally and regionally have declared a moratorium on any further commercialization of Indigenous human genetic materials until Indigenous communities have developed appropriate protection mechanisms."[70] Another declaration was issued after a Native Hawaiian Intellectual Property Rights Conference was held in October 2003, which further condemned the theft of "the biogenetic materials of our peoples, taken for medical research for breast cancer and other diseases attributable to western impact" as acts of "biocolonialism."[71]

These protests led the HGP to be discontinued. The strong response from the community surprised the project's founders, who seem to have genuinely believed that the "self-evident" medical and financial benefits to Native Hawaiians would accord them a willing participatory population. The response was thus very similar to a more famous example of genomic researchers' surprise: namely, in regard to the case protesters brought against the Human Genome Diversity Project (HGDP) shortly after its proposal in 1994.[72] Given the HGDP's sincere efforts to respond to the critiques ethically, scholar Jenny Reardon argues: "These were not self-seeking researchers who sought to extract the blood of indigenous peoples for the sake of financial and political gain. They were scientists who sincerely hoped to create a project that would deepen the stores of human knowledge while fighting racism and countering Eurocentrism. It would be historically inaccurate, and morally insensitive, to understand the Diversity Project as an extension of older racist practices by labeling the initiative the product of white scientists wielding the power of science to objectify and exploit marginalized groups."[73]

I doubt neither the sincerity of Luigi Luca Cavalli-Sforza and others' desire to conduct antiracist work nor the functional difference Reardon is pointing out between "research for research's sake" (or "research for humanity's good") and research to fuel a business's profits. Certainly both types of research exist within the genomics field—from rather questionable DNA ancestry tests offered by biogenetic companies on one end of the spectrum to federally funded top-tier genomics research on the other.[74] The wide variety of genomic scientists and entrepreneurs cannot all be branded the same. Nonetheless, we still urgently need critiques of scientific projects created with the best intentions but that perpetuate colonial damage on Indigenous peoples. For it is precisely this liberal universalism, and the incorporation of Polynesians into whiteness, that was so formative of the Polynesian Problem literature of the late nineteenth and early twentieth centuries. Decolonizing Hawai'i and Polynesia more broadly will continue to require wrestling with not only the problems of what Reardon terms "older racist practices" but also the more fundamental colonial practices that are compatible with and constitutive of contemporary liberalism and capitalism.

To begin with, the very invention of something that can be recognized as "the" Hawaiian genome, much less that thing's total sequencing and potential licensing/ownership, is something that deserves more reflection. For in the manifestation of a genome, concerns of possession and property reveal themselves in particularly complicated ways. A genome denotes an organism's complete set of genes, and thus genomics denotes the study of the interactions between those sets of genes, whereas genetics more specifically refers to the study of singular genes in relative isolation. A genome is at once a living part of a human being and an abstraction based on relative genetic similarities in a defined population—the population in this case being Native Hawaiians. Thus, a genome is a kind of organic "thing" that nonetheless can only be materialized and studied in the "captivity" of a laboratory. In the particular gene bank model that the Hawaiian Genome Project proposed, the DNA samples collected from Native Hawaiians likely would have been subject to "immortalization" in lymphoblastoid cell lines (LCLs), as the samples collected in the Human Genome Diversity Project were.[75] This immortalization allows the DNA sequences to be preserved and replicated, shared and sold among scientists according to the specific types of consent and ethical protocols under which the samples were collected.

As pitched to Native Hawaiians, we can understand the HGP as having offered Native Hawaiians a share in the ownership of a "Hawaiian genome." This genome was a newly conceptualized kind of privatized property potentially to be held in common by Native Hawaiians as a group, though the actual material of the genome would be located at the University of Hawai'i, in the care of scientists. Thus, ownership of the "Hawaiian Genome" is haunted by other types of ownership that turn out to be much more limited—as in the case of the Hawaiian Homes Commission Act, which leases homesteads to Native Hawaiians, homesteads that are perpetually owned and held in trust by the state, as discussed previously. The subtle, motivating logic of the HGP in exhorting Native Hawaiians' participation was classically liberal: since, theoretically, every Native Hawaiian would have access to the materials necessary to creating this genome in their own body, Native Hawaiians had a moral, national, civilizational duty to exploit those resources for their own and the common good. By refusing to license or lend their genome to the university, or even to acknowledge that such an entity exists and that it is perfectly described by Western science, Native Hawaiians risked seeming not only "stingy"—denying the common good of science—but also self-destructive, refusing a desperately needed opportunity that would potentially offer medical answers and treatments, as well as money.

Such subtly implied self-destruction uncannily recalls turn-of-the-century discourse on the reasons for the degeneration of the Polynesian race, discussed in chapters 1 and 2. For Native Hawaiians, degeneration was an especially influential discourse at the time of Hawai'i's annexation to the United States in 1898. Alexander Twombly, author of *The Native Hawaiian of Yesterday and To-Day*, published in 1901, put it this way: "Hawaiians die when the white man lives. The latter exercises a measure of self-control for selfish ends. The former shows little or no self-control for any ends. To sum up, the native Hawaiian of to-day is an anomaly in civilization.... The half-caste has not the same obstacles to contend with, and assimilates in greater degree with modern progress."[76]

Twombly demonstrates here his belief in the "half-caste" as the only possible future for the Hawaiian race because it is necessary to physically infuse the Hawaiian race with "a measure of self-control for selfish ends"—a critically apt description of the requirements of U.S. citizenship, for Twombly particularly saw Hawaiian degeneration in their failure to grasp the importance of owning land. He wryly noted: "It is a sign of the tendency to degenerate when men care little for the possession of land."[77] The apparently extreme depths of this degeneration, though described as moral, behavioral, or cultural failings, were ultimately blamed on the biological. Twombly, like many others, believed that nothing would be able to be done for Native Hawaiians until they had received a substantial racial infusion of whiteness. Ultimately, the Hawaiian race would disappear and be replaced by the growing numbers of "half-castes" more biologically disposed to become part of the white settler society.

In the context of genomics, Native Hawaiian refusal to participate in the development of biotechnology that might produce innovative new medical treatments for diseases that Native Hawaiians are susceptible to can still be read as a failure to exercise "a measure of self-control for selfish ends," and thus to give in to degeneration even when it is not environmentally inevitable. This situation also illustrates the point that whiteness is understood as a kind of property that one must carefully manage, protect, and control—because, as Margaret Radin and Cheryl Harris remind us, controlling one's whiteness is a mode of controlling one's expectations for the future, and one's very personhood depends on the realization of these expectations.[78] Seen this way, controlling, decoding, objectifying, and commercializing one's genome has developed as a new form of whiteness as property that one must carefully manage and protect.

Native Hawaiians refusing the HGP registers within a settler colonial framework as a refusal of development, reproduction, and life itself—a choice that scientists find difficult to parse, especially after they prove themselves eager to combat the valid problems of racism and colonialism. A few years after the proposed Hawaiian Genome Project, a similar situation also arose between the Native Hawaiian community and the University of Hawai'i when researchers there proposed to genetically modify kalo, the Hawaiian name for the taro plant, a traditional staple starch in the Hawaiian diet. As Noelani Goodyear-Ka'ōpua notes in her analysis of protests against GMO taro that took place beginning in 2006, "[c]ommunity organizers and farmers . . . saw in any move to commodify kalo connections to the encroaching forms of commercial agriculture practices by large biotechnology corporations [such as Monsanto], including genetic modification and field testing in Hawai'i."[79]

Native Hawaiian leaders including Walter Ritte spoke out against genetic modification of kalo, noting that genetic engineering was a kind of "mana māhele, which means owning and selling our mana or life force."[80]

Māhele here also evokes the Great Māhele, the change in land ownership laws in the Hawaiian Kingdom in 1848 that ultimately allowed white settlers to gain power in Hawai'i. In this respect, māhele signals a cautionary colonial tale for what Ritte is suggesting could be just as or more devastating at the genetic level. While Kānaka Maoli argued that kalo was sacred and inextricable from Kanaka Maoli lives, and thus it would be reprehensible to genetically modify it, researchers promoted the genetic modification as a biotechnological improvement that was "necessary to increase crop yields, improve pest and disease resistance and advance scientific research."[81] Though a provisional five-year moratorium on genetically modifying taro was passed in the state legislature in 2008, the Native Hawaiian case was often represented as simply a "cultural" one, whereas biotechnology proponents represented "progress"—delayed for now, but destined to win out, through more "culturally competent" means if necessary.[82]

Yet, on closer examination, the Native Hawaiian protests against the HGP and the genetic modification of kalo were significantly more complicated than their gloss as "cultural difference" implies. This is clear in a closer examination of the two statements issued in response to the HGP in 2003 by the association of Hawaiian Civic Clubs and the Native Hawaiian Intellectual Property Rights Conference. For the Hawaiian Civic Clubs, there is not a strict critique of capitalism or of a notion of isolating a Hawaiian genome. Their resolution, in fact, takes both the existence of a Hawaiian genome and the classification of this genome as property as given, stating: "The Hawaiian genome represents the genetic heritage of our ancestors and is the collective property of the Native Hawaiian people."[83] In this way, the Civic Clubs object less to the science of the HGP than to the assumption that a gene bank could commercialize the Hawaiian genome. In their account, the HGP is not viable until there are better protections in place for Native Hawaiians to be properly informed and benefit from or "equitably share" the results from such a project.[84]

The Paoakalani Declaration issued by the Native Hawaiian Intellectual Property Rights Conference (NHIPRC) goes farther in its critique, which it does not limit to the HGP. Nor does the declaration make reference to anything called a "Hawaiian genome." Rather, it forcefully problematizes "bioprospecting and biotechnology institutions and industries," which are "imposing western intellectual property rights over our traditional, cultural land-based resources. This activity converts our collective cultural property into individualized property for purchase, sale, and development."[85] Further, the NHIPRC group insists on a complete moratorium on any kind of gene bank project: "Kanaka Maoli human genetic material is sacred and inalienable. Therefore, we support a moratorium on patenting, licensing, sale or transfer of our human genetic material."[86] In the Paoakalani Declaration critique, it is not only the University of Hawai'i that is the subject of critique but also "the pharmaceutical, agricultural and chemical industries, the United States military, academic institutions and associated research corporations," all of which are implicated in biocolonialism in Hawai'i.[87]

While this Declaration draws on the notion of human rights and references other resolutions supporting Indigenous rights, as the Civic Clubs resolution also does, it also calls for a more fundamental unsettling of what humanity is. The NHIPRC authors reformulate the place of humanity within Hawaiian epistemology rather than accepting wholeheartedly the purportedly "universal" Western notion of humanity, writing that:

> According to the Kumulipo, a genealogical chant of creation, Po gave birth to the world. From this female potency was born Kumulipo and Po'ele. And from these two, the rest of the world unfolded in genealogical order. That genealogy teaches us the land is the elder sibling and the people are the younger sibling meant to care for each other in a reciprocal, interdependent relationship. Humanity is reminded of his place with the order of genealogical descent. The foundational principle of the Kumulipo is that all facets of the world are related by birth. And thus, the Hawaiian concept of the world descends from one ancestral genealogy.[88]

Thus, the Declaration repositions humanity as the apex of all organic life, siting humans as the "younger siblings" of the "elder sibling," land. In Hawaiian epistemology, then, land is not property but a form of genealogy and knowledge. This knowledge is actively formed and participated in, rather than simply accessed, shaped by a "reciprocal, interdependent relationship" between family members, humans, and the land. The Declaration reminds its readers that human life is interdependent with the life of the land; and land is indeed a living, knowing thing that all humans look up to as to a wiser elder sibling. The ways that this epistemology subverts popular heteropatriarchal notions of land as "virgin" or "mother" are also significant. The creator of the world was a "female potency," not necessarily a maternal figure. Land is not "Mother Earth," nor a sexualized thing to conquer and make reproduce, but humanity's sibling, someone with whom humans might have a complex, mutually sharing relationship.

Overall, what the Paoakalani Declaration envisions, then, is a form of Native Hawaiian indigeneity that is not property, as whiteness is. Indigeneity is constructed as something that is not possessable by whiteness at all, since it is premised on entirely different conceptualizations of land and the human. Compared to the Hawaiian Civic Clubs resolution, the Paoakalani Declaration intends to have a broader impact. For the Declaration recognizes, similarly to the Hawaiian Civic Clubs resolution, that Native Hawaiians need protections within laws that privilege the Western concept of Man, but refuses that they should *only* understand themselves, their "genetic material," and other "collective cultural property" within such colonial frameworks. The approaches of the Hawaiian Civic Clubs and the NHIPRC are both regenerative, in my analysis—both seek to avert new forms of colonialism and thus promote a different kind of future for Native Hawaiians. But where the Hawaiian Civic Clubs responded within the existing Western frameworks of institutional review boards and principles such as "reciprocity" and "equitable sharing," the NHIPRC challenged the very foundations of such principles. These divergent approaches thus parallel the differences between the *Day* plaintiffs arguing within the confines of blood quantum laws and the speakers at the DOI hearings against the entire system of U.S. settler colonialism. The Paoakalani Declaration argues that making genomic science more culturally competent and alert to Indigenous peoples' rights to free, prior, informed consent will not necessarily overturn the colonial basis of such science. In this way, the NHIPRC demonstrates an effective form of regenerative refusal, one that, like those examined in the preceding chapters, makes a strong stand against settler colonial logics and processes, even when such refusal is portrayed as ignorant or bad behavior by mainstream media and the state.

---

This chapter has argued for the importance of understanding the logic of possession through whiteness, first produced in the Polynesian Problem social scientific literature of the late nineteenth and early twentieth centuries, as continuing to inform knowledge production in genomics about both the specific ancient origins of Polynesians and broader notions about racial mixture and human "connectedness." While contemporary science insists that biological racism has long been debunked and imagines genomic population histories as a method of permanently eradicating racism and even the boundaries of ethnicity, this chapter illustrates that such eagerness to "move beyond race" and the apparent surprise of liberal scientists who find their "savior" efforts rebuffed by Indigenous protests really demonstrate the many ways that contemporary science remains rooted in Western, colonial, and racist definitions of Man. Even as we remain aware of how such ideologies have affected how Native Hawaiians ourselves understand our people and humanity more broadly, Native Hawaiians and other Polynesian peoples are among the global Indigenous peoples leading efforts to effectively decolonize both the practices of science and Western notions of humanity altogether.

The kinds of regenerative refusal highlighted in this chapter, from Lana Lopesi's refusal to let DNA ancestry test results determine how she identifies as a Sāmoan and Indigenous Pacific woman, to the refusal of the Tongan government's proprietary database of Tongan DNA, to the various Kanaka Maoli refusals to participate in the Hawaiian Genome Project, showed some of the specific ways that regenerative refusal operates in relation to Western scientific projects. Western science often narrates the significance of its studies as furthering universal knowledge, and pretends that its findings are unassailable truth. Indigenous people refusing such studies incur charges of being backward, anti-science, acting against their own best interests financially and medically, and so on. Yet the refusals considered in this chapter are not anti-science; rather, they demonstrate a commitment to protecting and fostering Indigenous knowledges and epistemologies. At the center of such epistemologies is the importance of relationality to other forms of life, like kalo, which Kānaka Maoli are meant to treat with respect and care as they would an elder sibling. Through refusing to allow capitalist and Western scientific norms to replace such practices of relationality, these forms of regenerative refusal model important ways of acting to perpetuate Indigenous narratives about how to be and thrive in the world.

CHAPTER 6

*Regenerating Indigeneity*
Challenging Possessive Whiteness in Contemporary
Pacific Art

A woman's body lies on the concrete tiles in front of the lei stands at the Honolulu International Airport, facing away from us, one arm stretched over her head (figure 6.1). Her body is covered with purple orchid lei. On the wall at her feet hang many more lei for sale: white tuberose, pink carnation, yellow-orange puakenikeni. Her face is not in view, only the top of her head. She might be gazing up at the sky. She might be dead. Is this a crime scene? Is this a joke? Not far away, a woman sitting below a large sign, "Pua Melia," strings a lei, unperturbed, and in the background, the sun shines on the parking lot, a bright blue sky peeking around the roof of the lei stands.

This scene describes a photograph by Native Hawaiian artist Adrienne Keahi Pao, titled *Lei Stand Protest/Lei Pua Kapa* (2004). Pao herself is the woman photographed, prostrate and covered by the ubiquitous, cheap, and hardy purple orchid lei, the type of lei most frequently given to tourists by tour companies on arrival. When I first encountered this work, I was delighted because the photo was incisive, familiar, and funny, even if possibly a little macabre. The purple orchid lei covering the artist's body immediately calls to my mind the routine, even banal, but nonetheless enraging symbol of the commodification of Native Hawaiian culture and Native Hawaiian women's bodies, so often used, scantily clad and pantomiming hula,

FIGURE 6.1. Adrienne Keahi Pao, *Lei Stand Protest/Lei Pua Kapa* (2004). Copyright Adrienne Keahi Pao.

in service of Hawai'i's tourism industry. As a Native Hawaiian woman, there are many such reminders of this commodification that I encounter daily, and I have often wished I could spontaneously protest or tear down such reminders, as Pao seems to have spontaneously done at the airport lei stands.

In an interview in *War Baby/Love Child*, Pao explains that the titular "protest" of this piece is not about the lei stands themselves, a site where, in addition to tourists, many local people stop to buy lei before picking up family members at the airports: "I'm not 'anti-lei stand.' Leis are incorporated into our family—we use them, we love them. I feel like that's a protest about the commodification of culture."[1] Pao is asserting a haunting presence, reminding viewers of the continued existence and belonging of Native Hawaiians even in spaces constructed with tourists in mind. Pao further points out that this photograph is purposefully humorous as well, as in the scene, her "protest" is evidently gathering no attention as the lei stand business goes on as usual.[2] She also notes that the lei stand workers found this performance funny and enjoyed helping place the orchids on her body.[3] Pao uses humor to leaven but not deny the routine painfulness of (and potential complicity of Native Hawaiians and other local residents of Hawai'i in) the commodification of Native Hawaiian culture and Native Hawaiian women's bodies.

The first time I shared my analysis of *Lei Stand Protest/Lei Pua Kapa* at an academic conference, one response I received was hesitant and concerned: "Couldn't this image also be co-opted? Couldn't tourists buy this image and just think it was pretty and cool, without understanding the critique?" That response has stuck with me for several years now. The concern is perhaps warranted. Yes, a tourist could buy this image without understanding it. Yes, this too, like so many things in Indigenous lives, can be co-opted. There is no space entirely outside of or safe from that risk of co-optation for many Indigenous people of the Pacific and elsewhere—not in contemporary Pacific art nor any of the more "traditional" arts. The risk of co-optation is an unavoidable fact of life for Indigenous people, and for many other marginalized communities. Yet this does not mean that no action is possible, or no counter-representation should be created. In fact, art such as Pao's can reflect critically and playfully on that risk. *Lei Stand Protest* shows how Native Hawaiian women live with and fight against the commodification of our bodies by the tourism industry every day, and how that routine living and fighting can manifest with complex emotions: despair, anger, hilarity, and gentleness all wrapped up under the cover of a purple orchid lei.

Though my response to Pao's artwork is partially the pleasure of recognition as a Native Hawaiian woman, her work is certainly not made only for Native Hawaiians. Indeed, the critical edge of the *Hawaiian Cover-Ups* series lies precisely in questioning the position and expectations of the viewer. Contemporary art scholar Jennifer Doyle raises important, related questions of the complicated feelings and positioning evoked by African American artist Carrie Mae Weems's series *From Here I Saw What Happened and I Cried*: "bearing witness might be a critical act, but it might also be a form of complicity depending on the spectator's location. At what point does witnessing switch from being a point of resistance to being a point of collusion? How does one know the difference—is it a matter of how we look at something, how we feel about what we are looking at? What is the relationship between one and the other?"[4]

Commissioned by the J. Paul Getty Museum as a response to their exhibition of mid-nineteenth-century photographs of African Americans, Weems's series presents several of those photographs (and others from other time periods) with commentary printed across them: "I SAW WHAT HAPPENED," "YOU BECAME A SCIENTIFIC PROFILE," "A NEGROID TYPE," "AN ANTHROPOLOGICAL DEBATE."[5] Doyle analyzes this series as one of many ways contemporary art can elicit difficult emotions in the viewers, in this case of how the art potentially implicates the viewer as spectator to "the ideological work of the colonial gaze."[6] Because the work, in its stark statements and unidentified and shifting use of "you" and "I" does not offer any simple, singular, or transparent response to the dehumanizing photographs of the nineteenth century, viewing the series "might be a critical act" or it "might be a form of complicity."

Similarly, this chapter is about how many contemporary Indigenous Pacific artists confront audiences with the ongoing violence of the colonial gaze on Indigenous bodies. Doyle's analysis resonates with Mohawk scholar Audra Simpson's theorizing of ethnographic refusal in anthropological settings, wherein she asks us to consider "stops" (such as the stops or silences in an interview) or "impediments to knowing" as expansive "in what they do not tell us."[7] In this chapter, I engage Doyle's theorizing of difficulty in contemporary art and Simpson's theories of refusal as regenerative "impediments to knowing" in conversation with the refusals evident in the visual art of Adrienne Keahi Pao and Yuki Kihara. I argue that their works illuminate important strategies Indigenous people can use to disrupt and refuse the relentless structure of possession through whiteness. Each of these Indigenous artists subvert viewers' expectations of receiving "authentic" information about Indigenous cultures or Indigenous feelings, as well as viewers' understandings that colonialism is a thing of the past, long since settled. This work is difficult, in Doyle's sense, in that it requires viewers to witness the colonial ideological production of the Polynesian and questions the viewers' complicity. I argue that Indigenous artists drawing attention to this production is necessary to the larger Indigenous project of regeneration: creating and imagining Indigenous futures where other relationships and different gazes might be possible.

Though there are many contemporary Indigenous Pacific artists I could write about here, this chapter focuses on two Polynesian artists, Yuki Kihara (Sāmoan) and Adrienne Keahi Pao (Kanaka Maoli).[8] I chose these artists because each presents compelling visual representations and performances of their own bodies that directly and indirectly speak back to the visual aesthetics of the logic of possession through whiteness and the many ways that logic has shaped race, gender, and sexuality for Polynesians. How they speak back is complex and regenerative, utilizing strategies of mimicry, obscuration, and juxtaposition of past, present, and future as well as of "nature" and the unnatural. Photography is a primary medium for each artist, though Kihara also uses video, sound, dance, and other performance mediums. These representations refuse to straightforwardly fulfill either a social scientific demand for authenticity or the related "mandate to represent their communities" common to minorities in multicultural regimes of recognition.[9] In these respects, Kihara and Pao refuse the logic of possession through whiteness, subverting representations of contemporary "mixed-race" identity and insisting on dynamic readings of Indigenous identity as an active, decolonial force.

Kihara and Pao thus demonstrate what Tavia Nyong'o has offered as the appropriate challenge to seeing a "hybrid future" of mixed-race people as an "American panacea" to its history of racism.[10] Nyong'o suggests that, instead of uncritically accepting racial hybridity as a sign of progress, we must innovate performative "tactics that are filled with the presence of the now and that thereby call the bluff of the ruse of postponement"—the postponement of racial justice to a mixed-race horizon promised in the future, as in the "New Race Growing Up in the Pacific" illustration analyzed in chapter 3.[11] Kihara and Pao seize the "presence of the now" in persuasive ways by using their own bodies staged on Indigenous land as it looks in the colonial present—whether it has been devastated by environmental disaster or by tourism. In doing so, their work diverges sharply from other mixed-race artists who remain wedded to seeing mixed-race bodies as heralds of a different, racism-free future. The next section in particular contrasts Kihara's work with that of Kip Fulbeck, a Chinese American artist whose well-known body of work *The Hapa Project* also attempts to subvert social scientific representations of race, though with less success. While multiracial heritage is often noted with pride in Kihara's and Pao's biographies, their work is primarily concerned with the racial and gendered power of imperialism and settler colonialism for Indigenous peoples, rather than with their "mixed" racial identities. Juxtaposing these Indigenous works with Fulbeck's, I reflect on how racial mixture is popularly performed under the Asian American use of Hapa to selectively appropriate but ultimately erase indigeneity, especially Kānaka Maoli. Overall, Kihara and Pao's works suggest practices that may expose and break the ways popular discourses about "mixed-race" often attach to and diminish indigeneity under the structure of possession through whiteness.

## ETHNOGRAPHIC REFUSAL AND REPLICATION IN CONTEMPORARY ART

Though Indigenous Pacific art is flourishing today, Indigenous Pacific contemporary artists, like other artists of color, feminist artists, and queer artists, face particular challenges in how their art is received in canonical art criticism.[12] As Karen Stevenson analyzes it, stereotypes about the Pacific have been constant factors that contemporary Indigenous artists have had to work against. For Stevenson, the symbol of the Pacific cliché is the frangipani, a flower with "bright, decorative appeal" that has also come to represent "a white attitude toward brown people ... a box within which Pacific artists were so easily imprisoned."[13] Similarly, Derek Conrad Murray and Soraya Murray analyze a prevalent, but mistaken, understanding among art theorists that political art is fundamentally a "trauma discourse," "a testimonial against an oppressive power," and that such artists are largely not interested in formal concerns, but only "idealize and ultimately make spectacles of their identities."[14] In short, there is a troubling expectation in the art world that Indigenous artists and other artists of color be native ethnographers for their community, and even that the art market preys upon such artists as unwitting pawns of passing white fetishes for the Other.[15]

Such assumptions are dismissive at best of the actual political work these artists forward. Jennifer Doyle argues that critics often miss the fact that this desire for ethnography in such artists' work are often "anticipated and refused."[16] This refusal resonates with Audra Simpson's theory of ethnographic refusal, which signifies in her work strategies used by Indigenous peoples to resist and defy stifling anthropological narratives.[17] Though largely contextualized in the anthropologist–interlocutor interview exchange and the broader politics of knowledge production within anthropology, Simpson's theory of ethnographic refusal is also relevant to the contemporary art context, given the heavy expectations of artists to be native or self-ethnographers. Specifically, Simpson's theory of ethnographic refusal refers both to a refusal on the part of an interlocutor to speak on a particular subject during an interview and to a more general refusal of the native anthropologist to produce certain types of knowledge that would render her home community representatives of an ahistorical "culture," rather than political subjects of a dynamic Indigenous nation.[18] In terms of visual art, we can understand ethnographic refusal as not necessarily limited to a refusal to say something or a refusal to look a certain way, but to a broader refusal to participate in the production of "natural," "authentic" Indigenous subjects who might be easily apprehended and utilized by either Western social scientific knowledge production or the Western contemporary art canon.

The works I examine in this chapter pursue ethnographic refusal by drawing attention to the ways that Indigenous Pacific identity irrupts and overflows the frame precisely when Western ethnographic desires attempt to force that identity into erasure via the "traditional," supposedly irretrievable past. Even as each of the works I analyze here includes the photographic representation of the artist's body, they also manage to perform evasion, rather than seek legibility. Again, more than revealing any kind of any ethnographic "truth," these works consistently draw viewers' attention instead to what Doyle describes as "the ideological work of the colonial gaze."

Before I move on to a closer analysis of Kihara and Pao's work, I want to briefly further situate ethnographic refusal in contemporary art, particularly in relation to discourses about racial science and racial mixture, by contrasting Yuki Kihara's series "A Study of a Samoan Savage" (2015) with Kip Fulbeck's *Part Asian, 100% Hapa* (2006), a book collection of his larger series *The Hapa Project*. Both series are framed as critiques of social scientific representations of Indigenous peoples and people of color. Each attempts to achieve this critique by closely mimicking late nineteenth-century and early twentieth-century Western scientific photographic forms, which in the case of Polynesians draws from the white settler representations of Polynesians as natural possessions of whiteness, as discussed in part I of this book. Kihara's work achieves this critique more effectively, demonstrating an uncanny ability to re-create but also subvert the desire of the Western gaze. Because Fulbeck's series maintains a desire to produce ethnographic truth about what he describes as an underrepresented community, "Hapa" or mixed-race Asian Americans, his series reinscribes some of the violence of the ethnographic form, even if unintentionally. Fulbeck's art therefore resembles the demand for recognition expressed by the plaintiffs in the *Day v. Apoliona* case, described in chapter 4, where the desire for greater self-determination was argued in court by acceding to the settler colonial blood quantum definitions of Native Hawaiians. Fulbeck similarly decides to pursue his desire to grant complex personhood and humanity to mixed-race Asian American people by acceding to the format of racial type photography, with similarly complex but ultimately disappointing results.

Let's begin with Yuki Kihara, an accomplished contemporary artist and the first Pacific Islander contemporary artist to have a solo exhibition at the Metropolitan Museum of Art.[19] Her series "A Study of a Samoan Savage" (2015) includes a number of photographs, most of which feature a Sāmoan man being subjected to anthropometric tools held by a white hand, jutting from a glimpse of a sleeve of a white lab coat. These tools explicitly reference not just anthropometry as a field but specifically the work of Louis Sullivan, the physical anthropologist who worked at the Bishop Museum in the early twentieth century and wrote a guide to anthropometry, as analyzed in chapter 2. The subject of Kihara's "Study" is an embodiment of Maui, the Polynesian demigod who slowed the sun and fished up islands. Like Sullivan's anthropometric photographs, Maui is photographed apparently nude. Unlike Sullivan's work, in Kihara's images, the anthropometric subject seems to glow in warm tones of brown skin that shine against a black backdrop. This warmth contributes to the portrayal of Maui as both human and otherworldly, and contrasts with the disembodied white hand, which stands out starkly against the black background. This Maui stares directly at the viewer or, in the portraits that are oriented in profile (as in *Nose Width with Vernier Caliper*, figure 6.2), directly at the off-screen scientist holding the calipers to measure the size of his nose. Played by the Sāmoan artist Ioane, his expressions appear defiant and annoyed at the probing metallic tools measuring his nose and skull. The tools appear sharp and potentially painful, though Maui's blank, resistant expressions betray no sign of being harmed.

Maui's countenance reminds viewers that he is a trickster and shapeshifter, who could likely easily escape not only the anthropologist's calipers

FIGURE 6.2. Yuki Kihara, *Nose Width with Vernier Caliper* (2015), from "A Study of a Samoan Savage" (2015) series. Courtesy of Yuki Kihara and Milford Galleries Dunedin, Aotearoa New Zealand.

but this bodily human form for another life form. The piece *Sprinting* deepens this association with shape-shifting by framing Maui running in a staggered, photographic sequence. This futurist-influenced image, like other works of Kihara's, shows him, still nude, in progressive actions of sprinting from a crouched start with one knee bent to a seemingly full sprint where he appears to be running full-tilt out of the frame. Most of the figures are staring directly at the viewer as he takes off, with an alert and wary expression, as if he is running away from both the viewer and the anthropologist. In the last two figures, Maui has turned his head to look forward and out of the frame, as he perhaps escapes the white settler gaze and the logic of possession through whiteness that Sullivan invested in through such anthropometric studies. By running out of the anthropological frame, Kihara's

Maui provides both a powerful rebuke to the violence of settler colonial science and a regenerative, alternative history in which Polynesian ancestors get to refuse and frustrate anthropometrists like Sullivan. Maui is an akua (god and ancestor) that most Polynesian peoples, and some Micronesian and Melanesian peoples, share across their histories. By choosing Maui as the imagined subject of settler colonial science, then, Kihara provides a broad swath of Pacific Islanders a connection to this series, and deliberately flaunts the designation of "Samoan Savage" that an anthropologist might use to label Maui. The joke here is on the scientist, who does not realize Maui's mana, or power, and by extension, the mana of all Indigenous Pacific Islanders.

Yet the representation of Maui by a Sāmoan male artist and the series title "Samoan Savage" also evokes more specific references to Sāmoan men, as Sāmoan scholar Fa'anofo Lisaclaire Uperesa has noted, connecting the series to the evaluation of Sāmoan men as "natural athletes" or "savage players." She argues, "foregrounding their punishing physical sporting performance may draw the cheers of the crowd in rugby and gridiron football, but it emerges from and remains tethered to racist imaginaries" that ultimately continue to "reinforce hierarchies, stereotypes and ceilings based on racialised opportunities in the settler colonial Pacific nations, as well as in the US, UK and beyond."[20] Here again we see antiblackness bleeding through the construction of an ideal, white Polynesian race that many actual Polynesians, and Polynesian men in particular, cannot fulfill in real life, as they are often are stigmatized and criminalized for their dark skin. Kihara's series therefore centers the gendered aspects of settler colonialism and racial anthropometry, in part by so powerfully focusing on the gendered and racialized body, as she does in her other works as well.

The skill of Kihara's work lies in how subtly but masterfully she reveals Sullivan's anthropometric studies to be steeped in the logic of possession through whiteness, which she suggests is still very much present today, in part by implicating the viewer's potential complicity with "savage" stereotypes of Sāmoan men as Maui stares out directly at the viewer. In this way, the violence of the logic of possession through whiteness is foregrounded in a provocative, unmissable way, but Kihara also imbues Maui with warmth and the agency to defy and refuse that violence as inevitable or as the only frame of reference. Maui is not possessed, or even possessable, in Kihara's vision, and neither are Indigenous Pacific people as a whole. This is at the heart of ethnographic refusal: the illustration of Indigenous self-determination to refuse anthropological and other scientific studies that, while dangerous in their creation of discourses about Indigenous peoples, never hold complete power to capture the "truth" or "essence" of Indigenous cultures or bodies. In staging its ethnographic refusal, "A Study of a Samoan Savage" is also regenerative in that it opens up different potential pasts, presents, and futures for Polynesians free from the logic of possession through whiteness.

Kip Fulbeck's *The Hapa Project* also attempts to restage anthropometric photographs from the early twentieth century, though he is less successful in critiquing the historical and ongoing forms of scientific racism such photographs evoke. His work features mixed-race Asian Americans, including a handful of mixed-race Pacific Islanders, as the subjects. *The Hapa Project* overall seeks to question how mixed-race Asian Americans are perceived today. This series therefore hauntingly echoes the interviews analyzed in chapter 3 with mixed-race Chinese and Native Hawaiians in the 1930s, especially in a key component of the work, a self-written statement in response to the question "What are you?" These statements accompany a headshot of a person apparently nude, from the shoulders up, devoid of any accessories, with rather blank facial expressions, and a list of the races the person identifies with (the person's name is not given). Fulbeck is less successful in mimicking and challenging the scientific frame than Kihara is, in part because he fails to reference and evoke a specific colonial or racist ideological production of mixed-race Asian American people. While the settler colonial gaze is skillfully re-created and rendered in Kihara's work in its specificity, it is not immediately clear from the *Hapa Project* photographs or the accompanying commentary (as exhibited solo, online, or in the book form) what specific context Fulbeck is re-creating in order to subvert.[21]

In part, this lack of contextual specificity is linked to the appropriated label "Hapa," and its rather arbitrary cobbling together of different Asian American and Pacific Islander constituencies, each with its own history in respect to racial and colonial power. It is worth explaining the context of Hapa's contested contemporary usage. As mentioned in chapter 2, *hapa* is a Hawaiian word meaning "part," and *hapa haole* was a term used to denote Native Hawaiians who also had white ancestry.[22] In the 1990s, Hapa (dropping the "haole" and capitalizing the H) became a popular identity for multiracial Asian Americans—primarily Asian Americans without Native Hawaiian ancestry and often for Asian Americans who have no connection to Hawai'i at all. Despite Native Hawaiian critiques of this appropriation, Asian American Hapa activists and artists have defended their use of Hapa largely by arguing that they are performing an empowering reclamation of the word. However, there is no evidence that *hapa* was ever used solely in a derogatory manner, nor have Native Hawaiians stopped using the term as a way of recognizing their expanding community and intentionally including Native Hawaiians with other racial backgrounds.

Kip Fulbeck has similarly been dismissive of such critiques, noting that his capitalized use of Hapa can distinguish it from the Native Hawaiian hapa. His book further includes an afterword in which scholar Paul Spickard makes the staggering suggestion that it is simply the nature of language to move and change, and as such, Hapa "is not anyone's property. Continental Americans might just as well complain about Hawaiians using 'TV and cell phone.'"[23] This comment conflates "continental Americans" as a group equivalent to Hawaiians (thus making Hawaiians simply a regional affiliation rather than an Indigenous nation), while simultaneously racially encoding Hawaiians as primitive and backward, people who should be grateful for "continental Americans" allowing them the use of TVs and cell phones! This logic is stunningly resonant with the logic of possession through whiteness: Native Hawaiians do not own Hawaiian language, lands, or identity, because these are really universal things that settlers can more properly and fairly manage. Thus, Hapa-identified people are more progressive than Native Hawaiians, who are backward in insisting on their specificity and ungrateful for the modern "gifts" of American technology. Though Hapa (in the mixed-race Asian American sense) are not (only) white, their visibility and recognition as Hapa depends on possessing Native Hawaiian-ness in the same terms as white settlers have done for centuries.

As demonstrated in part I of this book, racial mixture was a scientific discourse that developed in specific ways with respect to Polynesians. The logic of possession through whiteness, as generated in scientific knowledge, presupposed the extinction of Polynesian people as they were supposedly reabsorbed into the white race of their ancient ancestors. In the early to mid-twentieth century, racial mixture was the discourse that allowed scientists to measure and ensure the progress of this possession, especially through studying and meticulously documenting the blood quantum of mixed-race Native Hawaiians. Though Asian residents of Hawai'i were also part of such studies, their blood quantum was not tracked in any equivalent way, as there was no expectation that Asian races would become extinct. To recall the interviews analyzed in chapter 3, the prevailing discourse of Native Hawaiians as dying out encouraged mixed-race Hawaiians to stop identifying as Native Hawaiian and to align themselves more with Chinese or white American culture if they wanted to be part of the contemporary world. Thus, the problem with Fulbeck's use of Hapa is not simply a matter of appropriating Hawaiian language and identity in the word *hapa*; rather, in suggesting that scientific racism against "Hapa" people is equivalent, Fulbeck effectively erases the history and contemporary presence of the discourse around racial mixture in Hawai'i and Polynesia more broadly as a central structuring feature of settler colonialism, with particular violence wrought on Native Hawaiian and other Polynesian bodies.

In misunderstanding the nature of the history of racial mixture as a scientific discourse, *The Hapa Project* also fails to address gender and sexuality as constitutive of racial and colonial power—which Kihara's work, by contrast, addresses centrally. As I showed in chapter 3, mixed-race Native Hawaiian and Asian American women in particular were not the distanced objects of "human zoos," as Spickard claims in the afterword, but were, and in some respects still are, the desired ideal of Hawai'i as a welcoming, sexually fulfilling place for white American men.[24] Both Fulbeck and Spickard overlook the history of photographs portraying mixed-race women as sexual (as well as scientific) objects, and the fact that presenting themselves "nude from the collar-bone up" may be more invasive, and undesirable, for female, queer, and/or transgender subjects, especially if they are interested in creating unexoticized representations of Hapa identity. Though Fulbeck states that the subjects all volunteered to be photographed, the self-written statements intimate that they may not have known beforehand that they would be photographed partially nude and that they were not entirely comfortable with it. One subject writes as his answer to "What are you?": "I'm a grown man who just exposed my breasts to a complete stranger."[25] Another subject's answer to "What are you?" simply proclaims in all capital letters: "QUEER EURASIAN,"[26] anxious to write himself out of a presumed heteropatriarchal gaze and to highlight that perhaps his identity is more importantly formed intersectionally in relation to both his race and his sexuality, not his race alone. While these subjects' narratives point to the sexualization of mixed-race people both historically and in their personal experiences, the book seems to at once encourage this fetishizing and disavow having done so. In Kip Fulbeck's introduction, the foreword by Sean Lennon (John Lennon and Yoko Ono's son), and the afterword by Spickard, no mention is made of sex or gender at all. The subjects are presented partially nude but only because "I wanted us to look like *us*."[27]

Further, though *The Hapa Project* glosses the history of eugenics and other social sciences as "racist pseudo-science," it matters that these sciences were understood as quite progressive and liberal in their time, as chapters 2 and

3 have shown. Far from simply dehumanizing the subjects of their studies, social scientific knowledge production allowed white settlers to (selectively) identify with and as Polynesians. By misrecognizing the ways that eugenics discourses actually produced their ideologies, *The Hapa Project* is not able to effectively challenge those ideologies in mimicking them. Rather, it simply reproduces the logic that mixed-race people must be folded into a universal humanity that is always nonetheless white. In the afterword to the book from the series, Spickard claims that Fulbeck is "using the old form, but with exactly the opposite content."[28] However, the content of the photographs, with their tight attention to the physical features of mixed-race people, are in fact exactly the same content as older racial type photographs.

The one difference in the book is the addition of the photographic captions written by the subjects. The captions are important and interesting, showcasing a diverse range of ideas about Hapa identity. Yet they could be read as providing the ethnographic "truth" of a person's identity, thereby fulfilling the expectation of spectators to learn about the mixed-race subject from a distanced, anthropological standpoint, despite the stated intent of the project to overturn such a stance. In this sense, the captions also potentially prevent viewers of the series from questioning their complicity in the colonial gaze. Unlike the open, unresolved nature of the colonial mimicking in Kihara, the captions offer direct instructions and reassurances about how to read his portraits of mixed-race people. Spectators may initially feel uneasy looking at portraits reminiscent of the style of physical anthropological photographs, but the captions provide insight into the subjects' humanity, and thus allow viewers to put their initial discomfort aside. Nonetheless, media studies scholar Nicole Rabin notes that these self-descriptions are important not because they represent the space where the subjects reveal their truly "natural" selves, but rather because they actually show that "not all the participants seem to be 'at ease' with liminality."[29] Indeed, in many self-descriptions the subject highlights the absence of their own voice. Instead, they note the voice of someone (perhaps someone like the reader) confronting their physical appearance and racial identity. For example: "Really? You don't look Thai. Well let me look again. Yeah now I can see it around your eyes. You know Thai food is my favorite."[30] This self-description thus challenges and potentially implicates the viewer in the routine racism this woman experiences.

Yet what does such a challenge really accomplish beyond admonishing a reader to be more courteous to mixed-race people? *The Hapa Project*'s serialization of individual portraits diffuses the sources of the violence experienced by its subjects by pointing to a general sense of discrimination against mixed-race Asian American people. The response of viewers is an equally diffuse sense that mixed-race Asian Americans are discriminated against, and that people should be nicer to them. My point is that *The Hapa Project* is not difficult in Doyle's sense; it seeks less to unsettle the viewer, and more to ethnographically consolidate Hapa as an identity (and a proper response to that identity from those outside it). In doing so, it does not deflect the scientific gaze it purports to overturn, but simply makes multiracial people another group worthy of scientific and cultural study. Further, it does so by erasing historical and contemporary difference in terms of racial power and settler colonialism.

Beyond Kip Fulbeck's art itself, my critique seeks to offer productive suggestions to the expanding field of critical mixed race studies, for which Fulbeck and his art have so far served as a kind of standard-bearer.[31] Activism and academic studies centered around multiracial or mixed-race identity can often do important work, especially when aligned with the approach that race purity has always been a lie, and thus persons designated as "mixed-race" are thoroughly within the purview of studies and activism centered on race and racism, not magical exceptions. However, like Fulbeck, the field currently fails to recognize in substantial ways that mixed-race discourses have long been part of structuring and enlivening settler colonialism; that Indigenous-white people have long represented the desired settler future within the imaginaries of the settler nation-state. If critical mixed race studies is fixed too tightly on the articulation of a universal mixed-race subject being empowered through claiming a mixed-race identity (even if as only one identity among many), then this is fundamentally incompatible with, or even opposed to, the decolonization sought by many Indigenous people, for whom mixed-race identity has been imposed upon them as a structural feature of settler colonialism. For instance, critical mixed race studies could contextualize and problematize Fulbeck and others' use of Hapa, not just by highlighting the appropriation of Hawaiian language and identity, but by showing how the discourse of racial mixture is a central part of settler colonialism in Hawai'i. Again, this analysis echoes the analysis in chapter 3, which showed that mixed-race Hawaiian Chinese people often accepted and even celebrated as fact that their mixed heritage would lead to the extinction of "black" and backward Native Hawaiians.

## YUKI KIHARA'S SĀMOAN SALOME

Above I analyzed Kihara's series "Study of a Samoan Savage"; in this section I return to Kihara's work and its regenerative refusal of the logic of possession through whiteness by focusing on a recurring character she performs, which is inspired by a particular ethnographic photograph from 1886 by New Zealander Thomas Andrew, titled *Samoan Half Caste*.[32] The woman in Andrew's photo is wearing a Victorian-style mourning dress and staring directly into the camera. Both the dress and direct stare are unusual for nineteenth-century ethnographic photos, whose subjects were often required to undress or don "traditional" clothing in order to document supposedly disappearing Indigenous cultures. Kihara has used this image as inspiration for a character she performs in several of her works. Restaged, the Sāmoan half-caste of Andrew's photo becomes a character Kihara also refers to as a Sāmoan Salome, the classic femme fatale, dancing not the dance of the seven veils, but a taualuga, a Sāmoan dance often performed as a finale.[33]

In *Siva in Motion* (2012) and *Galu Afi* (2012), video works, Kihara embodies the Sāmoan Salome, wearing a heavy, formal, black Victorian mourning dress and performing a slow, mesmerizing taualuga. As described by Kihara, the dance both reenacts and mourns the devastating tsunami Galu Afi that hit Sāmoa in 2009.[34] Conventionally, the taualuga is usually performed at the end of a party or fund-raiser, and features one dancer performing subtly, largely with graceful hand movements, in the middle of a stage, while others join in a circle around that dancer, dancing more wildly and loudly. The taualuga in *Siva in Motion* is noticeably silent, performed very slowly, and shows only one dancer, though the hand motions are similar to those in conventional taualuga. By referencing the taualuga without showing the dancers who usually surround the solo dancer, the piece seems to invite viewers of the video to become dancers to surround the character in the video, and, more broadly, to surround Sāmoa in the lingering effects of the tsunami's devastation and the increasingly noticeable effects of climate change in the Pacific. But by referencing Salome in her descriptions of the character she is performing, Kihara also seems to embody the fierce destructive qualities of a femme fatale and a tsunami, such that neither she nor the Sāmoa she represents are innocent, passive victims, but complex characters who can respond, remember, mourn, and perhaps exact revenge. In this way, Kihara invites a response to the destruction of the tsunami alongside the character she performs, but refuses any straightforward, ethnographic account of the damage of the tsunami or the victimization of Sāmoan people.

Riffing off the genre of futurist photography from the late nineteenth century, *Siva in Motion* also challenges viewers' perceptions of time, space, and the movement of an individual body. The video was multitracked in post-production so that her figure grows and sprouts arms and heads moving in multiple directions. This gives the viewer a sense that tsunamis have happened more than once in Sāmoa, and will recur again and again—unless, perhaps, viewers take action. The mesmerizing growths and movements of Kihara's figure into someone with multiple heads and arms in the video suggests that the task of mourning and acting requires much more than any one ordinary person can give. Yet the quiet power of the performance also displays a confidence in the Sāmoan people to act as these multiple heads and arms to mourn and act.[35] When I have heard Kihara speak about her work, she often says that she is oriented by the Sāmoan principle that one must look to the past to go forward. Kihara's art pulls us into a Pacific in Indigenous time, where history, present, and future are entwined in nonlinear ways. Salesa notes of Indigenous time that "an ethical and full engagement with an indigenous past is through an indigenous present."[36] Kihara's works do precisely this. She has noted that her work seeks "for mystery and mana to draw people into exploring ancient Sāmoan principles by using today's cutting-edge technology. It is my hope that through dance I can trigger important discussions about the state of our world today."[37] This stance certainly guides this piece in its referencing of historic futurist photography as well as liberating the Sāmoan half-caste of the nineteenth-century ethnographic photograph into this futuristic space. The half-caste designation is noticeably reminiscent of the "Part Hawaiian" category analyzed in chapter 2 and the mixed-race Hawaiian Chinese figure in chapter 3. Though there was no blood quantum legislation in Sāmoa comparable to Hawai'i's Hawaiian Homes Commission Act, this photograph demonstrates that similar kinds of thinking about racial mixture, structured by the logic of possession through whiteness, also permeated other Polynesian places.

Kihara reprised her Salome character in her photograph series *Where Do We Come From? What Are We? Where Are We Going?* (2013). The series title references Paul Gauguin's 1897–98 painting of the same name, displaying Gauguin's hallmarks of largely naked female Tahitian figures lounging in a florid, tropical backdrop. Yet, instead of taking Gauguin's existential questions in the context of his views of Tahiti as a more "pure" society than the West, Kihara's series relays the title questions with the Sāmoan people in mind. The black-and-white photographs show Kihara as Salome, in the signature Victorian black mourning dress, in various locations around

FIGURE 6.3. Yuki Kihara, *Agelu I Tausi Catholic Church after Cyclone Evan Mulivai Safata* (2013), from *Where Do We Come From? What Are We? Where Are We Going?* series. Supported by Creative New Zealand and the Government of New Zealand. Courtesy of Yuki Kihara and Milford Galleries Dunedin, Aotearoa New Zealand.

Sāmoa shortly after the 2012 Cyclone Evan hit, though the series also often references the earlier 2009 tsunami Galu Afi. Her figure is usually photographed from behind, offering only glimpses of the side of her face, acting as an otherworldly guide to the viewer as she gazes upon still scenes. In one photo, standing in Apia's landmark Church of the Immaculate Conception of Mary, she gazes up at a chandelier that still hangs though, inches beyond, the roof has evidently blown away and water covers much of the floor (figure 6.3).[38] In another photo, she stands in the ruins of an elementary school devastated by Tsunami Galu Afi in 2009, where the remaining concrete walls now enclose a field of flowers (figure 6.4).[39] Such photos evoke mourning for what has been lost in the recent storms, but also suggest hope (in the figure's calm, upward gaze) and regeneration (in the new flowers growing in the school's ruins).

FIGURE 6.4. Yuki Kihara, *Saleapaga Primary School after Tsunami Galu Afi* (2013), from *Where Do We Come From? What Are We? Where Are We Going?* series. Supported by Creative New Zealand and the Government of New Zealand. Courtesy of Yuki Kihara and Milford Galleries Dunedin, Aotearoa New Zealand.

In other photos in the series, the central figure gazes at other locations of historical and contemporary importance in Sāmoa, such as the former Mau Headquarters (a center of activity in the movement for Sāmoa's independence in 1962) and the Faleolo International Airport (symbolic of the nation's increasing reliance on a tourist economy).[40] Though neither of these latter sites is visibly impacted by the storms—the landscaped grounds of the Mau Headquarters and an empty corridor of the departures wing of the airport are immaculate in the photos—the questions of the series title (*Where Do We Come From? What Are We? Where Are We Going?*) resonate just as much in these other locations. Though the series offers no simple answers to these questions or to the problem of climate change, Kihara's use of the Salome figure is powerful and evocative. Unlike the sexualized, exotic female figures in Gauguin's paintings, Kihara's Salome is composed, contemplative, and on the move, with evident deep reverence for and belief in Sāmoa that transcends time. Again, as with *Siva in Motion*, this series quietly refuses to portray Sāmoans as passive victims. Though the scenes engage the extent of loss after environmental destruction, by populating the evidently modern (not merely tropical à la Gauguin) Sāmoan landscape with an allegorical Sāmoan woman, the photos imbue the viewer with a haunting sense that, far from disappearing, Sāmoan people will always exert an active presence in their own land.

Kihara's use of her own body to create a symbolic guide to traverse Sāmoa is both inspiring and troubling. The black Victorian mourning dress makes her presence in these contemporary scenes seem out of place; yet at the same time, they make us see the various places as out of time—out of the linear, Western mode of understanding time and progress. These are hauntings, but they are not only haunting in the sense of seeing and fleeing from frightening ghosts who should not be there. They are haunting in the mode of Avery Gordon, or in Eve Tuck and C. Ree's sense: "Haunting doesn't hope to change people's perceptions, nor does it hope for reconciliation. Haunting lies precisely in its refusal to stop. Alien (to settlers) and generative (for ghosts), this refusal to stop is its own form of resolving. For ghosts, the haunting is the resolving, it is not what needs to be resolved."[41] Kihara's series theorizes a Pacific world in which Polynesian women refuse to stop. They do not stop showing up, thinking, moving, inhabiting, walking, dancing, or being despite the world around them demanding this deadening, Indigenous dispossession, at every turn. This refusal is, as Tuck and Ree write, not for the purpose of changing "people's perceptions" or for "reconciliation" but simply a generative mode of being for those whom the settler colonial world would kill, possess, or otherwise box in.

In the place of ethnographic information that would lend itself to the knowledge production of Polynesians as almost white, Kihara, in particular by mimicking Gauguin's navel-gazing questions in her series title—*Where Do We Come From? What Are We? Where Are We Going?*—overturns and refuses the Western project of extracting meaning about (white) humanity from those deemed Polynesian. While noting and critiquing such Western projects, symbolized in, for example, the tarnished grandeur of the Christian church, Kihara also shows and embodies a Polynesian female figure persistently present even when she is not supposed to be here or *be* at all. As Gauguin and his ilk gaze at Polynesian women, Polynesian women gaze too—and they do not simply gaze back, but elsewhere, creating, as Sarah Jane Cervenak suggests, "terrains where bodies are no longer the grounds for others' becomings."[42]

### ADRIENNE KEAHI PAO COVERS UP

Kanaka Maoli artist Adrienne Keahi Pao's work resonates in many ways with Kihara, particularly in her *Hawaiian Cover-Ups* series (2004–5), introduced at the beginning of this chapter, where she displays her own body photographed amid various scenes in the landscape of contemporary Hawai'i. Unlike the Kihara series I discussed above, however, the photos of Pao's *Hawaiian Cover-Ups* are in bright, glossy color, and her body is always shown prone, covered with materials other than clothing. The colorful landscapes in her photos often hint at the obviously unnatural, in stark contrast to the idyllic image of Hawai'i as a beach paradise, even as she stages many photographs at the beach. Pao uses her body to juxtapose, as art historian Margo Machida writes, "the perspectives of its actual inhabitants with the seductive notions of an unspoiled paradise so favored by tourist transients, for whom the realities of local life and history are characteristically hidden or willfully occluded."[43]

Yet Pao's work is not simply a "local" response to tourism, premised on a strict binary between tourists and Natives. More boldly, her work investigates the ways tourism also at times shapes and constrains the ways that Kānaka Maoli, especially those in diaspora, relate to the land and to Kanaka Maoli culture. As a Kanaka Maoli raised and still living in California, Pao's work is also shaped by her own partial dislocation from "local life," and the sometimes jarring, overlapping (but not equivalent) experiences of "tourist transients" and diasporic returns in spaces such as Honolulu International Airport. In an artist's statement about *Hawaiian Cover-Ups* she writes:

> As someone who is part Native-Hawaiian while born and raised in California, I wear many hats in relationship to the Hawaiian experience. I represent outsider and insider, tourist and indigenous person, colonizer and colonized. In this body of work, I use certain materials as cover-ups. These materials are consumed in two ways—one in direct relation to tourism and the other serving a purpose for the locals themselves.... I, as tourist, both comment on tourism, and photograph myself participating

in the most identifiable tourist act, posing within a landscape and capturing myself there.... As I become object and subject, I both question and participate in the commoditization of this land.[44]

Thus, Pao conceives of this series as simultaneously, on the one hand, the quintessential act of tourism—taking a photo of one's self in an exotic place—and, on the other, a quintessential act of indigeneity—of recognizing one's genealogy or connection with a place. Her pieces demonstrate that the line between these performances is sometimes startlingly thin, perhaps placing diasporic Native Hawaiians in a particularly difficult position in that their desires to return to and reconnect with the homeland are often mediated by tourism, not just as an industry that dominates the logistics of travel to Hawaiʻi but also more broadly in the ways that tourism participates in possession through whiteness—an epistemology that encourages visitors to perform and possess a transitory Native-ness.

Pao accordingly acknowledges the generative position of being both insider and outsider, and, as she notes in an interview, being able to "see through that lens. I can see the beauty, I can see the paradise, I can see the rapture in that place."[45] Nonetheless, like Kihara's *Where Do We Come From? What Are We? Where Are We Going?* series, Pao's *Hawaiian Cover-Ups* series refuses to entirely cede Hawaiian spaces to Western tourists and the Western gaze. In *Beachfront Property at Diamond Head/Leʻahi Kapa (Brow of Tuna Covering)*, Pao is photographed lying on the beach in Waikīkī, covered in strands of shiny, plastic beads (figure 6.5).[46] She is surrounded by sunbathing tourists and could be mistaken for one herself, but her pose is unnatural and stiff, and her legs mirror the lines of Diamond Head or Leʻahi off in the distance. Her eyes are closed, her head is fully exposed (unlike in most of the photos in this series), upturned and regal. She seems oblivious to the tourists, including a woman walking by with her back turned and "Aloha" written across the butt of her shorts. As with *Lei Stand Protest* discussed in this chapter introduction, everyone seems unaware of Pao's figure, and they continue sunbathing and enjoying the beach despite her perhaps reproachful, literal reenactment of Diamond Head, which is both funny and disturbing. It is disturbing that no one takes heed of Pao's figure, and the photo seems to question what it would take to decolonize Waikīkī, when the landscape itself has become so iconic of settler vacationing. Yet Pao's figure also is oblivious to the tourists, suggesting that attracting attention is not the aim of her performance anyway. The refusal of Pao's figure to acknowledge the tourists is, again, both humorous and powerful, remind-

FIGURE 6.5. Adrienne Keahi Pao, *Beachfront Property at Diamond Head/Le'ahi Kapa (Brow of Tuna Covering)*, from *Hawaiian Cover-Ups* series (2005). Copyright Adrienne Keahi Pao.

ing viewers of the oddity not just of this edgy performance art, which seems out of place on this sunny beach, but of the capitalist development of Waikīkī itself, and the premise that Kānaka Maoli do not belong there anymore.[47]

Though Pao's *Hawaiian Cover-Ups* are staged as photographs rather than interactive performance pieces in real time, her series evokes feminist performance art in its contention with issues of the beauty of paradise and its violation, and specifically the latent violence done to Kanaka Maoli female bodies in the Western imaginary of Hawai'i as paradise.[48] For example, in *Palm Fronds at Coconut Grove/Palama Kapa (Palm Frond Covering)*, only Pao's legs and part of her arm are visible under what appear to be fallen palm fronds from a few tall palm trees standing tall in the background against a perfect blue sky. "Coconut grove" could refer to many tourist sites around O'ahu, and one macabre suggestion of the photograph is that buried not far under the surface of all of those sites are Kanaka Maoli women's bodies, the objects of sexual violence that allow the tourist machine to churn.[49] The viewer of this photograph is positioned as if they had just happened upon the body, noticing the limbs sticking out of the palm leaves. Will the viewer uncover what potentially cruel, disturbing thing has happened to this figure, or will they keep strolling in the coconut grove, insisting on keeping the image of tranquil paradise intact?

Other pieces in *Hawaiian Cover-Ups* ask viewers to consider what has been obscured in other sacred or illicit sites in locations outside of the circuits regularly traveled by tourists. In *Sugar Plantation Surrounding Birthing Stones/Kopa'a Kapa (Hard Sugar Covering)*, Pao is photographed at Kūkaniloko, a sacred site which is acknowledged as the center of O'ahu and symbolizes the piko (navel/belly button) and birth of O'ahu (figure 6.6). It was also used by Native Hawaiian ali'i (rulers/royalty) as a birthing site, with stones at the site being used for backrests for ali'i women giving birth. In this piece, Pao is photographed lying in front of the birthstones, covered in sugar. Rather literally, she is covered in powdery whiteness, just as in *Beachfront Property* she is covered in white plastic beads simulating diamonds. The sugar references the fact that in the late nineteenth and early twentieth centuries, sugar plantations surrounded this sacred site, and that the white settler sugar plantation owners overthrew the Hawaiian monarchy in 1893. Thus, the piece foregrounds different, very old, and conflicting forms of power rooted in this specific place. The piece makes viewers question whether Pao's figure is one who would give birth at this site, or if she is the product of a birth at this site; and perhaps, whether births would be possible at this site again or whether the legacy of sugar has contaminated the productive power of Kūkaniloko. However, as with all of the images in the series, the very solid, seemingly immovable position of Pao's figure lying in the space reclaims and reinhabits the space with a Native Hawaiian body. Though the image is disturbing in its suggestion that perhaps these birthing stones no longer hold the same kind of power, given the influence of the sugar industry, there is an open question about whether the ultimate legacies or power of a place like Kūkaniloko make this an Indigenous performance. And staging an Indigenous body within an Indigenous performance rather than a settler performance that assumes Indigenous power is gone and Indigenous bodies have died and

FIGURE 6.6. Adrienne Keahi Pao, *Sugar Plantation Surrounding Birthing Stones/Kopa'a Kapa (Hard Sugar Covering)*, from *Hawaiian Cover-Ups* series (2005). Copyright Adrienne Keahi Pao.

disappeared into whiteness challenges the certainty and finality of the settler colonial process of possession through whiteness, despite its centuries-long hold on the Pacific.

Another series of Pao's *Family Portraits* (2008 and continuing) features family members of Pao, who live in Hawai'i, photographed in an apparently hybrid genre, with elements of the family photograph, the salvaged ethnographic photograph, and perhaps something of the fantastic, mythical, and/or absurd all at once. For example, *Aunty Wini Wearing Hina Hina (Pele's Hair)* portrays Pao's aunt in a pose both regal and funny, serious and childlike—she is standing between the stalks of a banyan tree, her head and much of her torso covered in long strings of hina hina (also called Spanish moss). In *Three Cousins as the Three Graces—Leilani, Malia and Pohai*, three young women greet the sunrise, posed with hands on each other's shoulders on rocks at Makapu'u Beach. They are dressed in bikinis—one with what appears to be an improvised skirt of different rainbow-colored lei, one whose bikini top is covered with two large white flowers, and one with a green haku lei on her head and ankles in traditional (kahiko) hula style. In this way, each photo carries a partial but earnest sense of make-believe. In this make-believe is a critique of the ethnographic photograph that assumes to capture "authentic" Kanaka Maoli culture; in the place of authenticity there seems to be a joyful embrace of the fantastic. At the same time, there remains a sly sense that perhaps these funny poses and attire could be passed on to anthropology and taken as "authentic"—which would be a great joke on anthropology.

Yet there is also an insistence that Kānaka Maoli, even those who live in Hawai'i—in contrast to the emphasis on Pao's position as diasporic in *Hawaiian Cover-Ups*—can also be complicit with, seduced, and shaped by the Western fantasy of Hawai'i as paradise. Of the *Family Portraits* series, Pao explains that she collaborated with her family members on the location and attire, and in doing so realized that it became "apparent to me how imbued the Hawaiian fantasy is with my family and myself."[50] Could these images be taken as, in Stevenson's words, "frangipani"—beautiful but ephemeral and lacking substance? Once again Pao provides unsettling and nondefinitive answers. Yes, these images could be co-opted, but maybe Native Hawaiian culture today is always already bound up in that co-optation. It is not only that non-Hawaiians regularly employ a settler colonial gaze in viewing Native Hawaiians, but also that Native Hawaiian themselves sometimes buy into and reproduce the colonial fictions imposed upon them. Pao's work considers this buying-in not from a place of reproach or absolutism but with humor, intimacy, and empathy. As with Kihara's work in restaging the Polynesianist gaze, the worlds inhabited by Native Hawaiians in Pao's works are never entirely free of settler colonialism, its violence, and its dislocations, but they are also attentive to Native Hawaiian desires, both serious and silly.

---

Kihara's and Pao's works speak to and with each other in multiple, resounding ways, each deploying various aspects of performance art to interrupt the ways Polynesian bodies are produced in relation to the settler colonial logic of possession through whiteness. Though each artist identifies in some way as multiracial, it is clear that the content of their work is deeply critical of discourses about racial mixture and the ways such discourses have (differently) shaped their communities, especially when compared to Kip Fulbeck's *Hapa Project* and its desire to create visibility for a new Hapa identity. Kihara's reembodiment of figures from ethnographic photographs of Sāmoa subtly undercuts the apparent "truth" such images attempted to capture by documenting the "natural" Polynesian within Western frameworks of race and gender. Thus, in Kihara's work her "mixed-race" body is not inherently surprising or a feature that distinguishes her from other Polynesian people; neither is embodying fa'afafine, as she notes, a gender without limits. Her work shows how she and other Polynesians exceed and flout Western racial categories and gender categories, being oriented instead by Indigenous Pacific epistemologies about the importance of relation to place and past as key to the future.

For Pao, multiraciality is similarly a common, rather unremarkable feature of contemporary Kanaka Maoli families. Yet she is also attentive to the ways that being multiracial and living in diaspora can create a sense of disconnection that cannot fully be repaired by visiting, given the dominance of tourist modes of visiting Hawai'i. Nonetheless, her work humorously and empathetically teases out the ways that Kānaka Maoli who live in Hawai'i or outside it are, for better or worse, at times romanced by the very fictions that have constituted their colonization. Like Kihara, Pao is attentive to the ways that the mixed-race female body is subject in potentially violent ways to the Western gaze of the white male ethnographer and/or tourist. For all the funny aspects of her photographs, her work insists too on questioning the price the post–World War II fantasy of the light-skinned hula girl awaiting each male tourist has enacted on Kanaka Maoli women.

All of these works are difficult. Without revealing much of the artists' emotions or offering any "authentic" representation of their community, these works demand much of viewers: to sit with the aesthetics of settler colonialism and its overt and subtle violences, to rethink how Western knowledge production has deeply structured the ways we see race, gender, and indigeneity, and to recognize that these forms of seeing are painfully overlaid onto Indigenous Pacific bodies daily. And yet violence is not the only thing richly present in these works. There is also abundant humor, as in Pao's performances in front of Diamond Head and the airport lei stands, and sheer loveliness, as in Kihara's mesmerizing dancing in *Siva in Motion*. These pieces demonstrate a variety of strategies to recognize the possessive violence of colonial mappings of Polynesia and the rest of the Pacific, and remapping Polynesia through the placement of Indigenous bodies in relation to Indigenous places. In each work are glimpses of other futures, other ways of relating to people and land, other aesthetics that cannot be fully apprehended or thwarted by settler colonialism, though these other futures may only be fully realized by destroying the dominant modes of knowing and seeing of the settler colonial world each artist inhabits. Will the viewer of these works recognize the artificiality of ethnographic productions of Indigenous Pacific peoples or will they continue to be seduced by colonial representations of Polynesia as paradise? As noted in this chapter's introduction, the risk of further appropriation and misreadings is one each artist boldly takes.

Overall, Kihara and Pao's rich, challenging, and often humorous work suggests that the possession of Indigenous peoples by whiteness—particularly in making Polynesians subjects of a touristic, erotic gaze—is profoundly unnatural and far from predestined. Audra Simpson has noted of refusal, in the context of her own interviews with Mohawk people: "There was something that seemed to reveal itself at the point of refusal—a stance, a principle, a historical narrative, and *an enjoyment in the reveal*."[51] In each of the works this chapter has discussed, I similarly see an enjoyment accompanying a confident refusal of the assumption that Indigenous peoples are doomed to disappear and become the possessions of whiteness enabling a strong enunciation of Indigenous identity and politics as a matter of ongoing engagement with the settler colonial world. Each work subtly marks an Indigenous presence not as a matter of unchanging authenticity, but existing in the midst of a modern landscape, long bound up with global capitalism and settler colonialism. Each shares "an enjoyment in the reveal" through the surprise of defying viewers' expectations of

Indigenous disappearance: Kihara's Victorian-clad Salome ready to board a plane at the Faleolo Airport; Pao's bodily reenactment of Diamond Head on the sand at Waikīkī. These artists provide regenerative models of refusing complacency and acknowledging loss and violence, but also enacting, with both reverence and irreverence, a continued Indigenous future.

CONCLUSION

*Regenerating an Oceanic Future in Indigenous Space-Time*

---

Standing on our mountain of connections, our foundation of history and stories and love, we can see both where the path behind us has come from and where the path ahead leads. This connection assures us that when we move forward, we can never be lost because we always know how to get back home. The future is a realm we have inhabited for thousands of years.
—BRYAN KAMAOLI KUWADA

---

We sweat and cry salt water, so we know that the ocean is really in our blood.
—TERESIA TEAIWA

---

In April 2015, mainstream media in Hawaiʻi began reporting on what they framed as a new and controversial standoff between Kānaka Maoli and science. The proposed Thirty Meter Telescope (TMT) was set to begin construction atop Mauna a Wākea (also known by the shortened version, Mauna Kea), a sacred mountain on Hawaiʻi Island. The TMT is sponsored by a number of international universities, including the University of Hawaiʻi, which leases the land on Mauna Kea to astronomers who flock to the site due to its ideal viewing conditions (e.g., free of too much ambient light). While conflict over using the mountain for telescopes has existed since the earliest construction of telescopes on the mountain in 1968 (thirteen telescopes were built prior to the TMT proposal), unprecedented numbers of Kānaka Maoli opposed the TMT given its incredible scale—covering five acres and standing eighteen stories tall—and potential for environmental and cultural damage to the mountain's sacred sites. Often these concerns have been dismissed by mainstream media and supporters of the TMT as superstitious and spurious, despite the official environmental impact statement noting that the project would cause adverse impact. Proponents of the project instead tout the importance of science for advancing humanity, and note that the TMT corporation donates over $1 million to Hawai'i schools annually to promote science education. This is another case in which the purported good and universal benefits of Western science claim authority over what mainstream discourse paints as backward cultural difference. The logic of possession through whiteness is at work in declaring that Mauna Kea properly belongs to science (long the domain of whiteness) rather than Kānaka Maoli, who in racist depictions are portrayed as superstitious for voicing substantiated concerns about the project's environmental impact and not knowing what is best for themselves when they disregard the TMT's annual million dollar donations.

Opposition to the TMT has existed since its initial proposal in 2010. In March 2015, kia'i (a Hawaiian language word for protectors) started camping out and blocking the road to the summit, preventing construction crews from beginning work on the TMT. Though subjected to periodic arrests by the police, the kia'i continued camping on Mauna Kea through late 2015, and were ultimately successful in postponing construction and forcing the project to proceed through court hearings to determine its legality, given its impact on land that is protected as a state conservation area. As of March 2016, the TMT corporation was said to be considering other sites outside of Hawai'i for the project.[1] However, in October 2018, the Hawai'i Supreme Court ruled in support of the TMT project. The Hawai'i Department of Land and Natural Resources stated after the ruling that the process for reviewing the construction plans to make sure they adhere to environmental and cultural protocols may take up to two years.[2] As of this writing, Kānaka Maoli and allies continue to organize to block the construction and protect Mauna Kea.

Some, including some Native Hawaiians, have stated their support for the TMT through references to navigation by the stars as a traditional art treasured by Polynesian navigators, arguing that the TMT would simply be an extension of such tradition.[3] In their letter of approval of the TMT project, the Hawai'i State Board of Land and Natural Resources argued, "Ancient Hawaiians intensely studied the stars in ways consistent with their technology," while also noting Kalākaua's support of astronomy and scientific innovation in his own era.[4] Such references ignore the material consequences of the TMT's construction while also discounting the contemporary viewpoints of many Kānaka Maoli who oppose the construction as against their own tradition. Many critiques in fact hinge on disparaging the authenticity of the kiaʻi and other Kānaka Maoli who are against the construction of the TMT. For example, a former state governor and longtime representative for Hawaiʻi in the U.S. House of Representatives, Neil Abercrombie, stated that the TMT project "will move forward. There will be no more obstruction from someone who found their cultural roots six minutes ago."[5] These comments reflect a white settler claim to Hawaiʻi that declares not only the prerogative to decide what happens to and on the land, but also an entitlement to decide Native Hawaiian cultural and biological authenticity. Abercrombie's quip that the kiaʻi at Mauna Kea "found their cultural roots six minutes ago" disparages the protectors by suggesting that they are naïve youth who are not deeply grounded in Native Hawaiian culture. In this logic, the kiaʻi are represented, like many white people who claim distant Native American ancestry, as not really serious about identifying with Native Hawaiian culture and perhaps not even actually having Native Hawaiian "roots." This is just one example of how the logic of possession through whiteness continues to operate in mundane ways in Hawaiʻi today. Even as Abercrombie would likely never attempt to identify as Native Hawaiian and represents himself as a supporter of Native Hawaiian rights (by which he means state and federal recognition for Native Hawaiians, which is complicated, as discussed in chapter 4), this is an instance of a male white settler still seeking to control Polynesian resources and identities through a questioning of Polynesian origins. While distant from the earliest Polynesian Problem literature by over two centuries, this settler logic of possession through whiteness is still alive and well today.

Significantly, this logic does not go unchallenged in contemporary times, just as it was never completely uncontested historically. The efforts of the kiaʻi and other activist, artist, and scholar allies prove this.[6] Bryan Kamaoli Kuwada has written powerfully of the false portrait painted of Kānaka Maoli by supporters of the TMT by positioning Kānaka as irrationally opposed to science and progress. Kuwada astutely notes how at Mauna Kea and in many other Indigenous fights to protect land, culture, and more, "we are dismissed as relics of the past, unable to hack it in the modern world with our antiquated traditions and practices."[7] Yet he makes clear that Kānaka Maoli and other Indigenous people operate on very different scales of progress, ones in which connections, in the various forms of "our relationships to our ancestors, our language, our culture, and our 'āina" are valued most. He explains:

> And when you see the possibility of "progress" in this more connected way, you see that we are actually the ones looking to the future. We are trying to get people back to the right timescale, so that they can understand how they are connected to what is to come. One of the urgencies for the construction company trying to break ground for the telescope on the mauna is that they have a limited time in which to execute the contract. But we are operating on geological and genealogical time. Protecting the 'āina, carrying on our traditions, speaking our language, and acting as kahu for our sacred places are not things measured in days, or weeks, or even years. This work spans generations and eras and epochs.[8]

Indeed, settler ideologies often dismiss Kanaka Maoli epistemologies as primitive and backward-looking, thereby mapping Indigenous peoples onto the past as ancient relics or exotic repositories of antiquated knowledge tragically unable to participate in the present or future, as chapter 1 explored. Yet, as Kuwada demonstrates, for Kānaka Maoli, regenerating connections to sacred places, ancestors, and traditions is not a mode of "being stuck in the past" but of mapping out different, desired futures. Further, he points out how this orientation is not meant just for Kānaka Maoli in isolation but for all people, all of whom are "connected to what is to come" and will be impacted by environmental destruction. Kuwada's analysis suggests that those who denigrate Kānaka Maoli who oppose the TMT, like Abercrombie, are perhaps not just ignorant racists who belittle Indigenous peoples but are significantly threatened by the ramifications of orienting themselves to the timescales and types of connection Kuwada describes, given how deeply these ideas undercut the core values of capitalism and settler colonialism.

Kuwada's analysis beautifully illustrates what Salesa has called Indigenous time, or more precisely, Indigenous space-time. Indigenous space-time operates on different scales of history and future, and different scales of space. As Salesa puts it, in Pacific Indigenous space-time, grounded in genealogies that cross historical and spiritual boundaries, "the past is not just a time but also a *place*."[9] Where the Polynesian Problem literature sought the racial origins of Polynesians across Asia or the Americas, Polynesians themselves always knew they came from Hawaiki, the ancestral homeland. Accordingly, as Salesa points out, "Not just genealogies of people, but genealogies of place tie Polynesia together."[10] This book started out as a critical history of how Polynesia became a settler colonial project, not a place. Recognizing, learning, and practicing Indigenous space-time is one method of making Polynesia an Indigenous Pacific project and destroying the settler colonial one.

Regenerative refusals operate in this kind of Indigenous space-time, as Kuwada shows us with the refusals of the kiaʻi at Mauna Kea. As argued throughout part II of this book, regenerative refusal is a significant strategy employed by Kānaka Maoli and other Indigenous peoples in order to challenge the settler colonial logic of possession through whiteness and enact different, more expansive forms of self-recognition and relationality. Saying no or aʻole to participation in federal recognition, genomic studies, or the TMT project are not simply empty, contrary, or ignorant objections, though this is how they are so often represented by the "reasonable" voices of authority in the mainstream media, science, and government. The refusals that I have analyzed in part II are not just about voicing dissent but also about enabling a transformed and liberatory future. Indigenous refusal, then, is not necessarily limited to a refusal to say something or a refusal to look a certain way, but, as Audra Simpson's notion of ethnographic refusal signals, a broader refusal to participate in the production of "natural," "authentic" Indigenous subjects who might be easily apprehended and utilized by Western social scientific knowledge production, Western contemporary art canons, or Western linear history. Regenerative refusals therefore push Indigenous and non-Indigenous peoples and places into relationships that deeply threaten settler colonial framings of time and space.

In refusing settler colonial knowledge production of the "Native," or the "Polynesian," Indigenous activists and artists do not just gaze back at the West but look elsewhere, to their own desires for themselves and their people. Regenerative refusals recognize violence and pain, but not to make that the center of Indigenous identity; rather, these refusals highlight the importance of envisioning and enacting different futures that are suffused with more love, humor, connection, and freedom. This is why the energy surrounding the kiaʻi at Mauna Kea and the powerful testimonies at the DOI hearings was electric, even for those watching and supporting from afar. For even in the face of what seemed to be unwinnable or unchangeable circumstances, in these cases people dared to refuse and demand a different future. Refusals allow for a blooming of desires beyond the strictures of settler colonialism that pretend to be eternal and unchangeable, and beyond the settler assumption that Polynesia and Polynesians are and will always be the possessions of whiteness.

Indigenous refusals create forms of regeneration that, as Kuwada writes, consciously remap Indigenous worlds onto a different time scale than settler time—on "geological and genealogical time" that "spans generations and eras and epochs." Again, this shift is a kind of Indigenous space-time generated through Indigenous actions. From the intergenerational testimonies at the federal recognition hearings in 2014 to the Indigenous contemporary art that speaks to both the colonial past and present and dream of radically decolonized futures, the activists, community members, and artists I consider in part II are engaged in work that slowly builds distinct ways of seeing and knowing. Those who dismiss such work as hopeless and naïve, while advocating moderate steps and acceding to settler forms of recognition, argue that we must grasp what is realizable now, within our lifetimes. But pursuing the expedient measures of the state or Western science too often interrupts the deeper, more significant forms of regeneration that require constant nurturing and care.

As many Kānaka Maoli who refused the Hawaiian Genome Project demonstrated, when promised solutions to structural problems violate deeply held understandings about our responsibilities to ourselves and other forms of life, they are not meaningful solutions. The evocation of the Kumulipo and the lesson that humans are the younger siblings of Hāloa or kalo in the Paoakalani Declaration pushes Kānaka Maoli to remember a different time scale and the long-term kuleana we have to care for the land. The Hāloa story also reminds Kānaka Maoli that we have many of the solutions to our own problems within our stories and our communities, as it also reminds us of the importance of sustainable and healthy food, noting that the revival of kalo farming and eating poi as a staple could help stem diabetes (one of the problems the Hawaiian Genome Project claimed it could potentially provide solutions to). Regenerative refusals such as these have the potential to offer different definitions not just of Native Hawaiian or Polynesian identity but of humanity itself, through an emphasis on relationality to other forms of life, not as superior to, but in reciprocal relationship with kalo, ʻāina, and other life.

Native Hawaiian writer Victoria Nālani Kneubuhl's short story "Hoʻoulu Lāhui" meditates on how genetic technologies may maintain the settler colonial importance of Hawaiian genes and "blood" into the future.[11] Published in 2000, the story takes place in a future Hawaiʻi, now independent from the United States but governed by a "New Hawaiian Nation" that privileges "pure" Hawaiian people to such an extent they have cloned thousands of "pure" Hawaiians to "ho'oulu lāhui," or "increase the race." As noted previously, Ho'oulu Lāhui, which was a slogan of King Kalākaua in the late 1800s, was part of his overall push to revitalize Native Hawaiian culture and hearten the Hawaiian people after several devastating epidemics. The main character of the story is Kahikina, an elderly woman who has just discovered that the egg she had donated to the nation as a young woman was fertilized by a "pure" Hawaiian man's sperm, and then replicated and cloned thousands of times to produce a new, "pure" race of Native Hawaiians, all without her knowledge or consent. She feels deeply violated, and the story follows her as she reconsiders her relationship to a beloved nephew who she has just discovered is one of these cloned children of hers, and to the man whose sperm was used to fertilize her egg, who she at first refuses to meet.

The story might be considered a retelling of a different version of the Kumulipo, in which kalo and humans are the children of Wākea (Sky Father) and his daughter Ho'ohokulani. Kneubuhl's story emphasizes that the future New Hawaiian Nation has chosen a sanitized version of this origin story, in which kalo and human beings are the product of Wākea and Papa (Earth Mother), not of Wākea and Ho'ohokulani. Kahikina notes that her grandmother told her the real story in secret, of how Wākea deceived Papa and slept with their daughter Ho'ohokulani, and from this union came the Hawaiian people. Her grandmother tells her, "She had children with her father.... Papa found out about the deception and spat in Wākea's face. People today don't like this story. They don't like that it tells how our people came from a lie, a lie to deceive women, but this is the story our ancestors told, my pua [flower, child]." Rather than shy away from this unflattering, troubling version of the story, Kahikina in fact identifies with Ho'ohokulani through the violation she has experienced and the cover-up perpetrated by the New Hawaiian Nation. When her nephew (who is actually her son), Alika, pushes Kahikina to forgive and welcome the man who also unknowingly fathered thousands of cloned children, Kahikina despairs that Alika doesn't know what it means to be "to be like a hole, a big gaping hole in the heavens through which thousands of offsprings pour! ... Elements are missing here, vital, aching, human elements: motherhood, pleasure, the feel of tiny feet and the closeness of small clinging limbs, the intoxicating smell of your flesh made flesh." Here we have Kahikina's reconfiguration of the human as, again, a matter of relationality, one that is deeply felt and offers pleasure, closeness, and connection. It is this relationality that has been denied to her in the use of her egg to create and clone thousands of children she has no relationship with.

Kanaka Maoli scholar Joyce Pualani Warren argues that this story "imagines how, when steeped in foreign constructions of identity, movements for political and cultural sovereignty could potentially intersect the future genetic engineering of a racially 'pure,' decolonized citizenry."[12] Kneubuhl and Warren thus gesture toward how important it is for Native Hawaiians ourselves to remain critical of how settler colonial notions of indigeneity based in race have warped how we understand our own people. Warren argues that, despite showing a nightmarish scenario of the future in which an independent Hawaiian nation is not really decolonized because it still operates according to settler colonial logics about race, Kneubuhl's story also shows how certain characters are able to refuse the ideology of purity by reorienting themselves to Kanaka Maoli epistemologies that, like the Paoakalani Declaration discussed in chapter 5, position Kānaka Maoli as the younger siblings of the land, genealogically linked to the universe through the Kumulipo.[13] Here again, both refusal of settler colonial logics and regeneration of Indigenous modes of recognition and space-time create possibilities for relating to each other differently, even in the face of genetic reification of Hawaiian blood and other kinds of violations that happen within Hawaiian communities.

Hence, regenerative refusals can strikingly reorient Kānaka Maoli and other Indigenous peoples away from investments in blood quantum and the burden of proving either purity or proximity to whiteness. In the logic of possession through whiteness, Kānaka Maoli are divided between Pure and Part Hawaiians, and legally between native Hawaiians and Native Hawaiians. This logic ensures that though Kānaka Maoli are said to be able to assimilate into whiteness, this assimilation is always deferred and incomplete. If there is a haunting quality to the logic of possession through whiteness in the persistence of settler colonial ideologies and practices, there is a responding, haunting quality to the ongoing challenge that Indigenous peoples exert in their responses to this colonial logic. The expected fading of Polynesians into whiteness never happens because of deep, intergenerational memories and the passing down of Indigenous identities and ways of life. Possession through whiteness is a one-way conduit that allows white settlers to claim ownership over indigeneity, while Indigenous people will never have secure ownership over whiteness as property. Yet in each of the last three chapters, Kānaka Maoli have shown that this divisive logic, which benefits white settlers by freeing up more resources and casting doubt on

Kānaka Maoli claims to indigeneity and authority, can and must be challenged. While chapter 4 looked at several Kānaka Maoli men who did seek to reinforce blood quantum policies, it also analyzed the pervasive sense among those testifying at the hearings on federal recognition that even those who are legally "native Hawaiian" and are homesteaders are often strong opponents of the 50 percent rule. Kneubuhl's short story suggests that internalizing notions of racial purity within Kānaka Maoli communities can lead to dystopian futures in which our vast genealogies and the knowledge associated with them are flattened and hollowed out. Yet, even in that apocalyptic future, Kānaka Maoli are not doomed. The story envisions a different path through recognizing colonial damage, regenerating our relationships with Hāloa and other forms of life, and thereby practicing different forms of humanness. Kneubuhl's story bolsters my belief that we Kānaka Maoli can end our investments in such internalized racial divisions and hierarchies, though this will require constant, difficult practice.

Settler colonial ideologies that valorize and universalize racial mixture can be just as dystopic and damaging as valorizing racial purity. Romanzo Adams's grand vision of Hawai'i in the early twentieth-century as a fantastic American melting pot free of racial problems did not do away with racism but encouraged it, especially for those who did not appear to be sufficiently "mixed," such as dark-skinned Native Hawaiian men. Meanwhile, mixed-race Native Hawaiian women were fetishized and represented in popular culture as the exotic rewards and possessions of deserving white American settler and military men in Hawai'i. Yet many Kānaka Maoli and others refuse to let indigeneity be erased and possessed through whiteness via settler colonial discourses of racial mixture. In chapter 6, I highlighted several mixed-race Indigenous Pacific artists whose work challenges the commodification of Indigenous identity, especially the ways that Polynesian women's bodies are represented as the soft, exotic possessions promised to white male settlers. Kihara and Pao each demonstrate that racial mixture does not make mixed-race Indigenous people immune from racial and settler colonial violence, but they also show that neither does it divorce mixed-race Indigenous people from finding strength and foundations in their genealogies and indigeneity. Their ethnographic refusals point out the fiction of imposed ideologies of race, while gesturing toward alternative Indigenous forms of recognition and relationality. Again, these kinds of activism, testimony, art, and literature described in part II are often evaluated as impractical and inauthentic in comparison to the supposedly more substantial change pursued through legislation and scientific study. Yet, as

Indigenous feminists remind us, the desires and dreams we have for our peoples matter profoundly for sustaining life and seeding decolonization.

In addition to regenerating our relationships to the ʻāina in Hawaiʻi, this book also suggests that Kānaka Maoli and others have more work to do in regenerating our genealogies and familial kuleana to the rest of Polynesia and the broader Oceania. In thinking about regenerating Polynesia, we must refuse the racial hierarchies that have been embedded in the imposed Polynesia/Melanesia/Micronesia divisions, and further work that recognizes all parts of Oceania as sites of expansive Indigenous relationality, deeply connected genealogically, ecologically, and otherwise. Too often, at least within continental U.S. popular discourse, Polynesians stand in for all Pacific Islanders, and similarly, Native Hawaiians too often stand in for all Polynesians and all Pacific Islanders. Native Hawaiians especially, then, have a responsibility to amplify other Polynesian and Pacific Islander voices and political struggles, and to forge lasting forms of solidarity based on mutual recognition of shared genealogies and interlocking, ongoing histories of colonialism and imperialism.

In part I, I analyzed how Kālakaua and Te Rangihīroa in their different ways sought and built Polynesian alliances and recognition. While we can take inspiration from them both, and recognize the difficult colonial contexts of their positions, we also must reject the superiority Kālakaua attributed to Kānaka Maoli over Sāmoans and the valorized whiteness of Polynesians maintained by Te Rangihīroa. This book has analyzed the origins and legacies of the logic of possession through whiteness in order to make clear how damaging and divisive such ideas about Polynesian proximity to whiteness have been to our communities. Accordingly, I argue that decolonization for Native Hawaiians and all Polynesians must center recognizing and deconstructing the racial and gendered hierarchies we have internalized through centuries of Western imperialism and colonialism. As the inspiring actions at Mauna Kea, Standing Rock, and many other Indigenous sacred sites have proven, our relationships with land, water, and each other are life-giving. Indigenous feminist scholar Mishuana Goeman elegantly puts it this way in describing why rebuilding relationships to land, and not just legal reclamations of land, is so important:

> Even if we were to recover the historical and legal dimensions of territory, for instance, I am not so sure that this alone would unsettle colonialism. Recovery has a certain saliency in Native American studies; it is appealing to people who have been dispossessed materially and culturally.

I contend, however, that it is also our responsibility to interrogate our ever-changing Native epistemologies that frame our understanding of land and our relationships to it and to other peoples. In this vein, (re)mapping is not just about regaining that which was lost and returning to an original and pure point in history, but instead understanding the processes that have defined our current spatialities in order to sustain vibrant Native futures.[14]

Goeman's (re)mapping resonates with this text's approach to regeneration, emphasizing not just a recovery of what was lost or damaged through colonialism, but deeper reckoning with what changes are needed in our own ways of thinking about our relationships. The point is not only to reestablish control over a piece of land, and to own it in the capitalist system, but to more fundamentally think through how to reestablish mutually caring relationships with land and with each other. This relationship building, too often dismissed as not essential or as not "material" (read: "masculine") to decolonial movements, is not something to do only because it may be considered "traditional" in some respects, but more importantly because it can, as Goeman says, "sustain vibrant Native futures."

In the Oceanic context, I argue that regeneration and (re)mapping requires turning critical attention to the regional and racial boundaries colonialism imposes, and acting on and renewing the ancestral and contemporary responsibilities and solidarities forged between Indigenous Pacific peoples, so that our struggles for decolonization are never made in isolation. There are a number of ongoing political actions and relationships being cultivated between Polynesians, Melanesians, and Micronesians that suggest that it is possible to reject the imposed regional divisions and racial hierarchies that have encouraged valorizing Polynesian proximity to whiteness and perpetuating antiblackness against Melanesians and, at times, Micronesians. For example, recently, a major focus of organizing among Pacific Islanders in New Zealand, Australia, and the United States has been the amplification of the Free West Papua struggle. Subject to genocide and settler colonialism at the hands of Indonesia since 1962, West Papuans are fighting for their freedom, but due to U.S. and UN complicity with Indonesia and tight restrictions on foreign journalists visiting West Papua, their struggle has been in isolation for far too long. Recently, however, other Pacific Islanders have learned more by meeting activists such as Benny Wenda, a West Papuan independence leader who lives in exile in the United Kingdom. One of the most inspiring groups that have organized to raise awareness and support for West Papua is Oceania Interrupted, a group of Māori and Pacific Islander women based in Auckland, New Zealand.[15] In 2015, they carried out fifteen public actions, inspired by the fact that the sentence under Indonesian rule for raising the Morning Star flag of West Papua is fifteen years in jail. These actions were inspiring public performances, using the Morning Star flag in a variety of ways, including strikingly painted over the women's faces, to draw attention to the cause and its erasure from mainstream discourse.

In Hawai'i, a similar solidarity group composed of Native Hawaiian and Pacific Islander artists, poets, scholars, and activists at the University of Hawai'i has also staged events to raise awareness for West Papua. In 2015, they published *Wansolwara: Voices for West Papua*, a collection of poems, lyrics, and art dedicated to fostering solidarity between Hawai'i and West Papua.[16] Kānaka Maoli poet Brandy Nālani McDougall and Chamorro poet Craig Santos Perez, in their poem "Morning Star" in this collection, write: "papuan cousins, / we're so sorry / we didn't see you— / but we see you now— / and imagine someday / we can talk story."[17] McDougall and Perez's poem acknowledges the wide differences between their lives in Hawai'i and the lives of West Papuans under occupation. While it marks the gaps between many Pacific Islanders and West Papuans, it also seeks to rectify previous blind spots and seeks to begin to build a deeper relationship with West Papuans as "cousins." Similarly, a poem by Kānaka Maoli poets No'u Revilla and Jamaica Osorio, titled "A Love Letter to West Papua," asks: "How do I learn to love you when / I know so little of your body? / None of your spine, terrain, lifelines." Revilla and Osorio evince a desire to know and love West Papua more deeply, imagining "Our touching a ceremony of resistance."[18] These are moving first steps in combating antiblackness among Pacific Islander peoples and models how Polynesians might regenerate meaningful relationships with Melanesians as Indigenous Pacific kin.

In another example, in recent years, Micronesian people living in Hawai'i have seen increasing daily discrimination from individuals and institutions. It seems that in the contemporary moment, Micronesians in Hawai'i are placed distinctly on the darker side of the Polynesian–Melanesian divide. A 2014 federal court decision declared that the state of Hawai'i does not have to provide Medicaid to Micronesian residents, who are nonetheless allowed to live and work in the United States on the basis of the Compact of Free Association between the United States and Palau, the Federated States of Micronesia, and the Marshall Islands. This health care denial is stunning in part because of the direct impacts the United States has had on Micronesians' health—namely, decades of nuclear testing in the Marshall Islands that devastated many islands and has caused cancer, reproductive deformities, and other health repercussions for Marshallese people.[19] Such denials are also enabled by antiblack welfare queen discourses that continue to posit Micronesians as undeserving, lazy, and nonheteronormative in order to deny them care.

A number of recent stories have also documented blatant anti-immigrant racism against Micronesians in Hawai'i, from radio programs making jokes about radiation damage to Micronesians to graffiti on Micronesian stores declaring, "Return my tax dollars."[20] Marshallese poet, activist, and scholar Kathy Jetñil-Kijiner responds powerfully to such racism in much of her work, including her spoken word poem "Lessons from Hawai'i," which parrots and critiques the things she hears daily about Micronesians in Hawai'i, including "You're actually kind of smart ... for a Micronesian," "You don't look Micronesian. You're much prettier," "Don't they know? This isn't their country, this is America," and "We should have just nuked their islands when we got the chance."[21] She further notes in an interview following the poem that she recognizes such racism from Hawaiians as stemming from "the government ... pushing our communities against each other," when it does not have to be that way: "I want to see us collaborate, I want to see us working together." Jetñil-Kijiner has indeed collaborated in a variety of ways with other Pacific Islander and Indigenous artists and activists. She has especially been recognized as a leader in the fight against climate change; she was invited to the opening of the UN Climate Change Summit in New York City in 2014 to read a poem about the effects of climate change in her home, and was visibly active with other Indigenous activists at the 2015 UN Climate Change Conference.

Jetñil-Kijiner is also a contributor to the Pacific-focused blog *Ke Kaupu Hehi Ale*, which includes a number of Pacific Islander authors writing on a number of issues that connect the Pacific (including Bryan Kamaoli Kuwada's writing about the future, noted above). The blog has often featured writing about overcoming the disconnections between different Pacific and non-Pacific peoples, especially highlighting the importance of challenging antiblackness within Pacific Islander communities and settler colonial nations including the United States, Australia, Fiji, and elsewhere. These connections are sparked by both the movement to free West Papua and the Black Lives Matter movement, an intersectional movement grounded in the continental United States that combats, among many other issues, the death of Black men and women at the hands of police. Many of the contributors find it urgent to be in solidarity with Black Lives Matter. Yet they also demonstrate that it is more than solidarity in a distanced fashion that they seek; rather, they hope their reflections will create stronger relationships within and among Pacific Islanders by challenging the internalization of colonial ideas of antiblackness and acknowledging a genealogy that includes blackness. For example, Kānaka Maoli and Black artist and scholar Joy Enomoto writes: "the first people of the Pacific were Black. Hawaii belongs to the Pacific. And so we must act against the genocide that is happening in West Papua being imposed by the Indonesian Army to protect mining interests, we must support the Kanak liberation struggle of New Caledonia as they continue their struggle for independence from France, we cannot forget the islands threatened by climate change in Vanuatu, Fiji, the Cook and Solomon Islands. BLACK LIVES MATTER IN OCEANIA."[22]

Enomoto thus directly challenges in her writing the imposed Western division of Polynesia, Melanesia, and Micronesia, emphasizing the connections between both the peoples and the many colonial struggles faced across Oceania. She also insists "that we all must expand our definitions of Blackness to include our Pacific sisters and brothers, whose lives have been marked as black while respecting how they define themselves."[23]

Another contributor to *Ke Kaupu Hehi Ale*, Fijian scholar and poet Tagi Qolouvaki, similarly writes that Black Lives Matter calls Pacific Islanders to recognize the legacies of past Black–Pacific alliances and foster more, while also needing to confront antiblackness in our own families and communities. She writes: "White supremacy and antiblackness continue to foster conditions where whiteness (and let's be honest, Polynesian-ness) is often judged superior and beautiful in the Indigenous homelands of brown and black children. . . . For decolonization in Oceania to succeed, we must root out antiblackness and white supremacy in our communities wherever they are. For true Oceanic unity in kinship, we must commit to loving blackness."[24] She notes the historical and ongoing placement of Polynesian-ness in close proximity to whiteness, and argues that this must be honestly confronted. She also argues for prioritizing loving blackness in Oceanic communities, seeing it as an urgent task for decolonial movements to attend to if we really want decolonization to succeed.

The above examples are just a few of the many regenerative ways that Pacific Islander activists, poets, artists, and scholars are doing the difficult but vital work of deconstructing the logic of possession through whiteness. Overall, there is no one "right" way to respond to being possessed by settler colonial whiteness. As a tool in service of decolonization, regeneration, as this book has theorized it, is not the opposite of power/knowledge but its haunting. It is a refusal to let the invisible lines undergirding the order of things established by scientific texts go unnoticed. Decolonization, if we look at it from an Indigenous feminist perspective, means more than just recovery of lost land and sovereignty, as Goeman notes above. Instead, decolonization will be a long-term practice that may not have any clear end in sight. Yet daily imagining and building decolonial futures is key to sustaining life, desire, and love within our Indigenous communities. Regenerative responses to the logic of possession through whiteness therefore allow us to reveal that science, heteropatriarchy, and whiteness (including but not reducible to white people) are inextricable parts of the story of settler colonialism in the Pacific, even (or especially) when science, heteropatriarchy, and whiteness present themselves as settler colonialism's solution, such as in the Hawaiian Genome Project's projected financial and medical benefits or the TMT's heralded donations to science education.

Eve Tuck and K. Wayne Yang write that "Decolonization is not an 'and.' It is an elsewhere."[25] Their sentiment resonates with Salesa's Indigenous space-time in that it asks readers to do the sometimes difficult and scary work of setting aside our understandings of time and space as we have come to know them through settler colonialism, imperialism, and other structures that promote white supremacy. Instead, Salesa, alongside the other Indigenous Pacific scholars, artists, and activists I have written about in this book, push us to see that change must be imagined and practiced at both micro and macro, short-term and long-term scales that unsettle any notion of simple solutions. Accordingly, this book has not attempted to offer policy solutions for how damaging scientific colonial ideologies and their legacies might be simply reconciled or reformed. Instead, I have tried to show, given the wide-reaching and ongoing legacies of the idea that Polynesians are conditionally white, that such reconciliation might not be possible or desirable but necessarily refused.

Rather than viewing such refusals as hopelessly backward (as many do in the standoff between Kānaka Maoli and the TMT), we might follow Indigenous Pacific peoples in setting aside such questions, at least at times. For refusals can also be paths to connection, in the context of settler colonial dispossession. Salesa concludes of Indigenous space-time that "Indigenous seaways and genealogies were always changing, but always connected here with there, and the present with ancestors."[26] Indeed, Polynesia radiates with these bright ties, linking both peoples and places. Sometimes refusals and boundaries are the best and clearest path to staying in good relation with people, with places, with knowledge. In Hawai'i, kapu (often translated into English as taboo or prohibition) recognizes precisely this: that there are limits passed down from ancestors that are honored and practiced because it protects not only a sacred place or person from harm but because it protects ourselves too.

What if we measured the success of our organizing, our research and writing, our relationships, and all our efforts toward decolonization in precisely these terms: Are we connecting here with there, the present with the ancestors? Are we keeping kapu and refusing what must be refused for our own freedoms, spirits, and bodies to be protected and loved? Indigenous feminists know that decolonization is never an overnight happening; it must be practiced and comprehended at Indigenous scales both intimate and grand. Both our ancestors and our next generations share these lessons in a million ways. While we march and protest and write against settler colonialism, there is also food to be made, children to bathe, elders to support. We fight not just to dismantle but to create the conditions for maintaining these practices of caring for each other, for sustaining more life. Whatever our ongoing strategies against the logic of possession through whiteness may be, we must anticipate being unsettled. But we also must rejoice in the fact that such unsettling is part of the collective work we must do, caringly and carefully, to realize our interconnected, expansive Oceanic future.

# NOTES

### INTRODUCTION: POLYNESIA IS A PROJECT, NOT A PLACE

1 In this book, I use Native Hawaiian, Kanaka Maoli, and Kanaka ʻŌiwi (the latter two Hawaiian language words suggesting "real people" and "people of the bone," respectively) interchangeably to refer to the Indigenous peoples of Hawaiʻi. Kānaka (with the macron or kahakō) denotes the plural form. Kanaka (without the kahakō) is used for singular and categorical forms.
2 Toni Morrison, *Playing in the Dark* (New York: Random House, 2007), 17.
3 In this book, I generally capitalize the word *Black* when referring to self-identified Black people and communities, following the practice of Black authors who have long capitalized Black as a matter of respecting and highlighting Black identity. This is similar to how I capitalize *Indigenous* when referring to self-identified Indigenous people and communities, again as is the established practice of Indigenous authors. I generally use a lower-case form of *black* when referring to colonial, racial ideologies about blackness imposed on people and communities, without those communities necessarily self-identifying as Black.
4 Noenoe Silva, *Aloha Betrayed: Native Hawaiian Resistance to American Colonialism* (Durham, NC: Duke University Press, 2004), 173–78.
5 Thor Heyerdahl, *Kon-Tiki: Across the Pacific by Raft* (Chicago: Rand McNally, 1950); Axel Andersson, *A Hero for the Atomic Age: Thor Heyerdahl and the Kon-Tiki Expedition* (Oxford: Peter Lang, 2010); Graham E. L. Holton, "Heyerdahl's Kon Tiki Theory and the Denial of the Indigenous Past," *Anthropological Forum* 14, no. 2 (2004): 163–81.

6 Later, Heyerdahl made similar trips on reed boats, supposedly emulating ancient Egyptian crafts, first from Morocco in an attempt to cross the Atlantic to South America in 1969, and then from the Tigris River in Iraq across the Arabian Sea to the Red Sea, in 1977. *Encyclopedia Britannica*, "Thor Heyerdahl," April 11, 2018, accessed August 8, 2018, https://www.britannica.com/biography/Thor-Heyerdahl.

7 Helen Altonn, "Heyerdahl's Book Stirs Pacific Debate Anew," *Honolulu Star-Bulletin*, May 27, 1962.

8 Polynesian Voyaging Society, "Hokulea," accessed June 29, 2018, http://www.hokulea.com/.

9 UNESCO Memory of the World, "Thor Heyerdahl Archives," accessed September 11, 2018, http://www.unesco.org/new/en/communication-and-information/memory-of-the-world/register/full-list-of-registered-heritage/registered-heritage-page-8/thor-heyerdahl-archives/.

10 Joachim Rønning and Espen Sandberg, *Kon-Tiki*, feature film, 2013.

11 Polynesian Voyaging Society, "Hokulea."

12 Quoted in Victor Bascara, *Model-Minority Imperialism* (Minneapolis: University of Minnesota Press, 2006), xxiii–xxiv.

13 For example, Epeli Hau'ofa's important scholarship has intervened into Western framings of the Pacific Islands as small islands in a far sea, reenvisioning the Pacific as an expansive world, as "our sea of islands." Yet Alice Te Punga Somerville has balanced such utopic framings of the Indigenous communities of Polynesia and Oceania more widely with a charge to engage the "disjunctures" and "rather embarrassing genealogies of suspicion, derision, and competition between our communities," which are also often undeniably present and structured by racism and colonialism. Epeli Hau'ofa, *We Are the Ocean: Selected Works* (Honolulu: University of Hawai'i Press, 2008); Alice Te Punga Somerville, *Once Were Pacific: Maori Connections to Oceania* (Minneapolis: University of Minnesota Press, 2012), xxiii.

14 In this book, I use the macron in the words *Sāmoa*, *Sāmoan*, and *Māori*, in keeping with contemporary orthographic standards in Sāmoan and Māori languages. In original sources, I have kept the spelling as originally published (e.g., *The Aryan Maori*).

15 Empowering Pacific Islander Communities, "A Community of Contrasts: Native Hawaiians and Pacific Islanders in the United States," 2014, https://www.scribd.com/document/214381774/a-Community-of-Contrasts-Native-Hawaiians-and-Pacific-Islanders-in-the-United-States.

16 Tonga did sign a Treaty of Friendship with the United Kingdom in 1900, making it a British protectorate until 1970. See Matt Matsuda, *Pacific Worlds: A History of Seas, Peoples, and Cultures* (Cambridge: Cambridge University Press, 2012), 304.

17 Hōkūlani Aikau, *A Chosen People, a Promised Land: Mormonism and Race in Hawai'i* (Minneapolis: University of Minnesota Press, 2012).

18 The last census that asked about ethnicity in French Polynesia was in 1988; it reported 66.5 percent of the population was Mā'ohi, and 11.9 percent were European. Māori comprised approximately 15 percent of New Zealand's population in 2013, whereas the "New Zealand European" population amounted to 68 percent in the 2013 census. In Hawai'i, Native Hawaiians (including those of mixed-race ancestry) make up approximately 21 percent of the population, whereas Asians make up 37 percent and white people make up 23 percent of the population, according to 2013 census data. See "French Polynesia Population 2018," World Population Review, accessed June 30, 2018, http://worldpopulationreview.com/countries/french-polynesia-population/; U.S. Census Bureau, "QuickFacts: Hawaii," accessed June 30, 2018, https://www.census.gov/quickfacts/fact/table/hi/PST045217; and Stats NZ, "2013 Census Ethnic Group Profiles," accessed June 30, 2018, http://archive.stats.govt.nz/Census/2013-census/profile-and-summary-reports/ethnic-profiles.aspx.

19 Sara Ahmed, *On Being Included: Racism and Diversity in Institutional Life* (Durham, NC: Duke University Press, 2012).

20 These physical anthropologists pushed UNESCO to modify their language around race's relation to biology in subsequent Statements on Race in 1951, 1964, and 1967. See Ashley Montagu, *Statement on Race: An Annotated Elaboration and Exposition of the Four Statements on Race Issued by the United Nations Educational, Scientific, and Cultural Organization* (New York: Oxford University Press, 1972).

21 Michelle Brattain, "Race, Racism, and Antiracism: UNESCO and the Politics of Presenting Science to the Postwar Public," *American Historical Review* 112, no. 5 (2007): 1386–413.

22 UNESCO, *What Is Race? Evidence from Scientists* (Paris: UNESCO, 1952), 37.

23 A. L. Kroeber, *Anthropology: Race, Language, Culture, Psychology, Prehistory* (New York: Harcourt, Brace, 1948); UNESCO, *What Is Race?*, 42.

24 "Referring to the list of racial characteristics on page 45, you might try to decide into what group you think the Polynesians should go and then compare the results with the work of Dr. Harry Shapiro." UNESCO, *What Is Race?*, 37, 45. The referenced list on page 45, titled "Physical Characteristics of the Three Main Races of Mankind," supplements the three circles diagram by describing the skin color, stature, head form, face, hair, eye color and eye fold shape, nose, and body build of the Caucasoid, Mongoloid, and Negroid.

25 Earnest Albert Hooton, *Up from the Ape* (New York: Macmillan, 1954).

26 Hooton, *Up from the Ape*, 617.

27 Kroeber, *Anthropology*, 140.

28 Although, lest readers confuse all Indigenous Pacific Islanders as Polynesian, the diagram also includes a separate dot for "Oceanic Mongoloids" and "Oceanic Negroids." Though unexplained in the *What Is Race?* booklet, Kroeber's text notes that Oceanic Negroids are "Papuo-Melanesian," who "are clearly close relatives" of Negroes—"A trained observer can distinguish them at sight,

but a novice would take a Papuan from New Guinea or a Melanesian from the Solomon or Bismarck islands to be an African." Kroeber does not elaborate on the Oceanic Mongoloid type. Kroeber, *Anthropology*, 137, 140.

29 "Race in a Genetic World," *Harvard Magazine*, May–June 2008, accessed June 29, 2018, https://harvardmagazine.com/2008/05/race-in-a-genetic-world-html.

30 Whiteness is a construction, not an agent in and of itself, which is why I generally use the phrasing "possession *through* whiteness," rather than "possession *by* whiteness."

31 Empowering Pacific Islander Communities, "A Community of Contrasts."

32 See, for example, on Louis Robert Sullivan: Warwick Anderson, "Racial Hybridity, Physical Anthropology, and Human Biology in the Colonial Laboratories of the United States," *Current Anthropology* 53, no. S5 (2012): S95–107; on Abraham Fornander: Silva, *Aloha Betrayed*, 71–72, and kuʻualoha hoʻomanawanui, *Voices of Fire: Reweaving the Literary Lei of Pele and Hiʻiaka* (Minneapolis: University of Minnesota Press, 2014), 45.

33 *Structure of dominance* being Stuart Hall's term, with which he describes racism. I am describing colonialism as a distinct but related structure of dominance. Stuart Hall, "Race, Articulation and Societies Structured in Dominance," in *Sociological Theories: Race and Colonialism*, edited by UNESCO (Paris: UNESCO, 1980), 305–45.

34 See, for example: Jon Kamakawiwoʻole Osorio, *Dismembering Lāhui: A History of the Hawaiian Nation to 1887* (Honolulu: University of Hawaiʻi Press, 2002); Lilikalā Kameʻeleihiwa, *Native Land and Foreign Desires = Ko Hawaiʻi ʻĀina a Me Nā Koi Puʻumake a Ka Poʻe Haole: A History of Land Tenure Change in Hawaiʻi from Traditional Times until the 1848 Māhele, Including an Analysis of Hawaiian Aliʻi and American Calvinists* (Honolulu: Bishop Museum Press, 1992); Silva, *Aloha Betrayed*.

35 John Roy Musick, *Hawaii, Our New Possessions: An Account of Travels and Adventure, with Sketches of the Scenery . . . an Appendix Containing the Treaty of Annexation to the United States* (New York: Funk and Wagnalls, 1898).

36 Mark Rifkin, "Settler Common Sense," *Settler Colonial Studies* 3, no. 3–4 (2013): 322–40.

37 Patrick Wolfe, *Settler Colonialism and the Transformation of Anthropology: The Politics and Poetics of an Ethnographic Event* (London: Cassell, 1999).

38 Scott Morgensen, "The Biopolitics of Settler Colonialism: Right Here, Right Now."

39 Maile Arvin, Eve Tuck, and Angie Morrill, "Decolonizing Feminism: Challenging Connections Between Settler Colonialism and Heteropatriarchy." See also Andrea Smith, "Queer Theory and Native Studies: The Heteronormativity of Settler Colonialism," *Settler Colonial Studies* 1, no. 1 (2011): 52–76.

40 Andrea Smith, *Conquest: Sexual Violence and American Indian Genocide* (Cambridge, MA: South End, 2005).

41 Denise Ferreira da Silva, *Toward a Global Idea of Race* (Minneapolis: University of Minnesota Press, 2007).

42 Jared Sexton, *Amalgamation Schemes: Antiblackness and the Critique of Multiracialism* (Minneapolis: University of Minnesota Press, 2008), 20.

43 Tavia Nyong'o, *The Amalgamation Waltz: Race, Performance, and the Ruses of Memory* (Minneapolis: University of Minnesota Press, 2009), 9–10.

44 Nyong'o, *The Amalgamation Waltz*, 9–10.

45 Nyong'o, *The Amalgamation Waltz*, 9–10.

46 Maile Arvin, Eve Tuck, and Angie Morrill, "Decolonizing Feminism: Challenging Connections between Settler Colonialism and Heteropatriarchy," *Feminist Formations* 25, no. 1 (2013): 8–34.

47 Lorenzo Veracini, "Introducing Settler Colonial Studies," *Settler Colonial Studies* 1, no. 1 (2011): 1–12.

48 Veracini, "Introducing Settler Colonial Studies," 4.

49 On California Indians, see Deborah Miranda, *Bad Indians: A Tribal Memoir* (Berkeley, CA: Heyday, 2013).

50 For more on the incommensurabilities of settler colonialism, see Eve Tuck and K. Wayne Yang, "Decolonization Is Not a Metaphor," *Decolonization: Indigeneity, Education and Society* 1, no. 1 (2012): 1–40.

51 Somerville, *Once Were Pacific*; ho'omanawanui, *Voices of Fire*; Ty Kāwika Tengan, *Native Men Remade: Gender and Nation in Contemporary Hawai'i* (Durham, NC: Duke University Press, 2008); Aikau, *A Chosen People, a Promised Land*.

52 Damon Salesa, "The Pacific in Indigenous Time," in *Pacific Histories: Ocean, Land, People*, edited by David Armitage and Alison Bashford (New York: Palgrave Macmillan, 2014), 41.

53 Salesa, "The Pacific in Indigenous Time," 43.

54 Many other Indigenous studies scholars have also significantly developed theories of regeneration, including Taiaiake Alfred and Andrea Smith, who have named regeneration or generative performance (respectively) as important characteristics of modern Native communities. However, as Alfred's formulation in particular promotes regeneration as a particular kind of political action/orientation, my own formulation of regeneration is distinct in that it is not necessarily or straightforwardly one type of political "resistance." See Taiaiake Alfred, *Wasáse: Indigenous Pathways of Action and Freedom* (Peterborough, ON: Broadview Press, 2005); Andrea Smith, *Native Americans and the Christian Right: The Gendered Politics of Unlikely Alliances* (Durham, NC: Duke University Press, 2008).

55 Naomi Klein, "Dancing the World into Being: A Conversation with Idle No More's Leanne Simpson," YES! *Magazine*, March 5, 2013, accessed June 29, 2018, http://www.yesmagazine.org/peace-justice/dancing-the-world-into-being-a-conversation-with-idle-no-more-leanne-simpson.

56 See also Noelani Goodyear-Ka'ōpua, *The Seeds We Planted: Portraits of a Native Hawaiian Charter School* (Minneapolis: University of Minnesota Press, 2013); ho'omanawanui, *Voices of Fire*.

57 J. Kēhaulani Kauanui, *Hawaiian Blood: Colonialism and the Politics of Sovereignty and Indigeneity* (Durham, NC: Duke University Press, 2008); Judy

Rohrer, "'Got Race?' The Production of Haole and the Distortion of Indigeneity in the Rice Decision," *Contemporary Pacific* 18, no. 1 (2005): 1–31.

58 Sarah Hunt, "More Than a Poster Campaign: Redefining Colonial Violence," *Decolonization: Indigeneity, Education and Society*, February 14, 2013, https://decolonization.wordpress.com/2013/02/14/more-than-a-poster-campaign-redefining-colonial-violence/; King, quoted in Leanne Simpson, "Anger, Resentment and Love: Fuelling Resurgent Struggle," NAISA paper presentation, June 5, 2015, accessed May 16, 2017, https://www.leannesimpson.ca/talk/anger-resentment-love-fuelling-resurgent-struggle.

59 Indigenous feminist scholar Eve Tuck reminds us that it is important to examine our underlying theories of change in our research. She describes damage-centered research as "research that operates, even benevolently, from a theory of change that establishes harm or injury in order to achieve reparation." She eloquently argues that when such research is framed "without the context of racism and colonization, all we're left with is the damage, and this makes our stories vulnerable to pathologizing analyses." Thus, such research has contributed to Indigenous and other colonized peoples "thinking of ourselves as broken," rather than actually transforming social and political relations. Eve Tuck, "Suspending Damage: A Letter to Communities," *Harvard Educational Review* 79, no. 3 (2009): 409–28.

60 Tuck, "Suspending Damage."

61 J. Kēhaulani Kauanui, *Hawaiian Blood*.

62 Damon Salesa, *Racial Crossings: Race, Intermarriage, and the Victorian British Empire* (Oxford: Oxford University Press, 2011).

63 Avery Gordon, *Ghostly Matters: Haunting and the Sociological Imagination* (Minneapolis: University of Minnesota Press, 2008), 5.

64 The *Oxford English Dictionary* credits Aryan philologist Max Müller (discussed further in chapter 1) with one of the first usages of the word *Austronesian*, as cited in an anthropology article in 1903. *Oxford English Dictionary*, "Austronesian."

65 Mark Munsterhjelm, *Living Dead in the Pacific: Contested Sovereignty and Racism in Genetic Research on Taiwan Aborigines* (Vancouver, BC: UBC Press, 2014), 135.

66 Silva, *Toward a Global Idea of Race*; Gordon, *Ghostly Matters*; Colin Dayan, *The Law Is a White Dog: How Legal Rituals Make and Unmake Persons* (Princeton, NJ: Princeton University Press, 2011); Stephan Palmié, *Wizards and Scientists: Explorations in Afro-Cuban Modernity and Tradition* (Durham, NC: Duke University Press, 2002).

67 Georg Wilhelm F. Hegel, *Lectures on the Philosophy of History*. Translated by J. Sibree (London: G. Bell, 1861).

68 Silva, *Toward a Global Idea of Race*, 22.

69 Silva notes that Foucault largely understood race as a mode of power that depended on the "symbolics of blood," in contrast to her own approach.

70 *Man* here is used not in the sense of all human beings but the specific description of the human by post-Enlightenment European philosophers, which Silva and others understand as the ruling onto-epistemology of the human in modernity. Silva, *Toward a Global Idea of Race*. See also Sylvia Wynter, "Unsettling the Coloniality of Being/Power/Truth/Freedom: Towards the Human, After Man, Its Overrepresentation—An Argument," CR: *The New Centennial Review* 3, no. 3 (2003): 257–337; and Michel Foucault, *The Order of Things: An Archaeology of the Human Sciences* (New York: Vintage, 1994).

71 Michel Foucault, *History of Sexuality* (New York: Vintage, 1990); Michel Foucault, *Security, Territory, Population: Lectures at the Collège de France 1977–1978* (New York: Picador, 2009); Michel Foucault, *The Birth of Biopolitics: Lectures at the Collège de France, 1978–1979* (New York: Picador, 2010).

72 Silva notes that, though she follows Foucault's methodology (tracking the analytics of raciality where Foucault tracks the analytics of sexuality) and "suggestion that attention to scientific signification can situate historicity (interiority-temporality)," "Foucault's excavations do not reach the place where European particularity is but an effect of the strategies of the productive ruler." Silva thus argues that "had he relinquished interiority, Foucault would have contributed to our understanding of how the productive force of the racial ensues from the haunting spatiality he spots at the core of modern thought, but would never fully explore." Silva, *Toward a Global Idea of Race*, 23–25.

73 Andrea Smith points out that in the U.S. context, though important works about whiteness as property (by Cheryl Harris) and the possessive investment in whiteness (by George Lipsitz) have deepened our understandings of how whiteness is protected juridically and economically, "these characterizations of whiteness as property generally fail to account for the intersecting logics of white supremacy and settler colonialism as they apply to Native peoples. In this intersection, whiteness may operate as a weapon of genocide used against Native peoples in which white people demonstrate their possessive investment not only in whiteness but also in Nativeness." Smith also notes, as I have above, that "The weapon of whiteness as a 'scene of engulfment' (Silva 2007) ensures that Native peoples disappear into whiteness so that white people in turn become the worthy inheritors of all that is indigenous." Andrea Smith, "Indigeneity, Settler Colonialism, White Supremacy," in *Racial Formation in the Twenty-First Century*, edited by Daniel Martinez HoSang, Oneka LaBennett, and Laura Pulido (Berkeley: University of California Press, 2012), 74; Cheryl Harris, "Whiteness as Property," *Harvard Law Review* 106, no. 8 (1993): 1707–91; George Lipsitz, *The Possessive Investment in Whiteness: How White People Profit from Identity Politics, Revised and Expanded Edition* (Philadelphia: Temple University Press, 2009).

74 See Mary Kawena Pukui and Samuel H. Elbert, *Hawaiian Dictionary: Hawaiian-English, English-Hawaiian* (Honolulu: University of Hawai'i Press, 1986), 58. For more on the production of haole identity in Hawai'i, see Rohrer,

"'Got Race?'" and Judy Rohrer, *Haoles in Hawai'i* (Honolulu: University of Hawai'i Press, 2010).
75 Rey Chow, *The Protestant Ethnic and the Spirit of Capitalism* (New York: Columbia University Press, 2002).
76 Andrea Smith, "Voting and Indigenous Disappearance," *Settler Colonial Studies* 3, no. 3–4 (2013): 352–68.
77 Harris, "Whiteness as Property."
78 Harris, "Whiteness as Property," 1711.
79 Aileen Moreton-Robinson, *The White Possessive: Property, Power, and Indigenous Sovereignty* (Minneapolis: University of Minnesota Press, 2015), xii.
80 See also Robin Kelley, "The Rest of Us: Rethinking Settler and Native," *American Quarterly* 69, no. 2 (2017): 267–76.
81 Ruth Wilson Gilmore, *Golden Gulag: Prisons, Surplus, Crisis, and Opposition in Globalizing California* (Berkeley: University of California Press, 2007).
82 Tracey Banivanua-Mar, *Violence and Colonial Dialogue: The Australian-Pacific Indentured Labor Trade* (Honolulu: University of Hawai'i Press, 2007), 17.
83 Gerald Horne, *The White Pacific: U.S. Imperialism and Black Slavery in the South Seas after the Civil War* (Honolulu: University of Hawai'i Press, 2007), 10.
84 Matsuda, *Pacific Worlds*, 227.
85 Robbie Shilliam, *The Black Pacific: Anti-Colonial Struggles and Oceanic Connections* (London: Bloomsbury, 2015).
86 Nitasha Sharma, "The Racial Imperative: Rereading Hawai'i's History and Black-Hawaiian Relations through the Perspective of Black Residents," in *Beyond Ethnicity: New Politics of Race in Hawai'i*, edited by Camilla Fojas, Rudy P. Guevarra Jr., and Nitasha Tamar Sharma (Honolulu: University of Hawai'i Press, 2018).
87 Candace Fujikane and Jonathan Y. Okamura, *Asian Settler Colonialism: From Local Governance to the Habits of Everyday Life in Hawai'i* (Honolulu: University of Hawai'i Press, 2008).
88 Gary Okihiro, *Cane Fires: The Anti-Japanese Movement in Hawaii, 1865–1945* (Philadelphia: Temple University Press, 1991); Ronald T. Takaki, *Pau Hana: Plantation Life and Labor in Hawaii, 1835–1920* (Honolulu: University of Hawai'i Press, 1983).
89 Victor Bascara, *Model-Minority Imperialism* (Minneapolis: University of Minnesota Press, 2006).
90 Pukui, *'Olelo No'eau: Hawaiian Proverbs and Poetical Sayings*, 129. See also ho'omanawanui, *Voices of Fire*, xxxvii.
91 Indeed, there is both an ancient and a more recent historical tradition of doing just that, as ku'ualoha ho'omanawanui has persuasively shown in her examination of Kanaka Maoli literary tradition through mo'olelo published in Hawaiian-language newspapers around the turn of the twentieth century. ho'omanawanui, *Voices of Fire*.
92 ho'omanawanui, *Voices of Fire*, xxix.
93 Nyong'o, *The Amalgamation Waltz*, 11.

94 Bronwen Douglas and Chris Ballard, *Foreign Bodies: Oceania and the Science of Race 1750–1940* (Canberra: ANU E Press, 2008); K. R. Howe, *The Quest for Origins: Who First Discovered and Settled the Pacific Islands?* (Honolulu: University of Hawai'i Press, 2003); Serge Tcherkézoff, "A Long and Unfortunate Voyage towards the 'Invention' of the Melanesia/Polynesia Distinction 1595–1832," *Journal of Pacific History* 38, no. 2 (2003): 175–96; Tom Ryan, "'Le Président des Terres Australes' Charles de Brosses and the French Enlightenment Beginnings of Oceanic Anthropology," *Journal of Pacific History* 37, no. 2 (2002): 157–86; Nicholas Thomas et al., "The Force of Ethnology: Origins and Significance of the Melanesia/Polynesia Division," *Current Anthropology* 30, no. 1 (1989): 27–41; Nicholas Thomas, *In Oceania: Visions, Artifacts, Histories* (Durham, NC: Duke University Press, 1997).

95 A similar critique has been made of the growing field of settler colonial studies, especially the work of Lorenzo Veracini. See, for example, Veracini, "Introducing Settler Colonial Studies"; Corey Snelgrove, Rita Dhamoon, and Jeff Corntassel, "Unsettling Settler Colonialism: The Discourse and Politics of Settlers, and Solidarity with Indigenous Nations," *Decolonization: Indigeneity, Education and Society* 3, no. 2 (2014): 1–32.

PART I. THE POLYNESIAN PROBLEM

1 William Lawrence Eisler, *The Furthest Shore: Images of Terra Australis from the Middle Ages to Captain Cook* (Cambridge: Cambridge University Press, 1995), 9–10; *Oxford English Dictionary*, "sciapodes."

2 Bronwen Douglas, "Geography, Raciology, and the Naming of Oceania," *The Globe: Journal of the Australian and New Zealand Map Society* 69 (2011), http://pacific-encounters.fr/pdf/Globe2011NamingOceania.pdf, 2.

3 Serge Tcherkézoff, "A Long and Unfortunate Voyage towards the 'Invention' of the Melanesia/Polynesia Distinction 1595–1832," *Journal of Pacific History* 38, no. 2 (2003): 188.

4 Tcherkézoff, "A Long and Unfortunate Voyage," 188.

5 Tcherkézoff, "A Long and Unfortunate Voyage," 188.

6 Charles de Brosses, *Histoire des navigations aux terres australes* (Paris: Durand, 1756).

7 Bronwen Douglas and Chris Ballard, *Foreign Bodies: Oceania and the Science of Race 1750–1940* (Canberra: ANU E Press, 2008), 6; Douglas, "Geography, Raciology, and the Naming of Oceania."

8 Tom Ryan, "'Le Président des Terres Australes': Charles de Brosses and the French Enlightenment Beginnings of Oceanic Anthropology," *Journal of Pacific History* 37, no. 2 (2002): 157–86.

9 Tcherkézoff, "A Long and Unfortunate Voyage," 179.

10 Tcherkézoff, "A Long and Unfortunate Voyage," 179.

11 Ryan, "'Le Président des Terres Australes,'" 180.

12 Ryan, "'Le Président des Terres Australes,'" 2; Bronwen Douglas has argued that the solidification of the boundaries and racial taxonomic labels of Polynesia

and Melanesia were developed slowly and unevenly across France, Britain, the United States, and Russia. Douglas and Ballard, *Foreign Bodies*.
13 Ryan, "'Le Président des Terres Australes.'"
14 Patty O'Brien, *The Pacific Muse: Exotic Femininity and the Colonial Pacific* (Seattle: University of Washington Press, 2006).
15 See, for example, Sylvia Wynter, "The Ceremony Must Be Found: After Humanism," *Boundary 2* 12, no. 3–13, no. 1 (1984): 19–70; Scott Morgensen, "The Biopolitics of Settler Colonialism: Right Here, Right Now," *Settler Colonial Studies* 1, no. 1 (2011): 52–76.
16 O'Brien, *The Pacific Muse*, 171.
17 Tcherkézoff, "A Long and Unfortunate Voyage," 185.
18 O'Brien, *The Pacific Muse*, 67.
19 Johann Reinhold Forster, *Observations Made during a Voyage Round the World* (Honolulu: University of Hawai'i Press, 1996; originally published 1778). On "hard" versus "exoticized" primitivisms regarding representations of Melanesians and Polynesians, respectively, see O'Brien, *The Pacific Muse*, 161.
20 Tcherkézoff, "A Long and Unfortunate Voyage," 175.
21 Tcherkézoff, "A Long and Unfortunate Voyage," 182.
22 Jules-Sébastien-César Dumont d'Urville, *Mémoire sur les iles du Grand Ocean* (Paris: Société de Géographie, 1831), 11–12; Horatio Hale, *United States Exploring Expedition during the Years 1838, 1839, 1840, 1841, 1842: Ethnography and Philology* (Philadelphia: C. Sherman, 1846), 73.
23 Tcherkézoff, "A Long and Unfortunate Voyage," 178.
24 Douglas and Ballard, *Foreign Bodies*, 12.
25 Tracey Banivanua-Mar, *Violence and Colonial Dialogue: Indigenous Globalisation and the Ends of Empire* (Cambridge: Cambridge University Press, 2016), 3.
26 Bronwen Douglas, "Comments," in John Edward Terrell, Kevin M. Kelly, and Paul Rainbird, "Foregone Conclusions? In Search of 'Papuans' and 'Austronesians,'" *Current Anthropology* 42, no. 1 (2001): 111.
27 S. J. Whitmee, "A Revised Nomenclature of the Inter-Oceanic Races of Men," *Journal of the Anthropological Institute of Great Britain and Ireland* 8 (1879): 360.
28 Whitmee, "A Revised Nomenclature," 360–69.
29 Ryan, "'Le Président des Terres Australes,'" 158.
30 Here again, my project dovetails with Banivanua-Mar's, in which she argued that "Melanesianism emphasizes the structural logic and continuity of representations across geographic and temporal change." Banivanua-Mar, *Violence and Colonial Dialogue*, 3.

## CHAPTER 1. HEIRLOOMS OF THE ARYAN RACE

1 John Dunmore Lang, *View of the Origin and Migrations of the Polynesian Nation; Demonstrating Their Ancient Discovery and Progressive Settlement of the Continent of America* (London: Cochrane and M'Crone, 1834), 63.

2  Edward Tregear, *The Aryan Maori* (Wellington, NZ: G. Didsbury, Government Printer, 1885), 4.
3  At the time of S. Percy Smith's writing, in 1911, he was president of the Polynesian Society, a New Zealand–based "learned society" focused on the study of Māori and other Pacific Island peoples. The Polynesian Society, founded in 1892 and still in existence today, built on earlier studies that similarly focused on deciphering "the mystery that surrounds their origins." See *Journal of the Polynesian Society*, accessed June 29, 2018, http://www.jps.auckland.ac.nz/.
4  *Oxford English Dictionary*, "heritage."
5  Denise Ferreira da Silva, *Toward a Global Idea of Race* (Minneapolis: University of Minnesota Press, 2007).
6  D. W. A. Baker, "Lang, John Dunmore (1799–1878)," *Australian Dictionary of Biography*, National Centre of Biography, Australian National University, accessed May 14, 2018, http://adb.anu.edu.au/biography/lang-john-dunmore-2326/text2953.
7  C. W. Salier, "The Australian Ideals of John Dunmore Lang," *Australian Quarterly* 10, no. 4 (1938): 70–76.
8  Jodi Byrd, *The Transit of Empire: Indigenous Critiques of Colonialism* (Minneapolis: University of Minnesota Press, 2011).
9  Lang, *View of the Origin and Migrations of the Polynesian Nation*, 3.
10  Reginald Horsman, "Scientific Racism and the American Indian in the Mid-Nineteenth Century," *American Quarterly* 27, no. 2 (1975): 154.
11  Howe, *The Quest for Origins: Who First Discovered and Settled the Pacific Islands?* (Honolulu: University of Hawai'i Press, 2003), 31.
12  Indeed, the eighteenth-century formulation of the Great Chain of Being itself was derived from Aristotle and Plato.
13  Howe, *The Quest for Origins*, 31.
14  Bronwen Douglas, "Comments," in John Edward Terrell, Kevin M. Kelly, and Paul Rainbird, "Foregone Conclusions? In Search of 'Papuans' and 'Austronesians,'" *Current Anthropology* 42, no. 1 (2001): 111–12.
15  Lang, *View of the Origin and Migrations of the Polynesian Nation*, 1.
16  Lang, *View of the Origin and Migrations of the Polynesian Nation*, 89.
17  Lang, *View of the Origin and Migrations of the Polynesian Nation*, 115. He later noted that "the forefathers of the Polynesian and Indo-American nations must have separated from the rest of mankind when the system of religious worship, that required the construction of pyramidal edifices, was generally prevalent—before the introduction of those more debasing systems of idolatry that characterized a later age, and in all probability within a few centuries of the deluge." Lang, *View of the Origin and Migrations of the Polynesian Nation*, 224–25.
18  Lang, *View of the Origin and Migrations of the Polynesian Nation*, 89.
19  Lang, *View of the Origin and Migrations of the Polynesian Nation*, 240–41.
20  Lang would take the diffusionist strain of thought one step further than most. He argued that ancient Polynesians did not stop in the Pacific after their migration from the west, but continued on to found the Americas. Lang

dismissed the Bering Strait theory because he could not reconcile the peoples of the Arctic with the "civilizations" of the Aztecs. Polynesians, in Lang's view, were civilized enough to be related to the Aztecs, though. Lang, *View of the Origin and Migrations of the Polynesian Nation*, 89.
21 Howe, *The Quest for Origins*, 53.
22 However, contrary to Lang, the Mormons believed that the Polynesians had migrated from the American continent into the Pacific, rather than from Asia across to the Americas.
23 Hōkūlani K. Aikau, *A Chosen People, a Promised Land: Mormonism and Race in Hawai'i* (Minneapolis: University of Minnesota Press, 2012), 46–47.
24 Aikau, *A Chosen People, a Promised Land*, 47.
25 Paul Reeve, *Religion of a Different Color: Race and the Mormon Struggle for Whiteness* (Oxford: Oxford University Press, 2015).
26 Kealani Cook, "Ke Ao a Me Ka Pō: Postmillennial Thought and Native Hawaiian Foreign Mission Work," *American Quarterly* 67, no. 3 (2015): 887–912.
27 Ballantyne notes that the concept of an Aryan people was not originally European, but Indian, embedded in Vedic tradition. Thus, Aryanism was fundamentally an Orientalist appropriation, born particularly in knowledge acquired by the British East India Company. Tony Ballantyne, *Orientalism and Race: Aryanism in the British Empire* (Houndmills, UK: Palgrave, 2002).
28 Lang, *View of the Origin and Migrations of the Polynesian Nation*, 29; Ballantyne, *Orientalism and Race*, 6–7.
29 Lang, *View of the Origin and Migrations of the Polynesian Nation*, 34.
30 Lang, *View of the Origin and Migrations of the Polynesian Nation*, 34.
31 Cathy Gere, *Knossos and the Prophets of Modernism* (Chicago: University of Chicago Press, 2009), 7. See also Lewis Henry Morgan, *Ancient Society; or, Researches in the Lines of Human Progress from Savagery, through Barbarism to Civilization* (New York: Henry Holt, 1877), vii. This text opens with a dramatic announcement of the radical potential of new scientific proof of mankind's underlying unity.
32 Gere, *Knossos and the Prophets of Modernism*, 11.
33 Gere, *Knossos and the Prophets of Modernism*, 8.
34 Gere, *Knossos and the Prophets of Modernism*, 8.
35 Gere, *Knossos and the Prophets of Modernism*.
36 Friedrich Max Müller, *India: What Can It Teach Us? A Course of Lectures Delivered before the University of Cambridge* (New York: Funk and Wagnalls, 1883), 47–48.
37 Müller, *India: What Can It Teach Us?*, 32–33.
38 Silva, *Toward a Global Idea of Race*.
39 Gere, *Knossos and the Prophets of Modernism*.
40 William Wyatt Gill, *Myths and Songs from the South Pacific* (London: Henry S. King, 1876).
41 Gill, *Myths and Songs from the South Pacific*, xii.
42 Gill, *Myths and Songs from the South Pacific*, vi–vii.

43 Gill, *Myths and Songs from the South Pacific*, xii.
44 Gill, *Myths and Songs from the South Pacific*, xviii. Gill similarly wrote in his introduction that though "there is much that is puerile and absurd in this heathen philosophy, there are evident glimmerings of primeval light." Gill, *Myths and Songs from the South Pacific*, xix.
45 Abraham Fornander and John F. G. Stokes, *An Account of the Polynesian Race, Its Origin and Migrations and the Ancient History of the Hawaiian People to the Times of Kamehameha I* (London: Trubner, 1880), vol. 2, vi.
46 Carol A. MacLennan, "Hawai'i Turns to Sugar: The Rise of Plantation Centers, 1860–1880," *Hawaiian Journal of History* 31 (1997): 97–126.
47 Fornander and Stokes, *An Account of the Polynesian Race*, vol. 2, xviii.
48 kuʻualoha hoʻomanawanui, *Voices of Fire: Reweaving the Literary Lei of Pele and Hiʻiaka* (Minneapolis: University of Minnesota Press, 2014), 45.
49 hoʻomanawanui, *Voices of Fire*; Noelani Arista, "Histories of Unequal Measure: Euro-American Encounters with Hawaiian Governance and Law, 1793–1827" (PhD diss., Brandeis University, Waltham, MA, 2010); Noenoe K. Silva, *Aloha Betrayed: Native Hawaiian Resistance to American Colonialism* (Durham, NC: Duke University Press, 2004).
50 Tregear, *The Aryan Maori*, 9.
51 Fornander and Stokes, *An Account of the Polynesian Race*, vol. 2, vii.
52 Fornander and Stokes, *An Account of the Polynesian Race*, vol. 2, vi.
53 Fornander and Stokes, *An Account of the Polynesian Race*, vol. 1, 59.
54 Fornander and Stokes, *An Account of the Polynesian Race*, vol. 1, 71, 98.
55 Yael Ben-zvi, "Where Did Red Go? Lewis Henry Morgan's Evolutionary Inheritance and US Racial Imagination," CR: *The New Centennial Review* 7, no. 2 (2007): 201–29; Jenny Reardon and Kim TallBear, "'Your DNA Is Our History': Genomics, Anthropology and the Construction of Whiteness as Property," *Current Anthropology* 53, no. S5 (2012): S233–45.
56 Henry Lewis Morgan, one of the most influential American anthropologists of the time, is exemplary of the redness as related to whiteness discourses for Reardon and TallBear in "Your DNA Is Our History."
57 Native Americans were also at times characterized as almost white in Western social scientific accounts, and as having migrated from Asia via the Bering Strait. Jodi Byrd examines the narrative the Bering Strait theory enables about Native Americans as the original "Yellow Peril," in *Transit of Empire: Indigenous Critiques of Colonialism* (Minneapolis: University of Minnesota Press, 2011), 200–201.
58 Tregear, *The Aryan Maori*, 5.
59 Philippa Mein Smith, *A Concise History of New Zealand* (Melbourne: Cambridge University Press, 2012).
60 K. R. Howe, "Tregear, Edward Robert," *Dictionary of New Zealand Biography*, 1993, accessed May 14, 2018, https://teara.govt.nz/en/biographies/2t48/tregear-edward-robert.
61 Tregear, *The Aryan Maori*, 38.
62 Tregear, *The Aryan Maori*, 4.

63 Tregear, *The Aryan Maori*, 4.
64 Tregear, *The Aryan Maori*, 4.
65 Tregear, *The Aryan Maori*, 4.
66 Tregear, *The Aryan Maori*, 7.
67 Tregear, *The Aryan Maori*, 90.
68 Tregear, *The Aryan Maori*, 91.
69 Ballantyne, *Orientalism and Race*, 76–77.
70 Ballantyne, *Orientalism and Race*, 76.
71 Ballantyne, *Orientalism and Race*, 76.
72 Silva, *Aloha Betrayed*, 71–72. Nonetheless, Silva notes that "Kanaka Maoli share with other Pacific Islanders theories about the migrations around the Pacific that are significantly different from those proposed by scholars such as Abraham Fornander." Silva, *Aloha Betrayed*, 97.
73 For example, "our Maori word for dog, kuri, is older than either" (Tregear, *The Aryan Maori*, 84), "our Polynesian Maui" (101), and "these uncivilized brothers of ours" (38) make clear that his audience is British settlers.
74 Tregear, *The Aryan Maori*, 81.
75 Tregear, *The Aryan Maori*, 103.
76 Tregear, *The Aryan Maori*, 103.
77 Kealani R. Cook, "Kahiki: Native Hawaiian Relationships with Other Pacific Islanders 1850–1915" (PhD diss., University of Michigan, Ann Arbor, 2011), 183.
78 Cook, "Kahiki," 181.
79 Cook, "Kahiki," 169.
80 Cook, "Kahiki," 166.
81 Cook, "Kahiki," 166.
82 Cook, "Kahiki," 165–66.
83 Cook, "Kahiki," 165–66.
84 Cook, "Kahiki," 170.
85 Cook, "Kahiki," 187.
86 Cook, "Kahiki," 187.
87 Stacy Kamehiro, *The Arts of Kingship: Hawaiian Art and National Culture of the Kalakaua Era* (Honolulu: University of Hawai'i Press, 2009), 65, 203. While I have not been able to find much information about Hale 'Ākala in the historical record, it is striking that he would choose to model his residence after a north Indian palace, given the contemporary theories about Aryans originating in northern India.
88 Cook, "Kahiki."
89 Silva, *Aloha Betrayed*, 173.
90 Cook, "Kahiki," 198.
91 Cook, "Kahiki," 235–36.
92 Cook, "Kahiki," 236.
93 Silva, *Aloha Betrayed*, 122.
94 Malama Meleisea, *The Making of Modern Samoa: Traditional Authority and Colonial Administration in the History of Western Samoa* (Suva, Fiji: Institute of Pacific Studies, University of the South Pacific, 1987), 2.

95 Meleisea, *The Making of Modern Samoa*, 2.
96 Cook, "Kahiki."
97 Virginia Dominguez, "Exporting US Concepts of Race: Are There Limits to the US Model?" *Social Research* 65, no. 2 (1998): 369–99.

CHAPTER 2. CONDITIONALLY CAUCASIAN

1 The very terminology of eugenics replaced other discourses that were more obviously tied to long-standing discourses about degeneration. For example, a 1911 collection published in Britain titled "The Methods of Race-Regeneration" began by using the language of "race regeneration"—thereby directly referencing and seeming to offer concrete solutions as to how to combat fears about degeneration. It argues that *eugenics* should replace *race regeneration* as a more scientific term. Caleb Williams Saleeby, *The Methods of Race-Regeneration* (New York: Moffat, Yard, 1911).
2 Gregory Moore, "Nietzsche, Degeneration, and the Critique of Christianity," *Journal of Nietzsche Studies*, no. 19 (2000): 1–18.
3 Jonathan Marks, "Historiography of Eugenics," *American Journal of Human Genetics* 52, no. 3 (1993): 650.
4 Robert Osgood, "Education in the Name of 'Improvement': The Influence of Eugenic Thought and Practice in Indiana's Public Schools, 1900–1930," *Indiana Magazine of History* 106, no. 3 (2010): 272–99.
5 Osgood, "Education in the Name of 'Improvement.'"
6 Quoted in Charles Benedict Davenport, *Scientific Papers of the Second International Congress of Eugenics Held at American Museum of Natural History, New York, September 22–28, 1921* (Baltimore: Williams and Williams, 1923), 484.
7 Quoted in Davenport, *Scientific Papers of the Second International Congress*, 484.
8 Christine Winter, "National Socialism and the German (Mixed-Race) Diasporas in Oceania," in *Europa jenseits der Grenzen: Festschrift für Reinhard Wendt*, edited by Michael Mann and Jürgen G. Nagel, 227–51 (Heidelberg: Draupadi Verlag, 2015).
9 Uldrick Thompson, *Eugenics for Young People: Twelve Short Articles on a Vital Subject* (Honolulu: Kamehameha Schools, 1913); Uldrick Thompson, *Eugenics for Parents and Teachers* (Honolulu: Kamehameha Schools, 1915); C. K. Szego, "The Sound of Rocks Aquiver? Composing Racial Ambivalence in Territorial Hawai'i," *Journal of American Folklore* 123, no. 487 (2010): 45; "Mr. and Mrs. Uldrick Thompson, Sr.: A Photograph Album from Their Relatives, and Kamehameha Schools Alumni and Staff" (Honolulu: Kamehameha Schools, n.d.), accessed June 29, 2018, http://kapalama.ksbe.edu/archives/albums/Thompson/album2/index.htm.
10 Szego, "The Sound of Rocks Aquiver?"
11 Szego, "The Sound of Rocks Aquiver?," 5.
12 Szego, "The Sound of Rocks Aquiver?," 5–6.
13 I have not found any evidence that this bill passed. Szego, "The Sound of Rocks Aquiver?," 46–47.

14 Osgood, "Education in the Name of 'Improvement,'" 282.
15 Noelani Goodyear-Kaʻōpua, "Domesticating Hawaiians: Kamehameha Schools and the 'Tender Violence' of Marriage," in *Indian Subjects: Hemispheric Perspectives on the History of Indigenous Education*, edited by Brenda J. Child and Brian Klopotek (Santa Fe: School for Advanced Research Press, 2014), 19.
16 Goodyear-Kaʻōpua, "Domesticating Hawaiians," 25.
17 Goodyear-Kaʻōpua, "Domesticating Hawaiians," 30.
18 Thompson, *Eugenics for Young People*, 9.
19 *Oxford English Dictionary*, "degenerate, v."
20 Herbert H. Gowen, *The Napoleon of the Pacific, Kamehameha the Great* (New York: Fleming H. Revell, 1919), 11, 316; quoted in Ty Kāwika Tengan, *Native Men Remade: Gender and Nation in Contemporary Hawaiʻi* (Durham, NC: Duke University Press, 2008), 71.
21 Thompson, *Eugenics for Young People*, 9–10.
22 Thompson, *Eugenics for Young People*, 9.
23 Thompson, *Eugenics for Young People*.
24 L. C. Dunn, for example, wrote, "The decrease in numbers of the native Hawaiians, and the increase in the number of hybrids indicate that the Hawaiian type will eventually exist only in hybrids between Hawaiians and other races." Dunn, quoted in Davenport, *Scientific Papers of the Second International Congress*, 110.
25 Szego, "The Sound of Rocks Aquiver?," 32.
26 Szego, "The Sound of Rocks Aquiver?," 47.
27 William Ellis, *Journal of William Ellis: Narrative of a Tour of Hawaiʻi, or Owhyhee: With Remarks on the History, Traditions, Manners, Customs, and Language of the Inhabitants of the Sandwich Islands* (Rutland, VT: Tuttle, 1979).
28 Jack London, *The House of Pride and Other Tales of Hawaii* (New York: Grosset and Dunlap, 1915); Jack London, *South Sea Tales* (New York: Regent, 1911).
29 Robert McRuer, "Compulsory Able-Bodiedness and Queer/Disabled Existence," *Disability Studies Reader* 3 (2010): 372.
30 Matthew Frye Jacobson, *Barbarian Virtues: The United States Encounters Foreign Peoples at Home and Abroad, 1876–1917* (New York: Hill and Wang, 2000).
31 Gregory Tomso, "The Queer History of Leprosy and Same-Sex Love," *American Literary History* 14, no. 4 (2002): 747–75; Neel Ahuja, "The Contradictions of Colonial Dependency: Jack London, Leprosy, and Hawaiian Annexation," *Journal of Literary and Cultural Disability Studies* 1, no. 2 (2007): 15–28.
32 Prince Morrow, "Leprosy and Hawaiian Annexation," *North American Review* 165, no. 492 (1897): 582.
33 Morrow, "Leprosy and Hawaiian Annexation," 582–83.
34 Thompson, *Eugenics for Young People*, 10.
35 Szego, "The Sound of Rocks Aquiver?," 49.
36 Szego, "The Sound of Rocks Aquiver?," 49.
37 Quoted in Davenport, *Scientific Papers of the Second International Congress*.

38 Clark Wissler, Clark Wissler to Herbert Gregory, December 9, 1919, and December 23, 1919, letters, Louis Robert Sullivan Staff File, Bishop Museum, Honolulu.
39 Louis R. Sullivan and Clark Wissler, *Observations on Hawaiian Somatology* (Honolulu: Bishop Museum Press, 1927).
40 Warwick Anderson, "Racial Hybridity, Physical Anthropology, and Human Biology in the Colonial Laboratories of the United States," *Current Anthropology* 53, no. S5 (2012): S99.
41 Anderson, "Racial Hybridity, Physical Anthropology," S95.
42 Anne Maxwell, "'Beautiful Hybrids': Caroline Gurrey's Photographs of Hawai'i's Mixed-Race Children," *History of Photography* 36, no. 2 (2012): 196.
43 Anderson, "Racial Hybridity, Physical Anthropology."
44 Anderson, "Racial Hybridity, Physical Anthropology."
45 Anderson, "Racial Hybridity, Physical Anthropology," S95.
46 Anderson, "Racial Hybridity, Physical Anthropology," S99–100.
47 Anderson, "Racial Hybridity, Physical Anthropology," S100.
48 *Twenty-Fifth Annual Report of the Trustees of the Bernice P. Bishop Museum*, December 31, 1921, 6, accessed at Bishop Museum Cultural Collections, September 2012.
49 *Twenty-Fifth Annual Report*, 6.
50 Louis Robert Sullivan, Louis Robert Sullivan to Herbert Gregory, June 22, 1922, letter, Louis Robert Sullivan Staff File, Bishop Museum, Honolulu.
51 Sullivan, Louis Robert Sullivan to Herbert Gregory, June 22, 1922.
52 Sullivan, Louis Robert Sullivan to Herbert Gregory, June 22, 1922.
53 Sullivan, Louis Robert Sullivan to Herbert Gregory, June 22, 1922.
54 Abraham Fornander and John F. G. Stokes, *An Account of the Polynesian Race, Its Origin and Migrations and the Ancient History of the Hawaiian People to the Times of Kamehameha I* (London: Trubner, 1880), vol. 2, vi.
55 Louis Robert Sullivan, "New Light on the Races of Polynesia," *Asia*, January 1923.
56 E. A. Hooton, "Louis Robert Sullivan," *American Anthropologist* 27, no. 2 (1925): 357–58; Charles B. Davenport and William K. Gregory, "Minute on the Death of Louis R. Sullivan," *Science* 62, no. 1617 (1925): 583.
57 After his death, the American Museum eventually replaced Sullivan's visiting position at the Bishop Museum with Harry Shapiro. Shapiro would continue many aspects of Sullivan's work, but appears to have been less invested in the Polynesian Problem line of inquiry. Instead, Shapiro would publish more generally on racial mixture, arguing for viewing racial mixture in a positive light, a legacy analyzed further in chapter 3 and the part II introduction.
58 Mary Kawena Pukui and Samuel H. Elbert, *Hawaiian Dictionary: Hawaiian-English, English-Hawaiian* (Honolulu: University of Hawai'i Press, 1986), 58.
59 ku'ualoha ho'omanawanui, "From Captain Cook to Captain Kirk, or, from Colonial Exploration to Indigenous Exploitation: Issues of Hawaiian Land,

Identity, and Nationhood in a 'Postethnic' World," in *Transnational Crossroads: Remapping the Americas and the Pacific*, edited by Camilla Fojas and Rudy P. Guevarra Jr., 229–68 (Lincoln: University of Nebraska Press, 2012).

60 Alexander Spoehr, "Foreword," in Peter Henry Buck, *Vikings of the Pacific* (Chicago: University of Chicago Press, 1959), v.
61 Spoehr, "Foreword," ix.
62 Spoehr, "Foreword," ix; Alice Te Punga Somerville, *Once Were Pacific: Maori Connections to Oceania* (Minneapolis: University of Minnesota Press, 2012), 12–14.
63 Somerville, *Once Were Pacific*, 13.
64 Peter Henry Buck, *The Coming of the Maori* (Wellington, NZ: Whitcombe and Tombs, 1949), 71; Buck, *Vikings of the Sunrise* (Christchurch, NZ: Whitcombe and Tombs, 1954), 21–22, 26.
65 Buck, *Vikings of the Pacific*, 13–14; Buck, *The Coming of the Maori*, 65.
66 Buck, *Vikings of the Pacific*, 15.
67 Buck, *Vikings of the Pacific*, 15.
68 Buck, *Vikings of the Pacific*, 54.
69 Buck, *Vikings of the Pacific*, 54.
70 Buck, *Vikings of the Pacific*, 55.
71 Somerville relates an anecdote in which Sāmoan hosts of an ʻava ceremony offered an "ʻava uso," which was "reserved for reunion between long-lost relatives." Somerville argues that this "act, securely located within Sāmoan epistemologies and hosting practices, reframed the entire encounter: Te Rangihīroa became the central member of the visiting party, and others were merely peripheral." Somerville, *Once Were Pacific*, 13.
72 Buck, *The Coming of the Maori*, 36.
73 Buck, *The Coming of the Maori*, 65.
74 Buck, *The Coming of the Maori*, 72.
75 Buck, *The Coming of the Maori*, 73.
76 Buck, *The Coming of the Maori*.
77 Buck, *Vikings of the Sunrise*, 17.
78 Buck, *Vikings of the Pacific*, 18.
79 Buck, *Vikings of the Pacific*, 5. Indeed, Te Rangihīroa was so fascinated with European explorers of the Pacific that he wrote another book on the topic, *Explorers of the Pacific* (Honolulu: Bishop Museum Press, 1953).
80 Buck, *Vikings of the Pacific*, 5.
81 Similarly, the back cover includes a blurb from a *New York Times Book Review* by Frederick A. Stokes, who begins with Te Rangihīroa's words in the quote above, repeating the "stone-age people" description.
82 "I may be criticized for applying the term vikings to the Polynesian ancestors," he noted, "but the term has come to mean bold, intrepid mariners and so is not the monopoly of the hardy Norsemen of the North Atlantic." Buck, *Vikings of the Sunrise*, x.
83 Buck, *Vikings of the Sunrise*, 12–13.

84 Buck, *Vikings of the Sunrise*, 12.
85 Buck, *Vikings of the Pacific*, x.
86 Somerville, *Once Were Pacific*, 14.
87 Buck, *Vikings of the Sunrise*, 15.
88 Buck, *Vikings of the Sunrise*, 17.
89 Buck, *Vikings of the Sunrise*, 36.
90 J. K. Kauanui, "'A Blood Mixture Which Experience Has Shown Furnishes the Very Highest Grade of Citizen-Material': Selective Assimilation in a Polynesian Case of Naturalization to U.S. Citizenship," *American Studies* 45, no. 3 (2004): 33–48.
91 Kauanui, "'A Blood Mixture.'"
92 Anderson, "Racial Hybridity, Physical Anthropology."
93 Anderson, "Racial Hybridity, Physical Anthropology," S105.
94 John Bell Condliffe, *Te Rangi Hiroa: The Life of Sir Peter Buck* (Wellington, NZ: Whitcombe and Tombs, 1971).

## CHAPTER 3. HATING HAWAIIANS, CELEBRATING HYBRID HAWAIIAN GIRLS

1 For more commentary on this incident, see Camilla Fojas, Rudy Guevarra Jr., and Nitasha Sharma, eds., *Beyond Ethnicity: New Politics of Race in Hawai'i* (Honolulu: University of Hawai'i Press, 2018), 4–7.
2 Christine Manganaro, "Assimilating Hawai'i: Racial Science in a Colonial 'Laboratory,' 1919–1939" (PhD diss., University of Minnesota, Minneapolis, 2012); Dean Itsuje Saranillio, "Seeing Conquest: Colliding Histories and Cultural Politics of Hawai'i Statehood" (PhD diss., University of Michigan, Ann Arbor, 2009).
3 Jonathan Okamura, *Ethnicity and Inequality in Hawai'i* (Philadelphia: Temple University Press, 2008), 10–11.
4 Manganaro, "Assimilating Hawai'i," 191–237.
5 David E. Stannard, *Honor Killing: Race, Rape, and Clarence Darrow's Spectacular Last Case* (New York: Penguin, 2006); John P. Rosa, "Local Story: The Massie Case Narrative and the Cultural Production of Local Identity in Hawai'i," *Amerasia Journal* 26, no. 2 (2000): 93–115.
6 Stannard, *Honor Killing*, 267.
7 Rosa, "Local Story," 102; Adria Imada, *Aloha America: Hula Circuits through the U.S. Empire* (Durham, NC: Duke University Press, 2012), 175.
8 I am indebted to Christine Manganaro's analysis and discovery of these interviews, discussed in her dissertation. Manganaro, "Assimilating Hawai'i."
9 Henry Yu, *Thinking Orientals: Migration, Contact, and Exoticism in Modern America* (New York: Oxford University Press, 2001), 81.
10 Yu, *Thinking Orientals*, 82.
11 Khalil Gibran Muhammad, *The Condemnation of Blackness: Race, Crime, and the Making of Modern Urban America* (Cambridge, MA: Harvard University Press, 2010), 236–38.

12 *Administration in Hawaii: Hearing before the Committee on Territories and Insular Affairs, United States Senate, Seventy-Second Congress, Second Session on S. 4309, S. 4310, S. 4312, S. 4314, S. 4315, and S. 4375*, January 16, 1933.
13 Shelley Sang-Hee Lee and Rick Baldoz, "'A Fascinating Interracial Experiment Station': Remapping the Orient-Occident Divide in Hawaii," *American Studies* 49, no. 3–4 (2008): 96.
14 Tavia Nyong'o, *The Amalgamation Waltz: Race, Performance, and the Ruses of Memory* (Minneapolis: University of Minnesota Press, 2009), 176.
15 Nyong'o, *The Amalgamation Waltz*, 26.
16 Damon Ieremia Salesa, *Racial Crossings: Race, Intermarriage, and the Victorian British Empire* (Oxford: Oxford University Press, 2011), 242.
17 As Silva argues, the "race relations cycle" rewrote "the play of engulfment as an eschatological narrative, thus deploying the logic of obliteration—which stipulates that the other of Europe will necessarily disappear." Denise Ferreira da Silva, *Toward a Global Idea of Race* (Minneapolis: University of Minnesota Press, 2007), 157.
18 Romanzo Colfax Adams, *The Japanese in Hawaii: A Statistical Study Bearing on the Future Number and Voting Strength and on the Economic and Social Character of the Hawaiian Japanese* (New York: National Committee on American Japanese Relations, 1924).
19 Adams, *The Japanese in Hawaii*.
20 Albert W. Palmer, *The Human Side of Hawaii: Race Problems in the Mid-Pacific* (Boston: Pilgrim, 1924), 144.
21 Manganaro, "Assimilating Hawai'i," 143.
22 Accessed at the University Archives, University of Hawai'i at Mānoa, Romanzo Adams Social Research Laboratory Records in 2013. There are 212 interviews in total, though a handful of interviewees were interviewed twice (possibly once by Margaret Lam and once by Doris Lorden). With the duplicates, 206 individuals were surveyed. It appears that Lam conducted the majority of the interviews, though it is sometimes unclear from the records.
23 However, many interviewees would venture an opinion on a racial category even if they confessed they did not really know anyone from that background (this was especially true of attitudes toward Hawaiians). The group interviewees were least likely to say they knew was Caucasian Hawaiians, and though opinions were generally negative, many also refrained from passing any judgment on them at all.
24 These percentages are based on my analysis of the data, not from the analysis of Lam or Adams.
25 Kahuna is defined in the Hawaiian dictionary as: "Priest, sorcerer, magician, wizard, minister, expert in any profession (whether male or female); in the 1845 laws doctors, surgeons, and dentists were called kahuna." Mary Kawena Pukui and Samuel H. Elbert, *Hawaiian Dictionary: Hawaiian-English, English-Hawaiian* (Honolulu: University of Hawai'i Press, 1986).
26 See Lam and Lorden, Interview #149, transcript: "Chinese-Hawaiians they are good, better than Hawaiian. (She doesn't have any who are friends.) Hapa-haole

(shakes her head). (Says in Chinese that they don't behave decently in public and they don't carry themselves in a dignified manner.)"
27 Lam and Lorden, Interview #47.
28 Lam and Lorden, Interview #47.
29 Lam and Lorden, Interview #47.
30 Lam and Lorden, Interview #47.
31 Lam and Lorden, Interview #23.
32 Lam and Lorden, Interview #56.
33 Lam and Lorden, Interview #56.
34 Lam and Lorden, Interview #106.
35 Lam and Lorden, Interview #48.
36 Lam and Lorden, Interview #130.
37 Lam and Lorden, Interview #90.
38 Lam and Lorden, Interview #43.
39 Lam and Lorden, Interview #71.
40 Lam and Lorden, Interview #19.
41 Porteus Hall at the University of Hawai'i was the subject of student protest in the 1970s due to the acknowledgment of his work as explicitly racist. They were unsuccessful in the 1970s, but rallied again in the 1990s and won. See Ibrahim G. Aoudé, ed., *The Ethnic Studies Story: Politics and Social Movements in Hawai'i: Essays* (Honolulu: University of Hawai'i Press, 1999).
42 David Stannard, "Honoring Racism: The Professional Life and Reputation of Stanley D. Porteus," in *The Ethnic Studies Story*, edited by Aoudé.
43 Stanley David Porteus and Marjorie Elizabeth Babcock, *Temperament and Race* (Boston: R. G. Badger, 1926); Stannard, "Honoring Racism."
44 Lam and Lorden, Interview #75.
45 Lam and Lorden, Interview #89.
46 Lam and Lorden, Interview #13.
47 Lam and Lorden, Interview #80.
48 Lam and Lorden, Interview #86.
49 Lam and Lorden, Interview #78.
50 Ellen D. Wu, *The Color of Success: Asian Americans and the Origins of the Model Minority* (Princeton, NJ: Princeton University Press, 2013).
51 Wu, *The Color of Success*, 239–40.
52 Recorded notes by the interviewers about respondents' views toward the Chinese included strong valorizations such as: "Admires this group and its ways of life very much," and "feels most at home with this group. Finds Chinese ways of life desirable." Lam and Lorden, Interviews #144, 162.
53 For example, one respondent's feeling toward Chinese Hawaiians is reported as: "Thinks they are a little better than the natives, but does not feel as congenial spiritually with them as he does with the Chinese." Lam and Lorden, Interview #175.
54 Wu, *The Color of Success*, 225.
55 Lam and Lorden, Interviews #22, 73, 79, 111.

56 *Poi dog* is a colloquial term for a mutt or mixed-breed dog but can also be used either pejoratively or affectionately to refer to multiracial people in Hawai'i. Lam and Lorden, Interview #58.
57 Lam and Lorden, Interview #66.
58 See, for example, Jane Desmond, *Staging Tourism: Bodies on Display from Waikiki to Sea World* (Chicago: University of Chicago Press, 1999).
59 Matthew Frye Jacobson, *Barbarian Virtues: The United States Encounters Foreign Peoples at Home and Abroad, 1876–1917* (New York: Hill and Wang, 2000); Noenoe K. Silva, *Aloha Betrayed: Native Hawaiian Resistance to American Colonialism* (Durham, NC: Duke University Press, 2004).
60 William Atherton Du Puy, *Hawaii and Its Race Problem* (Washington, DC: U.S. Government Printing Office, 1932), 131.
61 Henry Inn, "Hawaiian Medley," *Collier's*, December 11, 1943, 16–17.
62 Inn, "Hawaiian Medley," 16.
63 Inn, "Hawaiian Medley," 17.
64 Inn, "Hawaiian Medley," 17.
65 Nyong'o, *The Amalgamation Waltz*, 171–72.
66 Imada similarly notes a purposeful erasure of male hula performers in early twentieth-century hula circuits: "Euro-American promoters made a deliberate choice to cast young women rather than older male and female dancers. The ho'opa'a, men expert at the aural aspects of hula (chanted poetry and instrumentation), nearly disappear in the coverage of hula performances at the turn of the century. The men were eclipsed by the bodies of the female dancers, whose movements intrigued Euro-American observers." Imada, *Aloha America*, 68.
67 Silva, *Toward a Global Idea of Race*.
68 Henry Inn, *Hawaiian Types* (New York: Hastings, 1945).
69 Henry Inn and Katherine B. Allen, *Henry Inn* (Honolulu: Watumull Foundation Oral History Project, 1979).
70 Manganaro, "Assimilating Hawai'i," 168.
71 Inn, *Hawaiian Types*.
72 Stannard, *Honor Killing*.

PART II. REGENERATIVE REFUSALS

1 Denise Ferreira da Silva, *Toward a Global Idea of Race* (Minneapolis: University of Minnesota Press, 2007), 221–52.
2 Silva, *Toward a Global Idea of Race*, 231. "Racial democracy" in her usage refers to the sociological theory that Brazil's racial mix of Indians, blacks, and Portuguese was inherently democratic in contrast to the more strictly observed racial hierarchies of Europe.
3 Silva, *Toward a Global Idea of Race*, 246.
4 Silva, *Toward a Global Idea of Race*, 248.
5 Harry L. Shapiro, "Race Mixture," in UNESCO, *The Race Question in Modern Science: Race and Science* (New York: Columbia University Press, 1961), 388.

6 Leanne Simpson, *Dancing on Our Turtle's Back: Stories of Nishnaabeg Re-Creation, Resurgence and a New Emergence* (Winnipeg: Arbeiter Ring, 2011); Audra Simpson, *Mohawk Interruptus: Political Life across the Borders of Settler States* (Durham, NC: Duke University Press, 2014); Stephanie Nohelani Teves, *Defiant Indigeneity: The Politics of Hawaiian Performance* (Chapel Hill: University of North Carolina Press, 2018).
7 Teves, *Defiant Indigeneity*, 11.
8 Noelani Goodyear-Kaʻōpua, Ikaika Hussey, and Erin Kahunawai Wright, eds., *A Nation Rising: Hawaiian Movements for Life, Land and Sovereignty* (Durham, NC: Duke University Press, 2014).
9 Richard S. Hill, "Maori Urban Migration and the Assertion of Indigeneity in Aotearoa/New Zealand, 1945–1975," *Interventions* 14, no. 2 (2012): 256–78.
10 Robbie Shilliam, *The Black Pacific: Anti-Colonial Struggles and Oceanic Connections* (London: Bloomsbury, 2015).
11 Matsuda, *Pacific Worlds: A History of Seas, Peoples, and Cultures* (Cambridge: Cambridge University Press, 2012); Tracey Banivanua-Mar, *Decolonisation and the Pacific: Indigenous Globalisation and the Ends of Empire* (Cambridge: Cambridge University Press, 2016).
12 Lorenz Gonschor, "Mai Te Hau Roma Ra Te Huru: The Illusion of 'Autonomy' and the Ongoing Struggle for Decolonization in French Polynesia," *Contemporary Pacific* 25, no. 2 (2013): 259–96.
13 Setsu Shigematsu and Keith Camacho, eds., *Militarized Currents: Toward a Decolonized Future in Asia and the Pacific* (Minneapolis: University of Minnesota Press, 2010).

CHAPTER 4. STILL IN THE BLOOD

1 For further Native Hawaiian feminist analysis of Hoʻoulu Lāhui, see J. Kēhaulani Kauanui, "Blood Reproduction of (the) Race in the Name of Hoʻoulu Lāhui—A Hawaiian Feminist Critique," *Pacific Studies* 30, no. 1–2 (2007): 110–16.
2 See also Maile Arvin, "Sovereignty Will Not Be Funded: 'Good' Indigenous Citizenship in Hawaiʻi's Non-Profit Industrial Complex," MA thesis, University of California, San Diego, 2009.
3 Legal avenues include the Office of Federal Acknowledgment (the primary legal avenue for Native Americans), congressional legislation, and judicial recognition. Because Native Hawaiians are not a tribe, they cannot seek recognition through the Office of Federal Acknowledgment but do seek recognition through Congress and the Department of the Interior.
4 Brian Klopotek, *Recognition Odysseys: Indigeneity, Race, and Federal Tribal Recognition Policy in Three Louisana Indian Communities* (Durham, NC: Duke University Press, 2011), 3.
5 Klopotek, *Recognition Odysseys*, 3.
6 Klopotek, *Recognition Odysseys*, 249.

7 Office of Hawaiian Affairs website, accessed June 29, 2018, http://www.oha.org/DOI.
8 Judy Rohrer, "'Got Race?' The Production of Haole and the Distortion of Indigeneity in the Rice Decision," *Contemporary Pacific* 18, no. 1 (2005): 1–31; Judy Rohrer, *Staking Claim: Settler Colonialism and Racialization in Hawai'i* (Tucson: University of Arizona Press, 2016).
9 As Jodi Byrd has noted, though originally titled with language referring to recognition (and still popularly referred to as "federal recognition"), the Akaka Bill's shift toward "reorganization" in 2001 makes explicit that this legislation "draws upon the policies of the 1930s [regarding Native Americans] and not the post-termination policy era of the late twentieth century to incorporate Native Hawaiians further into the structures already established to maintain power over Indian lands and peoples under the rubric of 'reorganization.'" Jodi Byrd, *The Transit of Empire: Indigenous Critiques of Colonialism* (Minneapolis: University of Minnesota Press, 2011), 159.
10 Haunani-Kay Trask, "Pro, Con Articles on Akaka Bill Fail to Address Land Issues," *Honolulu Advertiser*, May 2, 2004.
11 Noelani Goodyear-Ka'ōpua, "Introduction," in *A Nation Rising: Hawaiian Movements for Life, Land, and Sovereignty*, edited by Noelani Goodyear-Ka'ōpua, Ikaika Hussey, and Erin Kahunawaika'ala Wright (Durham, NC: Duke University Press, 2014).
12 Jon Van Dyke, *Who Owns the Crown Lands of Hawai'i?* (Honolulu: University of Hawai'i Press, 2008), 9. See also Sydney Iaukea, *The Queen and I: A Story of Dispossessions and Reconnections in Hawai'i* (Berkeley: University of California Press, 2011).
13 Van Dyke, *Who Owns the Crown Lands?*, 9.
14 Melody MacKenzie, "Ke Ala Loa—The Long Road: Native Hawaiian Sovereignty and the State of Hawai'i," *Tulsa Law Review* 47, no. 3 (2012): 621–58.
15 Maile Arvin, "Sovereignty Will Not Be Funded"; Maile Arvin, "Spectacles of Citizenship: Native Hawaiian Sovereignty Gets a Makeover," in *Transnational Crossroads: Remapping the Americas and the Pacific*, edited by Camilla Fojas and Rudy Guevarra, 201–28 (Lincoln: University of Nebraska Press, 2012).
16 Kana'iolowalu: Native Hawaiian Roll Commission, "Kana'iolowalu: Act 195," accessed June 29, 2018, http://www.kanaiolowalu.org/about/act195/.
17 Kana'iolowalu, "Kana'iolowalu: Act 195."
18 Alexa Koenig and Jonathan Stein, "Federalism and the State Recognition of Native American Tribes: A Survey of State-Recognized Tribes and State Recognition Processes across the United States," *Santa Clara Law Review* 48, no. 1–2 (2008): 79–153.
19 Koenig and Stein, "Federalism and the State," 83.
20 The Paucatuck Eastern Pequot Nation, the Schaghticoke Indian Tribe, and the Golden Hill Paugussett. Koenig and Stein, "Federalism and the State Recognition," 117.

21 Koenig and Stein, "Federalism and the State Recognition," 87.
22 Alexandra Harmon, "Tribal Enrollment Councils: Lessons on Law and Indian Identity," *Western Historical Quarterly* 32, no. 2 (2001): 178.
23 Harmon, "Tribal Enrollment Councils," 179, 193.
24 Eva Marie Garroutte, "The Racial Formation of American Indians: Negotiating Legitimate Identities within Tribal and Federal Law," *American Indian Quarterly* 25, no. 2 (2001): 235.
25 Klopotek, *Recognition Odysseys*.
26 It also requires that the individual be eighteen years or older. Kanaʻiolowalu, "Kanaʻiolowalu: Act 195."
27 Sora Han's talk addressed the *Lawrence v. Texas* case of 2003, famous for striking down Texas's sodomy laws, by examining the initiation of the case as an account of racist profiling perpetuated by Robert Eubanks, a white man who had been sexually involved with Tyron Garner, a black man who was arrested for sodomy along with another sexual partner, John Lawrence, because Eubanks called the police on him. Han, as well as Moten in his own talk "On (Non) Violence," both asked what it meant that Eubanks essentially called the law on himself—by asking for homosexual sex (and his own former sexual partner) to be violently policed—and theorized that law was so effectively galvanized here precisely because Eubanks had framed the relationship between Garner and Lawrence as an injury to (his) whiteness.
28 On whiteness as legally protected property of white people, see Cheryl Harris, "Whiteness as Property," *Harvard Law Review* 106, no. 8 (1993): 1707–91; George Lipsitz, *The Possessive Investment in Whiteness: How White People Profit from Identity Politics*, rev. and exp. ed. (Philadelphia: Temple University Press, 2009).
29 See discussion about such lawsuits in Judy Rohrer, *Haoles in Hawaiʻi* (Honolulu: University of Hawaiʻi Press, 2010); Goodyear-Kāʻopua, Hussey, and Wright, eds., *A Nation Rising*.
30 Cathy J. Cohen, "Punks, Bulldaggers, and Welfare Queens: The Radical Potential of Queer Politics?," *GLQ: A Journal of Lesbian and Gay Studies* 3, no. 4 (1997): 437–65; Alexandra Harmon, *Rich Indians: Native People and the Problem of Wealth in American History* (Chapel Hill: University of North Carolina Press, 2010).
31 See, for example: Lydia Chavéz, *The Color Bind: California's Battle to End Affirmative Action* (Berkeley: University of California Press, 1998).
32 Glen Coulthard, "Subjects of Empire: Indigenous Peoples and the 'Politics of Recognition' in Canada," *Contemporary Political Theory* 6, no. 4 (2007): 437–60; Andrea Smith, *Native Americans and the Christian Right: The Gendered Politics of Unlikely Alliances* (Durham, NC: Duke University Press, 2008); Gerald Taiaiake Alfred, *Wasáse: Indigenous Pathways of Action and Freedom* (Peterborough, ON: Broadview Press, 2005).
33 Wendy Brown, "Suffering Rights as Paradoxes," *Constellations* 7, no. 2 (2000): 208–29. Brown is referencing Gayatri Spivak's argument that liberalism is "that

which we cannot not want." Gayatri Spivak, *Outside in the Teaching Machine* (New York: Routledge, 1993), 45–46.

34 Scott Richard Lyons, *X-Marks: Native Signatures of Assent* (Minneapolis: University of Minnesota Press, 2010).

35 See Defendant-Appellees Apoliona et al., Answering Brief (No. 08-16704, 01/05/2009, pp. 3–4).

36 Defendant-Appellees Apoliona et al., Answering Brief.

37 Van Dyke, *Who Owns the Crown Lands of Hawai'i?*

38 The Native Hawaiian Legal Corporation, Na Pua No'eau Education Program, and Alu Like. Walter Schoettle, *Day v. Apoliona* Appellants' Opening Brief (U.S. Court of Appeals for the Ninth Circuit, November 19, 2008).

39 Schoettle, *Day v. Apoliona* Appellants' Opening Brief.

40 Raymond Fisher, *Day v. Apoliona*, 10687 (U.S. Court of Appeals for the Ninth Circuit, 2009).

41 Wolfe, *Settler Colonialism and the Transformation of Anthropology: The Politics and Poetics of an Ethnographic Event* (London: Cassell, 1999), 3.

42 See, for example, Mishuana Goeman and Jennifer Nez Denetdale, "Guest Editors' Introduction: Native Feminisms: Legacies, Interventions, and Indigenous Sovereignties," *Wicazo Sa Review* 24, no. 2 (2009): 9–13; Andrea Smith and J. Kēhaulani Kauanui, "Native Feminisms Engage American Studies," *American Quarterly* 60, no. 2 (2008): 241–49.

43 Joanne Barker, "Gender, Sovereignty, Rights: Native Women's Activism against Social Inequality and Violence in Canada," *American Quarterly* 60, no. 2 (2008): 259–66; Audra Simpson, "Captivating Eunice: Membership, Colonialism, and Gendered Citizenships of Grief," *Wicazo Sa Review* 24, no. 2 (2009): 105–29.

44 Chris Finley, "Decolonizing the Queer Native Body (and Recovering the Native Bull-Dyke): Bringing 'Sexy Back' and Out of Native Studies' Closet," in *Queer Indigenous Studies: Critical Interventions in Theory, Politics, and Literature*, edited by Qwo-Li Driskill et al. (Tucson: University of Arizona Press, 2011), 31–42.

45 See, for example, Ani Mikaere, *Colonising Myths—Māori Realities: He Rukuruku Whakaaro* (Wellington, NZ: Huia, 2011); Ani Mikaere, *The Balance Destroyed: Consequences for Maori Women of the Colonisation of Tikanga Maori* (Auckland, NZ: International Research Institute for Maori and Indigenous Education, 2003); Teresia Teaiwa, "Reading Paul Gauguin's Noa Noa with Epeli Hau'ofa's Kisses in the Nederends: Militourism, Feminism, and the 'Polynesian' Body," in *Inside Out: Literature, Cultural Politics, and Identity in the New Pacific*, edited by Vilsoni Hereniko and Rob Wilson (Lanham, MD: Rowman and Littlefield, 1999); Dina El Dessouky, "Activating Voice, Body, and Place: Kanaka Maoli and Ma'ohi Writings for Kaho'olawe and Moruroa," in *Postcolonial Ecologies: Literatures of the Environment*, edited by Elizabeth DeLoughrey and George B. Handley (Oxford: Oxford University Press, 2011).

46 Lisa Kahaleole Hall, "Navigating Our Own 'Sea of Islands': Remapping a Theoretical Space for Hawaiian Women and Indigenous Feminism," *Wicazo Sa Review* 24, no. 2 (2009): 27.

47 ku'ualoha ho'omanawanui, *Voices of Fire: Reweaving the Literary Lei of Pele and Hi'iaka* (Minneapolis: University of Minnesota Press, 2014), 132.
48 Maile Arvin, Eve Tuck, and Angie Morrill, "Decolonizing Feminism: Challenging Connections between Settler Colonialism and Heteropatriarchy," *Feminist Formations* 25, no. 1 (2013): 9.
49 Arvin, Tuck, and Morrill, "Decolonizing Feminism," 18.
50 Ty Kāwika Tengan, *Native Men Remade: Gender and Nation in Contemporary Hawai'i* (Durham, NC: Duke University Press, 2008), 160.
51 Tengan, *Native Men Remade*, 160.
52 Tengan, *Native Men Remade*, 160.
53 Aikau, *A Chosen People, a Promised Land*, 178, 214.
54 *Day v. Apoliona*, No. 08-16704, U.S. Court of Appeals for the Ninth Circuit Hearing, 2009.
55 The judge speaking is not identified in the audio recording; it is either Judge Robert Beezer or Judge Raymond Fisher.
56 *Day v. Apoliona*.
57 *Day v. Apoliona*.
58 *Day v. Apoliona*.
59 *Day v. Apoliona*.
60 *Day v. Apoliona*.
61 *Day v. Apoliona*.
62 *Day v. Apoliona*.
63 *Day v. Apoliona*.
64 Here, "native Hawaiian" is my own interpretation of the judge's words, based on context.
65 *Day v. Apoliona*.
66 *Day v. Apoliona*.
67 As mentioned above, the 2000 Supreme Court case *Rice v. Cayetano* held that it was unconstitutional to limit voting for OHA trustees to Native Hawaiians, as limiting the vote according to "Hawaiian as a racial classification" violated the Fourteenth Amendment. See Rohrer, "'Got Race?'"
68 Schoettle, *Day v. Apoliona* Appellants' Opening Brief, 26.
69 *Day v. Apoliona*.
70 *Day v. Apoliona*.
71 Mentioned by Robert Klein, the defendants' attorney, in *Day v. Apoliona*.
72 *Day v. Apoliona*.
73 *Day v. Apoliona*.
74 Fisher, *Day v. Apoliona*, 10687.
75 "Platform of Unity," MANA: Movement for Aloha No Ka Aina, accessed January 16, 2015, http://www.manainfo.com/platform-of-unity.html.
76 Goodyear-Ka'ōpua, Hussey, and Wright, eds., *A Nation Rising*.
77 Goodyear-Ka'ōpua, *The Seeds We Planted: Portraits of a Native Hawaiian Charter School* (Minneapolis: University of Minnesota Press, 2013); Goodyear-Kā'opua, Hussey, and Wright, eds., *A Nation Rising*.

78 Lyons, *X-Marks*, 47.
79 The full text of the five questions was: "(1) Should the Secretary propose an administrative rule that would facilitate the reestablishment of a government-to-government relationship with the Native Hawaiian community? (2) Should the Secretary assist the Native Hawaiian community in reorganizing its government, with which the United States could reestablish a government-to-government relationship? (3) If so, what process should be established for drafting and ratifying a reorganized Native Hawaiian government's constitution or other governing document? (4) Should the Secretary instead rely on the reorganization of a Native Hawaiian government through a process established by the Native Hawaiian community and facilitated by the State of Hawaiʻi, to the extent such a process is consistent with Federal law? (5) If so, what conditions should the Secretary establish as prerequisites to Federal acknowledgment of a government-to-government relationship with the reorganized Native Hawaiian government?" Quoted in "Interior Considers Procedures to Reestablish a Government-to-Government Relationship with the Native Hawaiian Community," press release, Department of the Interior, June 18, 2014, accessed June 29, 2018, https://www.doi.gov/news/pressreleases/interior-considers-procedures-to-reestablish-a-government-to-government-relationship-with-the-native-hawaiian-community.
80 Lani Teves and Maile Arvin. "Recognizing the Aloha in 'No,'" *Hawaiʻi Independent*, July 7, 2014, http://hawaiiindependent.net/story/recognizing-the-aloha-in-no.
81 Noelani Goodyear-Kaʻōpua, "'Now We Know': Eight Reasons Why So Many Kānaka Maoli Oppose US Federal Recognition," *Ke Kaupu Hehiale*, September 26, 2016, accessed June 29, 2018, https://hehiale.wordpress.com/2016/09/26/now-we-know-eight-reasons-why-so-many-kanaka-maoli-oppose-us-federal-recognition/.
82 U.S. Department of the Interior, "Public Meeting Regarding Whether the Federal Government Should Reestablish a Government-to-Government Relationship with the Native Hawaiian Community, Kaunakakai Elementary School," 35.
83 U.S. Department of the Interior, "Public Meeting," 26.
84 U.S. Department of the Interior, "Public Meeting," 34.
85 U.S. Department of the Interior, "Public Meeting," 35.
86 Noenoe K. Silva, *Aloha Betrayed: Native Hawaiian Resistance to American Colonialism* (Durham, NC: Duke University Press, 2004).
87 U.S. Department of the Interior, "Public Meeting," 57.
88 U.S. Department of the Interior, "Public Meeting," 57.
89 U.S. Department of Interior, "Procedures for Reestablishing a Formal Government-to-Government Relationship with the Native Hawaiian Community," accessed June 29, 2018, https://www.doi.gov/sites/doi.gov/files/uploads/all_agency_combined_9.22.16_final_clean.pdf.
90 U.S. Department of the Interior, "Public Meeting," 46.
91 U.S. Department of the Interior, "Public Meeting," 31.
92 U.S. Department of the Interior, "Public Meeting," 36.

93 U.S. Department of the Interior, "Public Meeting," 28. See also a video of the Kaunakakai meeting: Akaku Maui Community Media, "Department of Interior Molokai Public Meeting 6-28-14," accessed June 29, 2018, https://vimeo.com/99599030.
94 U.S. Department of the Interior, "Public Meeting," 28.
95 For a deeper history of such comparisons between Native Americans and Native Hawaiians, see also David Chang, "'We Will Be Comparable to Indian Peoples': Recognizing Likeness between Native Hawaiians and American Indians, 1834–1923," *American Quarterly* 67, no. 3 (2015): 859–86.
96 U.S. Department of the Interior, "Public Meeting," 28.
97 U.S. Department of the Interior, "Public Meeting," 48.
98 U.S. Department of the Interior, "Public Meeting Regarding Whether the Federal Government Should Reestablish a Government-to-Government Relationship with the Native Hawaiian Community, Waimea High School," 14.
99 Poarch Creek Band of Indians, "History of the Poarch Creek Band of Indians," accessed June 29, 2018, http://pci-nsn.gov/westminster/tribal_history.html.
100 Rayna Green, "The Pocahontas Perplex: The Image of Indian Women in American Culture," *Massachusetts Review* 16, no. 4 (1975): 698–714; Chris Finley, "Violence, Genocide, and Captivity: Exploring Cultural Representations of Sacajawea as a Universal Mother of Conquest," *American Indian Culture and Research Journal* 35, no. 4 (2011): 191–208.
101 Akaku Maui Community Media, "Department of Interior Molokai Public Meeting 6-28-14," at 2:49. This comment is not identified in the official transcript because the transcript did not include the Q&A session, only the two-minute statements.
102 Akaku Maui Community Media, "Department of Interior Molokai Public Meeting 6-28-14."
103 Goodyear-Kāʻopua, "'Now We Know.'"

## CHAPTER 5. THE VALUE OF POLYNESIAN DNA

1 Department of Hawaiian Home Lands, "DHHL Proposed Rule Changes," 2015, accessed June 29, 2018, http://dhhl.hawaii.gov/wp-content/uploads/2015/10/DHHL-Admin-Rules-BC-Postcard-Web-Rev.pdf.
2 Jenny Reardon and Kim TallBear, "'Your DNA Is Our History': Genomics, Anthropology and the Construction of Whiteness as Property," *Current Anthropology* 53, no. S5 (2012): S235.
3 Kimberly TallBear, *Native American DNA: Tribal Belonging and the False Promise of Genetic Science* (Minneapolis: University of Minnesota Press, 2013), 71.
4 Both genetics and genomics are relevant here, and though at times "genetic" stands in for anything related to genes, it is useful to know the difference between genetics and genomics as distinct scientific fields. In general, genetics is the study of heredity, and genomics is the study of genes and their functions. The World Health Organization notes that the "main difference

between genomics and genetics is that genetics scrutinizes the functioning and composition of the single gene where as genomics addresses all genes and their interrelationships in order to identify their combined influence on the growth and development of the organism." World Health Organization, "WHO Definitions of Genetics and Genomics," accessed June 29, 2018, http://www.who.int/genomics/geneticsVSgenomics/en/.

5 Lealaiauloto Aigaletaulealea F. Tauafiafi, "'Polynesians Are All Samoans' Says Captain of Voyaging Canoe Hokule'a," *Pacific Guardians*, January 17, 2015, accessed June 29, 2018, http://pacificguardians.org/blog/2015/01/17/polynesians-are-all-samoans-says-captain-of-voyaging-canoe-hokulea/; "Ancient Chicken DNA Reveals Philippines Home to Polynesians," *Philippine Star Global*, March 18, 2014, accessed June 29, 2018, http://www.philstar.com/news-feature/2014/03/18/1302318/ancient-chicken-dna-reveals-philippines-home-polynesians; Brian Handwerk, "Polynesians Descended from Taiwanese, Other East Asians," *National Geographic News*, January 17, 2008, accessed June 29, 2018, http://news.nationalgeographic.com/news/2008/01/080117-polynesian-taiwan.html.

6 See, for example, Dan Salmon, *Made in Taiwan*, documentary film, 2006.

7 Mark Munsterhjelm, *Living Dead in the Pacific: Contested Sovereignty and Racism in Genetic Research on Taiwan Aborigines* (Vancouver, BC: UBC Press, 2014), 135.

8 TallBear, *Native American DNA*, 146.

9 TallBear, *Native American DNA*, 147.

10 Steve Olson, *Mapping Human History: Discovering the Past through Our Genes* (Boston: Houghton Mifflin, 2002), 39.

11 Olson, *Mapping Human History*, 149.

12 Science studies scholar Catherine Nash similarly notes that, "despite its positive connotations, the idea of a global human family is not unambiguously progressive. Nineteenth- and early twentieth-century imperial and racial discourses of the 'family of man' naturalized hierarchies of power and difference within a paternalistic model of the global human family." Catherine Nash, *Genetic Geographies: The Trouble with Ancestry* (Minneapolis: University of Minnesota Press, 2015), 91.

13 Olson, *Mapping Human History*, 223.

14 Olson, *Mapping Human History*, 224.

15 Nash, *Genetic Geographies*, 139.

16 Nash, *Genetic Geographies*, 139.

17 Olson, *Mapping Human History*, 223.

18 Olson, *Mapping Human History*, 223.

19 Olson notes that in Hawai'i, "It's as if a videotape of our species' history were being played backward at a fantastically rapid speed. Physical distinctions that took thousands of generations to produce are being wiped clean with a few generations of intermarriage." Olson, *Mapping Human History*, 226.

20 Olson, *Mapping Human History*, 236.

21 Shelley Sang-Hee Lee and Rick Baldoz, "'A Fascinating Interracial Experiment Station': Remapping the Orient-Occident Divide in Hawai'i," *American Studies* 49, no. 3/4 (2008): 87–109.
22 Denise Ferreira da Silva, *Toward a Global Idea of Race* (Minneapolis: University of Minnesota Press, 2007).
23 Olson, *Mapping Human History*, 237.
24 J. Koji Lum and Rebecca Cann, "MtDNA Lineage Analyses: Origins and Migrations of Micronesians and Polynesians," *American Journal of Physical Anthropology* 113, no. 2 (2000): 151–68.
25 Lana Lopesi, "My DNA Results Are In. I'm Whiter Than the Milkman," *E-Tangata*, April 24, 2016, accessed June 29, 2018, https://e-tangata.co.nz/news/my-dna-results-are-in-im-whiter-than-the-milkman.
26 It's unclear what type of test she took, but it does not seem like it was a mtDNA-focused test.
27 Lopesi, "My DNA Results Are In."
28 Lana Lopesi, "Is My Identity in My DNA?," *E-Tangata*, March 27, 2016, accessed June 29, 2018, http://e-tangata.co.nz/news/is-my-identity-in-my-dna.
29 Lopesi, "My DNA Results Are In."
30 Chad Cohen, *The Human Family Tree*, documentary film, 2009; Clive Maltby, *Journey of Man*, documentary film, 2003; Olson, *Mapping Human History*.
31 Kenneth Weiss, "Seeing the Forest through the Gene-Trees," *Evolutionary Anthropology: Issues, News, and Reviews* 19, no. 6 (2010): 212.
32 Kenneth Weiss and Jeffrey Long, "Non-Darwinian Estimation: My Ancestors, My Genes' Ancestors," *Genome Research* 19, no. 5 (2009): 703.
33 Weiss and Long, "Non-Darwinian Estimation," 705. See also Nash, *Genetic Geographies*, 25.
34 Weiss and Long, "Non-Darwinian Estimation," 707, 709.
35 See Alondra Nelson, *The Social Life of DNA: Race, Reparations, and Reconciliation after the Genome* (Boston: Beacon, 2016), for more on the three major types of genetic ancestry tests, which she calls spatiotemporal analysis, racial-composite analysis, and ethnic-lineage analysis.
36 Nash, *Genetic Geographies*, 53.
37 TallBear, *Native American DNA*, 71 (in reference to Donna Haraway's notion of gene fetishism).
38 Nelson, *The Social Life of DNA*.
39 Nash, *Genetic Geographies*, 51.
40 Olson, *Mapping Human History*, 233; Lum and Cann, "MtDNA Lineage Analyses."
41 Olson, *Mapping Human History*, 234.
42 Olson, *Mapping Human History*, 235–36.
43 Associated Press, "Rulemaking Under Way for DNA Testing for Hawaiian Homelands," *Honolulu Star-Advertiser*, December 28, 2015, accessed June 29,

2018, http://www.staradvertiser.com/breaking-news/rulemaking-under-way-for-dna-testing-for-hawaiian-homelands/.

44 Associated Press, "Rulemaking Under Way for DNA Testing."
45 Associated Press, "Rulemaking Under Way for DNA Testing."
46 TallBear, *Native American DNA*, 83.
47 TallBear, *Native American DNA*, 99.
48 TallBear, *Native American DNA*, 97.
49 Department of Hawaiian Home Lands. "Applying for Hawaiian Homelands," accessed May 15, 2017, http://dhhl.hawaii.gov/applications/applying-for-hawaiian-home-lands/.
50 Nelson, *The Social Life of DNA*, 81.
51 Jon Stokes, "Maori 'Warrior Gene' Claims Appalling, Says Geneticist," *New Zealand Herald*, August 10, 2006, accessed June 29, 2018, http://www.nzherald.co.nz/nz/news/article.cfm?c_id=1&objectid=10395491; "Once Were Warriors: Gene Linked to Maori Violence," *Sydney Morning Herald*, August 9, 2006, accessed June 29, 2018, https://www.smh.com.au/news/world/once-were-warriors-gene-linked-to-maori-violence/2006/08/08/1154802890439.html. Julian Sonny et al., "Why Polynesians Are Genetically Engineered to Be the Best Football Players in the World," *Elite Daily*, September 20, 2014, accessed June 29, 2018, http://elitedaily.com/sports/polynesians-genetically-engineered-best-football-players/778724/.
52 Lena Rodriguez and James Rimumutu George, "Is Genetic Labeling of 'Risk' Related to Obesity Contributing to Resistance and Fatalism in Polynesian Communities?," *Contemporary Pacific* 26, no. 1 (2014): 81.
53 Rodriguez and George, "Is Genetic Labeling of 'Risk' Related to Obesity?," 81.
54 Maile Tauali'i et al., "Native Hawaiian Views on Biobanking," *Journal of Cancer Education* 29, no. 3 (2014): 572.
55 Tauali'i et al., "Native Hawaiian Views on Biobanking," 572.
56 Health and Social Services Committee of the Navajo Nation Council, "Approving a Moratorium on Genetic Research Studies Conducted within the Jurisdiction of the Navajo Nation until Such Time That a Navajo Nation Human Research Code Has Been Amended by the Navajo Nation Council," Montezuma Creek, UT, April 2, 2002; John Bohannon, "A Home for Māori Science," *Science* 318, no. 5852 (2007): 907; Laura Arbour and Doris Cook, "DNA on Loan: Issues to Consider When Carrying Out Genetic Research with Aboriginal Families and Communities," *Community Genetics* 9, no. 3 (2006): 153–60.
57 Melissa A. Austin, Sarah Harding, and Courtney McElroy, "Genebanks: A Comparison of Eight Proposed International Genetic Databases," *Community Genetics* 6, no. 1 (2003): 37.
58 Gísli Pálsson and Paul Rabinow, "Iceland: The Case of a National Human Genome Project," *Anthropology Today* 15, no. 5 (1999): 14–18; Austin, Harding, and McElroy, "Genebanks."
59 Austin, Harding, and McElroy, "Genebanks," 42.

60 Lindsey Singeo, "The Patentability of the Native Hawaiian Genome," *American Journal of Law and Medicine* 33, no. 1 (2007): 121.
61 Singeo, "The Patentability of the Native Hawaiian Genome," 121.
62 "Licensing Hawaiian Genes for Medical Research," *Mālamalama, the Magazine of the University of Hawaiʻi System*, July 2003, 16.
63 Austin, Harding, and McElroy, "Genebanks."
64 "Tonga Sells Its Old, New Genes," *Wired*, November 27, 2000, accessed June 29, 2018, https://www.wired.com/2000/11/tonga-sells-its-old-new-genes/.
65 "Tonga Sells Its Old, New Genes."
66 Austin, Harding and McElroy, "Genebanks," 42.
67 Debra Harry, "Indigenous Peoples and Gene Disputes," *Chicago-Kent Law Review* 84, no. 1 (2009): 180.
68 Association of Hawaiian Civic Clubs, "A Resolution Urging the University of Hawaiʻi to Cease Development of the Hawaiian Genome Project or Other Patenting or Licensing of Native Hawaiian Genetic Material Until Such Time as the Native Hawaiian People Have Been Consulted and Given Their Full, Prior and Informed Consent to Such Project," Nukoliʻi, Kauaʻi, Hawaiʻi: Association of Hawaiian Civic Clubs, November 15, 2003.
69 Association of Hawaiian Civic Clubs, "A Resolution."
70 Association of Hawaiian Civic Clubs, "A Resolution."
71 "Paoakalani Declaration," https://190f32x2yl33s804xza0gf14-wpengine.netdna-ssl.com/wp-content/uploads/Paoakalani-Declaration.pdf.
72 The HGDP responded to such critiques by implementing a feasibility and ethics study led by a committee from the U.S. National Research Council (NRC) of the National Academy of Sciences (NAS) during 1994–97. The project proceeded in 1997 with strict ethical research guidelines established. See Luigi Luca Cavalli-Sforza, "The Human Genome Diversity Project: Past, Present and Future," *Nature Reviews: Genetics* 6, no. 4 (2005): 333–40.
73 Jenny Reardon, *Race to the Finish: Identity and Governance in an Age of Genomics* (Princeton, NJ: Princeton University Press, 2005), 2.
74 TallBear, *Native American DNA*.
75 Cavalli-Sforza, "The Human Genome Diversity Project."
76 Alexander Twombly, *The Native Hawaiian of Yesterday and To-Day* (New York, 1901), 10.
77 Twombly, *The Native Hawaiian of Yesterday and To-Day*, 8.
78 Cheryl Harris, "Whiteness as Property," *Harvard Law Review* 106, no. 8 (1993): 1730.
79 Noelani Goodyear-Kaʻōpua, *The Seeds We Planted: Portraits of a Native Hawaiian Charter School* (Minneapolis: University of Minnesota Press, 2013), 229–30.
80 Goodyear-Kaʻōpua, *The Seeds We Planted*, 230.
81 Mark Niesse, "Hawaiʻi Targets Taro Genetic Modification," *USA Today*, April 7, 2008, http://www.usatoday.com/money/economy/2008-04-07-3677522660_x.htm.
82 Mark Niesse, "Hawaiʻi Targets Taro Genetic Modification." On Kānaka Maoli's genealogical relationship to kalo, see Noenoe Silva, *Aloha Betrayed:*

*Native Hawaiian Resistance to American Colonialism* (Durham, NC: Duke University Press, 2004), 101–2; Goodyear-Kaʻōpua, *The Seeds We Planted*.
83 Association of Hawaiian Civic Clubs, "A Resolution."
84 Association of Hawaiian Civic Clubs, "A Resolution."
85 "Paoakalani Declaration," 2.
86 "Paoakalani Declaration," 6.
87 "Paoakalani Declaration," 6.
88 "Paoakalani Declaration," 3.

CHAPTER 6. REGENERATING INDIGENEITY

1 Laura Kina, "Hawaiian Cover-Ups: An Interview with Adrienne Pao," in *War Baby/Love Child: Mixed Race Asian American Art*, edited by Laura Kina and Wei Ming Dariotis (Seattle: University of Washington Press, 2013), 127.
2 Kina, "Hawaiian Cover-Ups," 127.
3 Kina, "Hawaiian Cover-Ups," 127.
4 Jennifer Doyle, *Hold It against Me: Difficulty and Emotion in Contemporary Art* (Durham, NC: Duke University Press, 2013), 116.
5 Doyle, *Hold It against Me*, 116.
6 Doyle, *Hold It against Me*, 117.
7 Audra Simpson, *Mohawk Interruptus: Political Life across the Borders of Settler States* (Durham, NC: Duke University Press, 2014), 113.
8 Kihara was previously known as Shigeyuki Kihara. I have favored Yuki Kihara, given her official name change (from Shigeyuki to Yuki) with the New Zealand government in 2014.
9 Megan Wilson, quoted in Sarita Echavez See, *The Decolonized Eye: Filipino American Art and Performance* (Minneapolis: University of Minnesota Press, 2009), 128.
10 Tavia Nyong'o, *The Amalgamation Waltz: Race, Performance, and the Ruses of Memory* (Minneapolis: University of Minnesota Press, 2009), 27.
11 Nyong'o, *The Amalgamation Waltz*, 12.
12 Many people may not associate Indigenous peoples from the Pacific with contemporary art, which is confined in many people's minds to the rarefied spaces of the Western museum and art gallery, and concerned with modernism and postmodernism, abstraction and urbanity. However, there has been a rich and ever-expanding field of contemporary Indigenous Pacific art since the 1980s, located in the Pacific Islands as well as spaces of diaspora and centers of canonical art like the Venice Biennale. Urban spaces of Pacific diaspora, such as Honolulu, Auckland, and Brisbane, have been hubs of contemporary Pacific art, along with art centers such as the Oceania Centre at the University of the South Pacific in Suva, Fiji, and the Tjibaou Cultural Center in Noumea, New Caledonia.
13 Karen Stevenson, *The Frangipani Is Dead: Contemporary Pacific Art in New Zealand, 1985–2000* (Wellington, NZ: Huia, 2008), 32–34; see also Karen

Stevenson, *Pacific Island Artists: Navigating the Global Art World* (Oakland, CA: Masalai, 2011).

14 Derek Conrad Murray and Soraya Murray, "Uneasy Bedfellows: Canonical Art Theory and the Politics of Identity," *Art Journal* 65, no. 1 (2006): 27–28.

15 Murray and Murray, "Uneasy Bedfellows," 35.

16 Doyle, *Hold It against Me*, 21.

17 Audra Simpson, "On Ethnographic Refusal: Indigeneity, 'Voice,' and Colonial Citizenship," *Junctures* 9 (2007): 67; Simpson, *Mohawk Interruptus*.

18 Simpson, *Mohawk Interruptus*.

19 A. Marata Tamaira, "From Full Dusk to Full Tusk: Reimagining the 'Dusky Maiden' through the Visual Arts," *Contemporary Pacific* 22, no. 1 (2010): 19.

20 Fa'anofo Lisaclaire Uperesa, "Of Savages and Warriors," in *Yuki Kihara: A Study of the Samoan Savage* (exhibition booklet), edited by Andrew Clifford, Te Uru Waitakere Contemporary Gallery, February 27–May 22, 2016.

21 There is one possible exception to this lack of context for *The Hapa Project*. In 2011, the Smithsonian Museum of Natural History included images from *The Hapa Project* in their exhibit *Race: Are We So Different?* This set *The Hapa Project* within a very broad discussion of race and racism, with some panels on the history of eugenics. Asian American studies scholar Leilani Nishime argues that in this context *The Hapa Project* functions as an explicit challenge to viewers as to "whether we have truly left technologies of race in the past." However, given the exhibit's broad focus on explaining race as it pertains universally to all people, my critique seems to hold even here, as the particular histories and discourses that shaped different racial and colonial understandings were not investigated in depth. For more, see Leilani Nishime, *Undercover Asian: Multiracial Asian Americans in Visual Culture* (Urbana: University of Illinois Press, 2014), 133–60.

22 ku'ualoha ho'omanawanui, "From Captain Cook to Captain Kirk, or, From Colonial Exploration to Indigenous Exploitation: Issues of Hawaiian Land, Identity, and Nationhood in a 'Postethnic' World," in *Transnational Crossroads: Remapping the Americas and the Pacific*, edited by Camilla Fojas and Rudy P. Guevarra Jr. (Lincoln: University of Nebraska Press, 2012), 229–68.

23 Kip Fulbeck, *Part Asian, 100% Hapa* (San Francisco: Chronicle, 2006), 262.

24 Fulbeck, *Part Asian, 100% Hapa*, 261.

25 Fulbeck, *Part Asian, 100% Hapa*, 86.

26 Fulbeck, *Part Asian, 100% Hapa*, 182.

27 Fulbeck, *Part Asian, 100% Hapa*, 16.

28 Fulbeck, *Part Asian, 100% Hapa*, 260–61.

29 Nicole Miyoshi Rabin, "Picturing the Mix: Visual and Linguistic Representations in Kip Fulbeck's *Part Asian, 100% Hapa*," *Critical Studies in Media Communication* 29, no. 5 (2012): 11.

30 Fulbeck, *Part Asian, 100% Hapa*.

31 Nishime, *Undercover Asian*, 133. See also Kina and Dariotis, eds., *War Baby/Love Child*.

32 Utah Museum of Fine Arts, *salt 8: Shigeyuki Kihara* (exhibit catalogue), Utah Museum of Fine Arts, 2013.
33 Utah Museum of Fine Arts, *salt 8: Shigeyuki Kihara*.
34 Utah Museum of Fine Arts, *salt 8: Shigeyuki Kihara*.
35 As an exhibition catalogue from the Utah Museum of Fine Arts notes, "while memorializing the victims of the natural disaster and lamenting a lost sense of security, the steady deliberateness of the dance is also a meditation on future action … [and] the rhythm of the dance is calming, suggesting … a belief in the resilience of an already tested people." Utah Museum of Fine Arts, *salt 8: Shigeyuki Kihara*.
36 Damon Salesa, "The Pacific in Indigenous Time," in *Pacific Histories: Ocean, Land, People*, edited by David Armitage and Alison Bashford (New York: Palgrave Macmillan, 2014), 40.
37 Salesa, "The Pacific in Indigenous Time," 40.
38 Shigeyuki Kihara, *Agelu I Tausi Catholic Church after Cyclone Evan, Mulivai Safata*, 2013, included in Utah Museum of Fine Arts, *salt 8: Shigeyuki Kihara*.
39 Shigeyuki Kihara, *Saleapaga Primary School after Tsunami Galu Afi Saleapaga*, 2013, included in Utah Museum of Fine Arts, *salt 8: Shigeyuki Kihara*.
40 Shigeyuki Kihara, *Mau Headquarters, Vaimoso*, 2013, included in Hocken Collections, University of Otago, *Shigeyuki Kihara: Undressing the Pacific, A Mid-Career Survey Exhibition* (exhibit catalogue), 2013; Shigeyuki Kihara, *Departure, Faleolo International Airport*, 2013, included in Utah Museum of Fine Arts, *salt 8: Shigeyuki Kihara*.
41 Avery Gordon, *Ghostly Matters: Haunting and the Sociological Imagination* (Minneapolis: University of Minnesota Press, 2008); Eve Tuck and C. Ree, "A Glossary of Haunting," in *Handbook of Autoethnography*, edited by Stacy Holman Jones, Tony E. Adams, and Carolyn Ellis (London: Routledge, 2013), 642.
42 Sarah Jane Cervenak, *Wandering: Philosophical Performances of Racial and Sexual Freedom* (Durham, NC: Duke University Press, 2014), 172.
43 Margo Machida, "Remixing Metaphors: Negotiating Multiracial Positions in Contemporary Native Hawaiian Art," in *War Baby/Love Child*, edited by Kina and Dariotis, 121.
44 Adrienne Pao, accessed April 20, 2015, http://adriennepao.com/wordpress/?page_id=127.
45 Margo Machida, "Remixing Metaphors: Negotiating Multiracial Positions in Contemporary Native Hawaiian Art," 125.
46 Adrienne Pao, accessed February 16, 2015, http://adriennepao.com/?page_id=127.
47 For more on the history of Waikīkī, see Gayle Chan and Andrea Feeser, *Waikīkī: A History of Forgetting and Remembering* (Honolulu: University of Hawai'i Press, 2006).
48 Pao's insistence on putting her own, seemingly passive body into the frame of the tourist gaze, raising uncomfortable questions for the viewer as to how

not to be complicit with that gaze, resonates with other feminist performance art, including the well-known work of Marina Abramović and Yoko Ono.

49 Perhaps the most well known is the coconut grove on the grounds of the Royal Hawaiian Hotel in Waikīkī, described by the hotel's website as "serenely quiet," and "once the playground of Hawai'i's kings and queens," now a venue for wedding receptions. See Royal Hawaiian website, accessed April 20, 2015, http://www.royal-hawaiian.com/meetings/overview/coconut-grove.

50 Adrienne Pao, accessed April 20, 2015, http://adriennepao.com/?page_id=177.

51 Simpson, *Mohawk Interruptus*, 107.

## CONCLUSION: REGENERATING AN OCEANIC FUTURE IN INDIGENOUS SPACE-TIME

1 KAHEA: The Hawaiian-Environmental Alliance, "Timeline of Mauna Kea Legal Actions since 2011," September 10, 2016, accessed June 29, 2018, http://kahea.org/issues/sacred-summits/timeline-of-events. See also Joseph Iokepa Casumbal-Salazar, "Multicultural Settler Colonialism and Indigenous Struggle in Hawai'i: The Politics of Astronomy on Mauna a Wakea" (PhD diss., University of Hawai'i at Manoa, 2014).

2 "Hawaii Supreme Court issues ruling allowing TMT to be built on Mauna Kea," KHON 2 News, accessed Feb 20, 2019. https://www.khon2.com/news/local-news/hawaii-supreme-court-issues-ruling-allowing-tmt-to-be-built-on-mauna-kea/1562984067.

3 "Thirty Meter Telescope (TMT)," *Star Gaze Hawaii*, accessed June 29, 2018, https://www.stargazehawaii.com/thirty-meter-telescope-tmt/.

4 "TMT Approval Letter from the Hawaii BLNR," September 2017, accessed June 29, 2018, https://www.scribd.com/document/360186974/TMT-approval-letter-from-the-Hawaii-BLNR.

5 ku'ualoha ho'omanawanui, "'Continue to Be Steadfast in Your Love for the Land' (E Ho'omalu i ke kūpa'a no ka 'Āina)," *Hawaii Independent*, April 10, 2015, accessed June 29, 2018, http: //hawaiiindependent.net/story/continue-to-be-steadfast-in-your-love-for-the-land-e-hoomalu-i-ke-kuupaa-no.

6 See, for example, Casumbal-Salazar, "Multicultural Settler Colonialism and Indigenous Struggle in Hawai'i"; David Maile, "Science, Time and Mauna a Wākea: The Thirty-Meter Telescope's Capitalist-Colonialist Violence," *Hawaii Independent*, May 13, 2014; Noelani Goodyear-Ka'ōpua, "Trapped in an Abusive Relationship? Divest!," *Ke Kaupu Hehi Ale*, May 28, 2015, accessed June 29, 2018, https://hehiale.wordpress.com/2015/05/28/trapped-in-an-abusive-relationship-divest-a-call-to-action/; No'u Revilla, "Do-It-Ourselves, Do-It-Now: Zines and Aloha 'Āina," *Ke Kaupu Hehi Ale*, May 27, 2015, accessed June 29, 2018, https://hehiale.wordpress.com/2015/05/26/do-it-ourselves-do-it-now-zines-aloha-%CA%BBaina/.

7 Bryan Kamaoli Kuwada, "We Live in the Future. Come Join Us," *Ke Kaupu Hehi Ale*, April 3, 2015, accessed June 29, 2018, https://hehiale.wordpress.com/2015/04/03/we-live-in-the-future-come-join-us/.
8 Kuwada, "We Live in the Future."
9 Damon Salesa, "The Pacific in Indigenous Time," in *Pacific Histories: Ocean, Land, People*, edited by David Armitage and Alison Bashford (New York: Palgrave Macmillan, 2014), 43.
10 Salesa, "The Pacific in Indigenous Time," 44.
11 Victoria Nālani Kneubuhl, "Hoʻoulu Lāhui," in *Hoʻokupu: An Offering of Literature by Native Hawaiian Women*, edited by Miyoko Sugano and Jackie Pualani Johnson (Honolulu: Mutual Publishing, 2009), 91–101.
12 Joyce Pualani Warren, "Embodied Cosmogony: Genealogy and the Racial Production of the State in Victoria Nalani Kneubuhl's 'Hoʻoulu Lāhui,'" *American Quarterly* 67, no. 3 (2015): 949.
13 Warren, "Embodied Cosmogony," 949.
14 Mishuana Goeman, *Mark My Words: Native Women Mapping Our Nations* (Minneapolis: University of Minnesota Press, 2013), 3.
15 Oceania Interrupted, https://www.facebook.com/pg/OceaniaInterrupted/about/.
16 *Wansolwara: Voices for West Papua*, published by *Hawaiʻi Review*, 2015.
17 *Wansolwara*, 16.
18 *Wansolwara*, 13–14.
19 Jon Letman, "Micronesians in Hawaii Face Uncertain Future," *Al Jazeera*, October 2013, accessed June 29, 2018, http://www.aljazeera.com/humanrights/2013/10/micronesians-hawaii-face-uncertain-future-201310191535637288.html.
20 Will Caron, "Racism in Hawaiʻi Is Alive and Well," *Hawaii Independent*, June 2, 2014, accessed June 29, 2018, http://hawaiiindependent.net/story/racism-in-hawaii-is-alive-and-well; Craig Santos Perez, "'Catering to Our Own People': On Micronesia Mart," *Kenyon Review*, August 3, 2013, accessed June 29, 2018, https://www.kenyonreview.org/2013/08/catering-to-our-own-people-on-micronesia-mart/.
21 Kathy Jetñil-Kijiner, "Video Poems," accessed June 29, 2018, http://jkijiner.wordpress.com/video-poems/.
22 Joy Enomoto, "Where Will You Be? Why Black Lives Matter in the Hawaiian Kingdom," *Ke Kaupu Hehi Ale*, February 2, 2017, accessed June 29, 2018, https://hehiale.wordpress.com/2017/02/01/where-will-you-be-why-black-lives-matter-in-the-hawaiian-kingdom/.
23 Enomoto, "Where Will You Be?"
24 Tagi Qolouvaki, "Dreaming Black Love," *Ke Kaupu Hehi Ale*, August 11, 2015, accessed June 29, 2018, https: //hehiale.wordpress.com/2015/08/10/dreaming-black-love/.
25 Eve Tuck and K. Wayne Yang, "Decolonization Is Not a Metaphor," *Decolonization: Indigeneity, Education and Society* 1, no. 1 (2012): 36.
26 Salesa, "The Pacific in Indigenous Time," 50.

BIBLIOGRAPHY

ARCHIVES

Bishop Museum Archives, Honolulu, HI.
Newberry Library, Chicago, IL.
University of Hawaiʻi at Mānoa, University Archives and Hawaiian and Pacific Collections, Honolulu, HI.

OTHER RESOURCES

Adams, Romanzo Colfax. "Hawaii as a Racial Melting Pot." *The Mid-Pacific* 32, no. 3. (1926): 213–16.
Adams, Romanzo Colfax. *Interracial Marriage in Hawaii: A Study of the Mutually Conditioned Processes of Acculturation and Amalgamation*. New York: Macmillan, 1937.
Adams, Romanzo Colfax, and Dan Kane-Zo Kai. *The Education of the Boys of Hawaii and Their Economic Outlook: A Study in the Field of Race Relationship*. Research Publications. Honolulu: University of Hawaiʻi Press, 1928.
Adams, Romanzo Colfax, and National Committee on American Japanese Relations. *The Japanese in Hawaii: A Statistical Study Bearing on the Future Number and Voting Strength and on the Economic and Social Character of the Hawaiian Japanese*. New York: National Committee on American Japanese Relations, 1924.
Ahmed, Sara. *On Being Included: Racism and Diversity in Institutional Life*. Durham, NC: Duke University Press, 2012.

Ahuja, Neel. "The Contradictions of Colonial Dependency: Jack London, Leprosy, and Hawaiian Annexation." *Journal of Literary and Cultural Disability Studies* 1, no. 2 (2007): 15–28.

Aikau, Hōkūlani K. *A Chosen People, a Promised Land: Mormonism and Race in Hawai'i.* Minneapolis: University of Minnesota Press, 2012.

Alexander, W. D. "The Origin of the Polynesian Race." *Journal of Race Development* 1, no. 2 (1910): 221–30.

Alfred, Taiaiake. *Wasáse: Indigenous Pathways of Action and Freedom.* Peterborough, ON: Broadview Press, 2005.

Anderson, Warwick. "Hybridity, Race, and Science: The Voyage of the Zaca, 1934–1935." *Isis* 103, no. 2 (2012): 229–53.

Anderson, Warwick. "Racial Hybridity, Physical Anthropology, and Human Biology in the Colonial Laboratories of the United States." *Current Anthropology* 53, no. S5 (2012): S95–107.

Andersson, Axel. *A Hero for the Atomic Age: Thor Heyerdahl and the Kon-Tiki Expedition.* Oxford: Peter Lang, 2010.

Aoudé, Ibrahim G. *The Ethnic Studies Story: Politics and Social Movements in Hawai'i: Essays in Honor of Marion Kelly.* Honolulu: University of Hawai'i Press, 1999.

Arbour, Laura, and Doris Cook. "DNA on Loan: Issues to Consider When Carrying Out Genetic Research with Aboriginal Families and Communities." *Community Genetics* 9, no. 3 (2006): 153–60.

Archey, Gilbert, and Auckland Institute and Museum. *South Sea Folk: Handbook of Maori and Oceanic Ethnology,* 2nd ed. Auckland: Auckland War Museum, 1949.

Arista, Noelani. "Histories of Unequal Measure: Euro-American Encounters with Hawaiian Governance and Law, 1793–1827." PhD diss., Brandeis University, Waltham, MA, 2010.

Arista, Noelani. "Captive Women in Paradise 1796–1826: The Kapu on Prostitution in Hawaiian Historical Legal Context." *American Indian Culture and Research Journal* 35, no. 4 (2011): 39–55.

Arvin, Maile. "Sovereignty Will Not Be Funded: Indigenous Citizenship in Hawai'i's Non-Profit Industrial Complex." MA thesis, University of California, San Diego, 2009.

Arvin, Maile. "Spectacles of Citizenship: Native Hawaiian Sovereignty Gets a Makeover." In *Transnational Crossroads: Remapping the Americas and the Pacific,* edited by Camilla Fojas and Rudy Guevarra, 201–28. Lincoln: University of Nebraska Press, 2012.

Arvin, Maile, Eve Tuck, and Angie Morrill. "Decolonizing Feminism: Challenging Connections between Settler Colonialism and Heteropatriarchy." *Feminist Formations* 25, no. 1 (2013): 8–34.

Association of Hawaiian Civic Clubs. "A Resolution Urging the University of Hawai'i to Cease Development of the Hawaiian Genome Project or Other Patenting or Licensing of Native Hawaiian Genetic Material Until Such Time as the nature Hawaiian People Have Been Consulted and Given Their Full,

Prior and Informed Consent to Such Project." Nukoliʻi, HI: Association of Hawaiian Civic Clubs, November 15, 2003.

Austin, Melissa A., Sarah E. Harding, and Courtney E. McElroy. "Monitoring Ethical, Legal, and Social Issues in Developing Population Genetic Databases." *Genetics in Medicine* 5, no. 6 (2003): 451–57.

Austin, Melissa A., Sarah Harding, and Courtney McElroy. "Genebanks: A Comparison of Eight Proposed International Genetic Databases." *Community Genetics* 6, no. 1 (2003): 37–45.

Ballantyne, Tony. *Orientalism and Race: Aryanism in the British Empire*. Houndmills, UK: Palgrave, 2002.

Banivanua-Mar, Tracey. *Decolonisation and the Pacific: Indigenous Globalisation and the Ends of Empire*. Cambridge: Cambridge University Press, 2016.

Banivanua-Mar, Tracey. *Violence and Colonial Dialogue: The Australian-Pacific Indentured Labor Trade*. Honolulu: University of Hawaiʻi Press, 2007.

Barker, Joanne. "Gender, Sovereignty, Rights: Native Women's Activism against Social Inequality and Violence in Canada." *American Quarterly* 60, no. 2 (2008): 259–66.

Barker, Joanne. *Native Acts: Law, Recognition, and Cultural Authenticity*. Durham, NC: Duke University Press, 2011.

Barker, Joanne. *Sovereignty Matters: Locations of Contestation and Possibility in Indigenous Struggles for Self-Determination*. Lincoln: University of Nebraska Press, 2005.

Bascara, Victor. *Model-Minority Imperialism*. Minneapolis: University of Minnesota Press, 2006.

Ben-zvi, Yael. "Where Did Red Go? Lewis Henry Morgan's Evolutionary Inheritance and U.S. Racial Imagination." *CR: The New Centennial Review* 7, no. 2 (2007): 201–29.

Brattain, Michelle. "Race, Racism, and Antiracism: UNESCO and the Politics of Presenting Science to the Postwar Public." *American Historical Review* 112, no. 5 (2007): 1386–413.

Brosses, Charles de. *Histoire des navigations aux terres australes*. vol. 1. Paris: Durand, 1756.

Brown, Wendy. "'The Most We Can Hope For . . .': Human Rights and the Politics of Fatalism." *South Atlantic Quarterly* 103, no. 2–3 (2004): 451–63.

Buck, Peter Henry. *The Coming of the Maori*. Wellington, NZ: Whitcombe and Tombs, 1949.

Buck, Peter Henry. *Explorers of the Pacific*. Honolulu: Bishop Museum Press, 1953.

Buck, Peter Henry. *Vikings of the Sunrise*. Christchurch, NZ: Whitcombe and Tombs, 1954.

Byrd, Jodi A. *The Transit of Empire: Indigenous Critiques of Colonialism*. Minneapolis: University of Minnesota Press, 2011.

Cavalli-Sforza, Luigi Luca. "The Human Genome Diversity Project: Past, Present and Future." *Nature Reviews: Genetics* 6, no. 4 (2005): 333–40.

Cervenak, Sarah Jane. *Wandering: Philosophical Performances of Racial and Sexual Freedom*. Durham, NC: Duke University Press, 2014.

Chang, David. "'We Will Be Comparable to the Indian Peoples': Recognizing Likeness between Native Hawaiians and American Indians, 1834–1923." *American Quarterly* 67, no. 3 (2015): 859–86.

Chavez, Lydia. *The Color Bind: California's Battle to End Affirmative Action*. Berkeley: University of California Press, 1998.

Chow, Rey. *The Protestant Ethnic and the Spirit of Capitalism*. New York: Columbia University Press, 2002.

Coan, Titus Munson. "Hawaiian Ethnography." *Journal of the American Geographical Society of New York* 31, no. 1 (1899): 24–30.

Coan, Titus Munson. "The Natives of Hawaii: A Study of Polynesian Charm." *Annals of the American Academy of Political and Social Science* 18 (1901): 9–17.

Cohen, Cathy J. "Punks, Bulldaggers, and Welfare Queens: The Radical Potential of Queer Politics?" *GLQ: A Journal of Lesbian and Gay Studies* 3, no. 4 (1997): 437–65.

Cohen, Chad. *The Human Family Tree*. Documentary film, National Geographic Channel, 2009.

Condliffe, John Bell. *Te Rangi Hiroa: The Life of Sir Peter Buck*. Wellington, NZ: Whitcombe and Tombs, 1971.

Contreras, Sheila Marie. *Blood Lines: Myth, Indigenism, and Chicana/o Literature*. Austin: University of Texas Press, 2009.

Cook, Kealani R. "Kahiki: Native Hawaiian Relationships with Other Pacific Islanders 1850–1915." PhD diss., University of Michigan, Ann Arbor, 2011.

Cooper, George, and Gavan Daws. *Land and Power in Hawaii: The Democratic Years*. Honolulu: University of Hawai'i Press, 1990.

Cooper, Melinda. *Life as Surplus: Biotechnology and Capitalism in the Neoliberal Era*. Seattle: University of Washington Press, 2008.

Corntassel, Jeff. "Re-Envisioning Resurgence: Indigenous Pathways to Decolonization and Sustainable Self-Determination." *Decolonization: Indigeneity, Education and Society* 1, no. 1 (2012).

Coulthard, Glen S. "Subjects of Empire: Indigenous Peoples and the 'Politics of Recognition' in Canada." *Contemporary Political Theory* 6, no. 4 (2007): 437–60.

Coulthard, Glen Sean. *Red Skin, White Masks: Rejecting the Colonial Politics of Recognition*. Minneapolis: University of Minnesota Press, 2014.

Countryman, Edward. "Indians, the Colonial Order, and the Social Significance of the American Revolution." *William and Mary Quarterly* 53, no. 2 (1996): 342–62.

Davenport, Charles Benedict. *Scientific Papers of the Second International Congress of Eugenics Held at American Museum of Natural History, New York, September 22–28, 1921*. Baltimore: Williams and Williams, 1923.

Davenport, Charles B., and William K. Gregory. "Minute on the Death of Louis R. Sullivan." *Science* 62, no. 1617 (1925): 583.

*Day v. Apoliona*, No. 08-16704, Hearing, U.S. Court of Appeals for the Ninth Circuit, 2009.

Dayan, Colin. *The Law Is a White Dog: How Legal Rituals Make and Unmake Persons.* Princeton, NJ: Princeton University Press, 2011.

Denetdale, Jennifer Nez. "Securing Navajo National Boundaries: War, Patriotism, Tradition, and the Diné Marriage Act of 2005." *Wicazo Sa Review* 24, no. 2 (2009): 131–48.

Denis, Claude. *We Are Not You: First Nations and Canadian Modernity.* Toronto: University of Toronto Press, 1997.

Desmond, Jane. *Staging Tourism: Bodies on Display from Waikiki to Sea World.* Chicago: University of Chicago Press, 1999.

Diaz, Vicente M. "'To "P" or Not to "P"?': Marking the Territory between Pacific Islander and Asian American Studies." *Journal of Asian American Studies* 7, no. 3 (2004): 183–208.

Diaz, Vicente M., and J. Kēhaulani Kauanui. "Native Pacific Cultural Studies on the Edge." *Contemporary Pacific* 13, no. 2 (2001): 315–42.

Dixon, Roland B. "'A New Theory of Polynesian Origins': A Review." *Journal of the Polynesian Society* 30, no. 2 (1921): 79–90.

Dominguez, Virginia R. "Exporting US Concepts of Race: Are There Limits to the US Model?" *Social Research* 65, no. 2 (1998): 369–99.

Douglas, Bronwen. "Geography, Raciology, and the Naming of Oceania." *The Globe: Journal of the Australian and New Zealand Map Society* 69 (2011). http://pacific-encounters.fr/pdf/Globe2011NamingOceania.pdf.

Douglas, Bronwen, and Chris Ballard. *Foreign Bodies: Oceania and the Science of Race 1750–1940.* Canberra: ANU E Press, 2008.

Doyle, Jennifer. *Hold It against Me: Difficulty and Emotion in Contemporary Art.* Durham, NC: Duke University Press, 2013.

Drinnon, Richard. *Facing West: The Metaphysics of Indian-Hating and Empire Building.* Norman: University of Oklahoma Press, 1997.

Driskill, Qwo-Li, Chris Finley, and Brian Joseph Gilley. *Queer Indigenous Studies: Critical Interventions in Theory, Politics, and Literature.* Tucson: University of Arizona Press, 2011.

Dunn, Leslie C. "An Anthropometric Study of Hawaiians of Pure and Mixed Blood." *Papers of the Peabody Museum of American Archaeology and Ethnology* 11, no. 3 (1928).

Du Puy, William Atherton. *Hawaii and Its Race Problem.* Washington, DC: U.S. Government Printing Office, 1932.

Dvorak, Greg. "'The Martial Islands': Making Marshallese Masculinities between American and Japanese Militarism." *Contemporary Pacific* 20, no. 1 (2008): 55–86.

Eisler, William Lawrence. *The Furthest Shore: Images of Terra Australis from the Middle Ages to Captain Cook.* Cambridge: Cambridge University Press, 1995.

El Dessouky, Dina. "Activating Voice, Body, and Place: Kanaka Maoli and Ma'ohi Writings for Kaho'olawe and Moruroa." In *Postcolonial Ecologies: Literatures of the Environment,* edited by Elizabeth DeLoughrey and George B. Handley. Oxford: Oxford University Press, 2011.

Ellis, William. *Journal of William Ellis: Narrative of a Tour of Hawaii, or Owhyhee: With Remarks on the History, Traditions, Manners, Customs, and Language of the Inhabitants of the Sandwich Islands*. Rutland, VT: Tuttle, 1979.

Ellis, William. *Polynesian Researches: Hawaii*. Rutland, VT: Tuttle, 1969.

Emory, Kenneth P. "Origin of the Hawaiians." *Journal of the Polynesian Society* 68, no. 1 (1959): 29–35.

Empowering Pacific Islander Communities (EPIC) and Asian Americans Advancing Justice. "A Community of Contrasts: Native Hawaiians and Pacific Islanders in the United States." 2014. https://www.scribd.com/document/214381774/a-Community-of-Contrasts-Native-Hawaiians-and-Pacific-Islanders-in-the-United-States.

Fanon, Frantz. *Black Skin, White Masks*. New York: Grove, 2008.

Fanon, Frantz. *The Wretched of the Earth*. New York: Grove, 2004.

Finley, Chris. "Decolonizing the Queer Native Body (and Recovering the Native Bull-Dyke): Bringing 'Sexy Back' and Out of Native Studies' Closet." In *Queer Indigenous Studies: Critical Interventions in Theory, Politics, and Literature*, edited by Qwo-Li Driskill, Chris Finley, Brian Joseph Gilley, and Scott Laura Morgensen, 31–42. Tucson: University of Arizona Press, 2011.

Finley, Chris. "Violence, Genocide, and Captivity: Exploring Cultural Representations of Sacajawea as a Universal Mother of Conquest." *American Indian Culture and Research Journal* 35, no. 4 (2011): 191–208.

Fitzpatrick, Peter. *The Mythology of Modern Law*. London: Routledge, 1992.

Fojas, Camilla, and Rudy P. Guevarra Jr. *Transnational Crossroads: Remapping the Americas and the Pacific*. Lincoln: University of Nebraska Press, 2012.

Fojas, Camilla, Rudy P. Guevarra Jr., and Nitasha Tamar Sharma, eds. *Beyond Ethnicity: New Politics of Race in Hawai'i*. Honolulu: University of Hawai'i Press, 2018.

Fornander, Abraham, and John F. G. Stokes. *An Account of the Polynesian Race, Its Origins and Migrations, and the Ancient History of the Hawaiian People to the Times of Kamehameha I*. London: Trubner, 1880.

Forster, Johann Reinhold. *Observations Made during a Voyage Round the World*. Honolulu: University of Hawai'i Press, 1996. Originally published 1778.

Foucault, Michel. *The Birth of Biopolitics: Lectures at the Collège de France, 1978–1979*. New York: Picador, 2010.

Foucault, Michel. *The History of Sexuality: An Introduction*, vol. 1. New York: Vintage, 1990.

Foucault, Michel. *Language, Counter-Memory, Practice: Selected Essays and Interviews*. Ithaca, NY: Cornell University Press, 1980.

Foucault, Michel. *The Order of Things: An Archaeology of the Human Sciences*. New York: Vintage, 1994.

Foucault, Michel. *Security, Territory, Population: Lectures at the Collège de France 1977–1978*. New York: Picador, 2009.

Foucault, Michel, Mauro Bertani, Alessandro Fontana, and François Ewald. *Society Must Be Defended: Lectures at the Collège de France, 1975–76*. New York: Picador, 2003.

Franklin, Cynthia G., Njoroge Njoroge, and Suzanna Reiss. "Tracing the Settler's Tools: A Forum on Patrick Wolfe's Life and Legacy." *American Quarterly* 69, no. 2 (2017): 235–47.

"French Polynesia Population 2018." World Population Review. Accessed June 30, 2018. http://worldpopulationreview.com/countries/french-polynesia-population/.

Fujikane, Candace, and Jonathan Y. Okamura. *Asian Settler Colonialism: From Local Governance to the Habits of Everyday Life in Hawai'i*. Honolulu: University of Hawai'i Press, 2008.

Fulbeck, Kip. *Part Asian, 100% Hapa*. San Francisco: Chronicle, 2006.

Gagne, Karen M. "Falling in Love with Indians: The Metaphysics of Becoming America." *CR: The New Centennial Review* 3, no. 3 (2003): 205–33.

Garner, Steve. *Whiteness: An Introduction*. Abingdon, UK: Routledge, 2007.

Geiger, Jeffrey. *Facing the Pacific: Polynesia and the American Imperial Imagination*. Honolulu: University of Hawai'i Press, 2007.

Geiger, Jeffrey. "Imagined Islands: 'White Shadows in the South Seas' and Cultural Ambivalence." *Cinema Journal* 41, no. 3 (2002): 98–121.

Gere, Cathy. *Knossos and the Prophets of Modernism*. Chicago: University of Chicago Press, 2009.

Gere, Cathy, and Bronwyn Parry. "The Flesh Made Word: Banking the Body in the Age of Information." *BioSocieties* 1, no. 1 (2006): 41–54.

Gill, William Wyatt. *Myths and Songs from the South Pacific*. London: Henry S. King, 1876.

Gilmore, Ruth Wilson. *Golden Gulag: Prisons, Surplus, Crisis, and Opposition in Globalizing California*. Berkeley: University of California Press, 2007.

Goeman, Mishuana. *Mark My Words: Native Women Mapping Our Nations*. Minneapolis: University of Minnesota Press, 2013.

Goeman, Mishuana. "Notes toward a Native Feminism's Spatial Practice." *Wicazo Sa Review* 24, no. 2 (2009): 169–87.

Goeman, Mishuana. "(Re)Mapping Indigenous Presence on the Land in Native Women's Literature." *American Quarterly* 60, no. 2 (2008): 295–302.

Goeman, Mishuana, and Jennifer Nez Denetdale. "Guest Editors' Introduction: Native Feminisms: Legacies, Interventions, and Indigenous Sovereignties." *Wicazo Sa Review* 24, no. 2 (2009): 9–13.

Gonschor, Lorenz. "Mai Te Hau Roma Ra Te Huru: The Illusion of 'Autonomy' and the Ongoing Struggle for Decolonization in French Polynesia." *Contemporary Pacific* 25, no. 2 (2013): 259–96.

Gonzalez, Vernadette Vicuña. *Securing Paradise: Tourism and Militarism in Hawai'i and the Philippines*. Durham, NC: Duke University Press, 2013.

Goodyear-Ka'ōpua, Noelani. "Domesticating Hawaiians: Kamehameha Schools and the 'Tender Violence' of Marriage." In *Indian Subjects: Hemispheric Perspectives on the History of Indigenous Education*, edited by Brenda J. Child and Brian Klopotek, 16–47. Santa Fe: School for Advanced Research Press, 2014.

Goodyear-Ka'ōpua, Noelani. *The Seeds We Planted: Portraits of a Native Hawaiian Charter School*. Minneapolis: University of Minnesota Press, 2013.

Goodyear-Kāʻopua, Noelani, Ikaika Hussey, and Erin Kahunawaikaʻala Wright, eds. *A Nation Rising: Hawaiian Movements for Life, Land, and Sovereignty*. Durham, NC: Duke University Press, 2014.

Gordon, Avery. *Ghostly Matters: Haunting and the Sociological Imagination*. Minneapolis: University of Minnesota Press, 2008.

Gormley, Melinda. "Scientific Discrimination and the Activist Scientist: L. C. Dunn and the Professionalization of Genetics and Human Genetics in the United States." *Journal of the History of Biology* 42, no. 1 (2009): 33–72.

Gould, Stephen Jay. *The Mismeasure of Man*, rev. and expanded. New York: W. W. Norton, 1996.

Gowen, Herbert H. *The Napoleon of the Pacific: Kamehameha the Great*. New York: Fleming H. Revell, 1919.

Green, Rayna. "The Pocahontas Perplex: The Image of Indian Women in American Culture." *Massachusetts Review* 16, no. 4 (1975): 698–714.

Grewal, Inderpal. "'Women's Rights as Human Rights': Feminist Practices, Global Feminism, and Human Rights Regimes in Transnationality." *Citizenship Studies* 3, no. 3 (1999): 337–54.

Guerrero, M. A. Jaimes. "Global Genocide and Biocolonialism." In *Violence and the Body: Race, Gender, and the State*, edited by Arturo Aldama, 171–88. Bloomington: University of Indiana Press, 2003.

Gulick, Sidney Lewis. *Mixing the Races in Hawaii: A Study of the Coming Neo-Hawaiian American Race*. Honolulu: Hawaiian Board Book Rooms, 1937.

Hale, Horatio. *United States Exploring Expedition during the Years 1838, 1839, 1840, 1841, 1842: Ethnography and Philology*, vol. 6. Philadelphia: C. Sherman, 1846.

Hall, Lisa Kahaleole. "'Hawaiian at Heart' and Other Fictions." *Contemporary Pacific* 17, no. 2 (2005): 404–13.

Hall, Lisa Kahaleole. "Navigating Our Own 'Sea of Islands': Remapping a Theoretical Space for Hawaiian Women and Indigenous Feminism." *Wicazo Sa Review* 24, no. 2 (2009): 15–38.

Hall, Lisa Kahaleole. "Strategies of Erasure: U.S. Colonialism and Native Hawaiian Feminism." *American Quarterly* 60, no. 2 (2008): 273.

Hall, Stuart. "Race, Articulation and Societies Structured in Dominance." In *Sociological Theories: Race and Colonialism*, edited by UNESCO, 305–45. Paris: UNESCO, 1980.

Halualani, Rona Tamiko. *In the Name of Hawaiians: Native Identities and Cultural Politics*. Minneapolis: University of Minnesota Press, 2002.

Handy, Edward S. "Some Conclusions and Suggestions Regarding the Polynesian Problem." *American Anthropologist*, n.s. 22, no. 3 (1920): 226–36.

Haney-López, Ian. *White by Law: The Legal Construction of Race*. New York: NYU Press, 2006.

Haraway, Donna. "The Promises of Monsters: A Regenerative Politics for Inappropriate/d Others." In *Cultural Studies*, edited by Lawrence Grossberg, Cary Nelson, and Paula Treichler, 295–337. New York: Routledge, 1992.

Harmon, Alexandra. *Rich Indians: Native People and the Problem of Wealth in American History*. Chapel Hill: University of North Carolina Press, 2010.

Harmon, Alexandra. "Tribal Enrollment Councils: Lessons on Law and Indian Identity." *Western Historical Quarterly* 32, no. 2 (2001): 175–200.
Harris, Cheryl. "Whiteness as Property." *Harvard Law Review* 106, no. 8 (1993): 1707–91.
Harry, Debra. "Indigenous Peoples and Gene Disputes." *Chicago-Kent Law Review* 84, no. 1 (2009): 147–96.
Harry, Debra, and Le'a Malia Kanehe. "Asserting Tribal Sovereignty over Cultural Property: Moving towards Protection of Genetic Material and Indigenous Knowledge." *Seattle Journal for Social Justice* 5, no. 1 (2006): 27–55.
Hau'ofa, Epeli. *We Are the Ocean: Selected Works*. Honolulu: University of Hawai'i Press, 2008.
Health and Social Services Committee of the Navajo Nation Council. "Approving a Moratorium on Genetic Research Studies Conducted within the Jurisdiction of the Navajo Nation until Such Time That a Navajo Nation Human Research Code Has Been Amended by the Navajo Nation Council." Montezuma Creek, UT, April 2, 2002.
Hegel, Georg Wilhelm F. *Lectures on the Philosophy of History*. Translated by J. Sibree. London: G. Bell, 1861.
Heyerdahl, Thor. *Kon-Tiki: Across the Pacific by Raft*. Chicago: Rand McNally, 1950.
Hill, Richard S. "Maori Urban Migration and the Assertion of Indigeneity in Aotearoa/New Zealand, 1945–1975." *Interventions* 14, no. 2 (2012): 256–78.
Hinsley, Curtis M. *Savages and Scientists: The Smithsonian Institution and the Development of American Anthropology, 1846–1910*. Washington, DC: Smithsonian Institution Press, 1981.
Holton, Graham E. L. "Heyerdahl's Kon Tiki Theory and the Denial of the Indigenous Past." *Anthropological Forum* 14, no. 2 (2004): 163–81.
ho'omanawanui, ku'ualoha. "From Captain Cook to Captain Kirk, or, From Colonial Exploration to Indigenous Exploitation: Issues of Hawaiian Land, Identity, and Nationhood in a 'Postethnic' World." In *Transnational Crossroads: Remapping the Americas and the Pacific*, edited by Camilla Fojas and Rudy P. Guevarra Jr., 229–68. Lincoln: University of Nebraska Press, 2012.
ho'omanawanui, ku'ualoha. *Voices of Fire: Reweaving the Literary Lei of Pele and Hi'iaka*. Minneapolis: University of Minnesota Press, 2014.
Hooton, E. A. "Louis Robert Sullivan." *American Anthropologist* 27, no. 2 (1925): 357–58.
Hooton, E. A. *Up from the Ape*. New York: Macmillan, 1954.
Horne, Gerald. *The White Pacific: U.S. Imperialism and Black Slavery in the South Seas after the Civil War*. Honolulu: University of Hawai'i Press, 2007.
Horsman, Reginald. "Scientific Racism and the American Indian in the Mid-Nineteenth Century." *American Quarterly* 27, no. 2 (1975): 152–68.
HoSang, Daniel Martinez, Oneka LaBennett, and Laura Pulido. *Racial Formation in the Twenty-First Century*. Berkeley: University of California Press, 2012.
Howard, Alan, and Robert Borofsky, eds. *Developments in Polynesian Ethnology*. Honolulu: University of Hawai'i Press, 1989.

Howe, K. R. *The Quest for Origins: Who First Discovered and Settled the Pacific Islands?* Honolulu: University of Hawai'i Press, 2003.

Hunt, Sarah. "More Than a Poster Campaign: Redefining Colonial Violence." Decolonization: Indigeneity, Education and Society, February 14, 2013. https://decolonization.wordpress.com/2013/02/14/more-than-a-poster-campaign-redefining-colonial-violence/.

Iaukea, Sydney. *The Queen and I: A Story of Dispossessions and Reconnections in Hawai'i.* Berkeley: University of California Press, 2011.

#IdleNoMore Hawai'i. Oiwi TV, 2013. http://vimeo.com/57654871.

Imada, Adria L. *Aloha America: Hula Circuits through the U.S. Empire.* Durham, NC: Duke University Press, 2012.

INCITE! Women of Color against Violence. *Color of Violence: The INCITE! Anthology.* Boston: South End, 2006.

INCITE! Women of Color against Violence. *The Revolution Will Not Be Funded: Beyond the Non-Profit Industrial Complex.* Cambridge MA: South End, 2007.

Inn, Henry. "Hawaiian Medley." *Collier's*, December 11, 1943, 16–17.

Inn, Henry. *Hawaiian Types.* New York: Hastings, 1945.

Inn, Henry, and Katherine B. Allen. *Henry Inn.* Honolulu: Watumull Foundation Oral History Project, 1979.

Jackson, Shona N. *Creole Indigeneity: Between Myth and Nation in the Caribbean.* Minneapolis: University of Minnesota Press, 2012.

Jacobson, Matthew Frye. *Barbarian Virtues: The United States Encounters Foreign Peoples at Home and Abroad, 1876–1917.* New York: Hill and Wang, 2000.

Jones, William, Anna Maria Jones, and John Shore Teignmouth. *The Works of Sir William Jones: In Six Volumes.* London: Printed for G. G. and J. Robinson . . . and R. H. Evans, 1799.

Jung, Moon-Kie. *Reworking Race: The Making of Hawaii's Interracial Labor Movement.* New York: Columbia University Press, 2006.

Kame'eleihiwa, Lilikalā. *Native Land and Foreign Desires =Ko Hawai'i 'Āina a Me Nā Koi Pu'umake a Ka Po'e Haole: A History of Land Tenure Change in Hawai'i from Traditional Times until the 1848 Māhele, Including an Analysis of Hawaiian Ali'i and American Calvinists.* Honolulu: Bishop Museum Press, 1992.

Kamehiro, Stacy L. *The Arts of Kingship: Hawaiian Art and National Culture of the Kalakaua Era.* Honolulu: University of Hawai'i Press, 2009.

Kanehe, Le'a Malia. "From Kumulipo: I Know Where I Come From: An Indigenous Pacific Critique of the Genographic Project." In *Pacific Genes and Life Patents: Pacific Indigenous Experiences and Analysis of the Commodification and Ownership of Life*, edited by Aroha Te Pareake Mead and Steven Ratuva, 114–29. Wellington, NZ: Call of the Earth and the United Nations University Institute of Advanced Studies, 2007.

Kasindorf, Martin. "Racial Tensions Are Simmering in Hawaii's Melting Pot." *USA Today*, March 6, 2007.

Kauanui, J. K. "'A Blood Mixture Which Experience Has Shown Furnishes the Very Highest Grade of Citizen-Material': Selective Assimilation in a Polynesian Case of Naturalization to U.S. Citizenship." *American Studies* 45, no. 3 (2004): 33–48.

Kauanui, J. Kēhaulani. "Blood Reproduction of (the) Race in the Name of Hoʻoulu Lāhui—A Hawaiian Feminist Critique." *Pacific Studies* 30, nos. 1 and 2 (2007): 110–16.

Kauanui, J. Kēhaulani. "Diasporic Deracination and 'Off-Island' Hawaiians." *Contemporary Pacific* 19, no. 1 (2007): 138.

Kauanui, J. Kēhaulani. "'For Get' Hawaiian Entitlement: Configurations of Land, 'Blood,' and Americanization in the Hawaiian Homes Commission Act of 1921." *Social Text* 59 (1999): 123–44.

Kauanui, J. Kēhaulani. *Hawaiian Blood: Colonialism and the Politics of Sovereignty and Indigeneity*. Durham, NC: Duke University Press, 2008.

Kauanui, J. Kēhaulani. "The Multiplicity of Hawaiian Sovereignty Claims and the Struggle for Meaningful Autonomy." *Comparative American Studies* 3, no. 3 (2005): 283–99.

Kauanui, J. Kēhaulani. "Native Hawaiian Decolonization and the Politics of Gender." *American Quarterly* 60, no. 2 (2008): 281–87.

Kauanui, J. Kēhaulani. "NO: Unnecessary Bargain Extinguishes All Claims in Exchange for Recognition." *Honolulu Advertiser*, April 25, 2004.

Kauanui, J. Kēhaulani. "Precarious Positions: Native Hawaiians and US Federal Recognition." *Contemporary Pacific* 17, no. 1 (2005): 1.

Kawaharada, Dennis. "Local Mythologies: 1979–2000." *Hawaii Review* 56 (2001). http://www2.hawaii.edu/~dennisk/texts/localmythologies.html.

Kazanjian, David. *The Colonizing Trick: National Culture and Imperial Citizenship in Early America*. Minneapolis: University of Minnesota Press, 2003.

Kelley, Robin D. G. "The Rest of Us: Rethinking Settler and Native." *American Quarterly* 69, no. 2 (2017): 267–76.

Kim, Claire Jean. "The Racial Triangulation of Asian Americans." *Politics and Society* 27, no. 1 (1999): 105–38.

Kina, Laura, and Wei Ming Dariotis, eds. *War Baby/Love Child: Mixed Race Asian American Art*. Seattle: University of Washington Press, 2013.

Kino-nda-niimi Collective. *The Winter We Danced*. Winnipeg: Arbeiter Ring, 2014.

Kirch, Patrick V. "Peopling of the Pacific: A Holistic Anthropological Perspective." *Annual Review of Anthropology* 39 (2010): 131–48.

Klein, Christina. *Cold War Orientalism: Asia in the Middlebrow Imagination, 1945–1961*. Berkeley: University of California Press, 2003.

Klein, Naomi. "Dancing the World into Being: A Conversation with Idle No More's Leanne Simpson." *YES! Magazine*, March 5, 2013. Accessed March 25, 2013. http://www.yesmagazine.org/peace-justice/dancing-the-world-into-being-a-conversation-with-idle-no-more-leanne-simpson.

Kline, Wendy. *Building a Better Race: Gender, Sexuality, and Eugenics from the Turn of the Century to the Baby Boom*. Berkeley: University of California Press, 2001.

Klopotek, Brian. *Recognition Odysseys: Indigeneity, Race, and Federal Tribal Recognition Policy in Three Louisiana Indian Communities*. Durham, NC: Duke University Press, 2011.

Koenig, Alexa, and Jonathan Stein. "Federalism and the State Recognition of Native American Tribes: A Survey of State-Recognized Tribes and State Recognition Processes across the United States." *Santa Clara Law Review* 48, no. 1–2 (2008): 79–153.

Kroeber, A. L. *Anthropology: Race, Language, Culture, Psychology, Prehistory.* New York: Harcourt, Brace, 1948.

Kualapai, Lydia. "The Queen Writes Back: Lili'uokalani's *Hawaii's Story by Hawaii's Queen.*" *Studies in American Indian Literatures*, ser. 2, 17, no. 2 (2005): 32–62.

Lambert, S. M. *The Depopulation of Pacific Races.* Honolulu: Bishop Museum, 1934.

Lang, John Dunmore. *On the Origin and Migrations of the Polynesian Nation; Demonstrating Their Original Discovery and Progressive Settlement of the Continent of America.* Sydney: George Robertson, 1876.

Lang, John Dunmore. *View of the Origin and Migrations of the Polynesian Nation; Demonstrating Their Ancient Discovery and Progressive Settlement of the Continent of America.* London: Cochrane and M'Crone, 1834.

Latour, Bruno. *We Have Never Been Modern.* Cambridge, MA: Harvard University Press, 2012.

Ledward, B. C. "On Being Hawaiian Enough: Contesting American Racialization with Native Hybridity." *Hūlili: Multidisciplinary Research on Hawaiian Well-Being* 4, no. 1 (2007): 107–43.

Ledward, B. C. "Inseparably Hapa: Making and Unmaking a Hawaiian Monolith." PhD diss., University of Hawai'i at Manoa, 2007.

Lee, Shelley Sang-Hee, and Rick Baldoz. "'A Fascinating Interracial Experiment Station': Remapping the Orient-Occident Divide in Hawai'i." *American Studies* 49, no. 3–4 (2008): 87–109.

Lévi-Strauss, Claude. *Race and History.* Paris: UNESCO, 1952.

Lévy-Bruhl, Lucien. *How Natives Think.* Princeton, NJ: Princeton University Press, 1985.

"Licensing Hawaiian Genes for Medical Research." *Mālamalama, the Magazine of the University of Hawai'i System*, July 2003.

Lili'uokalani. *Hawaii's Story by Hawaii's Queen, Lili'uokalani.* Boston: Lee and Shepard, 1898.

Lind, Andrew William. *An Island Community: Ecological Succession in Hawaii.* New York: Greenwood, 1968.

Linnekin, Jocelyn S. "Defining Tradition: Variations on the Hawaiian Identity." *American Ethnologist* 10, no. 2 (1983): 241–52.

Lipsitz, George. *The Possessive Investment in Whiteness: How White People Profit from Identity Politics*, rev. and exp. ed. Philadelphia: Temple University Press, 2009.

Lock, Margaret. "The Alienation of Body Tissue and the Biopolitics of Immortalized Cell Lines." *Body and Society* 7, no. 2–3 (2001): 63–91.

London, Jack. *South Sea Tales.* New York: Regent, 1911.

London, Jack. *The House of Pride and Other Tales of Hawaii.* New York: Grosset and Dunlap, 1915.

Lovejoy, Arthur Oncken. *The Great Chain of Being: A Study of the History of an Idea.* Cambridge, MA: Harvard University Press, 1936.

Lum, J. Koji, and Rebecca L. Cann. "MtDNA Lineage Analyses: Origins and Migrations of Micronesians and Polynesians." *American Journal of Physical Anthropology* 113, no. 2 (2000): 151–68.

Lum, J. Koji, Rebecca L. Cann, Jeremy J. Martinson, and Lynn B. Jorde. "Mitochondrial and Nuclear Genetic Relationships among Pacific Island and Asian Populations." *American Journal of Human Genetics* 63, no. 2 (1998): 613–24.

Lum, J. K., O. Rickards, C. Ching, and R. L. Cann. "Polynesian Mitochondrial DNAs Reveal Three Deep Maternal Lineage Clusters." *Human Biology* 66, no. 4 (1994): 567–90.

Lyons, Laura E., and Cynthia G. Franklin. "Land, Leadership, and Nation: Haunani-Kay Trask on the Testimonial Uses of Life Writing in Hawai'i." *Biography* 27, no. 1 (2004): 222–49.

Lyons, Scott Richard. *X-Marks: Native Signatures of Assent.* Minneapolis: University of Minnesota Press, 2010.

MacKenzie, Melody. "Ke Ala Loa—The Long Road: Native Hawaiian Sovereignty and the State of Hawai'i." *Tulsa Law Review* 47, no. 3 (2012): 621–58.

MacLennan, Carol A. "Hawai'i Turns to Sugar: The Rise of the Plantation Centers, 1860–1880." *Hawaiian Journal of History* 31 (1997): 97–126.

Maltby, Clive. *Journey of Man.* Documentary film, PBS, 2003.

Manganaro, Christine. "Assimilating Hawai'i: Racial Science in a Colonial 'Laboratory,' 1919–1939." PhD diss., University of Minnesota, Minneapolis, 2012.

Marks, Jonathan. "Historiography of Eugenics." *American Journal of Human Genetics* 52, no. 3 (1993): 650–52.

Marks, Jonathan. "The Origins of Anthropological Genetics." *Current Anthropology* 53, no. S5 (2012): S161–72.

Marques, A. "The Population of the Hawaiian Islands: Is the Hawaiian a Doomed Race? Present and Future Prospects." *Journal of the Polynesian Society* 2, no. 4 (1893): 253–70.

Marsh, Selina Tusitala. *Fast Talking PI.* Auckland: Auckland University Press, 2009.

Mast, Robert H., and Anne B. Mast. *Autobiography of Protest in Hawai'i.* Honolulu: University of Hawai'i Press, 1996.

Matsuda, Matt K. *Empire of Love: Histories of France and the Pacific.* Oxford: Oxford University Press, 2004.

Matsuda, Matt K. *Pacific Worlds: A History of Seas, Peoples, and Cultures.* Cambridge: Cambridge University Press, 2012.

Maude, H. E. "Pacific History—Past, Present and Future." *Journal of Pacific History* 6 (1971): 3–24.

Maxwell, Anne. "'Beautiful Hybrids': Caroline Gurrey's Photographs of Hawai'i's Mixed-Race Children." *History of Photography* 36, no. 2 (2012): 184–98.

Maxwell, Anne. *Colonial Photography and Exhibitions: Representations of the Native and the Making of European Identities.* Leicester, UK: Leicester University Press, 2000.

Maxwell, Anne. *Picture Imperfect: Photography and Eugenics, 1870–1940*. Brighton, UK: Sussex Academic Press, 2010.

McDougall, Brandy Nālani. "Moʻokūʻauhau versus Colonial Entitlement in English Translations of the Kumulipo." *American Quarterly* 67, no. 3 (2015): 749–79.

McRuer, Robert. "Compulsory Able-Bodiedness and Queer/Disabled Existence." *Disability Studies Reader* 3 (2010): 383–92.

Mead, Aroha Te Pareake, and Steven Ratuva, eds. *Pacific Genes and Life Patents: Pacific Indigenous Experiences and Analysis of the Commodification and Ownership of Life*. Wellington, NZ: Call of the Earth and the United Nations University Institute of Advanced Studies, 2007.

Meleisea, Malama. *The Making of Modern Samoa: Traditional Authority and Colonial Administration in the History of Western Samoa*. Suva, Fiji: Institute of Pacific Studies, University of the South Pacific, 1987.

Meyer, Manu Aluli. "Our Own Liberation: Reflections on Hawaiian Epistemology." *Contemporary Pacific* 13, no. 1 (2001): 124.

Mignolo, Walter. *Local Histories/Global Designs: Coloniality, Subaltern Knowledges, and Border Thinking*. Princeton, NJ: Princeton University Press, 2000.

Mikaere, Ani. *The Balance Destroyed: Consequences for Maori Women of the Colonisation of Tikanga Maori*. Auckland, NZ: International Research Institute for Maori and Indigenous Education, 2003.

Mikaere, Ani. *Colonising Myths—Maori Realities: He Rukuruku Whakaaro*. Wellington, NZ: Huia, 2011.

Miller, Bruce J. *Invisible Indigenes: The Politics of Nonrecognition*. Lincoln: University of Nebraska Press, 2003.

Million, Dian. "Felt Theory: An Indigenous Feminist Approach to Affect and History." *Wicazo Sa Review* 24, no. 2 (2009): 53–76.

Million, Dian. *Therapeutic Nations: Healing in an Age of Indigenous Human Rights*. Tucson: University of Arizona Press, 2013.

Miranda, Deborah A. *Bad Indians: A Tribal Memoir*. Berkeley, CA: Heyday, 2013.

Montagu, Ashley. *Statement on Race: An Annotated Elaboration and Exposition of the Four Statements on Race Issued by the United Nations Educational, Scientific, and Cultural Organization*. New York: Oxford University Press, 1972.

Moore, Gregory. "Nietzsche, Degeneration, and the Critique of Christianity." *Journal of Nietzsche Studies*, no. 19 (2000): 1–18.

Moreton-Robinson, Aileen. *The White Possessive: Property, Power, and Indigenous Sovereignty*. Minneapolis: University of Minnesota Press, 2015.

Morgan, Lewis Henry. *Ancient Society; or, Researches in the Lines of Human Progress from Savagery, through Barbarism to Civilization*. New York: Henry Holt, 1877.

Morgensen, Scott. "The Biopolitics of Settler Colonialism: Right Here, Right Now." *Settler Colonial Studies* 1, no. 1 (2011): 52–76.

Morgensen, Scott Lauria. "Settler Homonationalism: Theorizing Settler Colonialism within Queer Modernities." *GLQ: A Journal of Lesbian and Gay Studies* 16, no. 1–2 (2010): 105–31.

Morgensen, Scott Lauria. *Spaces between Us: Queer Settler Colonialism and Indigenous Decolonization*. Minneapolis: University of Minnesota Press, 2011.
Morrison, Toni. *Playing in the Dark*. New York: Random House, 2007.
Morrow, Prince A. "Leprosy and Hawaiian Annexation." *North American Review* 165, no. 492 (1897): 582–90.
Muhammad, Khalil Gibran. *The Condemnation of Blackness: Race, Crime, and the Making of Modern Urban America*. Cambridge, MA: Harvard University Press, 2010.
Müller, Friedrich Max. *India: What Can It Teach Us? A Course of Lectures Delivered before the University of Cambridge*. New York: Funk and Wagnalls, 1883.
Munsterhjelm, Mark. *Living Dead in the Pacific: Contested Sovereignty and Racism in Genetic Research on Taiwan Aborigines*. Vancouver, BC: UBC Press, 2014.
Murray, Derek Conrad, and Soraya Murray. "Uneasy Bedfellows: Canonical Art Theory and the Politics of Identity." *Art Journal* 65, no. 1 (2006): 22–39.
Musick, John Roy. *Hawaii, Our New Possessions: An Account of Travels and Adventure, with Sketches of the Scenery . . . an Appendix Containing the Treaty of Annexation to the United States*. New York: Funk and Wagnalls, 1898.
Nash, Catherine. *Genetic Geographies: The Trouble with Ancestry*. Minneapolis: University of Minnesota Press, 2015.
*Native Hawaiian Federal Recognition: Joint Hearing before the Committee on Indian Affairs, United States Senate, and the Committee on Resources, United States House of Representatives, One Hundred Sixth Congress, Second Session, on S. 2899 . . . and H.R. 4904*. Washington, DC: U.S. Government Printing Office, 2001.
Naval Historical Center. "Works by McClelland Barclay in the Navy Art Collection." Online archive, May 17, 2005. http://www.history.navy.mil/ac/artist/b/barclay/barclay%20n.html.
Nelson, Alondra. *The Social Life of DNA: Race, Reparations, and Reconciliation after the Genome*. Boston: Beacon, 2016.
Niezen, Ronald. *The Origins of Indigenism: Human Rights and the Politics of Identity*. Berkeley: University of California Press, 2003.
Nihipali, Kunani. "Stone by Stone, Bone by Bone: Rebuilding the Hawaiian Nation in the Illusion of Reality." *Arizona State Law Journal* 34, no. 1 (2002): 27–46.
Nishime, LeiLani. *Undercover Asian: Multiracial Asian Americans in Visual Culture*. Urbana: University of Illinois Press, 2014.
Nyong'o, Tavia. *The Amalgamation Waltz: Race, Performance, and the Ruses of Memory*. Minneapolis: University of Minnesota Press, 2009.
O'Brien, Patty. *The Pacific Muse: Exotic Femininity and the Colonial Pacific*. Seattle: University of Washington Press, 2006.
Okamura, Jonathan Y. *Ethnicity and Inequality in Hawai'i*. Philadelphia: Temple University Press, 2008.
Okihiro, Gary Y. *Cane Fires: The Anti-Japanese Movement in Hawaii, 1865–1945*. Philadelphia: Temple University Press, 1991.
Olson, Steve. *Mapping Human History: Discovering the Past through Our Genes*. Boston: Houghton Mifflin, 2002.

Omi, Michael, and Howard Winant. *Racial Formation in the United States: From the 1960s to the 1990s*, 2nd ed. New York: Routledge, 1994.

Osgood, Robert. "Education in the Name of 'Improvement': The Influence of Eugenic Thought and Practice in Indiana's Public Schools, 1900–1930." *Indiana Magazine of History* 106, no. 3 (2010): 272–99.

Osorio, Jon Kamakawiwoʻole. *Dismembering Lāhui: A History of the Hawaiian Nation to 1887*. Honolulu: University of Hawaiʻi Press, 2002.

Palmer, Albert W. *The Human Side of Hawaii: Race Problems in the Mid-Pacific*. Boston: Pilgrim, 1924.

Palmié, Stephan. *Wizards and Scientists: Explorations in Afro-Cuban Modernity and Tradition*. Durham, NC: Duke University Press, 2002.

Pálsson, Gísli, and Paul Rabinow. "Iceland: The Case of a National Human Genome Project." *Anthropology Today* 15, no. 5 (1999): 14–18.

"Paoakalani Declaration." Ka ʻAha Pono Native Hawaiian Intellectual Property Rights Conference, 2003. https://190f32x2yl33s804xzaogfi4-wpengine.netdna-ssl.com/wp-content/uploads/Paoakalani-Declaration.pdf.

Parker, Elizabeth Maria Bonney Wills. *The Sandwich Islands as They Are, Not as They Should Be*. San Francisco: Burgess, 1852.

*Policy of the United States Regarding Relationship with Native Hawaiians and to Provide a Process for the Recognition by the United States of the Native Hawaiian Governing Entity: Hearing before the Committee on Indian Affairs, United States Senate, One Hundred Eighth Congress, First Session on S. 344, Expressing the Policy of the United States Regarding the United States Relationship with Native Hawaiians and to Provide a Process for the Recognition by the United States of the Native Hawaiian Governing Entity, February 25, 2003*. Washington, DC: U.S. Government Printing Office, 2003.

Porteus, Stanley David, and Marjorie Elizabeth Babcock. *Temperament and Race*. Boston: R. G. Badger, 1926.

Povinelli, Elizabeth A. *The Cunning of Recognition: Indigenous Alterities and the Making of Australian Multiculturalism*. Durham NC: Duke University Press, 2002.

Pukui, Mary Kawena. *ʻŌlelo Noʻeau: Hawaiian Proverbs and Poetical Sayings*, vol. 71. Honolulu: Bishop Museum Press, 1983.

Pukui, Mary Kawena, and Samuel H. Elbert. *Hawaiian Dictionary: Hawaiian-English, English-Hawaiian*. Honolulu: University of Hawaiʻi Press, 1986.

Rabin, Nicole Miyoshi. "Picturing the Mix: Visual and Linguistic Representations in Kip Fulbeck's *Part Asian, 100% Hapa*." *Critical Studies in Media Communication* 29, no. 5 (2012): 387–402.

Rajan, Kaushik Sunder. *Biocapital: The Constitution of Postgenomic Life*. Durham, NC: Duke University Press, 2006.

Reardon, Jenny. *Race to the Finish: Identity and Governance in an Age of Genomics*. Princeton, NJ: Princeton University Press, 2005.

Reardon, Jenny, and Kim TallBear. "'Your DNA Is Our History': Genomics, Anthropology and the Construction of Whiteness as Property." *Current Anthropology* 53, no. S5 (2012): S233–45.

Reece, Ernest J. "Race Mingling in Hawaii." *American Journal of Sociology* 20, no. 1 (1914): 104–16.
Reeve, W. Paul. *Religion of a Different Color: Race and the Mormon Struggle for Whiteness*. Oxford: Oxford University Press, 2015.
Rifkin, Mark. "Settler Common Sense." *Settler Colonial Studies* 3, no. 3–4 (2013): 322–40.
Rodriguez, Lena, and James Rimumutu George. "Is Genetic Labeling of 'Risk' Related to Obesity Contributing to Resistance and Fatalism in Polynesian Communities?" *Contemporary Pacific* 26, no. 1 (2014): 65–93.
Rohrer, Judy. "'Got Race?' The Production of Haole and the Distortion of Indigeneity in the Rice Decision." *Contemporary Pacific* 18, no. 1 (2005): 1–31.
Rohrer, Judy. *Haoles in Hawai'i*. Honolulu: University of Hawai'i Press, 2010.
Rohrer, Judy. *Staking Claim: Settler Colonialism and Racialization in Hawai'i*. Tucson: University of Arizona Press, 2016.
Rønning, Joachim, and Espen Sandberg, directors. *Kon-Tiki*. Feature film, 2013.
Rosa, John P. "Local Story: The Massie Case Narrative and the Cultural Production of Local Identity in Hawai'i." *Amerasia Journal* 26, no. 2 (2000): 93–115.
Ross, Luana. "From the 'F' Word to Indigenous/Feminisms." *Wicazo Sa Review* 24, no. 2 (2009): 39–52.
Ryan, Tom. "'Le Président des Terres Australes': Charles de Brosses and the French Enlightenment Beginnings of Oceanic Anthropology." *Journal of Pacific History* 37, no. 2 (2002): 157–86.
Sahlins, Marshall D. "Poor Man, Rich Man, Big-Man, Chief: Political Types in Melanesia and Polynesia." *Comparative Studies in Society and History* 5, no. 3 (1963): 285–303.
Said, Edward W. *Orientalism*. New York: Vintage, 1994.
Saleeby, Caleb Williams. *The Methods of Race-Regeneration*. New York: Moffat, Yard, 1911.
Salesa, Damon. "The Pacific in Indigenous Time." In *Pacific Histories: Ocean, Land, People*, edited by David Armitage and Alison Bashford, 31–52. New York: Palgrave Macmillan, 2014.
Salesa, Damon Ieremia. *Racial Crossings: Race, Intermarriage, and the Victorian British Empire*. Oxford: Oxford University Press, 2011.
Salier, C. W. "The Australian Ideals of John Dunmore Lang." *Australian Quarterly* 10, no. 4 (1938): 70–76.
Salmon, Dan. *Made in Taiwan*. Documentary film, NZ On Screen, 2006.
Sanders, Elizabeth Elkins. *Remarks on the "Tour around Hawaii."* Salem, MA: Author, 1848.
Saranillio, Dean Itsuje. "Seeing Conquest: Colliding Histories and Cultural Politics of Hawai'i Statehood." PhD diss., University of Michigan, Ann Arbor, 2009.
Searle, G. S. "Mount and Morris Exonerated: A Narrative of the Voyage of the Brig 'Carl' in 1871, with Comments Upon the Trial Which Followed the Massacre on Board That Vessel." Melbourne: Evans Brothers, 1875.
See, Sarita Echavez. *The Decolonized Eye: Filipino American Art and Performance*. Minneapolis: University of Minnesota Press, 2009.

Selcer, Perrin. "Beyond the Cephalic Index: Negotiating Politics to Produce UNESCO's Scientific Statements on Race." *Current Anthropology* 53, no. S5 (2012): S173–84.

Selden, Steven. "Selective Traditions and the Science Curriculum: Eugenics and the Biology Textbook, 1914–1949." *Science Education* 75, no. 5 (1991): 493–512.

Sexton, Jared. *Amalgamation Schemes: Antiblackness and the Critique of Multiracialism*. Minneapolis: University of Minnesota Press, 2008.

Shapiro, Harry L. *Race Mixture*. Paris: UNESCO, 1953.

Sharma, Nitasha. "Pacific Revisions of Blackness: Blacks Address Race and Belonging in Hawai'i." *Amerasia Journal* 37, no. 3 (2011): 43–60.

Sharma, Nitasha. "The Racial Imperative: Rereading Hawai'i's History and Black-Hawaiian Relations through the Perspective of Black Residents." In *Beyond Ethnicity: New Politics of Race in Hawai'i*, edited by Camilla Fojas, Rudy P. Guevarra Jr., and Nitasha Tamar Sharma. Honolulu: University of Hawai'i Press, 2018.

Shigematsu, Setsu, and Keith Camacho. *Militarized Currents: Toward a Decolonized Future in Asia and the Pacific*. Minneapolis: University of Minnesota Press, 2010.

Shilliam, Robbie. *The Black Pacific: Anti-Colonial Struggles and Oceanic Connections*. London: Bloomsbury, 2015.

Silva, Denise Ferreira da. "An Outline of a Global Political Subject: Reading Evo Morales' Election as a (Post-)Colonial Event." *Seattle Journal for Social Justice* 8 (2009): 25–47.

Silva, Denise Ferreira da. *Toward a Global Idea of Race*. Minneapolis: University of Minnesota Press, 2007.

Silva, Noenoe K. *Aloha Betrayed: Native Hawaiian Resistance to American Colonialism*. Durham, NC: Duke University Press, 2004.

Simpson, Audra. "Captivating Eunice: Membership, Colonialism, and Gendered Citizenships of Grief." *Wicazo Sa Review* 24, no. 2 (2009): 105–29.

Simpson, Audra. "From White into Red: Captivity Narratives as Alchemies of Race and Citizenship." *American Quarterly* 60, no. 2 (2008): 251.

Simpson, Audra. *Mohawk Interruptus: Political Life across the Borders of Settler States*. Durham, NC: Duke University Press, 2014.

Simpson, Audra. "On Ethnographic Refusal: Indigeneity, 'Voice,' and Colonial Citizenship." *Junctures* 9 (2007): 67–80.

Simpson, Audra. "To the Reserve and Back Again: Kahnawake Mohawk Narratives of Self, Home and Nation." PhD diss., McGill University, Montreal, 2003.

Simpson, Leanne. "Anger, Resentment and Love: Fuelling Resurgent Struggle." NAISA paper presentation, June 5, 2015. Accessed May 16, 2017. https://www.leannesimpson.ca/talk/anger-resentment-love-fuelling-resurgent-struggle.

Simpson, Leanne. *Dancing on Our Turtle's Back: Stories of Nishnaabeg Re-Creation, Resurgence and a New Emergence*. Winnipeg: Arbeiter Ring, 2011.

Singeo, Lindsey. "The Patentability of the Native Hawaiian Genome." *American Journal of Law and Medicine* 33, no. 1 (2007): 119.

Smith, Andrea. *Conquest: Sexual Violence and American Indian Genocide*. Cambridge, MA: South End, 2005.

Smith, Andrea. "Indigeneity, Settler Colonialism, White Supremacy." In *Racial Formation in the Twenty-First Century*, edited by Daniel Martinez HoSang, Oneka LaBennett, and Laura Pulido, 66–90. Berkeley: University of California Press, 2012.

Smith, Andrea. *Native Americans and the Christian Right: The Gendered Politics of Unlikely Alliances*. Durham, NC: Duke University Press, 2008.

Smith, Andrea. "Voting and Indigenous Disappearance." *Settler Colonial Studies* 3, no. 3–4 (2013): 352–68.

Smith, Andrea, and J. Kēhaulani Kauanui. "Native Feminisms Engage American Studies." *American Quarterly* 60, no. 2 (2008): 241–49.

Smith, Philippa Mein. *A Concise History of New Zealand*. Melbourne: Cambridge University Press, 2012.

Snelgrove, Corey, Rita Dhamoon, and Jeff Corntassel. "Unsettling Settler Colonialism: The Discourse and Politics of Settlers, and Solidarity with Indigenous Nations." *Decolonization: Indigeneity, Education and Society* 3, no. 2 (2014): 1–32.

Somerville, Alice Te Punga. *Once Were Pacific: Maori Connections to Oceania*. Minneapolis: University of Minnesota Press, 2012.

Spivak, Gayatri. *Outside in the Teaching Machine*. New York: Routledge, 1993.

Stannard, David E. *Honor Killing: Race, Rape, and Clarence Darrow's Spectacular Last Case*. New York: Penguin, 2006.

Stannard, David E. "Honoring Racism: The Professional Life and Reputation of Stanley D. Porteus." In *The Ethnic Studies Story: Politics and Social Movements in Hawai'i: Essays*, edited by Ibrahim Aoudé, 85–125. Honolulu: University of Hawai'i Press, 1999.

Stats NZ. "2013 Census Ethnic Group Profiles." Accessed June 30, 2018. http://archive.stats.govt.nz/Census/2013-census/profile-and-summary-reports/ethnic-profiles.aspx.

Stevenson, Karen. *The Frangipani Is Dead: Contemporary Pacific Art in New Zealand, 1985–2000*. Wellington, NZ: Huia, 2008.

Stevenson, Karen. *Pacific Island Artists: Navigating the Global Art World*. Oakland, CA: Masalai, 2011.

Sullivan, Louis R. "New Light on the Races of Polynesia." *Asia*, January 1923.

Sullivan, Louis R. *The Racial Diversity of the Polynesian Peoples*. Paper presented to the Australasian Association for the Advancement of Science, Wellington, NZ, 1923.

Sullivan, Louis R., Edward Winslow Gifford, and W. C. McKern. *A Contribution to Samoan Somatology*. Honolulu: Bishop Museum Press, 1921.

Sullivan, Louis R., E. S. Craighill Handy, and Willowdean C. Handy. *Marquesan Somatology with Comparative Notes on Samoa and Tonga*. Honolulu: Bishop Museum Press, 1923.

Sullivan, Louis R., and Harry L Shapiro. *Essentials of Anthropometry: A Handbook for Explorers and Museum Collectors*. New York: American Museum of Natural History, 1928.

Sullivan, Louis R., and Clark Wissler. *Observations on Hawaiian Somatology*. Honolulu: Bishop Museum Press, 1927.

Szego, C. K. "The Sound of Rocks Aquiver? Composing Racial Ambivalence in Territorial Hawai'i." *Journal of American Folklore* 123, no. 487 (2010): 31–62.

Takaki, Ronald T. *Pau Hana: Plantation Life and Labor in Hawaii, 1835–1920*. Honolulu: University of Hawai'i Press, 1983.

TallBear, Kimberly. "DNA, Blood, and Racializing the Tribe." *Wicazo Sa Review* 18, no. 1 (2003): 81–107.

TallBear, Kimberly. "Narratives of Race and Indigeneity in the Genographic Project." *Journal of Law, Medicine and Ethics* 35, no. 3 (2007): 412–24.

TallBear, Kimberly. *Native American DNA: Tribal Belonging and the False Promise of Genetic Science*. Minneapolis: University of Minnesota Press, 2013.

TallBear, Kim, and Deborah Bolnick. "'Native American DNA' Tests: What Are the Risks to Tribes?" *Native Voice*, December 3–17, 2004, D2.

Tamaira, A. Marata. "From Full Dusk to Full Tusk: Reimagining the 'Dusky Maiden' through the Visual Arts." *Contemporary Pacific* 22, no. 1 (2010): 1–35.

Tcherkézoff, Serge. "A Long and Unfortunate Voyage towards the 'Invention' of the Melanesia/Polynesia Distinction 1595–1832." *Journal of Pacific History* 38, no. 2 (2003): 175–96.

Teaiwa, Teresia. "Bikinis and Other s/Pacific n/Oceans." *Contemporary Pacific* 6, no. 1 (1994): 87–109.

Teaiwa, Teresia. "Reading Paul Gauguin's Noa Noa with Epeli Hau'ofa's Kisses in the Nederends: Militourism, Feminism, and the 'Polynesian' Body." In *Inside Out: Literature, Cultural Politics, and Identity in the New Pacific*, edited by Vilsoni Hereniko and Rob Wilson, 249–64. Lanham, MD: Rowman and Littlefield, 1999.

Tengan, Ty Kāwika. *Native Men Remade: Gender and Nation in Contemporary Hawai'i*. Durham, NC: Duke University Press, 2008.

Tengan, Ty Kāwika. "Re-Membering Panalā'au: Masculinities, Nation, and Empire in Hawai'i and the Pacific." *Contemporary Pacific* 20, no. 1 (2008): 27–53.

Terrell, John Edward, Kevin M. Kelly, and Paul Rainbird. "Foregone Conclusions? In Search of 'Papuans' and 'Austronesians.'" *Current Anthropology* 42, no. 1 (2001): 97–124.

Teves, Stephanie Nohelani. "Aloha State Apparatuses." *American Quarterly* 67, no. 3 (2015): 705–26.

Teves, Stephanie Nohelani. *Defiant Indigeneity: The Politics of Hawaiian Performance*. Chapel Hill: University of North Carolina Press, 2018.

Thomas, Greg. "Erotics of Aryanism/Histories of Empire: How 'White Supremacy' and 'Hellenomania' Construct 'Discourses of Sexuality.'" *CR: The New Centennial Review* 3, no. 3 (2003): 235–55.

Thomas, Nicholas. *In Oceania: Visions, Artifacts, Histories*. Durham, NC: Duke University Press, 1997.

Thomas, Nicholas, Allen Abramson, Ivan Brady, R. C. Green, Marshall Sahlins, Rebecca A. Stephenson, Friedrich Valjavec, and Ralph Gardner White. "The Force of Ethnology: Origins and Significance of the Melanesia/Polynesia Division [and Comments and Replies]." *Current Anthropology* 30, no. 1 (1989): 27–41.

Thompson, Uldrick. *Eugenics for Parents and Teachers*. Honolulu: Kamehameha Schools, 1915.

Thompson, Uldrick. *Eugenics for Young People: Twelve Short Articles on a Vital Subject*. Honolulu: Kamehameha Schools, 1913.

Tomso, Gregory. "The Queer History of Leprosy and Same-Sex Love." *American Literary History* 14, no. 4 (2002): 747–75.

Trask, Haunani-Kay. *From a Native Daughter: Colonialism and Sovereignty in Hawaiʻi*. Honolulu: University of Hawaiʻi Press, 1999.

Trask, Haunani-Kay. "Natives and Anthropologists: The Colonial Struggle." *Contemporary Pacific* 3, no. 1 (1991): 159–67.

Trask, Haunani-Kay. "Pro, Con Articles on Akaka Bill Fail to Address Land Issues." *Honolulu Advertiser*, May 2, 2004.

Tregear, Edward. *The Aryan Maori*. Wellington, NZ: G. Didsbury, Government Printer, 1885.

Tregear, Edward. "Polynesian Origins. (Continued.)." *Journal of the Polynesian Society* 13, no. 3 (1904): 133–52.

Tuck, Eve. "Suspending Damage: A Letter to Communities." *Harvard Educational Review* 79, no. 3 (2009): 409–28.

Tuck, Eve, and C. Ree. "A Glossary of Haunting." In *Handbook of Autoethnography*, edited by Stacy Holman Jones, Tony E. Adams, and Carolyn Ellis, 639–58. London: Routledge, 2013.

Tuck, Eve, and K. Wayne Yang. "Decolonization Is Not a Metaphor." *Decolonization: Indigeneity, Education and Society* 1, no. 1 (2012): 1–40.

Twombly, Alexander Stevenson. *The Native Hawaiian of Yesterday and To-Day*. Publisher unknown. University of Hawaiʻi Hawaiian Collections. 1901.

UNESCO. *Four Statements on the Race Question*. Paris: UNESCO, 1969.

UNESCO. *The Race Question in Modern Science; Race and Science*. New York: Columbia University Press, 1961.

UNESCO. *What Is Race? Evidence from Scientists*. Paris: UNESCO, 1952.

Uperesa, Faʻanofo Lisaclaire. "Fabled Futures: Migration and Mobility for Samoans in American Football." *Contemporary Pacific* 26, no. 2 (2014): 281–301.

U.S. Census Bureau. "QuickFacts: Hawaii." Accessed June 30, 2018. https://www.census.gov/quickfacts/fact/table/hi/PST045217.

Van Dyke, Jon M. *Who Owns the Crown Lands of Hawaii?* Honolulu: University of Hawaiʻi Press, 2008.

Veracini, Lorenzo. "Introducing Settler Colonial Studies." *Settler Colonial Studies* 1, no. 1 (2011): 1–12.

Warren, Joyce Pualani. "Embodied Cosmogony: Genealogy and the Racial Production of the State in Victoria Nalani Kneubuhl's 'Hoʻoulu Lāhui.'" *American Quarterly* 67, no. 3 (2015): 937–58.

Weiss, Kenneth M. "Seeing the Forest through the Gene-Trees." *Evolutionary Anthropology: Issues, News, and Reviews* 19, no. 6 (2010): 210–21.

Weiss, Kenneth M., and Jeffrey C. Long. "Non-Darwinian Estimation: My Ancestors, My Genes' Ancestors." *Genome Research* 19, no. 5 (2009): 703–10.

Werry, Margaret. *The Tourist State: Performing Leisure, Liberalism, and Race in New Zealand*. Minneapolis: University of Minnesota Press, 2011.

Whitmee, S. J. "The Ethnology of Polynesia." *Journal of the Anthropological Institute of Great Britain and Ireland* 8 (1879): 261–75.

Whitmee, S. J. "On Some Characteristics of the Malayo-Polynesians." *Journal of the Anthropological Institute of Great Britain and Ireland* 7 (1878): 372–78.

Whitmee, S. J. "A Revised Nomenclature of the Inter-Oceanic Races of Men." *Journal of the Anthropological Institute of Great Britain and Ireland* 8 (1879): 360–69.

Winter, Christine. "Lingering Legacies of German Colonialism." In *Mixed Race Identities in Australia, New Zealand and the Pacific Islands*, edited by Kirsten McGavin and Farida Fozdar, 147–61. New York: Routledge, 2017.

Winter, Christine. "National Socialism and the German (Mixed-Race) Diasporas in Oceania." In *Europa jenseits der Grenzen: Festschrift für Reinhard Wendt*, edited by Michael Mann and Jürgen G. Nagel, 227–51. Heidelberg: Draupadi Verlag, 2015.

Wolfe, Patrick. *Settler Colonialism and the Transformation of Anthropology: The Politics and Poetics of an Ethnographic Event*. London: Cassell, 1999.

Wolfe, Patrick. *Traces of History: Elementary Structures of Race*. London: Verso, 2016.

Wood, Houston. *Displacing Natives: The Rhetorical Production of Hawai'i*. Lanham, MD: Rowman and Littlefield, 1999.

Wu, Ellen D. *The Color of Success: Asian Americans and the Origins of the Model Minority*. Princeton, NJ: Princeton University Press, 2013.

Wynter, Sylvia. "The Ceremony Must Be Found: After Humanism." *Boundary 2* 12, no. 3–13, no. 1 (1984): 19–70.

Wynter, Sylvia. "Unsettling the Coloniality of Being/Power/Truth/Freedom: Towards the Human, after Man, Its Overrepresentation—An Argument." *CR: The New Centennial Review* 3, no. 3 (2003): 257–337.

Yamashiro, Aiko, and Noelani Goodyear-Kaʻōpua. *The Value of Hawaii 2: Ancestral Roots, Oceanic Visions*. Honolulu: University of Hawaiʻi Press, 2014.

Yu, Henry. *Thinking Orientals: Migration, Contact, and Exoticism in Modern America*. New York: Oxford University Press, 2001.

# INDEX

Abercrombie, Neil, 141, 226
"accidental drift" theory, 6–7
*An Account of the Polynesian Race: Its Origin and Migrations and the Ancient History of the Hawaiian People to the Times of Kamehameha* (Fornander), 53–54
Adams, Romanzo: assimilation research by, 97, 99–104, 119, 125, 175; on Chinese Hawaiians, 105–6, 114; on intermarriage and racism, 172; "neo-Hawaiian race," concept of, 115, 122–23, 156
Admission Act, 146
African Americans: assimilation and, 100–104; genetic testing and, 179–80; Hawaiian identity and, 4, 30; photographs of, 198; Polynesian and Melanesian identity and, 29; slavery and, 21–23
African Ancestry, 179
Aikau, Hōkūlani, 49, 149
Akaka, Daniel, 136–37

Akaka Bill, 136–40, 146, 152–53
Alaska Native Claims Settlement Act, 140–41, 164
Alaska Native model: Native Hawaiian identity recognition and, 140–46, 164–66, 185
almost whiteness: antiblackness linked to, 68–69; logic of possession and, 13, 59–60; Polynesian identity and, 41, 92–93, 95; settler colonialism and, 9, 22, 33
Alu Like, 151–52
American Museum of Natural History, 78–81, 257n56
Anderson, Warwick, 78, 81, 94
Andrew, Thomas, 210
annexation of Hawai'i, 75–76, 115
anthropology: eugenics and, 66, 94–95; historical evolution of, 51; racial theory and, 67–95; Te Rangihīroa's contributions to, 88–90

*Anthropology* (Kroeber), 11
anthropometric techniques: in contemporary art, 202–3; Sullivan's eugenics research and, 78–86, 94, 202; Te Rangihīroa's research and, 87–93
anti-affirmative action legislation, 145–46
antiblackness: in Australia, 28; in Brazil, 127–29; defined, 28; in Fornander's research, 54–56; geographic mapping of Polynesia and, 39–40; law, violence, the state, and, 144–46; Micronesian identity and, 235–36; possessive spirit of whiteness and, 23–31; racial mapping of Pacific Islands and, 36–40; views of Native Hawaiians and, 107–11
antiracist sociology: assimilation and, 100–104
aʻole, 228; as intergenerational regeneration, 159–66
Apology Bill, 138, 140
artistic production: ethnographic refusal and replication in, 200–209; regenerative refusal and, 131–32, 195–223
Aryanism: Austronesian research and, 24; Fornander's research and, 54–56; Māori people and, 56–61; origins of, 50–51, 252n27; Polynesian identity and, 14–19, 29, 33–34, 43–44, 50–66, 83–86, 123, 173. *See also* whiteness
*The Aryan Maori* (Tregear), 53–54, 56–61, 173
Asian Americans: Fulbeck's *Hapa Project* photographs and, 204–9; *Hapa* (mixed-race identity) and, 32, 200–202; Hawaiian identity and, 30–31; model minority stereotype of, 111–14, 122; race relations cycle and, 99–100; racial mixture discourse and, 205–9
Asian/Pacific Islanders: decolonization and activism of, 132–33; Kihara's photography and, 203–4; racial triangulation and, 30–31; regenerative refusal and, 129–33; terminology for, 8

assimilation: Chinese Hawaiians and, 112–14; in Hawaiʻi, 96–104, 174–77; Kānaka Maoli refusal of, 231–39
Association of Hawaiian Civic Clubs, 187, 191–93
*Aunty Wini Wearing Hina Hina* (*Pele's Hair*) (Pao), 220
Australasia: British settler colonialism and, 46–50; racial mapping of, 37–40
Australia: Native title law in, 28
Austronesian discourse, 23–24
Autogen company, 184

Ballantyne, Tony, 58–59, 252n27
Banivanua-Mar, Tracey, 28–29, 39
Bayonet Constitution, 63
*Beachfront Property at Diamond Head/ Leʻahi Kapa* (*Brow of Tuna Covering*) (Pao), 216–21
Beamer, Harriet, 80
Bering Strait theory, 251n20, 253n57
biopolitics, 26
Bishop, Bernice Pauahi, 70–72
Bishop, Charles, 72
Bishop Museum: Shapiro at, 125–26; Sullivan's affiliation with, 69–71, 77–86; Te Rangihīroa's affiliation with, 87–93
blackbirding (forced labor), 28–29
Black identity, 4, 30–31; defined, 241n3; Pacific Islanders and, 236–37; Sullivan's eugenics and, 84–86. *See also* antiblackness
Black Lives Matter movement, 236–37
Black Panthers, 30
blood quantum laws, 17–18, 64, 94–95; *Day v. Apoliona* case and, 153–56; DNA testing and, 168–70; genealogical verification and, 142–46; Hawaiian Homes Commission Act and, 135–38; Kānaka Maoli indigeneity and, 231–39; land and homestead rights and, 138–40, 146–49, 168–70, 173; Native Hawaiian identity and, 22,

126–29, 146–49; regenerative refusal of, 157–58, 162
Boas, Franz, 81–82, 98
Bougainville, Louis-Antoine de, 37–38
Bory de Saint-Vincent, Jean-Baptiste, 39
Boyd, Charles, 184–85
Brazil: racial mixture discourse and, 127–29
Breyer, Stephen (Justice), 153–54
Buck, Sir Peter Henry. *See* Te Rangihīroa

Callender, John, 37
Cannon, George, 49
Caribbean region: racial mixture discourse and, 127–29
Caucasian identity: Polynesians' link to, 67–70, 83–86, 89, 94–95, 123; valorization of, 111–14
Cherokee tribe: federal recognition of, 143
Chicago School discourse: melting pot ideology and, 99–106, 175
Chinese Hawaiians, 30–31, 104–11; valorization of, 111–14
Christian missionaries: Polynesian identity and, 49–50, 66
Christian theology: British settler colonialism and, 47–50
Church of Jesus Christ of Latter-Day Saints, 9, 49
citizenship: Native Hawaiians and, 136–38, 189–90
classical mythology: Polynesians and, 43–44
class politics: eugenics and, 72–77
climate change activism, 236–37
*Collier's* magazine: "Hawaiian Medley" article in, 115–22
Cologne, Phyllis U'ilani Ka'ahanui, 162
*The Coming of the Maori* (Te Rangihīroa), 88–89
Compact of Free Association between the United States and Palau, the Federated States of Micronesia and the Marshall Islands, 235–36
contemporary Pacific art: ethnographic refusal and replication in, 200–209;

regeneration of indigeneity through, 195–223; stereotypes about, 200, 274n12
Cook, James (Captain), 2, 28, 35, 37, 47, 173–75
Cook, Kealani, 49–50, 61–63
Council for Native Hawaiian Advancement (CNHA), 138–41
coverture: heteropatriarchy and, 16–17
criminology, 51; Chicago School research in, 100–104
critical mixed race studies, 209. *See also* racial mixture discourse
Cyclone Evan (2012), 212–14

Dampier, William, 36
Darwin, Charles, 51
Davenport, Charles, 70, 81
Davis, Gene Ross, 162–64
Davis, Kanoelani, 159–60
Dawes Act, 143
Day, Virgil, 136
*Day v. Apoliona* case, 22, 131; gender and race and, 146–49; Native Hawaiian identity and, 136–39, 143–46, 162–67; testimony in, 149–56, 161–62, 202
De Brosses, Charles, 36, 40
DeCODE project, 184–87
decolonization: regeneration and, 232–39
deductive reasoning, 51
defiant indigeneity theory, 130
degeneration discourse: eugenics and, 67–70, 72–77, 95, 255n1; evolutionary perspective on, 51; in Hawaiian racial discourse, 98–99, 189–90; imperialism and, 45–50
de las Casas, Bartolomé, 38
Department of Hawaiian Home Lands (DHHL), 168, 180–82
Department of the Interior (DOI): recognition of Native Hawaiians and, 139–43, 166–67; regenerative refusal of directives from, 157–58, 162–66
Department of Land and Natural Resources, 225

de Rienzi, Louis Domeney, 39
diabetes risk of Polynesians, 182–83
diffusionism ideology: Aryanism and, 58–61, 251n20; imperialism and, 48–50
direct-to-consumer (DTC) genetic ancestry tests: limitations of, 178–82
disease: genetics and, 184–93; race and, 75–77
diversity rhetoric: Polynesian identity and, 10
Douglas, Bronwen, 34, 40
Doyle, Jennifer, 198–201, 209
d'Urville, Jules-Sébastien-César Dumont, 37–39

EasyDNA test, 177
education: Hawaiian identity and, 108–11
Egypt: Polynesian identity and, 43–44
Elderts, Kollin, 122
Emory, Kenneth, 5
empiricism: race and whiteness and, 26
Enlightenment philosophy: Polynesian identity and, 38
Enomoto, Joy, 237
Espanola, Wendy, 161
*E-Tangata* (online news journal), 177
ethnicity: genetics and, 174–77; regenerative refusal and replication in contemporary art and, 200–209
ethnographic refusal, 228; art and, 200–209; Kānaka Maoli indigeneity as, 232–39
ethnology: Te Rangihīroa's research in, 88
eugenics, 66; blood quantum laws and legacy of, 147–49; in *The Hapa Project*, 207–9; physical anthropology and, 67–70; social science and, 71–77; Sullivan's work in, 77–86; terminology of, 255n1; Thompson's work in, 70–77
European identity: Kalākaua's research on, 62–65; logic of possession through whiteness and, 64–65; Polynesian link to, 43–54; stereotypes of, 100–104

fa'afafine, 221
*Family Portraits* (Pao), 220
federal recognition of Native Hawaiian identity, 138–46; genetic testing and, 185; regenerative refusal of, 157–58
feminist scholarship: blood quantum laws and, 147–49; Kanaka Maoli indigeneity and, 232–39; regenerative refusal and, 20–23, 130–33
Fiji: forced labor on, 28–29
Filipinos: in Hawai'i, 31
forced labor in Melanesia, 28–29
Fornander, Abraham, 14, 44, 46, 51, 53–55, 65–66, 83; Te Rangihīroa's critique of, 87
Forster, Johann Reinhold, 38, 48
founder effects in genetic testing, 184
Frazier, E. Franklin, 100
Free West Papua struggle, 234–37
French Polynesia: as Hawaiki ancestral homeland, 89; imperialist identity of, 9–10; Mā'ohi activism in, 132; population demographics in, 243n18
Freyre, Gilberto, 128
*From Here I Saw What Happened and I Cried* (Weems), 198
Fulbeck, Kip, 131, 200–201, 205–9, 221–23

Galton, Francis, 51
Galton Society, 78, 94
*Galu Afi* (Kihara video work), 210–14
Galu Afi tsunami, 210–14
gaming rights for Native American tribes, 144–46
Gauguin, Paul, 10, 211–14
gender: in contemporary Polynesian art, 221–23; disease and, 75–77; Hawaiian stereotypes and, 99; omission in *The Hapa Project* of, 207–9; Polynesian stereotypes and, 91–93; race and, 75–77, 146–49; settler colonialism and, 17–19
genealogical verification: genetic testing and, 179–82; land rights and, 192–93; Native Hawaiian identity and, 142–46

genetic ancestry tests: state-recognized indigeneity and, 177–82
genetics: DNA testing policy and, 168–70; feminist perspectives on, 148–49; genetic modification of plants and, 190–92; racial mixture discourse and, 128–29; regenerative refusal and, 131–32
genome biobanking, 170, 183
genomics: ancient migrations and, 172; Polynesian identity and, 23–24
geographic boundaries: genetics and, 171; Oceanic remapping of, 234–39; racial mapping of Pacific islands and, 36–40; regional geography of Oceania and, 4, 7–8
Gill, W. W., 52
Ginés de Sepúlveda, Juan, 50
Glissant, Édouard, 7, 43
Goeman, Mishuana, 233–34
Goodyear-Kaʻōpua, Noelani, 72, 158, 166, 190–91
Gordon, Avery, 23, 214
Gowen, Herbert, 73
Graber, Susan (Justice), 150–56
Great Britain: Māori Aryanism linked to, 59–61; settler colonialism and, 46–50
Great Chain of Being: Pacific Islanders and, 47–48
Great Māhele, 150, 190–91
Greece: Polynesian identity and, 43–44
Gregory, Herbert, 78, 82

Hale ʻĀkala, 62, 254n87
Hale Nauā, 61
half-caste ideology: in contemporary art, 210–11; Native Hawaiian identity and, 189–90
Hansen's disease, 75–76
*haole* (whiteness), 26–27, 72
*Hapa* (mixed-race identity), 32, 200–202, 205–9
hapa haole: Hawaiian identity and, 205–9; Part Hawaiian as, 85–86

*The Hapa Project* (Fulbeck), 200, 205–9, 221, 275n21
haunting: regenerative refusal and, 214
Hawaiʻi: Micronesians in, 234–36; population demographics in, 243n18; race and assimilation in, 96–99; statehood for, 42, 75–76, 97, 102–4, 115, 132, 140; as white possession, 15–19
*Hawaiian Cover-ups* series, 198, 215–21
*Hawaii and Its Race Problem* (State Department), 115
"Hawaiian Genome" as property, 189–91
Hawaiian Genome Project, 170, 182–93, 194, 229
Hawaiian Homes Commission Act, 94, 126–27, 135–38, 142–46, 162–66, 182, 189
Hawaiian identity: stereotypes about, 2–3, 99–104
Hawaiian Kingdom: ceded lands dispute and, 140–41, 146–50; Great Māhele and, 150, 190–91; Native Hawaiian identity linked to, 155–56, 159–66; settler colonialism and destruction of, 15–19; overthrow of, 4–5, 64–65, 72, 138, 140, 158
Hawaiian Renaissance, 132
*Hawaiian Types* (Inn), 118, 173
Hawaiki (Polynesian ancestral homeland), 87–89
Hegel, G. W. F., 25–26
heteronormativity: eugenics and, 72–77
heteropatriarchy: gender and race and, 148–49; settler colonialism and, 16–19
heterosexuality: reproductive politics and, 101–4, 147–49; stereotypes of Hawaiian women and, 117–22; whiteness and, 75–76
Heyerdahl, Thor, 5–7
*Histoire des navigations aux terres australes* [A History of Voyages to the Southern Lands] (De Brosses), 37, 40
Hodges, William, 2
*Hōkūleʻa* voyage, 7

Holocaust: Sāmoan German diaspora and, 70
homophobia: social impact of, 18–19
*Honolulu Star-Advertiser*, 180–81
*Honolulu Star-Bulletin*, 5–6
Hoʻohokulani (goddess figure), 230–31
Hoʻohuli, Josiah, 136
Hoʻomanawanui, Mel, 136
Hoʻopiʻi, Richard Kealoha, Sr., 159–60
Hooton, E. A., 11
Hoʻoulu Lāhui: Rise, Be Heard motto, 137, 230–39
"Hoʻoulu Lāhui" (Kneubuhl), 229–32
Howe, K. R., 34, 47–48
hula girl stereotype, 114–22, 221–23
Human Genome Diversity Project (HGDP), 187–89
*The Human Side of Hawaii* (Palmer), 103–4
Huxley, Thomas, 51
hybridity discourse: art as rejection of, 199–223; genetics research and, 173–77; Hawaiian stereotypes of, 99, 115–22; racial policies and, 17–18, 104–6, 256n24
hygiene: eugenics and, 74–77
hyperdescent, logic of, 17–18
hypodescent of blackness, 17

Icelandic population: genetic testing of, 184–87
Ida, Horace, 98
immigrant experience: assimilation and, 100–104; Sullivan's work in, 82
imperialism: Polynesian degeneration myth and, 45–50
incest, 74–77
India: Māori people and, 56–61; Polynesian links to, 89; retrospective prophecy theory and colonialism in, 51–52
indigeneity: artistic production and, 198–223; Austronesian discourse and, 24; colonialism and, 50; contested terms of recognition and, 136–38; DNA testing and, 169–70; genetics ancestry tests and, 177–83; Hawaiian Genome Project as threat to, 189–92; hyperdescent of, 17; Kānaka Maoli claims to, 231–39; logic of elimination and genocide in, 16–19; Native Hawaiians and, 176–77; ocean exploration and, 6–13, 224–39; Polynesian identity and, 9–13, 20–23; regeneration and, 20–23, 195–223; sovereignty and, 153–56; Terra Australis mythology and, 35; whiteness and possession of, 23–31
Indigenous feminism: genetics and, 148–49; regeneration and, 20–22; regenerative refusals and, 129–31; (re)mapping and, 233–34
Indigenous time, concept of, 20, 227–39
"Indonesians of Polynesia": Sullivan's concept of, 82–86
informed consent: genetic testing and, 183–84
Inn, Henry, 119, 173
intelligence testing: racial research and, 109–11
intermarriage: genetics and, 174–77; race relations and, 99–104, 172; whitening process and, 14, 18
ʻIolani Palace, 62

Japan: Kalākaua's visit to, 62–65
Japanese in Hawaiʻi, 31, 103–4; valorization of, 111–14
Japanese Problem, 103–4
Jetñil-Kijiner, Kathy, 236–37
*John Doe v. Kamehameha Schools* (2003–6), 139, 144–46
Johnson, Charles, 100
Jones, William (Sir), 50
Jordan, David Starr, 70
Joy, Wilma Noelani, 125–26, 162
J. Paul Getty Museum, 198

Kahahawai, Joseph, 98, 122
Kahawaiolaʻa, Patrick, 136
Ka Lāhui Hawaiʻi, 140

Kalākaua, David (King), 4, 45, 53; astronomy and science supported by, 225–26; Hoʻoulu Lāhui: Rise, Be Heard motto of, 137; Polynesian confederation proposed by, 64; Polynesian origins, scholarship of, 61–65, 91, 233–39; settler colonialism and, 53–54; worldwide tour by, 62
Kalama, Camille, 181
kalo (taro): genetic modification of, 190–92, 229; in Hawaiian culture, 229–31
Kamehameha I (King), 64, 73
Kamehameha Schools, 68–70, 70–77; federal recognition cases and, 139, 144–46
Kanaʻiolowalu. *See* Native Hawaiian roll commission
Kānaka Maoli: blood quantum politics and, 148–49; contemporary artistic representations of, 215–23; defined, 241n1; erasure in Hawaiʻi of, 63–65, 96–97, 200; eugenics and, 72–77; Hawaiian Genome Project and, 170, 182–94; Hawaiian identity and, 9; Hawaiian Renaissance and, 132; kalo modification and, 190–91; literary representations of, 229–39; in New Zealand, 9–10; police violence against, 122–23; as political concept, 155–56; Polynesian identity and, 9, 21–23, 48–50, 65–66; regenerative refusal and, 130–33, 159–66, 229–39; Thirty Meter Telescope opposed by, 225–28
Kanaka ʻŌiwi: defined, 241n1
*Ke Kaupu Hehi Ale* blog, 236–38
kiaʻi (protectors): Thirty Meter Telescope project and, 225–28
Kihara, Yuki, 131, 133, 198–204, 210–14, 221–23
kinship: in Māori culture, 88; Polynesian and Asian identity and, 62–65
Kneubuhl, Victoria Nālani, 229–32

knowledge: agency in colonialism of, 24–25; land linked to, 192–93
Koniag (Alaska Native) base roll, 143
*Kon-Tiki* expedition, 5–7
Kroeber, A. L., 11–13
Kūʻe Petitions, 161–66
Kūkaniloko sacred site, 218–21
kuleana (indigenous responsibility), 21
Kumulipo, 229–31
Kuwada, Bryan Kamaoli, 224, 226–28, 236–37

Laiʻohi, George, 162
Lam, Margaret, 96, 99, 104–11
land rights for Native Hawaiians: blood quantum laws and, 168–70; ceded lands dispute and, 138, 140, 146–49; degeneration discourse and, 189–90; genealogy and knowledge linked to, 192–93; genetic testing and, 180–82
Lang, John Dunmore, 43, 46–48, 50–51, 65–66, 83, 251n17
Latin America: racial mixture discourse and, 127–29
Leclerc, Georges-Louis, Comte de Buffon, 37
*Lei Stand Protest/Lei Pua Kapa* (Pao), 195–98, 216
lei stands, 195–97
leprosy: Native Hawaiians linked to, 74–77
"Lessons from Hawaiʻi" (Jetñil-Kijiner), 236
Lewontin, Richard, 13
Liliʻuokalani (Queen), 4, 16, 115, 146, 158, 160
Lind, Andrew, 119–22
linguistics: Māori people and, 56–61; Polynesian identity and, 23–24, 50–51; Te Rangihīroa's research on, 87–93
London, Jack, 75–76, 83
Lopesi, Lana, 177, 179, 182, 194
Lorden, Doris, 99, 104–11
Lost Tribes of Israel: Polynesians linked to, 49

māhele: genetic engineering and, 190–91
Man, Western ideal of: eugenics and, 70–77; genetics research and inclusive perspective on, 170–77
mana wahine, 148–49
Manganaro, Christine, 97–98
Māʻohi people, 9, 132–33
maoli designation: Native Hawaiian identity and, 141
Māori culture, 9; Polynesian Problem research by, 61–66; population demographics for, 243n18; regenerative refusal in, 132–33; self-identification by, 22–23, 30; Te Rangihīroa's identification with, 88–93, 95; Tregear's research on, 44, 46, 53–54, 56–61, 65; warrior gene mythology and, 182–83
*Mapping Human History* (Olson), 172–73, 180
Marshall Islands: U.S. nuclear weapons testing in, 184, 235–36
Massie, Thalia, 98, 115, 118
Massie affair, 98–99, 115, 118
Matsuda, Matt, 29
Maui (Polynesian demigod), 202–4
Mau Movement, 132, 213
Mauna Kea: Thirty Meter Telescope project and, 225–28
McDougall, Brandy Nālani, 235
Melanesia: antiblackness in history of, 28–29; history of, 7; racial mapping of, 36–40; regeneration of, 233–39; regional geography of, 4
Melanesian identity: blackness associated with, 54–66, 109–11; Polynesian identity and, 29–30; racial labeling of, 36, 39–40; Te Rangihīroa on origins of, 89–90, 92–93
melting pot ideology: in Adams's research, 96–100, 104, 110, 123–25; Asian American assimilation and, 112–14; Brazil as example of, 127–29; genomic studies of Hawaiians and, 170–77; Hawaiʻi as model for, 129, 153–56;

hybridity of Hawaiian women, 114–22; whiteness and, 33–34
"Memory of the World Register," 7
*mestizaje* discourse, 19
Metropolitan Museum of Art, 202
Micronesia: history of, 7; racial mapping of, 36–40; regional geography of, 4
Micronesian identity: genomics and, 176–77, 180–82; regeneration of, 233–39; separation from Polynesian identity, 36, 92–93
middle class ideology: eugenics and, 72–77
miscegenation: colonialism and, 128–29
misogyny: social impact of, 18–19
"mitochondrial Eve" project, 180
mixed race ideology. *See* racial mixture discourse
*Modern Geography* (Pinkerton), 37
Moreau de Maupertuis, Pierre Louis, 37
Moreton-Robinson, Aileen, 27–28
Morgan, Henry, 169
Mormon Church: Polynesians and, 9, 49, 252n22
Morrow, Prince, 76
Moten, Fred, 144–46, 155–56, 265n27
Movement for Aloha No Ka ʻĀina, 155–56
Müller, Max, 51–54
*Myths and Songs from the South Pacific* (Gill), 52

naʻaupō (ignorance and backwardness), 49–50
Native Americans: as almost white, 253n57; DNA testing and, 169–70, 181; federal recognition process and, 138–46, 157–58; gaming rights for, 144–46; land dispossession of, 150; Native Hawaiian identity linked to, 140–46, 164–66; "redness" of, 55–56; settler colonial stereotypes of, 50, 164–65; state tribal recognition laws and, 141–46
Native Hawaiian Government Reorganization Act. *See* Akaka Bill

Native Hawaiian Intellectual Property Rights Conference, 187, 191–93
Native Hawaiian Legal Corporation, 151–52, 181
*The Native Hawaiian of Yesterday and To-Day* (Twombly), 189–90
Native Hawaiian roll commission (Kanaʻiolowalu), 141–46, 161–62
Native Hawaiians: in Adams's research, 99–106; African Americans and, 30; anthropometric measurements and, 78–86; assimilation imperative and, 102–4; blood quantum laws and, 94–95; contemporary artists' representations of, 215–21; cultural commodification of, 195–98; eugenics and, 72–77, 93–95; federal and state recognition of, 138–43; Fornander's research on, 54–56; gender and, 115–22, 146–49; genetic testing and, 169–70, 180–82; Hawaiian Genome Project and, 183–93; Hawaiian Homes Commission Act definition of, 135–38; indigeneity and, 176–78; Kalākaua's interest in, 61–65; Kānaka Maoli and, 231–39; land and homestead rights for, 138–40, 146–49, 168–70, 173; leprosy and, 74–77; negative stereotypes about, 106–11; origins and terminology of, 9–13; as political construction, 154–56; racial mixture discourse and, 126–27; racial superiority linked to, 63–65; regeneration of indigeneity and, 22–23, 130–33; Sullivan's advocacy for, 68–70; Thirty Meter Telescope project and, 225–28; Thompson's advocacy for, 70–77; whiteness and, 111–14; Native Hawaiian women, stereotypes about, 114–22
Native title law (Australia), 28
Nāwahī, Emma, 161
"neo-Hawaiian race": Adams' concept of, 115, 122–23

"New Light on the Races of Polynesia" (Sullivan), 84
"New Race Growing Up in the Pacific" illustration, 100–102, 199
New Zealand: Māori Aryanism and, 56–61; Polynesian identity and, 9; racial amalgamation policies and, 102
*Nose Width with Vernier Caliper* (Kihara), 202–3
Nyongʻo, Tavia, 17, 33, 101–2, 117–18, 199–200

*Oakland Tribune*: construction of neo-Hawaiian race in, 100–102, 114, 123
Obama, Barack, 94
obesity: Polynesian genetic susceptibility to, 182–83
Oceania: antiblackness in history of, 28; geographic boundaries of, 39; Polynesian identity and connections in, 232–39; racial identity in, 69–70; regional geography of, 4, 7–8
Oceania Interrupted, 235
Office of Federal Acknowledgment, 263n3
Office of Hawaiian Affairs (OHA), 136–40, 143–44, 146–49, 152–56
O'Hara, Samuel Kealoha, 136, 164
Olson, Steve, 172–77, 180
*On the Origin of Species* (Darwin), 51
Orientalism: Aryanism and, 64–65, 252n27; assimilation imperative and, 102–4
origin narrative: Mormon-Polynesian ties and, 49–50
Osborn, Henry Fairfield, 78, 81–82

Pa, Kekane, 163
Pacific Biomedical Research Center, 184–85
Pacific islands: racial mapping of, 36–40
"Pacific muse," 38
Palmer, Albert, 103–4
*Palm Fronds at Coconut Grove/Palama Kapa* (*Palm Frond Covering*) (Pao), 217–21

Pang Kee, Leighton, 180–81
Pao, Adrienne Keahi, 131, 195–223
Paoakalani Declaration, 191–93, 229, 231
Park, Robert, 97, 99–104
*Part Asian, 100% Hapa* (Fulbeck), 200
Part Hawaiian discourse, 231–32; blood quantum laws and, 135; eugenics and concept of, 72, 74–77, 93–95; Sullivan's research on, 77, 84–86
paternity testing, 181
Perez, Craig Santos, 235
Peru: mythical links to Hawai'i, 5–6; Rapa Nui forced labor in, 29
photography: eugenics research and use of, 77–86; as regenerative refusal, 199–223
physical anthropology. *See* anthropology
Piailug, Mau, 7
Pinkerton, John, 37
plaster casts: eugenics research and use of, 77–86
political agendas: art and, 200–209; genetics research and, 171–77
Polynesia: regeneration of, 233–39; terminology about, 37–40, 47
Polynesian identity: Aryanism and, 14–19, 29, 33–34, 43–44, 50–66, 173; in cultural studies, 1–5; exceptionalism and, 29–30, 39–40, 65, 69–70; football skill stereotype and, 182–83, 204; gender stereotypes and, 91–93; genetics research and, 171–77, 180–82; Native Hawaiian identity and, 102–4; possessive spirit of whiteness and, 23–31; racial labeling of, 36, 69–70; racial mixture discourse and, 126–27; regeneration of, 233–39; scientific perspectives on, 40–42; self-regeneration of, 20–23; settler colonialism perspectives on, 5–13; stereotypes of, 100–104; Sullivan's eugenics and, 77–86; Taiwan and, 171–77; Te Rangihīroa's research on, 88–93; transnational and regional formations of, 1–5, 7–13; in Western social science, 7–19, 31–34; whiteness and, 13–19, 54–66, 109–11
Polynesian mythology and genealogy, 88–89
*Polynesian* newspaper, 59
Polynesian origins and terminology: Western perspectives on, 7–13
Polynesian Panthers, 30, 132
Polynesian Problem scholarship, 5–19, 34; Adams and, 123–24; anti-Hawaiian perspective in, 107–11; Austronesian discourse and, 24; British settler colonialism and, 46–50; Chicago School and, 103–4; eugenics and, 81–86; Fornander and, 54–56; genetics research and, 169–77, 193–94; Polynesian participation in, 61–65; racial mapping of Pacific Islands and, 36–40, 227–28; scientific discourse and, 40–42; Sullivan's eugenics research and, 80–86; Te Rangihīroa's research, 69–70, 86–93
Polynesian Society, 251n3
popular media: genetic testing in, 178–82
Porteus, Stanley, 109–11
positivism: race and whiteness and, 26
possession, logic of: antiblackness and, 23–31; Austronesian discourse and, 24; Chicago School and, 103–4; global development of, 64–65; regenerative refusal and, 23, 129–33, 195–223; settler colonialism and, 3–5, 15–19; whiteness and, 31–34, 231–39
post-racial discourse, 11; racial mixture and, 127–29
Prince, Venus, 164–65
property: "Hawaiian Genome" as, 189–91; whiteness as, 27, 190–93, 247n73
Pure Hawaiians, 231–32; anti-Hawaiian stereotypes and, 107–11; Chinese Hawaiian attitudes about, 105–6; Kneubuhl's fictive portrayal of, 229–31; Sullivan's concept of, 77–86, 93–95

Qolouvaki, Tagi, 237
Quiros, Pedro Fernandez de, 36

race and racism: anthropometric measurements and, 78–86; Chinese Hawaiian views on, 112–14; disease and, 75–77; eugenics and, 67–70; gender and, 146–49; genetic testing and, 170–82; in Hawai'i, scholarship on, 96–99; Kalākaua's views on, 64–65; Micronesians and, 235–37; Native Hawaiian concepts of, 22–23; physical anthropology theories on, 67–95; Polynesian identity and, 1–7; Polynesian origins and terminology in context of, 7–13; racial mapping of Pacific islands and, 36–40; racial mixture theory and, 17–18; as scientific problem, 40–42; social and scientific perspectives on, 13, 25–26; Te Rangihīroa's research on, 87–93
*Race Mixture* (Shapiro), 128–29
race relations cycle, 99–100, 260n17
racial mixture discourse: art as refusal of, 199–223; contemporary art and, 201–9, 221–23; eugenics and, 76–77, 94–95; genetics and, 174–77; Kānaka Maoli indigeneity and, 232–39; Native Hawaiian women and, 114–22; settler colonialism and, 17–19, 69–70; Shapiro and, 125–27; sociology and fictions in, 96–124; as solution and threat, 127–29; Sullivan and, 77–86; valorization of Chinese and Caucasians and, 111–14; women in, 101–2. *See also* critical mixed race studies
Rapa Nui people, 29
Rastafari identity, 30
Reardon, Jenny, 55, 169, 183, 187–88
regeneration: a'ole as, 159–66; cultural production as tool for, 195–223; Native Hawaiian initiatives for, 155–56; ocean exploration and, 224–39; in Oceanic context, 234–39; Polynesian identity and, 20–23; theories of, 245n54. *See also* degeneration
regenerative refusal, 23, 129–33; a'ole as, 159–66; in contemporary Polynesian art, 200–209, 214–23; cultural production and, 198–200; DNA testing and, 178–82, 189–94; Indigenous spacetime and, 228–39; models for, 236–39; to state and federal governments, 157–58; of whiteness, 229–39
reproductive politics: blood quantum laws and, 146–49; eugenics and, 71–77
retrospective prophecy, 51–52
Rice, Harold F., 144
*Rice v. Cayetano* (1996–2000), 139, 144, 153, 267n67
Ritte, Walter, 190–91
Rome: Polynesian identity and, 43–44
Ryan, Tom, 37, 40

Salesa, Damon, 20, 22–23, 102, 227–28, 238–39
*Samoan Half Caste* (Andrew), 210–11
Sāmoans: Aryanism and, 59–61, 63–65, 233–39; German diaspora of, 70; Kihara's art as expression of Sāmoan identity, 210–14; Sāmoan independence and, 132–33
Sāmoan Salome: Kihara's depiction of, 210–14
Sanskrit: Polynesian languages linked to, 54–55, 66
Satawal people: ocean exploration and, 6–7
Schoettle, Walter, 150–56
school curriculums: eugenics in, 71–77
sciapods, mythology of, 35–36
scientific research: eugenics and, 71–77; genetics research in Hawai'i and, 170–77, 184–93; in *The Hapa Project*, 207–9; Polynesian identity in context of, 40–42
Second International Eugenics Congress, 80

settler colonialism: Aryan framing of Polynesians and, 45–54, 65–66; Asian Americans and, 30–31; assimilation imperative in, 102–4; in contemporary Indigenous art, 200–223; degeneration and, 46–50; feminist perspectives on, 148–49; in Hawaiʻi, 96–99; Hawaiian Genome Project and, 190–93; Hawaiian race and racism and, 96–99; Kānaka Maoli indigeneity and, 229–32; knowledge as agency in, 24–25; logic of race and, 106–11; Māori Aryanism and, 56–61; Polynesian identity and, 9–13; possession through whiteness and, 3–5, 13–19; racial mixture discourse and, 17–19, 69–70; regeneration of indigeneity and, 21–23; regenerative refusal of, 158, 230–39; theory and terminology of, 15–19; Thirty Meter Telescope project and, 226–28

sex and sexuality: omission in *The Hapa Project* of, 207–9; reproductive politics and, 101–4, 147–49; stereotypes of Hawaiians and, 98–99, 115, 117–22, 173–77; whiteness and, 75–76

Shapiro, Harry, 13, 125–29, 174, 257n56

Silva, Denise Ferreira da, 25–26, 45, 52, 246n69, 247n72; racial mixture discourse and, 127–29, 175

Simpson, Audra, 130, 198, 200–201, 228

Simpson, Leanne, 20, 130

*Siva in Motion* (Kihara video work), 210–14, 222

slavery: genetic testing and, 179; transformation of indigeneity and, 21. *See also* forced labor in Melanesia

Smith, S. Percy, 43–44, 251n3

social science: Chicago School and, 100–104; contemporary art and, 201–9; hula girl stereotype and, 114–22; race and history of, 25–26

Somerville, Alice Te Punga, 87, 92–93, 242n13, 258n71

Spirit (Hegel), 25–26

*Sprinting* (Kihara), 203–4

state government recognition of Native Hawaiian identity, 138–46; regenerative refusal of, 157–58

statehood for Hawaiʻi: assimilation discourse and, 97, 102–4; land rights and, 140–41, 146–49; Native Hawaiian identity and, 42, 132, 146–49; neo-Hawaiian concept and, 115; whiteness discourse and, 75–76

Stephen, Alfred Milner, 93

sterilization: Thompson's belief in, 71–77

"A Study of a Samoan Savage" (Kihara), 201–4, 210–23

*Sugar Plantation Surrounding Birthing Stones/Kopaʻa Kapa* (*Hard Sugar Covering*) (Pao), 218–21

Sullivan, Louis Robert, 14, 22; anthropometric techniques of, 78–86, 94, 202–4; eugenics research by, 67–71, 89, 93–94, 98, 107; Hawaiian Homes Commission Act, 94; Part Hawaiian, concept of, 77, 84–86, 135

*Sunday Night Football*, 2

*Tahiti Revisited* (Hodges), 2

Taiwan: in Austronesian discourse, 23–24; indigenous groups in, 171

TallBear, Kimberly, 55, 169, 171–72, 181, 183

taulaluga, 210–14

Te Rangihīroa: early career and life of, 87; on Polynesian mythology and genealogy, 88–89; Polynesian origin research of, 61–65, 69–70, 86–93, 95, 233–39; U.S. citizenship denied to, 92–93

Terra Australis, mythology of, 35–36

*terra nullis*, colonial concept of, 28

Teves, Lani, 130, 158

Thirty Meter Telescope (TMT), 224–28

Thompson, Uldrick, 68–77, 93–94, 108, 136

*Three Cousins as the Three Graces—Leilani, Malia and Pohai* (Pao), 220

tiki culture, 1; white supremacy and, 15

Tongan Genome Project, 133, 186, 194
Tongans: identity of, 9
tourism: artistic representations of, 215–23
transcendence: evolution and, 52
Trask, Haunani-Kay, 140, 148
Treaty of Waitangi, 56
Tregear, Edward: Māori research of, 44, 46, 53–54, 56–61, 65–66, 173; Te Rangihīroa's critique of, 87
tribal recognition laws, 141–46
Tuck, Eve, 22, 214, 246n59
23andMe, 181
Twombly, Alexander, 189–90

United Nations Educational, Scientific and Cultural Organization (UNESCO), 7, 10; Statement on Race, 10–13
"Unite the Right" event (Charlottesville), 14–15
Universal Declaration of Human Rights, 10
universalizing narratives: genetics research and, 171–77, 188–93
University of Chicago, 99–104
University of Hawai'i: genetic modification of kalo project, 190–92; hula girl stereotype and, 114–22; intelligence research at, 109–11; race relations studies at, 99–104, 119; solidarity groups at, 235; Thirty Meter Telescope and, 224–28
*Up from the Ape* (Hooton), 11

Valladolid debates, 50
Veracini, Lorenzo, 18
*Vikings of the Pacific/Vikings of the Sunrise* (Te Rangihīroa), 88, 90, 258n81

Wākea (Sky Father), 230–31
*Wansolwara: Voices for West Papua*, 235
Weems, Carrie Mae, 198
Wenda, Benny, 234–35
Western ethnic and scientific discourse: contemporary artistic responses to, 200–223, 274n12; framing of Polynesian identity through, 7–19, 31–34, 47–50; regenerative refusal and, 131–32; Thirty Meter Telescope project and, 225–28
West Papua: activism on behalf of, 234–35
*What Is Race?* (UNESCO), 10–13, 126, 172
*Where Do We Come From? What Are We? Where Are We Going?* (Kihara photographic series), 211–14, 216
whiteness: anti-Hawaiian stereotypes linked to, 107–11; Chicago School and role of, 103–4; contemporary Polynesian artists' representations of, 221–23; degeneration discourse and, 48–50; DNA testing and, 177–82; eugenics and role of, 77–86; in Fornander's research, 55–56; genetic testing and, 188–93; geographic mapping of Polynesia and, 37–40; logic of possession and, 23–34, 231–39; Native Hawaiian identity and, 114–22, 190; Polynesian identity and, 3–5, 9–13; racial mixture discourse and, 129; regeneration of indigeneity and, 22–23, 195–223; settler colonial possession and, 3–5, 13–19; Sullivan's eugenics and, 84–86; Te Rangihīroa and conditionality of, 86–93; women and, 114–22. *See also* Aryanism
white supremacy: resurgence of, 14–15; structural forms of, 26–27
Whitmee, S. J., 40
Wissler, Clark, 78
Wolfe, Patrick, 16
women: blood quantum laws and, 147–49; disease and, 75–77; erasure of, in race cycle theory, 101–4; genetics research and role of, 173–77; Native American women, stereotypes of, 164–65; Native Hawaiian women, stereotypes of, 99, 114–22; in Pao's photography, 216–21; Polynesian women, stereotypes of, 91–93; reproduction of Native Hawaiians and, 71–77; settler colonialism and, 17–19
Wu, Ellen, 111–14

www.ingramcontent.com/pod-product-compliance
Lightning Source LLC
Chambersburg PA
CBHW051048230426
43666CB00012B/2613